INDECENT DETROIT

INDECENT DETROIT

Race, Sex, and Censorship
in the Motor City

BEN STRASSFELD

INDIANA UNIVERSITY PRESS

This book is a publication of

Indiana University Press
Office of Scholarly Publishing
Herman B Wells Library 350
1320 East 10th Street
Bloomington, Indiana 47405 USA

iupress.org

© 2023 by Ben Strassfeld

All rights reserved
No part of this book may be reproduced or utilized in any form or by any means, electronic or mechanical, including photocopying and recording, or by any information storage and retrieval system, without permission in writing from the publisher. The paper used in this publication meets the minimum requirements of the American National Standard for Information Sciences—Permanence of Paper for Printed Library Materials, ANSI Z39.48-1992.

Manufactured in the United States of America

First printing 2023

Cataloging information is available from the Library of Congress.

ISBN 978-0-253-06783-8 (hardback)
ISBN 978-0-253-06784-5 (paperback)
ISBN 978-0-253-06785-2 (ebook)

For Eema and Tatti

CONTENTS

Acknowledgments   ix

Introduction   1

1. "Burn the House to Roast the Pig": Literary Censorship and Juvenile Delinquency   17
2. "We're Not Really Censors": The (Il-)Legality of Detroit Police Movie Censorship   74
3. "The Blight of Indecency": Anti-Porn Politics and the Urban Crisis in Detroit   135
4. Topless Detroit: Regulating Industry and Exotic Dance   157
5. Erogenous Zoning: The Creation and Dispersal of the "Detroit Model"   202

    Epilogue: The Election of Coleman Young and the Politics of Pornography and Race   271

Bibliography   283

Index   291

ACKNOWLEDGMENTS

BY THE TIME THIS BOOK is released out into the world, it will have been nearly a decade since I wrote the first words for what would ultimately become this manuscript. The intervening years have seen this project evolve in ways I never could have predicted, moving away from my initial focus (postwar film exhibition in Detroit) to become the book you are now reading. In part these changes have been a result of the research process, which always seems to pull in unexpected directions. But, more importantly, this project has been shaped by the countless individuals whose support made this book possible. These acknowledgments are my earnest, if inevitably insufficient, effort to thank them.

My time as a graduate student in the Department of Film, Television, and Media (née Screen Arts and Cultures) at the University of Michigan shaped me and this project in innumerable ways. Matthew Solomon was immensely supportive as my adviser during my first few years at Michigan, and his boundless curiosity and love of learning are qualities I continue to try to emulate. Phil Hallman helped steer me toward studying Detroit and film exhibition history. Nicole Scholtz taught me literally everything I know about digital mapping and GIS. I am indebted to much of the faculty in the department, including Johannes von Moltke, Giorgio Bertellini, Caryl Flinn, Yeidy Rivero, Dan Herbert, Mark Kligerman, and Sheila Murphy, for shaping my thinking through my coursework as well as through informal hallways chats. Tremendous thanks go to my colleagues and friends who helped me get through graduate school, including Erin Hanna, Nathan Koob, Dimitri Pavlounis, Josh Morrison, Yuki Nakayama, and Richard Mwakasege-Minaya. Thanks in particular to Mike Arnold and Peter Alilunas for their friendship and for influencing what I wound up studying and to Katy Peplin for being such a tremendous cohort mate.

This project would not be what it is without the support and guidance I received from my dissertation committee. Matthew Lassitter pushed me to think through how my work intersected with urban history, while Eric Schaefer did the same with the history of exploitation cinema, and this project is immeasurably better as a result. I am immensely grateful to Gayle Rubin and Colin Gunckel for their generous support and thoughtful feedback through the years. Richard Abel has always been there with advice and guidance since the day I stepped foot at Michigan, and I will forever be thankful for that.

Since leaving the University of Michigan, I have had the pleasure of teaching at Queens College. Thanks to Mara Einstein for the opportunity and to both her and Amy Herzog for the continued support. My thanks as well go to Noah Tsika, who, in addition to being an inspiration with his work, also has been incredibly supportive of me. Last, I am grateful to my students, whom I am constantly learning from.

Thanks to everyone at Indiana University Press who has worked to make this book happen, including the copyeditor, graphic designer, and so many others who shaped this book into the form it now takes. Particular thanks to Allison Blair Chaplin for all the help through this process and for patiently answering my many questions. I thank anonymous Readers 1 and 2 for their immensely helpful feedback on my manuscript. My thanks especially to Reader 1 for generously taking the time to read through a revised version of the manuscript and for suggesting changes that made this project much stronger.

Thanks also to the many friends who have supported me over the years. They number too many to name each here, but in brief, my thanks to Jeremy Borovitz, Jeff Kaplan, Eric Markowitz, Jesse Axelrod, and Jake Meier. Appreciation as well to Jesse for suggesting the title to chapter 5 and to Sarah Ketchen Lipson for her help in the early days of this project.

There were times while working on this project that I felt more than a bit like the Georges Seurat of Stephen Sondheim's imagination from the musical *Sunday in the Park with George*. Like George at work finishing the hat, I often found myself watching the rest of the world from a window while I wrote and finished the book. What made that possible was the love and support of my partner, Joanna Barlow. She has been unbelievably helpful throughout this process. Most importantly, to paraphrase Sondheim, Joanna has been, for me, precisely the kind of woman willing to wait and that you want to find waiting to return you to the night. Thanks for making this book possible, and I cannot wait to see where life takes us next.

Finally, profound thanks to my family. Thanks to my brothers, Max and Noam, whose kindness, generosity, and intelligence are qualities I aspire to. Thanks to my stepparents, Michael Ramella and Joy Levitt, and my stepsisters, Sara and Ruthie Friedlander, who are hardly deserving of the modifier *step*. Last, thanks to my parents, Eema and Tatti. Eema has been a rock throughout my life, there for me in good times and bad, and has never for a minute stopped believing in me. Tatti is the person I strive to emulate every day, a real-life walking *Lamed Vavnik* in our time. I cannot possibly repay the debt I owe both of you, and so I will just try to continue to express gratitude and return your love in kind. This book is dedicated to you both.

INDECENT DETROIT

INTRODUCTION

COMING OUT OF THE SECOND World War, Detroit was seemingly in the midst of a period of boundless economic prosperity that was powered by the automobile industry, which had made Detroit famous around the world. This economic growth had led to Detroit being one of the fastest-growing cities over the first half of the twentieth century, with its population peaking in 1950 at 1.85 million, when it was the fifth-largest city in the United States. In the midst of this postwar prosperity, however, some city officials and grassroots activists saw a threat that, they feared, might doom the city—and perhaps even the nation as a whole. Rather than forces like deindustrialization, white flight, or systemic racism, these activists identified a different threat imperiling the city: "indecent" media.

Activists at the local level mounted campaigns to fight the scourge of indecent media across the whole of Detroit and its suburbs throughout the late 1940s and 1950s. They included volunteer Catholic and Protestant women making visits to bookstores and retailers to make sure they were not carrying any publications deemed immoral and to beseech store owners to change their ways if stores did carry such material. Also participating in the fight were the hundreds of thousands of Catholics across Detroit who each year, in the weeks leading up to Christmas, renewed their pledge to support the Legion of Decency in its campaign against "indecent" and "immoral" motion pictures. Meanwhile, this era also saw the Detroit Parent-Teacher Association enlist thousands of its members in a crusade against comic books, which were seen as unfit reading material for children. Across all these efforts, activists used rhetoric emphasizing how these various forms of media transgressed norms of morality and decency, often with religious, and specifically Catholic, undertones.

Acting in response to these grassroots activists, and oftentimes working directly with them, was the Detroit Police Department's Censor Bureau. Throughout this period, the roughly dozen police officers that made up the Censor Bureau were charged with keeping the city free from all forms of indecent media. This included inspecting all movies intended for theatrical exhibition before their release in the city, with the bureau cutting or banning titles found to be morally wanting. The Censor Bureau also waged a constant hunt for pornographic stag films circulating clandestinely through nontheatrical circuits in the city, arresting those found to be exhibiting or distributing them. During this era, in response to community activism, the Censor Bureau also set up a comprehensive system to review and censor paperback books and comic books before they made it on to store shelves in the city. Meanwhile, the Censor Bureau also was charged with reviewing the city's live entertainment offerings, with police officers routinely inspecting stage productions and burlesque theaters in search of any risqué dialogue or female performers not wearing "proper" attire. These efforts relied on city and state ordinances that permitted the banning of any works that were judged to be "obscene," "indecent," or "immoral."

By the early 1970s, Detroit was a city in crisis. The structural forces that had been weakening the city for decades had become evident to all by this point, particularly following the violence that shook the city in the summer of 1967. For some Detroiters, though, the most pressing problem facing the city was not the flight of industry from Detroit or the city's deeply embedded racial inequities, but rather the fact that the whole of Detroit, from its downtown to its residential neighborhoods, was increasingly dotted with adult businesses offering up all manner of pornographic attractions. To these activists, the spread of adult entertainment in the city was not an unrelated distraction pulling attention from the larger forces causing Detroit's decline: rather, the growing number of adult businesses was one of the prime causes of Detroit's woes. And so, rather than rooting their arguments against pornography strictly in the traditional morality-focused and religious-based procensorship rhetoric of old, these activists instead used seemingly morality-neutral arguments emphasizing economic concerns and the rights of homeowners. This new form of discourse was needed in the wake of the sexual revolution and societal changes that had rendered "censorship" practically a four-letter word. Though morality was never absent from the anti-porn arguments they now made, anti-porn activists of the early 1970s nevertheless consciously sought to distance themselves from the stereotype of the bluenose censor seeking to curtail free speech in the name of prudishness and religious doctrine. As part of their campaign against pornography, these homeowner activists mounted protests outside adult movie theaters and bookstores and wrote letters en masse to city officials urging them to take action.

The problem for city officials in Detroit in the early 1970s who were hoping to regulate the spread of adult entertainment was that the legal landscape for censorship had changed drastically since the immediate postwar era. Across the country, the preceding decades had seen a spate of legal rulings that had significantly curtailed the ability of cities to censor movies or prosecute the purveyors of pornography. This included numerous cases that winnowed down the scope of obscenity law, the exception to the First Amendment that had long been a favored means of censoring media. Among these was an influential 1957 United States Supreme Court ruling that declared that Michigan's obscenity law—which the Detroit Police Censor Bureau had been using to censor literature—was unconstitutional. The 1950s and 1960s also saw repeated rulings by the Supreme Court that made it increasingly difficult for cities and states to continue to operate movie censorship boards in a constitutional manner, ultimately resulting in Detroit's movie censorship law being declared unconstitutional by a lower court in 1969. All this meant that by the early 1970s, the Detroit Police Department's censorship operation was a shell of what it had once been, and so pressure mounted on the city's elected officials to find a new method of regulating indecent media. The solution that the city council and mayor eventually adopted was a novel one. Rather than using obscenity law, they passed new anti-porn legislation that used zoning law to try to disperse adult businesses rather than banning them outright. Through this approach, the city could—in cold legal terms if not in actual practice—elide free speech concerns by claiming the legislation was concerned only with the economic effect of the conglomeration of adult businesses in a neighborhood rather than the constitutionally protected content housed in these businesses. A legal challenge eventually made its way to the United States Supreme Court, which, in 1976, in a narrow five-to-four ruling, sided with the city in declaring its anti-porn zoning ordinance constitutional, after which most cities across the country copied Detroit's approach to regulating adult entertainment.

This book charts these changes in the politics of censorship alongside the legal means used to regulate indecent media through a case study of Detroit and its suburbs. I argue that the period from the late 1940s through the 1970s saw a dramatic change in the rhetoric used by those aiming to suppress indecent media. The overt moralizing associated with the censorship of the immediate postwar era grew out of step with the times in the wake of the sexual revolution and broader societal changes. As a result, those advocating censorship developed novel discursive strategies that could distance them from any associations with puritanism and prudishness. Likewise, new legal methods for regulating indecent media were also developed over the course of this period, ones that moved away from obscenity law and other direct forms of censorship. Crucially, this new zoning-based approach to regulating sex media was designed to mimic the shift in the rhetoric deployed by censorship advocates by denying that it was a form of censorship or that it was in any way concerned with morality. Nevertheless, zoning adult businesses ultimately still sought the same goals of older forms of censorship by curtailing, if not halting entirely, the spread of indecent media. That these changes happened within the context of a Detroit in the midst of a rapid economic decline was no coincidence, as the urban crisis facing cities across the United States at this time became inextricably intertwined with the anti-porn politics of this era.

In mapping out this history of media censorship, I argue that a crucial animating force, particularly in the new form of procensorship rhetoric that emerged in the 1970s, was white racial politics. To illustrate this, it is worth pivoting to the story of L. Brooks Patterson. For urban historians and Detroit-area natives, Patterson is best known as one of the era's most prominent opponents of efforts to combat racism and end segregation in the region. A Detroit native who decamped as a young adult to Oakland County, the suburbs located just north of Detroit, Patterson made a name for himself politically in the early 1970s as the attorney for the National Action Group, an organization that fought back against proposals to use busing programs to desegregate schools. Patterson used the notoriety he gained from this role as a springboard to successfully run for Oakland County prosecutor in 1972, a position he held for the next sixteen years. During that time, Patterson adopted a "tough-on-crime" persona and advocated for harsher criminal sentencing guidelines. He also become one of Detroit's most vocal detractors, frequently courting controversy with language that his critics argued amounted to thinly veiled racism. Despite this history of lambasting a predominantly Black city and fighting against measures to redress racial disparities, Patterson always made sure to deny that he, himself, was racist, pointedly telling one journalist in the late 1980s, "I'm color-blind." Patterson instead used the same rhetorical strategies emphasizing the rights of homeowners and economic concerns that had come to dominate white racial politics of the day. This color-blind conservative discourse sought to distance Patterson and his compatriots from their explicitly racist political forebearers while ultimately continuing in the same tradition of white backlash to racial integration and Black political gains.[1]

Though he is best known for his racial politics, which acted to pathologize and demonize a Detroit that was becoming increasingly Black, as Oakland County prosecutor in the 1970s, Patterson also attracted popular attention through his war against pornography and adult entertainment. Soon after taking office, Patterson mounted a campaign to shut down Oakland County's adult movie theaters and bookstores as well as its topless bars. Even as he did so, Patterson was quick to distance himself from any associations with the censorship efforts of old. As he later claimed, his effort to stamp out pornography in Oakland County "had nothing to do with morality." As he explained, "I wasn't getting on my white horse. This was always an economic issue. It was about the effect these places have on the business climate in these communities." Just as Patterson denied that he was racist while simultaneously seeking to combat efforts to redress racism, he also denied the centrality of morality and free speech while seeking to suppress the spread of sex media and adult entertainment.[2]

Beyond illustrating how white racial politics inflected the politics of media censorship, Patterson's anti-porn activity also highlights how the regulation of media and the proliferation of adult entertainment have long been intertwined with urban and suburban politics. One long-standing question in the field of urban studies has been how both suburbanites and city dwellers construct notions of their own neighborhoods as distinct from one another, even as the line between the two is often blurry, if not invisible. This question is particularly relevant to Detroit, a city that is huge in landmass and thus contains many residential neighborhoods that, even at the peak of the city's population size and economic fortunes, more closely resembled the look and feel of suburbs rather than a bustling city center. Most urban historians answer this question by pointing to political culture as the impetus for the imagined dividing line between city and suburb.[3] In his public comments, though, Patterson gave another explanation for this distinction. As he said, "I used to say to my kids, 'First of all, there's no reason for you to go to Detroit. We've got restaurants out here.' They don't even have movie theatres in Detroit—not one." Patterson's negative opinion of Detroit, then, was based not only on economics and politics but also on the city's supposed cultural deficit, symbolized here through a dearth of movie houses. In his specific mention of Detroit not having any movie theaters (which, it is worth pointing out, was simply not true), Patterson indicated the way culture, or a perceived lack thereof, was critical to his understanding of the distinction between Detroit and the suburbs of Oakland County.[4]

At the same time, Patterson also drew on a very different form of popular entertainment when giving another reason for how he distinguished the suburbs of Oakland County from the city of Detroit. In 1973, in the midst of his efforts as Oakland County prosecutor to shut down adult businesses, Patterson specified that his actions were designed to prevent the suburbs he represented from being overrun with pornography in the way he believed Detroit had. As he said, "The county's policy is preventative medicine. We don't want the problems Wayne County [containing Detroit] has. I have no intention of becoming an art critic or assuming the role of a censor. But I'm charged with the responsibility of enforcing all laws including state obscenity laws." This was not the last time Patterson would point to the availability of adult entertainment in drawing a distinction between Oakland County and its urban neighbor to the south. In a 2014 *New Yorker* article, Patterson noted the lack of strip clubs on the Oakland County side of Eight Mile Road in comparison with their abundance on the Detroit side of the city-suburb dividing line, saying of adult entertainment, "It destroys neighborhoods. There's not a topless bar in Oakland County, not an X-rated movie theater, not a house of ill repute. I shut 'em down.... I'm not a prude. I'm a guy who wants to protect my neighbors, protect my community." Beyond just reiterating how he actively sought to distance himself from associations with censorship or prudishness, Patterson's comments here also point to the way indecent media and adult entertainment have often been a means for the supposedly sexless and sedate suburbs to distinguish themselves from the commercial-sex-ridden urban center. Of course, in reality the suburbs were never as free from sex media as has often been imagined. Nevertheless, Patterson's statements indicate how the availability of "respectable" entertainment options like mainstream movie theaters or "illicit" entertainment options like adult businesses or topless bars could come to popularly define the distinct identities of city and suburb.[5]

—⚏—

This book first and foremost fits within and is influenced by scholarship on the history of media censorship. In particular, I draw upon works focused on the history of local film censorship. Much of this work is centered on the period stretching from the beginning of the transitional era of cinema around 1908 up through the end of the pre–Production Code era in 1934, a period that saw the creation of numerous city and state movie censorship boards.[6] As Eric Smoodin writes, in what he facetiously calls the "happy end" to this narrative of film censorship, governmental censorship efforts were supposedly "made more or less obsolete" following Hollywood's full adoption of the self-censoring

Production Code midway through 1934. As he notes, though, in reality governmental censorship of movies continued to occur in a variety of different forms for years to come.[7] Though there has been some work on the operation of local movie censor boards after 1934, most scholarship on censorship after that time tends to focus on either state movie censor boards or Hollywood self-censorship through the Production Code and later the ratings system.[8] Work on local movie censor boards post-1934 has tended to focus on the way race was embedded in the censorship of cinema in southern cities like Memphis and Atlanta.[9] As I contend in this book, though, censorship of movies continued in Detroit for decades after the Production Code Administration was formed in 1934 and was just as informed by constructions of race and whiteness as in southern cities.

This book also argues that histories of film censorship have too often ignored connections with other forms of media censorship. The same Detroit Police Department's Censor Bureau that was tasked with censoring movies was also in charge of censoring literature, comic books, live theater, exotic dance, and pornography, and these various areas of regulation had significant overlap and linkages. Likewise, when Detroit's city council and mayor enacted new forms of censorship in the early 1970s, they targeted not just indecent movies but rather all forms of sex media. This project therefore argues against isolating the history of different forms of media censorship from one another, showing how the systems of regulation of various types of popular media and entertainment have long been closely intertwined.

Relatedly, I also make the case for moving away from a focus on the censorship of "great works" to instead examine the totality of works being censored as well as the system of censorship itself. Though, to be sure, the Censor Bureau banned many celebrated books and films by prestigious authors and directors, far more common was the censorship of less heralded or high-minded works. Similarly, Detroit's anti-porn zoning law sought to regulate all forms of adult entertainment just the same, with no attention paid to particularly notable adult films of the era. Rather than walling off the censorship of pornography and lowbrow media from the censorship of mainstream and art-house movies, then, I show how there has always been a fluid relationship between these various forms of regulation. To do so, I focus on the system of censorship in Detroit, detailing the city's operation rather than focusing on the story of any one work subject to censorship.

Given the way this book foregrounds the study of interrelated systems of media censorship, I also draw centrally on work in the emerging field of porn studies—in particular work that focuses on the regulation of pornography and adult entertainment. A question that scholars in this area have long grappled with is how to define *pornography* when the word has been applied to so many different types of objects over time. This is certainly a challenge for this project given that Detroit officials and activists advocating for censorship used the term *pornography* to refer to a wide swath of different types of media objects. In the 1950s, this included referring to cheap paperback novels as pornographic, which few would label them as today. Though by the 1970s the term *pornography* was mainly being used in ways similar to its modern-day usage, those in favor of censorship at times still applied the label to mainstream Hollywood films due to their sexual content. To square the many ways the term has been used, Walter Kendrick, in his book *The Secret Museum*, argues that *pornography* is a "fighting word," meaning that calling a work pornographic inevitably implicates efforts to suppress the work in question. In Kendrick's view, "pornography" is simply whatever media a dominant class or group of people wants to keep out of the hands of those who are viewed as threatening the social order at a given point in time. Whitney Strub takes a similar approach in his book *Perversion for Profit*, which examines the linkages between conservative and anti-porn politics. As Strub writes, "Language in this book is intended to be read as always immersed in historically bound contestations over meaning." Likewise, throughout this book I use terms like *pornographic* and *indecent* as, in Kendrick's formulation, "fighting words" evoking the censorship debates surrounding them rather than terms whose meaning is self-evident or proscribed by me.[10]

To this scholarship on the history of anti-porn politics as well as work on film and media censorship I add a focus on the impact of urban history on the censoring of film, media, and pornography. Using this lens, I argue that a better understanding can be gained of the ways race and urban politics have long been intertwined with censorship campaigns. In the immediate postwar era, with the city near the height of its economic power, censorship was a way to try to maintain Detroit's standing by protecting the "masses"—with all the racist, sexist, homophobic, ableist, and classist connotations contained therein—from being perverted by the licentious powers of indecent media. Once Detroit's economic decline had become evident to all by the early 1970s, the city's censorship efforts took on a new valence, with the regulation of sex media and adult entertainment seen as a means of restoring the city's economic fortunes and turning back the tide to an older (and, though rarely explicitly acknowledged, whiter) time in the city's history. That those efforts were ultimately in vain only reinforces the importance of examining closely how Detroit and cities like it have long used media censorship as a misguided means to try to maintain their prosperity and halt the tide of economic decline and urban decay. In the end, as explored in this book's epilogue, those efforts at censoring media would largely be sidelined once Detroit's first African American mayor was elected, a fact that speaks to the all-consuming whiteness of much of the history of media censorship.

Detroit is an illustrative case study for how urban political contexts impacted local media censorship given that Detroit has long held a prominent position in the field of urban history. Thomas Sugrue's seminal 1996 book, *The Origins of the Urban Crisis*, established Detroit as perhaps the central locale for studying postwar urban economic decline and racial conflict. Subsequent work in the field has deepened our understanding of Detroit's racial politics, its at-times adversarial relationship with the surrounding suburbs, and the history of organized labor in the city. This project draws on this scholarship focused on Detroit's history while seeking to further our understanding of how debates over media censorship became an avenue for Detroit to grapple with broader, thornier issues.[11]

Within the field of urban history, I build upon a growing body of scholarship that has sought to study sex and sexuality in urban space—in particular the history of pornography and censorship in cities. Most of this work has focused on New York City, San Francisco, and Los Angeles, which have long been known as hotbeds of emergent sexualities and various forms of commercial sex. By contrast, to date no scholar has looked centrally at the history of censorship in Detroit, and there are only a few works more broadly on sex and sexuality in Detroit.[12] I argue that a focus on Detroit is an important addition to this existing scholarship for two primary reasons. The first is that there has been an overemphasis on the major coastal cities in work on the history of the regulation of pornography at the municipal level. A focus on Detroit can help move scholars' gaze toward the middle of the country, toward an industrial city, and toward a city with a complex and fluid relationship between city and suburb.

The second major reason for the focus on Detroit is that the city had an outsized influence on the history of media censorship, one that has been unexamined by scholars to date. As detailed in chapter 1, Detroit's list of banned books circulated so widely that the city became something akin to the de facto literary censor for the entire country. Detroit's literary operation was challenged in a case that ultimately wound up before the Supreme Court, whose 1957 decision set an important precedent for the laws governing censorship. In the wake of this ruling and others over the course of the 1950s and 1960s that curtailed the use of obscenity law and direct forms of media censorship, cities across the country found themselves struggling with how to regulate the rapidly growing number of adult businesses dotting the urban landscape. It was within this context, as detailed in the final chapter, that Detroit passed its anti-porn zoning law. A legal challenge to that ordinance made its way to the Supreme Court, which in 1976 affirmed the constitutionality of Detroit's law. Soon after that decision, countless cities both large and small across the country replicated Detroit's zoning-based approach to regulating pornography.

Despite this immense influence, Detroit's regulation of media and adult entertainment has received little scholarly attention to date. Detroit's literary censorship regime of the 1950s has garnered only passing mention in the past half century outside of legal histories, which focus only on the legacy of the 1957 Supreme Court ruling and not on Detroit's literary censorship operation itself.[13] Likewise, Detroit's anti-porn zoning law has primarily been discussed by legal historians, who again elide the particular roots of the law in Detroit to instead study the legal precedent it eventually set in the Supreme Court.[14] The only other place that Detroit's zoning law tends to come up is when it is briefly mentioned as the progenitor to similar laws passed in other cities, as in the work of Marilyn Adler Papayanis on New York City, Josh Sides on San Francisco, and Robert Self on Los Angeles.[15] In all these cases, though, the particularities and local contexts for how these forms of censorship were first practiced in Detroit are ignored. I argue here that these prominent Supreme Court censorship cases emanating out of Detroit cannot be understood without a close examination of their origins in the city itself and the political contexts from which they were born. Meanwhile, Detroit's movie censorship board and the city's regulation of topless dancing, both of which I examine in this book, have garnered no scholarly attention of any kind in recent decades, legal or otherwise.

While this book does speak centrally to the legal history of censorship, I also point to the limitations of such an approach. For one, as scholar Whitney Strub has noted, a legalistic history of censorship leaves out the historical contexts through which sex media circulates and is regulated.[16] Beyond this, my project also demonstrates a further shortcoming with legal histories of censorship that focus primarily on the major court cases and the implications of their rulings for obscenity law and the First Amendment. Namely, as I often point to in this book, just because a court, or even the Supreme Court itself, issued a ruling on how censorship should be practiced constitutionally does not mean that censorship was then actually practiced in such a manner at the local level. This was particularly the case in Detroit, where, until the end of the 1960s, it was police officers who were in charge of censoring media. As the early chapters of this book demonstrate, the Detroit Police Department quite often enacted censorship far outside the accepted legal boundaries set by the Supreme Court. I therefore discuss the history of policing and how the Censor Bureau ignoring or violating the laws of censorship fits within a broader history of police misconduct.[17] The legal and extralegal censorship practiced in Detroit demonstrates how examining only the most significant rulings can leave out the realities of how censorship actually functioned at the ground level.

Legal histories also tend to ignore the fact that systematic forms of media censorship do not typically happen merely as a result of the predilections of a few city officials; rather, they emerge out of the concerted efforts of grassroots activists. As detailed in chapters 1 and 2, Detroit's censorship of literature and movies during the 1950s was born out of the sustained advocacy of Catholic groups who argued for the need to keep the city free from indecent media. They were joined by many Detroit residents across the religious spectrum alongside many leaders in local parent-teacher associations. In the early 1970s, Detroit's new zoning-based approach to regulating adult businesses developed out of the activism of neighborhood residents, with thousands of Detroiters writing to city officials using rhetoric that Detroit's city council would transform into policy. A similar story played out in Oakland County, where L. Brooks Patterson's war against pornography was waged in concert with angry anti-porn residents who sent letters, circulated petitions, and organized pickets outside adult theaters. In the midst of a protracted battle over Patterson's attempt to ban the adult film *Naked Came the Stranger* (1975), residents of Ferndale in Oakland County organized a meeting to call for a crackdown on pornography. Patterson was invited to speak at the gathering, where he told residents to write letters putting political pressure on the judges involved in the case and handed out some seven hundred copies of a petition calling for adult movies to be kept out of Oakland County. Across these examples in both Detroit and Oakland County, then, censorship came about due to the sustained efforts of residents who successfully pushed their city and elected officials to take action against indecent media. Even as this project reiterates the ways censorship is, at its core, an elitist top-down affair, with those in power deciding what the masses can watch and read, I also show the dynamic interplay between grassroots activists and those formally in charge of censoring media.[18] In writing a history of censorship from below, I argue for the need to see censorship not merely as a war over high-minded ideas or legal principles but rather as an embodied, material practice with its own institutions and political economy, as something not just about sex and free speech but also police budgets, real estate property values, the political ambitions of elected officials, and the activism of homeowners and religious groups.[19]

Chapter 1 of this book focuses on the history of literary censorship in Detroit. I open with the history of how the city censored movies during the early twentieth century, discussing how the Detroit Police Department was pushed by Catholic groups toward literary censorship in the late 1930s before fully embracing its role as literary censor in the postwar era. I attempt to reconstruct the inner workings of the Censor Bureau, a task made more difficult by the secrecy that surrounded police censorship in Detroit. This secrecy allowed the Detroit Censor Bureau to quietly become perhaps the country's most important center of literary censorship during the postwar period, influencing the circulation and censorship of literature across the country. I also demonstrate how literary censorship in Detroit relied on the cooperation of a number of key constituencies, including local Catholic groups, the print industry, and the city's newspapers. I use a leaked version of the city's banned book list to examine the types of titles that were targeted by the Censor Bureau, paying particular attention to the ways the banned book list reflected the priorities and biases of the Detroit Police Department. Censorship, though, is as much concerned with the perceived audience for a controversial work as it is the content of the work itself, and so I delve into popular conceptions of the demographic and psychological makeup of the people who were imagined to be the intended audience of these books. Finally, I end by examining the Supreme Court decision that both halted this type of literary censorship by the Censor Bureau and simultaneously set an important legal precedent that limited the scope of obscenity law and the way media could be regulated.

In chapter 2, I tell the parallel story of postwar movie censorship in Detroit. In particular, I look closely at how the Censor Bureau went about censoring movies before their theatrical release. This censorship operation was made possible by a 1907 Detroit ordinance that empowered the Detroit Police Department to act as movie censors, and it was through this ordinance that the Detroit police would censor movies deemed "indecent or immoral" until the end of the 1960s. Importantly, even as the Censor Bureau was nominally following Detroit law in censoring movies, I show that they also spent decades ignoring Supreme Court rulings that should have hemmed in their work. Simultaneously, this chapter also shows how the Detroit Police Department used state obscenity law to arrest and prosecute those found to be disseminating pornographic materials. Again, though, the Detroit police quite often ignored the actual strictures of obscenity law to instead apply the law entirely at their own discretion. This chapter, then, is both a study of movie censorship laws as well as an examination of how movie censorship was often practiced in Detroit far outside the boundaries of the law.

Whereas the early chapters of this book focus on censorship in Detroit during the 1950s and 1960s, later chapters turn to the early 1970s, by which time the overt moralizing underlying censorship efforts of old had become antiquated. Chapter 3 explores the development of a new form of procensorship and anti-porn politics through a case study of the protests of one neighborhood in northwest Detroit against an adult bookstore that had opened in its midst. In the months after the Adult World Bookstore set up shop in the neighborhood of Redford, residents mounted a campaign aimed at stamping out the adult business, inundating the offices of the mayor and city council with hundreds of letters calling for the city to take action against the spread of pornography. Rather than using traditional religious-inflected and morality-based anti-porn rhetoric, residents' letters were steeped in seemingly more mundane concerns surrounding declining property values, neighborhood deterioration, and white flight. In so doing, these residents managed to adopt and adapt the color-blind discourse that had become central to white racial politics of the era. This chapter therefore argues for the need to situate the politics of censorship in the early 1970s within the context of urban history and contemporaneous battles over racial integration.

In chapter 4, I examine the city's regulation of topless bars. Controversy surrounding exotic dance in Detroit, and the perceived need for the city to regulate it, had been present throughout much of the 1950s and 1960s, but the debate escalated after dancers in the city started performing topless in 1969. In the years that followed, the legal decisions of judges, alongside the legislative priorities of city officials, worked to create new restrictions on exotic dance in Detroit. However, topless-bar owners and dancers fought back using economic-based arguments to make the case for not enacting new legislation against the industry. Meanwhile, the regulations placed on exotic dance in Detroit led more suggestive dancing to at times flee to suburban locales with laxer restrictions, challenging notions of the city as a bastion of adult entertainment while the suburbs were, by comparison, supposedly staid and buttoned up.

Chapter 5 examines the zoning law Detroit passed in 1972 to regulate adult businesses. I begin by looking at the lead-up to the adoption of the law, demonstrating how liberal politicians not only failed to mount a defense of the free speech rights of pornography at this time but actually led the campaign against porn in the city. I show how this was rooted in responding to the type of grassroots anti-porn protests seen in chapter 3, with liberal politicians hoping to mollify constituents' concerns by curtailing the spread of pornography. Zeroing in on the inner workings of the city council, I explore how its members tried to use obscenity law to ban pornography only to be stymied by adverse court decisions. This led to an approach based in zoning law—one that could harness the type of anti-porn discourse explored in chapter 3 and turn its rhetoric into legislation. I then look at the legal challenge to the zoning law as the case made its way up to the Supreme Court, which affirmed the legality of the ordinance in 1976. I conclude by exploring the influence of Detroit's zoning approach by discussing how the law was copied by numerous cities across the country.

Finally, the epilogue continues the story of the political maneuverings examined in the fifth chapter by detailing the 1973 mayoral race in Detroit. The election of Coleman Young that year as the city's first Black mayor not only marked a historic moment for Detroit, but his victory also spoke to the limits of the politics of pornography. All the various city officials who, in chapter 5, saw anti-porn politics as a stepping stone to higher office were stymied by a city ready for Black political leadership. Still, as indicated by Young's inaugural address and his invocation of blaxploitation cinema, the politics of indecent media continued to be central to this new era, even as the ways this indecency was defined took on more explicitly racial terms.

Ultimately, I argue throughout this book for the need to better understand the politics of censorship within the context of urban history. I do so by charting the evolution in both the rhetoric deployed against indecent media—from a religious- and morality-based discourse to one centered around economics and the rights of homeowners—as well as the legal mechanisms used to regulate adult media—from an approach based in obscenity to one utilizing zoning law. I argue that these changes were inextricably linked with shifts in racial politics during this era. Finally, this project argues for the central importance of Detroit to the broader history of anti-porn politics, demonstrating how the city had an influence stretching far beyond its borders, shaping the methods used to regulate pornography and adult entertainment across the country.

NOTES

1. Paige Williams, "Drop Dead, Detroit!," *New Yorker*, January 27, 2014; Ze'ev Chafets, *Devil's Night: And Other True Tales of Detroit* (New York: Random House, 1990), 132.

2. Williams, "Drop Dead, Detroit!," 36.

3. See Kevin M. Kruse and Thomas J. Sugrue, "Introduction: The New Suburban History," in *The New Suburban History*, ed. Kevin M. Kruse and Thomas J. Sugrue (Chicago: University of Chicago Press, 2006), 5; David M. P. Freund, *Colored Property: State Policy and White Racial Politics in Suburban America* (Chicago: University of Chicago Press, 2010), 29.

4. Williams, "Drop Dead, Detroit!," 32.

5. Jackie Klein, "Patterson Begins War to Eliminate Obscenity," *Southfield News & Observer*, July 25, 1973; Williams, "Drop Dead, Detroit!," 37.

6. For just some examples of this work, see Mary P. Erickson, "'In the Interest of the Moral Life of Our City': The Beginning of Motion Picture Censorship in Portland, Oregon," *Film History* 22, no. 2 (2010): 148–69; Daniel Czitrom, "The Politics of Performance: From Theater Licensing to Movie Censorship in Turn-of-the-Century New York," *American Quarterly* 44, no. 4 (1992): 525–53; Kathleen D. McCarthy, "Nickel Vice and Virtue: Movie Censorship in Chicago, 1907–1915," *Journal of Popular Film* 5, no. 1 (January 1976): 1907–15; R. Bruce Brasell, "'A Dangerous Experiment to Try': Film Censorship during the Twentieth Century in Mobile, Alabama," *Film History* 15, no. 1 (January 2003): 81–102.

7. Eric Smoodin, "Going Hollywood Sooner or Later: Chinese Censorship and *The Bitter Tea of General Yen*," in *Looking Past the Screen: Case Studies in American Film History and Method*, ed. Jon Lewis and Eric Smoodin (Durham, NC: Duke University Press, 2007), 170.

8. For work on the Production Code, see Thomas Doherty, *Pre-Code Hollywood: Sex, Immorality, and Insurrection in American Cinema; 1930–1934* (New York: Columbia University Press, 1999); Thomas Doherty, *Hollywood's Censor: Joseph I. Breen and the Production Code Administration* (New York: Columbia University Press, 2007); Leonard J. Leff and Jerold L. Simmons, *The Dame in the Kimono: Hollywood, Censorship, and the Production Code* (Lexington: University Press of Kentucky, 2001); Gregory D. Black, *Hollywood Censored: Morality Codes, Catholics, and the Movies* (Cambridge: Cambridge University Press, 1996). For scholarship on the ratings system, see Jon Lewis, *Hollywood v. Hard Core: How the Struggle over Censorship Created the Modern Film Industry* (New York: New York University Press, 2000); Justin Wyatt, "The Stigma of X: Adult Cinema and the Institution of the MPAA Ratings System," in *Controlling Hollywood: Censorship and Regulation in the Studio Era*, ed. Matthew Bernstein (New Brunswick, NJ: Rutgers University Press, 1999), 238–63; Kevin S. Sandler, *The Naked Truth: Why Hollywood Doesn't Make X-Rated Movies* (New Brunswick, NJ: Rutgers University Press, 2007); Christie Milliken, "Rate It X?: Hollywood Cinema and the End of the Production Code," in *Sex Scene: Media and the Sexual Revolution*, ed. Eric Schaefer (Durham, NC: Duke University Press, 2014), 25–52.

9. Whitney Strub, "Black and White and Banned All Over: Race, Censorship and Obscenity in Postwar Memphis," *Journal of Social History* 40, no. 3 (2007): 685–715; Margaret T. McGehee, "Disturbing the Peace: Lost Boundaries, Pinky, and Censorship in Atlanta, Georgia, 1949–1952," *Cinema Journal* 46, no. 1 (2006): 23–51.

10. Walter Kendrick, *The Secret Museum: Pornography in Modern Culture* (Berkeley: University of California Press, 1987), 223–24, 235; Whitney Strub, *Perversion for Profit: The Politics of Pornography and the Rise of the New Right* (New York: Columbia University Press, 2011), 4.

11. See Thomas J. Sugrue, *The Origins of the Urban Crisis: Race and Inequality in Postwar Detroit* (Princeton, NJ: Princeton University Press, 1996); Freund, *Colored Property*; Heather Ann Thompson, *Whose Detroit?: Politics, Labor, and Race in a Modern American City* (Ithaca, NY: Cornell University Press, 2004); June Manning Thomas, *Redevelopment and Race: Planning a Finer City in Postwar Detroit* (Detroit: Wayne State University Press, 2013); Sidney Fine, *Violence in the Model City: The Cavanagh Administration, Race Relations, and the Detroit Riot of 1967* (East Lansing: Michigan State University Press, 2007).

12. Notable works on sex and sexuality in Detroit include Tim Retzloff, "City, Suburb, and the Changing Bounds of Lesbian and Gay Life and Politics in Metropolitan Detroit, 1945–1985" (PhD diss., Yale University, 2014); Marlon M. Bailey, *Butch Queens Up in Pumps: Gender, Performance, and Ballroom Culture in Detroit* (Ann Arbor: University of Michigan Press, 2013).

13. Richard F. Hixson, *Pornography and the Justices: The Supreme Court and the Intractable Obscenity Problem* (Carbondale: Southern Illinois University Press, 1996), 20–21; Clay Calvert, "Of Burning Houses and Roasting Pigs: Why Butler v. Michigan Remains a Key Free Speech Victory More Than a Half-Century Later," *Federal Communications Law Journal* 64, no. 2 (March 2012): 247–74.

14. Hixson, *Pornography and the Justices*, 135–46; Lewis, *Hollywood v. Hard Core*, 273–75; Strub, *Perversion for Profit*, 173–74; Jeremy Geltzer, *Dirty Words and Filthy Pictures: Film and the First Amendment* (Austin: University of Texas Press, 2016), 282–84.

15. Marilyn Adler Papayanis, "Sex and the Revanchist City: Zoning Out Pornography in New York," *Environment and Planning D: Society and Space* 18, no. 3 (2000): 343–45; Josh Sides, "Excavating the Postwar Sex District in San Francisco," *Journal of Urban History* 32, no. 3 (2006): 369–71; Robert O. Self, "Sex in the City: The Politics of Sexual Liberalism in Los Angeles, 1963–79," *Gender & History* 20, no. 2 (2008): 303.

16. Strub, *Perversion for Profit*, 3.

17. For more on the relationship between cinema history and policing, see Noah Tsika, *Screening the Police: Film and Law Enforcement in the United States* (New York: Oxford University Press, 2021).

18. "Porno Fight Joined," *Detroit Free Press*, October 7, 1975, 3; "Pickets, Michigan Paper Denounce X-Film Showing at Studio North," *Boxoffice*, October 27, 1975, ME-2; Timothy J. McNulty, "23 Judges Join Battle over 'Naked Stranger,'" *Detroit Free Press*, September 21, 1975, 8; "Restrain Raids on 'Stranger' but 'Guerilla Warfare' Looms," *Variety*, September 24, 1975, 36.

19. Enormous thanks to reader 1 for their generous suggestion of this language.

ONE

"BURN THE HOUSE TO ROAST THE PIG"
Literary Censorship and Juvenile Delinquency

THROUGHOUT MUCH OF THE 1950S, the men of the Detroit Police Department's Censor Bureau read through every comic book and paperback novel entering the city, eyeing them for four-letter words as well as violent and sexual content, banning those that fell afoul of their censorial standards. Their list of banned titles circulated widely and was enforced in towns and cities both large and small across Michigan and the whole of the United States. Their power and influence as literary censors were such that publishers and distributors willingly cooperated by sending their entire line of new publications to Detroit's Censor Bureau, knowing full well the harsh economic consequences of appearing on the banned list. Perhaps the most remarkable detail about Detroit's literary censorship operation was that hardly anyone in Detroit knew it was going on at the time, and even fewer know about it today.

This chapter seeks to recover a history that has long since been forgotten, a history in which Detroit, for a time, established itself as the de facto literary censor for the entire country. No scholars have written in detail on the topic: in fact, it has garnered little more than passing mention in over half a century. In large part, this is due to the secrecy that Detroit's Censor Bureau cultivated during its heyday, which left only a handful of sources detailing the bureau's operations, particularly in its early years. This chapter relies on these select few sources from the era, in particular a three-part exposé on Detroit censorship published in the *Minneapolis Star*, transcripts from the testimony of the head of the Censor Bureau before a congressional hearing, sporadic articles covering the bureau that appeared in the *Detroit Free Press* and the *Detroit News*, and the documentation generated by the United States Supreme Court case that would ultimately end the city's literary censorship setup. All these sources have their blind spots, but together they paint a complex and detailed portrait of Detroit's literary censorship practices.

As I do throughout this book, in this chapter I argue for the outsized role played by Detroit in the broader history of media censorship in the United States. Detroit's Censor Bureau was highly influential during the early 1950s, both in terms of its widely disseminated list of banned books and as a model of effective police censorship for other cities across the country. Still, even as I make the case for the exceptionalism of Detroit's censorship of literature in that era, I also demonstrate how broader national trends shaped the city's censorship practices. The growing popularity of comic books and paperback books during the postwar era spurred concerns over the impact they were having on both children and "weak-minded" adults, concerns that molded the rhetoric and strategies used by Detroit's Censor Bureau. The particular form of literary censorship in Detroit, however, was also shaped by key local contexts. Among these was that the city housed a large and active Catholic population at the time, and Catholic groups in Detroit not only encouraged the city to take action against indecent literature but also actively partnered with the Censor Bureau by monitoring newsstands and book dealers. Literary censorship in Detroit was also inevitably shaped by the fact that the Censor Bureau was housed in the Detroit Police Department, with the particular predilections of the police influencing what books were targeted for censorship.

I begin this chapter by briefly examining the history of the Detroit Police Department's Censor Bureau, starting with the censorship of movies during the silent era of cinema and continuing through the rise of literary censorship in the latter half of the 1930s and the comic book scare of the late 1940s. I then detail the working practices of the Censor Bureau during the early 1950s, showing how various forms of "cooperation" greased the wheels of Detroit's censorship machine, allowing Detroit to emerge as the country's most influential literary censor while making possible the secrecy that surrounded the bureau's work. From here, I look at what books were banned by the city alongside what was thought to be the effect of this indecent literature on its intended readers. I conclude by looking at the United States Supreme Court's 1957 decision in *Butler v. Michigan*, which both effectively ended systematic literary censorship in Detroit and marked an important legal precedent that constrained obscenity law as a means of media censorship.

SILENT CENSORSHIP

Before turning to the literary censorship of the postwar era, it is necessary to first discuss the origins of film censorship in Detroit within the context of the history of Detroit and its police department. In the early twentieth century, Detroit enjoyed a booming economy fueled by the meteoric rise of the automobile industry. The demand for workers across the city's numerous factories led to the rapid growth of Detroit's population, with the number of residents of the city surging from 285,000 in 1900 all the way up to 993,000 in 1920. Migrants came to Detroit from across the United States as well as from Europe, and the city was increasingly made up of a heterogeneous mix of different ethnicities and nationalities, including a large number of first- and second-generation immigrants. The Detroit Police Department, however, reflected little of the city's demographic diversity. Between 1910 and 1918, some 93 percent of Detroit police officers were native born, in contrast to 66 percent of the city as a whole. The police were, in the words of historian Rebecca Reed, "overwhelmingly male, white, working class, and native born." The police also tended to be poorly educated as well as poorly trained for their jobs. As historian Robert Conot writes, "Not until 1911 had Detroit . . . pioneered in the establishment of a training school for police. Before then, men had been given a revolver, a club, a pair of handcuffs and a badge, and instructed to go out and enforce the law. What the law was, normally was left to the discretion of the sergeant or lieutenant." Given this, the Detroit Police Department of the early twentieth century often acted as a force of repression that targeted the city's immigrants and African Americans, who suffered arrests, harassment, and beatings at the hands of the police at much higher rates than native-born white Detroiters.[1]

It was within this context that the regulation of motion pictures developed in Detroit. Detroit's first movie theater, the Casino, opened in 1906; not long after, calls to regulate the new medium of motion pictures began to circulate in the city. Early on, many of these demands for regulation focused on the physical dangers that movie theaters were perceived as posing to audiences. The flouting of fire safety codes in many nickelodeon theaters, combined with high-profile tragedies at other theaters around the country, led the city's regulatory forces to focus their attention on basic renovations to theater architecture to ensure the safety of patrons. This was largely in keeping with the dominant approach to the regulation of cinema happening in cities across the country, where to regulate the movies largely meant to regulate movie theaters. However, this began to change during what film historians have called the "transitional era" of cinema, lasting from roughly 1908 to 1917. As Lee Grieveson writes, the period saw a "shift from a regulatory focus on buildings and space, to a focus both on the social function of cinema characteristic of the transitional era, and on representations and effects that have subsequently dominated policy discussions of cinema."[2]

Detroit was at the forefront of this trend, shifting regulatory focus from theaters to the movies themselves. On September 3, 1907, just a few short months before Chicago passed its own movie censorship ordinance, the Detroit City Council passed a law requiring "proprietors of moving picture shows to submit films it is proposed using to the commissioner of police for approval." The ordinance imposed a penalty of $200 or six months in a house of correction for failure to comply. Importantly, the ordinance in many ways extended the existing powers of the Detroit Police Department to censor other forms of public entertainment. As the *Detroit Free Press* wrote at the time, "The measure is in reality an amendment to the old ordinance covering places of amusement." Given that the Detroit police had started assigning two detectives to the censorship of legitimate theater in the city some four years prior, it evidently seemed easy enough to all involved to simply expand the police's jurisdiction to cover movies as well. Weeks later, the city council adopted a measure extending the police's censorship powers to also include penny arcades.[3]

And so, the Detroit Police Department came to be in charge of movie censorship in Detroit. A comprehensive system for censorship would be developed in the years ahead, particularly starting in 1912, after which any film hoping to play in Detroit first needed to be submitted to what came to be known as the Detroit Police Department's Censor Bureau. There, the film would be examined for content deemed "indecent" or "immoral," the standards under which they could censor a picture. Given the haziness of these standards, the police had enormous leeway to censor whatever they saw fit. As the *Detroit Free Press* said in 1913, the "censors are pretty much a law unto themselves" and "have authority to take any action they feel is warranted by conditions." If a film featured material deemed unfit for public exhibition, the film would either be banned outright or the distributor would be asked to cut out a particular shot or scene to avoid a ban. Once a film was found to be suitable for public exhibition the police would issue a permit, without which a film could not be shown commercially in Detroit. To check on compliance, members of the Censor Bureau would regularly pay visits to theaters, which were required to publicly display permits for all movies showing at the theater. These spot visits also gave the Censor Bureau occasion to pass judgment on the tastefulness of theaters' advertising displays.[4]

That the police should willingly take on the work of censoring movies fits with the broader practices and priorities of the Detroit Police Department at the time. Importantly, as was the case in numerous other cities, motion pictures during this era attracted all manner of audiences given that the standard price for a ticket was a mere five cents. This in turn made movies a unique threat for the censorial minded. The *Free Press*, in an October 1913 article on what they called "Movie Mad" Detroit, described the diverse audience for movies thus: "Rich and poor flock to the picture play houses. . . . Here come all classes and conditions—rich and poor, American and foreign born, of high or low station." Those in the latter of these binary pairings—the poor, the foreign born, and those of low station—were disproportionately targeted by the Detroit Police Department throughout this era, with the police frequently harassing and arresting immigrants and the working class. As Rebecca Reed writes, the Detroit police of this era evinced a "flagrant fear and suspicion" of "the sizable foreign-born population of the city," blaming them for crime in the city. The Detroit police also routinely cataloged the physical characteristics of poor men boarding in rooming houses, believing them to be potential criminals. Police regulation of the movies, the most popular form of entertainment for these groups, can therefore be seen as one other means of controlling these populations. Likewise, the popularity of the movies with the youth of Detroit also meant that censorship aligned with police interests. Juvenile delinquency was a major concern for the police throughout this era, with a specialized juvenile court having been created in Detroit in 1907, and movie censorship in Detroit was often proffered as necessary to protect children from indecent cinema. All in all, the shape of movie censorship in Detroit reflected the priorities of the police. As one Detroit film exhibitor said in 1913, "The rules on censorship here are quite strict. Four-fifths of the patronage of moving picture houses are children. No pictures are shown here where a criminal is depicted as a hero or too much degradation of women is shown, and ridicule of police authority, etc., is discouraged."[5]

The fear that immoral movies might have a negative impact on children led the Detroit Federation of Women's Clubs (DFWC) to argue that they would be a better fit for the job of movie censor in Detroit than the police were. Throughout much of the 1910s, the DFWC lobbied strongly and steadfastly for a representative from their ranks to be made film censor. As R. H. Ashbaugh, president of the DFWC, said in 1913, "The right kind of a woman as censor of moving picture films would be an inestimable moral force." The rationale she put forward was that the duty of movie censor was to protect the minds of innocent children and that women—or, more accurately, white, married mothers—had a special understanding of the needs of children that a police officer could never match. Speaking to the type of woman imagined as suitable for this work, Ashbaugh said, "A woman censor should be a Christian woman, not in the orthodox sense, but in the big, broad sense." This notion of a female movie censor was actually supported initially by the police commissioner, John Gillespie, who in 1913 proposed creating a censorship board of three people, one of them a woman drawn from the ranks of the DFWC. Gillespie said of his rationale, "Regarding the appointment of a woman censor of motion pictures and houses, it seems to me as a particularly good idea. Women are the natural guardians of children, the best qualified to know what will hurt or benefit them."[6]

That a woman did not end up acting as movie censor was the result of local film distributors and exhibitors vehemently opposing the notion, preferring to continue dealing with police censors, particularly since they feared (in oftentimes plainly sexist terms) being subject to the whims of a female censor. As the manager of the Detroit Universal Film Exchange said, "I have no criticism of the police censorship in Detroit. It has been very satisfactory, but if a woman were appointed on a censorship board she must be very strong to withstand the opinions of other women who will bring pressure upon her." Meanwhile, the threat of the Michigan legislature setting up its own movie censorship board for the entire state also encouraged the industry to call for the Detroit police to continue to act as censors. *Motion Picture News* reported on a meeting of local exhibitors and distributors on this issue in May of 1914, saying of the argument made by one exhibitor, "Mr. McCarren declared he believed in choosing the lesser of two evils. . . . To abandon local censorship, he said, would be to open up the way for state censorship and a bunch of farmers would be passing on the films." In large part because of the industry's objections, movie censorship in Detroit stayed in the hands of the Detroit Police Department, with no female censor or state censor board intruding on police authority.[7]

Beyond their fear of having to deal with a female censor or a state censor board, Detroit distributors and exhibitors also preferred to keep police censorship in place because, for the most part, the police censors had been good to them. Indeed, what is perhaps most striking about the history of Detroit's censorship of movies from the 1910s through the early 1930s was the degree to which the city's police censors were friendly with local film exhibitors and distributors. This is illustrated through the case of Lieutenant Royal A. Baker, who acted as the Detroit Police Department's chief film censor for much of this period. Baker's path to becoming Detroit's police censor was circuitous. At age fourteen Baker had dropped out of school to try to enter the entertainment industry, ignoring the exhortations of his father to follow in his footsteps by becoming a police officer. At various points over the next decade, Baker worked as an actor, managed a vaudeville house, and wrote scenarios for plays and films, all before eventually becoming a police officer. Baker's experience in the industry, in turn, led to him being chosen as Detroit's first head of film censorship.[8]

Baker would be in charge of movie censorship in Detroit for much of the next twenty-five years, which is not to say he gave up his ambitions of making it in the entertainment industry. Baker was the credited writer on three films released in 1912: the Kalem Company's *The Girl Deputy*, the Biograph Company's *Like the Cat, They Came Back*, and the Vitagraph Company's *Timid May*. In 1913, just two years after essentially creating the position of film censor in Detroit, Baker left the job to become business director of the Columbia Educational Motion Picture Company. As *Moving Picture World* wrote at the time, "Readers of *The Moving Picture World* will recall Mr. Baker as the genius who formulated the rules of censorship for pictures to govern the work of the Detroit police censorship. Now he is going into the business of making pictures, which would indicate that he is not afraid to take a dose of his own medicine." By August of 1914, Baker was back with the police while still insisting to *Moving Picture World* that "he was devoting considerable of his spare time to writing scenarios, and that he was working out a number of new and original ideas." Baker would continue to work on the side as an aspiring writer for decades to come. In 1922, he sold a story to the Irons-Clamage Amusement Company and a year later another story to Preferred Pictures. In 1931, *Variety* reported that Baker was writing "a musical comedy which he hopes to have finished in time for production this year." By 1934, Baker could also boast of being a radio author for local station WXYZ. After announcing his retirement from the police force in 1935, *Billboard* said of Baker's plans, "He will devote his time to painting and writing music and screen plays; a scenario for a musical comedy is now accepted for production."[9]

Perhaps not surprisingly, Baker's dalliances with show business led to a somewhat cozy relationship with the entertainment industry in his role as police censor. Baker was known for his relatively lax attitude to his job of censoring the movies, with the *Detroit Free Press* in 1921 noting that the movie censors in Detroit "are lenient compared to those in Illinois and Ohio." Baker also routinely went out of his way to compliment the work of producers whose films he favored—for instance, by publicly praising *The Last of the Mohicans* (1920), *The Sheik* (1921), and *Great Expectations* (1934). In return, the industry also embraced Baker. Few challenges to Baker's censorship decisions ever emerged, with Baker saying, "It is a pleasure to make cuts without getting any squawks from the exhibitors." As *Exhibitors Herald* reported, "Detroit exchanges and exhibitors are not afraid of unfair censorship while Royal A. Baker is on the job."[10]

Baker's relatively lenient approach to his job occasionally drew the ire of local groups who sought stricter censorship. This was particularly so during the early 1930s, a period during which Hollywood made increasingly sexually explicit and violent movies until being curtailed by the industry's adoption of the Production Code in 1934. In 1933, the DFWC sought to supplant Baker and establish a stricter censorship of movies in Detroit only to be overruled by the police commissioner, who firmly backed Baker and the current setup. In early 1934, Judge John J. Maher—in a written opinion sentencing the manager of the Adams Theater to ninety days' jail time for displaying stills from the exploitation film *Elysia (Valley of the Nude)* (1933) in his theater's lobby—expressly called for the city to supplant Baker by creating a new board of censorship modeled after the one proposed by Detroit club women. In response, Mayor Frank Couzens expressed that he was satisfied with the present system of movie censorship and with Baker, and so no changes were made.[11]

The most strenuous objections to Baker's role as censor undoubtedly came from Catholic groups in Detroit hell-bent on cleaning up the movies. In 1934, the local chapter of the Catholic Legion of Decency began to organize a citywide campaign to protest indecent movies, soon getting some 350,000 Catholics in Detroit to pledge themselves to boycott immoral films while also picking up support from other religious groups. This development drew the ire of Baker, who gave what would prove to be a controversial interview to *Billboard* in May of 1934 in which he said, "It's all right for the Catholic Church to make rules and set standards for its own members . . . but they have no right to interfere with what another person shall see." He went on to say, "What is immorality to one person is not so to another. . . . The kind of films the Catholics accept as clean under the strictest standards would not interest me, nor most people." Local Catholic leaders expressed their outrage over Baker's remarks, with Bishop Michael Gallagher, head of the Diocese of Detroit, saying, "It is the height of presumption for a Detroit policeman to set up his opinion on morals against that of all the churches in the United States." It is a testament to the power of the Catholic Church in Detroit at that time that Baker was forced to walk back his comments, claiming he had been misquoted and demanding a retraction from *Billboard*. Needless to say, no retraction from the journal ever came, and given Baker's public statements elsewhere, there is no reason to think the views expressed in the *Billboard* interview were not his own.[12]

Baker tended to talk less like a bluenose censor than an advocate for the interests of the film industry. As Baker told the *Free Press* in 1921, "They're all [deluded] when they say the motion pictures influence persons to commit crimes. It is just as sensible to think that seeing a man jump from a 10-story window would make me want to jump from that height." In his controversial interview with *Billboard* in 1934, Baker similarly said, "I don't think anyone ever did wrong because he saw a picture. I've seen more than most people for 27 years, and I haven't become a gangster yet."[13] Such comments, of course, directly contradicted the notion at the center of almost all movie censorship, which is that movies have a direct effect on people, with immoral movies leading to immoral behavior by viewers. Baker repeatedly aligned himself with industry interests and against those advocating for more stringent film censorship. In an interview given to *Billboard* upon his retirement in 1935, Baker said of the era's growing calls for harsher censorship of movies: "Such finely detailed art cannot be chopped to pieces to satisfy reformers who know nothing of the technical work involved. If the form of prohibition shown by contemporary demands for stricter regulation is to grow continuously, where is the stopping place? It will happen to our free press. It will destroy the free speech of this country. The creative writer and artist must have freedom of self-expression. We must not set up such barriers." In the same article, Baker responded specifically to mounting pressure for national censorship of motion pictures by saying, "But if national censorship is threatened, let the theaters strike. I would dare all houses to close for 30 days. The public protest would be so overwhelming that the move for censorship of this kind would be at an end forever."[14]

Despite the seeming paradox of a censor decrying censorship, in truth Baker's words fit perfectly with his approach to censorship for over two decades. From his start as censor in 1911 to his retirement in 1935—the news of which was greeted with the *Variety* headline "Lieut. Baker, a Liberal, Resigns as Det. Censor"—Baker continually took a tolerant stance toward the industry, defending it even when, as during the early 1930s, calls for greater censorship of cinema were being heard in Detroit and across the country. More broadly, Baker's views in many ways were indicative of the Detroit Police Department's approach to media censorship during this era. Though the 1910s, 1920s, and early 1930s certainly saw plenty of films cut, books banned, and plays postponed for required revisions, this era in Detroit nevertheless was marked by a relatively lax approach to the censorship of media by the city. However, this permissive approach to media censorship would be drastically altered by the end of the 1940s due to a host of shifts in the media landscape and an altered political climate.[15]

CATHOLIC ACTION AND THE RISE OF LITERARY CENSORSHIP

During the 1930s, Catholics were an ascendant power in Detroit society and politics. The previous decade had seen the Diocese of Detroit nearly double in size, from 386,000 Catholics in 1919 to 725,000 in 1929, and by the start of the 1930s, roughly 40 percent of Detroit was Catholic. Alongside these growing numbers came Catholics' growing political power in the city. The 1920s had seen Catholics achieve some gains in political representation, most notably the 1924 election of the Catholic John W. Smith even in the face of concerted opposition led by the Ku Klux Klan. In the 1930s, though, Catholic political influence become a dominant force in Detroit politics, a trend aided by the nationwide rise of the Democratic Party, which had long-standing ties with Catholics. Catholic Frank Murphy's election as mayor in 1930 was seen as a landmark, particularly given that Murphy closely aligned himself with Catholic leaders and ideology. Meanwhile, as historian Henry J. Pratt noted, "The Depression era saw a significant rise in the number of Catholics on the [Detroit] city council: from a low point of two in 1922 to four (among nine to ten members) throughout most of the 1930s." All told, writes Leslie Tentler, "Catholics were an integral part of Detroit's political establishment after 1930." Detroit's status as a hub of Catholic activity and power would be cemented in 1937 when the Diocese of Detroit was elevated to archdiocese status.[16]

This growing prominence of Catholics in Detroit in the 1930s coincided with the rise of the Catholic Action movement throughout the United States. Developing in the early 1930s in the midst of the Great Depression, Catholic Action called for laity to take on more of an active role in shaping American society. The call to Catholic Action encompassed a number of different efforts by Catholics, including charitable work, a campaign against communism, activism against birth control, and finally a war against movie immorality. Though numerous groups in the early 1930s called for a cleanup of the movies, Catholics undoubtedly led the charge. The threat of a mass boycott of Hollywood cinema by Catholics—a move spearheaded by the Legion of Decency—had been crucial in persuading the film industry to adopt the Production Code midway through 1934. The code itself bore heavy Catholic influence, having been cowritten by Father Daniel A. Lord and *Motion Picture Herald* editor and Catholic layman Martin Quigley, with the two imbuing the document with Catholic views on decency and morality. Once the Production Code era was ushered in, another Catholic, Joseph I. Breen, was put in charge of the enforcement of the code as head of the Production Code Administration. Though the Legion of Decency would continue to keep Hollywood in check for decades to come, there was some sense that the battle against movie immorality had been won and that a new battlefront was needed in the broader war over the morality of popular entertainment in American society. Catholic leaders and organizations soon found their new target in indecent literature (see fig. 1.1).

Central to the Catholic war on obscene literature was the formation of the National Organization for Decent Literature (NODL) in 1938 as the literary counterpart to the Legion of Decency. Among local chapters of the NODL

Figure 1.1. Comic in *Drive for Decency in Print* (1938).

across the country, Detroit was renowned for having, in the words of historian Thomas O'Connor, "a very active parish-level campaign" against obscene literature, with "enthusiastic lay and clerical leadership." Detroit's NODL chapter officially launched their campaign on March 26, 1939, with parishioners across Detroit treated to a sermon condemning obscene literature and encouraging them to take the NODL pledge, which read: "I promise to refrain from purchasing and reading all reading matter which violates the Code of the National

Organization for Decent Literature, and I promise not to enter places where such literature continues to be sold."[17]

The campaign, though, was not limited to boycotts of obscene literature and the establishments selling them. Catholic leaders in Detroit worked with and at times against various parts of the city government in their campaign. One city institution the NODL found fault with was the Detroit Public Library, which came under fire after one Alban J. Norris wrote to the *Michigan Catholic* telling of the "trash" his daughter had brought home from the library, including *The Friendly Tree* by C. Day Lewis and *I Am the Fox* by Winifred Van Etten. Though nationally the NODL made a point to not target public libraries, Catholic leaders in Detroit apparently had no such qualms. What ensued was a series of letters between Anthony Beck, editor of the *Michigan Catholic*, and Adam Strohm of the Detroit Public Library. For Beck, a major issue was the public availability of these books. As he said, "The books in question are not works in the research section but books in general circulation and available to young folks." Strohm responded by noting that one of the missions of a public library is that of "developing broad-minded intelligence and willingness to consider all sides of a problem and its presentation." Ultimately Strohm held out in refusing to remove the books, though there would be more battles to come between the Detroit Public Library and Catholic pressure groups.[18]

Detroit-area Catholic groups tended to find more success in their campaign against indecent literature when they joined forces with other local organizations. Among these were other religious groups, as in 1936 when the League of Jewish Women's Organizations joined Catholics in their plea for the city council to act against obscene literature. Likewise, the late 1930s saw the Detroit Council of Churches, composed of approximately four hundred Protestant congregations, pass a resolution to "commend our Catholic men for their campaign" against indecent literature. Such efforts to reach across religious lines were part of a broader NODL strategy to court allies. As Thomas O'Connor writes, "Catholics were always in the majority in NODL, but Protestants and Jews were also encouraged to participate. It was for this reason that the organization was deliberately not called the Catholic Organization for Decent Literature." This strategy allowed Catholic leaders to not only forge alliances in the war against obscene literature but also position the cause as uniting a variety of religious institutions, rather than this being just another instance of Catholics trying to force their moral standards upon the rest of the country.[19]

Still, the most important ally for Catholic organizations in the city was undoubtedly the Literary Censorship Bureau of the Detroit Police Department, which had been formed in 1937 largely in response to Catholic efforts to combat the perceived flood of illicit reading material entering the city. The collaboration between the police and Catholic groups was made clear at a meeting of representatives from numerous local religious and civic organizations who gathered in early 1938 to discuss the war on obscene literature. At the meeting, Raymond Cameron, president of the Detroit Council of Catholic Organizations and lay director of the Detroit chapter of the NODL, presented a list of thirty-four "objectionable" periodicals along with a list of a further eighty-two periodicals falling under the heading of "questionable." After some individuals at the meeting questioned the rationale behind placing certain titles on the list, Cameron "revealed that he had prepared the list with the aid of Sergt. Newton Peters, police book censor." This would be far from the last time that the local NODL and the Detroit Police Department's censors would work in concert with one another.[20]

In 1938, the local Catholic literary censorship campaign began to bear fruit when Detroit's censors decided to ban Ernest Hemingway's *To Have and Have Not*. The incident started when Catholic organizations in the city launched a concerted attack on the book. The *Michigan Catholic* harshly criticized Hemingway's novel, calling for it to be removed from high school classrooms and public libraries. Arthur D. Maguire, chair of the board of directors of the Detroit Council of Catholic Organizations, wrote a letter to the Detroit Public Library demanding that they remove the book from circulation and declaring that "what we are asking for is plain American decency and we propose to get it." The Detroit Council of Catholic Organizations also sent a letter of complaint to Judge Thomas M. Cotter of the recorder's court in Detroit, who in turn forwarded the complaint to Wayne County prosecutor Duncan C. McCrea. Following this, McCrea, in conjunction with the police Literary Censorship Bureau, banned the book from Detroit on the grounds that it violated state and city law prohibiting the sale or distribution of any book containing "obscene, immoral, lewd or lascivious language, manifestly tending to the corruption of the morals of youth."[21]

The ban on *To Have and Have Not* would soon be challenged in court, with the Wayne County Circuit Court ultimately ruling in favor of Detroit and Michigan, upholding the constitutionality of the state law under which the book was banned even as the court refused to rule on whether the book itself was or was not obscene. In the wake of the decision, William Dowling, chief assistant prosecutor for Wayne County, wrote a letter to Reverend John A. Donovan, secretary to Detroit archbishop Edward A. Mooney, lauding him for his role in the campaign against the book. As Dowling wrote, "I feel that this victory is due in large measure to the efforts of men like yourself in bringing the subject to the attention of your parishioners and especially in enlisting their support in the drive for clean literature. For this kind assistance please accept my sincere thanks."[22]

The Archdiocese of Detroit's interest in banning *To Have and Have Not* was ostensibly due to their view of the book as being indecent and obscene. Still, others saw a different motivation behind their push for censorship. In a letter to the editor published in *Nation*, writers Van Wyck Brooks, Archibald MacLeish, and Thornton Wilder argued that the city's action had less to do with the book itself than it did Hemingway's political leanings. As they wrote, "The real reason for the suppression is Mr. Hemingway's known sympathy for the Spanish government in the civil war in Spain and his activity in securing ambulances for the service of the Spanish army and the bombed population." Supporting this notion was the fact that Catholics in Detroit had mounted a major drive in support of Franco, and there was significant overlap between the local Catholic leadership on the twin issues of the Spanish Civil War and literary indecency. Regardless of the true reason for the Archdiocese of Detroit's interest, though, what is clear is the degree to which Catholic organizations in the city held sway over the censorial activity of those in power, with their campaign against obscene literature achieving concrete results.[23]

Local Catholic activism against obscene literature gained an important ally in 1937 when Herbert W. Case joined the newly formed Literary Censorship Bureau. Case was a native of the area, having gone to the University of Michigan as an undergraduate before attending the Detroit College of Law and joining the Detroit Police Department in 1931. In time, Case would be the driving force behind the expansion of Detroit police censorship and later became perhaps the country's most important literary censor. Notably, too, he was nothing if not a friend to Catholic advocates of censorship, with one 1955 article calling him "the most important ally the NODL has found to date." During the late 1930s and throughout much of the 1940s, though, Case and the Literary Censorship Bureau's activities remained rather limited, and for the most part only minor censorial action occurred during this time. Besides the ban on *To Have and Have Not*, the other notable exception was the 1944 banning of Lillian Smith's novel *Strange Fruit*, which dealt with racism and the topic of interracial romance. This brief episode saw Case employ a number of the tactics he would refine over the course of his career, even as he was faced with constraints that distinguished the incident from his later censorial exploits.[24]

Rather than outright banning *Strange Fruit*, Case asked stores and libraries to voluntarily remove the book. As he said of his reasoning, "I didn't want to ban the book because that only creates that much more public interest. I went to bookstores and the library seeking their co-operation after receiving complaints from a number of people, including some parents, and got agreements in most places not to sell the book." Such reliance on the cooperation of distributors and book dealers would be a hallmark of Case's brand of censorship, as he sought to avoid formal legal action and the attendant free publicity for the banned work.[25]

Still, even as the banning of *Strange Fruit* in certain ways resembled the mechanisms of censorship Case would employ during the 1950s, in other ways it fell short of his later, more successful efforts. A key difference was that whereas Case here acted in response to complaints his office had received, as we shall see, later on no such impetus would be required for censorial action. Perhaps more centrally, though, while Case may have sought to sidestep a public debate over the merits of *Strange Fruit*, his efforts in this regard were an abject failure. After the Detroit Public Library and the labor-run Union Book Store both refused to cooperate with the ban on the book, the story was extensively covered in both local newspapers and national trade magazines. Mounting public pressure ultimately forced Case to lift the ban on the book, after which it immediately (and rather predictably) "leaped to first place on the local best seller list."[26]

Beyond signaling a number of the major strategies Case would go on to deploy in censoring literature, Detroit's ban on *Strange Fruit* also speaks to the way racism often inflected censorship in Detroit. Case claimed that *Strange Fruit* had been banned because the word *fuck* appears once in the novel. Others contended that this was a pretext for the real reason the book was banned, with the *Michigan Chronicle*, Detroit's largest African American newspaper, writing in an editorial, "We believe that this four-letter word would have been overlooked if it were not for the fact that the book tells the story of love between the races." Detroit's banning of *Strange Fruit* thus speaks to the myth of the racist exceptionalism of the South. Whereas studies of the civil rights movement for some time pitted an imagined racist South versus a racially liberal and tolerant North, in recent years scholars have begun to push back on this notion. As Thomas Sugrue writes, this myth of Southern exceptionalism "ignores the long and intense history of racial violence and conflict in northern towns and cities." The case of the banning of *Strange Fruit* is illustrative in this regard. In the North, the book was banned not only in Detroit but also in Boston, prompting author Lillian Smith to remark, "I had been uneasy about how the South might take my book.... But I had not even thought that *Strange Fruit* would find official disfavor in Boston." That Smith had not contemplated the possibility of her book getting banned in a

Northern city speaks to the power of the myth of Southern racist exceptionalism. Beyond this, the very fact that Detroit chose to ban an anti-racist book illustrates the way whiteness and the need to preserve the racial status quo were central to the city's censorship efforts. As the same *Michigan Chronicle* editorial went on to say of Detroit's ban on the book, "The simple truth is that there are many whites who do not want the world to know the ugly truths of race relations in the South where the lust and lynch-spirit of white men have made a living hell. Detroit is becoming a Southern town and those who want to shape it after Southern patterns are protesting the sale of this book because its truths cut deep into the heart of bigotry."[27]

COMICS AND CRIMINALITY

The year 1948 marked a turning point in Detroit police censorship with the retirement of Charlie Snyder, who had started as film censor in 1935 before ascending to head of the Censor Bureau in 1943. Snyder left the police force to become the "goodwill ambassador" for Allied Theatres of Michigan, a trade group representing the state's film exhibitors, thereby continuing in the tradition of Royal Baker in moving through the revolving door between Detroit's police censors and the industries they were charged with regulating. Coupled with the announcement of Snyder's move was speculation in the industry regarding his replacement as head of censorship in Detroit, with *Variety* writing that the "best guess is that it will be Lt. Herbert Chase [sic], Snyder's assistant." In 1948, Case took over as head censor, tasked to lead the newly formed License and Censor Bureau, which was in charge of all media censorship activity in the city. And, as luck would have it, just as Case was promoted, there emerged a perfect target for the new regime: comic books.[28]

During the era immediately preceding the Second World War, comic books achieved their "gold-rush period," as the number of published titles ballooned from 150 in 1937 to nearly 700 by 1940. Attendant with this burgeoning popularity was growing concern over the impact comics were having on the youth of America, leading to some of the first calls for comic book censorship. Still, the coming of the war largely set these concerns aside. As David Hajdu writes, "By the end of 1941, American families were absorbed with dangers clearer and more present than comic books. Much as the First World War had snuffed early criticism of newspaper strips, the Second damped the debate over comic books before it caught fire. In fact, the idea of superheroes began to seem acutely patriotic—a simple, democratic, home-grown symbol of American might and surety of purpose."[29]

The good times would not last, though, as the end of the war brought with it renewed calls for comic book censorship. This was largely tied to growing fears of an alleged epidemic of juvenile delinquency. The most famous purveyor of the idea that comic books were linked to, and indeed the cause of, juvenile delinquency was Fredric Wertham. In his public comments, Wertham drew on his background in psychiatry, as well as pseudoscientific data, to argue vociferously that comic books were a key driver behind the supposedly skyrocketing rates of juvenile delinquency. Between his writing in popular magazines of the day, his 1954 testimony before the United States Senate Subcommittee on Juvenile Delinquency, and his book *Seduction of the Innocent*, Wertham managed to galvanize public opinion against comic books. This public outrage over comic books in turn fed a movement to censor comics, a movement that the city of Detroit and its Censor Bureau eagerly joined.[30]

In April of 1948, Detroit police commissioner Harry S. Toy announced that the police would begin inspecting comic books for objectionable material, making Detroit one of the first major cities to take such action. This crackdown on comics was the result of Toy's view of comic books as being "loaded with communistic teachings, sex and racial discrimination." Just a few years earlier, critics of comic books had accused them of having fascist leanings, with *Time* magazine in 1945 publishing an article asking, "Are Comics Fascist?" The postwar era brought with it new enemies, though, and so the "fascist tendencies" of war-era comic books morphed into communist ones once the country's war turned cold.[31]

Reflecting the variety of concerns posed by indecent comic books, the city's war on comics was waged jointly by the Detroit Police Department's anticommunist Red Squad, the Censor Bureau, and the Juvenile Crime Prevention Bureau (see fig. 1.2). The last of these was headed by Lieutenant Ralph Baker, who stated that comic books "contribute directly to juvenile delinquency." As an example, Baker cited the case of "three brothers who broke into 20 homes in their neighborhood [and] admitted that they 'learned how' by reading comic books." Such anecdotal tales of comic book–inspired juvenile criminality drove censorship efforts in Detroit, leading Commissioner Toy to announce in April of 1948 that thirty-six comic books had been banned for being "corrupting to youth," with another nineteen given the label "partially objectionable" and a further ten categorized as "questionable." Prosecutor James N. McNally listed out what he saw as the four types of objectionable comics:

1. Those planning or perpetrating a crime.
2. Those involving youth in crime.

Figure 1.2. Detective Doyle McKinney and Lieutenant Herbert Case inspect newsstand comic books. *Detroit Free Press*, April 14, 1948.

3. Entire comic[s] dealing with crime or criminal deeds.
4. Those portraying gruesome or brutal conduct on women, children or race.

The fear that youth would simply copy the crimes they saw depicted in comic books was frequently invoked by Detroit police officials to justify their censorship campaign. Similarly, the list of banned comics—including titles like *Crime Exposed Comics*, *True Crime Comics*, and *Gangster Comics*—bears out the centrality of fears of juvenile delinquency in Detroit's efforts to censor comic books.[32]

This tumult also led other cities in Michigan to follow Detroit's lead. Some, including Ann Arbor, mimicked Detroit's approach in having their police departments inspect individual comic book titles. Still others directly copied Detroit's list of banned comic books, as in the case of Hillsdale. The headlines generated by Detroit's censorship of comics meant that the city's Censor

Bureau received, in the words of Case, "in excess of 10,000 letters.... We had them from the Hawaiian Islands, from the university over there, from practically every State in the United States." Undoubtedly, then, there was considerable interest in what Detroit was doing far outside of the city itself, including outside of the state of Michigan.[33]

Detroit's censorship of comic books relied on the cooperation of a number of key local organizations. As Commissioner Toy publicly stated at the time, "We need the full co-operation of the parents, churches, schools and civic groups if we are going to rid the city of this menace. The Police Department cannot do it alone." The Archdiocese of Detroit in turn offered their assistance, telling Toy that they were behind him "all of the way." The Detroit Parent-Teacher Association (PTA) also provided vocal support, promising to "enlist 18,000 members to march behind Police Commissioner Harry S. Toy in his crusade against unfit comic books." The statewide PTA similarly pledged to "mobilize 163,000 members to back Toy's drive." This public backing of groups like these not only lent political support to police efforts to clear away indecent comics but also provided the legwork the police could not manage on their own, with private citizens inspecting magazine racks all over the city to make sure dealers and store owners kept in line.[34]

Critically, in announcing the ban of thirty-six comic books, Prosecutor McNally also revealed that the Ludington News Co. and Detroit News Co., two major comic book distributors in the region, would voluntarily remove those comics from sale immediately. The two firms' cooperation with the police soon went beyond just removing offending titles from store shelves, though. By September of 1948, just months after the start of the campaign, Herbert Case was quoted as saying, "Ninety percent of the comic distributors and publishers cooperate with our department, with most publishers sending us advance copies of their magazines two months before publication for our approval." The industry evidently reasoned that it was cheaper and easier to cooperate rather than instigate a lengthy and expensive battle in court. This move by comic book publishers and distributors was indicative of a larger industrywide effort to clean up comic books in the face of increasing scrutiny and censorial activity. Eventually, these efforts would coalesce into the comic book industry adopting the self-regulatory Comics Code Authority in 1954. This would, in turn, lessen the need for the type of local censorship of comic books seen in Detroit in much the same way that the adoption of the Production Code had once done the same, at least to some extent, for Hollywood. If the local regulatory focus on comics would not last long, then, for Detroit's Censor Bureau, this moment nevertheless marked a shift away from a system of censorship based on complaints to one based on proactive and preventive censorship. Rather than waiting for the public to express outrage over specific titles, the police began to scan and pass judgment on works before the public had a chance to complain, a practice that would soon become a hallmark of literary censorship in Detroit.[35]

POCKET-SIZED PORNOGRAPHY

In time, the uproar over comic books in Detroit calmed down. Quickly there to take its place was a new controversy surrounding indecent paperback books. Cheap paperbacks exploded in popularity during the postwar era, though their existence as a popular form of mass entertainment was hardly new. As Michael Denning explores in his book *Mechanic Accents*, the nineteenth century saw paperback dime novels, with their inexpensive price tag, become hugely popular with ethnic groups and the working class. This, in turn, generated concern from middle-class reformers over the impact these books were having on the minds of the working masses. As Denning writes, the battles over dime novels "marked a social conflict over the relations between the dominant genteel culture, the relatively autonomous and 'foreign' working class cultures, and the new commercial culture, the new 'mass culture.'"[36]

Though the dime novels Denning focuses on had subsided in popularity by the beginning of the twentieth century, a half century later, a new type of paperback novel had revived the format's popularity and its prominent place in working-class culture. The term "mass market paperback" was introduced in 1939, though the format was already rapidly gaining in popularity by that time. During the postwar era the format would truly come into its own as a new consumer culture took hold, washing away the lean years of the war. As historian Kenneth C. Davis writes, "Paperback books and the baby boomers were made for each other, a mass medium for a mass generation." The inexpensive price of these paperbacks, in the words of Davis, "democratized reading in America," helping make literature available to a generation of Americans unable to afford the high price of hardcovers. Paperbacks of the era came in a variety of forms, ranging from inexpensive versions of literary classics to paperback-only genre books typically doling out equal measures of tawdry sex and violence. And, just like their dime novel forbearers, reformers soon seized on fears regarding the impact these paperback books were having on working-class readers.[37]

It was within this context that Detroit began to wade into the censorship of paperback books in 1950. As one news story stated, "In the fall of 1950, Case says, the police department received complaints 'from individual citizens as well as

Table 1.1 Detroit Police Department Censorship

Year	Books Reviewed	Books Withheld from Circulation (Number of Copies)	Magazines (Including Comics) Reviewed	Magazines Withheld from Circulation (Number of Copies)	Feet of Film Eliminated	Cabaret Corrections
1943	7	3 (250 copies)	387	9 (54,000 copies)	26,600	–
1944	15	1 (250)	352	5 (16,700)	19,840	152
1945	20	0	318	1 (2,500)	4,220	153
1946	19	0	343	2 (10,500)	12,500	121
1947	25	2 (15,000)	364	3 (24,000)	11,750	116
1948	17	1 (3,000)	778	53 (636,000)	59,300	66
1949	23	3 (26,000)	488	8 (90,000)	39,950	63
1950	167	30 (295,000)	334	8 (85,000)	26,340	91
1951	726	39 (400,000)	394	5 (54,600)	17,299	71
1952	1,131	58 (569,000)	501	19 (175,000)	37,600	72
1953	1,109	58 (501,000)	493	13 (123,000)	16,650	82
1954	–	60 (–)[1]	–	–	27,200	88
1955	1,010	– (455,000)	–	–	44,380	89
1956	1,084	72 (708,000)	836	104 (576,000)	–	88
1957	593	15 (150,000)	795	53 (233,000)	–	145

Note: All figures come from the Detroit Police Department *Annual Reports* except where noted. En dashes signify incomplete data.
[1] Dave Smith, "Detroit Renews Book Ban Despite Court's Decision," *Michigan Journalist*, March 27, 1957, 4.

from church and civic groups and the board of education.' Since then the censor bureau has attempted to pass judgment on all the pocket-size books that enter Detroit." This entailed a movement away from a complaint-based operation to a proactive examination of all paperbacks before their release, a shift presaged by the city's censorship of comic books.[38]

The increased scrutiny of paperback books was part of a broader trend after Case became head of the Detroit Police Department's Censor Bureau in 1948. Namely, even as Detroit's censorship of other entertainment formats stayed at a relatively stable rate during the late 1940s and 1950s, this period saw a marked rise in literary censorship (see table 1.1). A spike in the number of magazines banned in 1948 corresponds to the comic book scare of that year. Likewise, the number of books reviewed, as well as the number banned—or, in the euphemism employed by the police department in their annual reports, the number "withheld from circulation"—skyrocketed beginning in 1950 as the police began to take a closer look at paperbacks. Between 1943 and 1949, the Censor Bureau annually reviewed 18 books, banning on average just under 1½ per year. The year 1950 acted as something of a transition period, with the department beginning to examine all paperbacks in the fall; the number of books reviewed reached 167 and the number of books banned totaled 30, both figures higher than the previous seven years combined. Between 1951 and 1956, the year preceding the United States Supreme Court ruling that severely curtailed Detroit's censorial activity, the Censor Bureau, on average, reviewed 1,012 books each year and banned around 57, increases of roughly 5,500 and 3,500 percent, respectively, from the period of 1943 through 1949. Within the span of less than a decade, Detroit went from only banning the rare book that drew numerous complaints and controversy to making the censorship of literature a major priority. The reasons for this are many—including increased concern over juvenile delinquency and the rapid growth in the popularity of paperbacks—but just as important as why this increased focus on literary censorship occurred is exactly how it occurred. To appropriate what film critic and theorist André Bazin once said of the Hollywood studio system, what truly set Detroit's literary censorship operation apart was the "genius of the system."

THE CENSORSHIP MACHINE

As the perceived threat posed by indecent literature increased, the Detroit Police Department's Censor Bureau grew in response. By 1952, twelve men worked under Case to keep Detroit free from indecent media, with the whole operation costing the city around $70,000—equaling roughly ten times that amount in today's dollars adjusted for inflation. More important than the growth of the department itself was the development of a system of censorship shaped by the knowledge Inspector Case had amassed during his time as police literary censor. This censorship machine was built with thoroughness in mind, and the tall task of inspecting every comic and paperback book entering the city was made possible through an assembly-line approach to censorship modeled after Detroit's most famous export, Fordism. It was built to operate seemingly without personal discretion or human bias, with dispassionate legal guidelines belying the notion that any judgments of morality or value were taking place at all. And last, but perhaps most important, this machine was built to operate silently, with its smooth workings giving off none of the noise that might draw the public's attention.[39]

The assembly line began once paperbacks and comic books were first submitted to the Censor Bureau for inspection in advance of their distribution in Detroit. The police officers who made up the bureau would then read through the books, managing to cover between 90 and 125 books a month between them. While reading, officers were actively searching for objectionable material, a process Case would describe to *Newsweek* as "skimming off the filth, so to speak, at the top." Wayne County assistant prosecutor John J. Rusinack would then inspect the objectionable passages that had been highlighted by the officers. Crucially, Rusinack only examined those highlighted passages rather than the book as a whole, with a 1955 *Newsweek* article saying of Rusinack's role, "In a sense, the prosecutor is the unsung hero of the Case censorship operation, because he never gets to read anything in business hours but pure, distilled pornography. Not a nickel's worth of context. Just dirt, or what the clockers think is dirt." The practice of declaring a work obscene based solely on passages taken out of context was clearly unconstitutional given previous court rulings that had made clear that works needed to be "taken as a whole" rather than declared obscene due to a stray salacious passage. Nevertheless, based solely on these excerpts, Rusinack would give his opinion as to whether the book was, under Michigan law, obscene. If Rusinack did find the book obscene (and he almost always sided with the police censors), the distributor would be asked to withhold the book from circulation in Detroit. Distributors would then be faced with the choice of challenging the bureau, thereby paying enormous court costs and further garnering the anger of Detroit's censors, or simply withdrawing the book quietly. Almost without fail, distributors chose the latter option.[40]

Through this process, the Censor Bureau would create two lists of books, the first being books officially banned in Detroit and the second being books that did not quite qualify for banned status but were nevertheless labeled "objectionable." Distributors or bookstore owners caught selling a banned book would quickly find themselves in court, though it hardly ever came to that. For those books on the objectionable list, however, dealers were told that any complaints from residents would necessitate the book's immediate removal. Once again, though, it was rare that things ever got to that point. As one article on Detroit's censorship practices stated, "The dealer often simply withholds the book on the theory that it might be more nuisance than its sales are worth. To that extent, the 'objectionables' are effectively banned." The result was that hundreds of banned and objectionable books never made it onto store shelves in Detroit.[41]

In interviews, Case was careful to maintain that the entire censorship process was based on the law, rather than his own views and the views of the officers working below him. As Case said, "We primarily are police officers, and we try never to forget that we're going to act according to law and not according to our personal opinions. My personal opinion means absolutely nothing." Elaborating on this elsewhere, Case said, "We do not, in any instance, act solely upon our personal views or preferences." Case's protests notwithstanding, this alleged objectivity is belied by the very nature of media censorship and the subjective decision of what falls under the category of "obscene." This was made clear by the statement of one member of the Censor Bureau, Sergeant Richard Loftus, who said in a 1954, "The standards [for censorship] are usually those set up by the state law. When it comes to applying standards I suppose it is the personal judgment of the person reviewing the material." Here, then, was the inherent fallacy at the heart of Case's claims that this was an objectively run operation—in the end, the standards for determining obscenity always come down to "personal judgment." Indeed, Rusinack, the Wayne County assistant prosecutor who was tasked with giving official legal recommendations as to what was and was not obscene, made the subjective nature of the task all too clear in comments he made to the *Detroit News* in 1955 in which he said: "If I feel that I wouldn't want my 13-year-old daughter reading it, I decide it's illegal. Mind you, I don't say that it is illegal in fact, I merely say that in my opinion it would be a violation of the law to distribute it." Needless to say, Michigan's obscenity law did not, in fact, include any mention of the Wayne County assistant prosecutor's daughter as the appropriate barometer for determining whether a book was obscene or not. Rusinack's comments make clear the arbitrariness that is always characteristic of media censorship efforts, even one seemingly practiced as systematically as the Detroit Censor Bureau did during this period.[42]

Just as significantly, in spite of Case's protestations that censorship in Detroit was not based on personal opinion but rather on the law alone, the city's censorship practices were designed to avoid having to prove the obscene nature of any banned book in a courtroom. This stands in opposition to Case's argument that his office was in the business of legal rather than moral judgment and his statement that "only a judge or jury can say whether a thing is obscene." The genius of Detroit's censorship system was that no judge or jury ever had to.[43]

Though the officers of the Censor Bureau occasionally made unannounced visits to retailers to check that no banned titles were making it on to store shelves, given that estimates pegged the number of outlets in Detroit selling paperbacks or comics at somewhere between 1,800 and 2,500, it was hardly feasible for them to regularly check every retailer in the city. And so, the Censor Bureau relied on what Rusinack called a "watchdog system," in which "numerous civic and church groups" in the city helped keep an eye on bookstores and newsstands. At first, it was almost exclusively allied Catholic organizations that took on this work. Beginning around 1951, the Archdiocese of Detroit and the NODL organized its members to canvass retailers for indecent material on a weekly basis. Despite the largely male leadership of these Catholic organizations, in practice this work of visiting stores was almost exclusively carried out by Catholic women, who acted as the ground force for this watchdog system. This organizational structure was typical of many anti-porn groups of the era, such as Citizens for Decent Literature, which similarly had men at the top of the organizational hierarchy who were reliant on the largely unheralded labor of female volunteers.[44]

In 1954, Reverend Clement Esper, assistant pastor of St. Aloysius Church and a leader in the Detroit chapter of the NODL, explained how this canvassing of retailers worked in practice, saying, "Our council of Catholic Women checks closely and constantly on the distributors' shelves, newsstands, drugstores and candy stores near schools. Whenever they find an objectionable book they urge the dealer to take it off his stand and, in the event of a refusal, we complain to the police." In another interview that same year, Clement explained how Catholics' work monitoring retailers served to extend literary censorship beyond the legal limits of the Detroit Police Department. As he said, "We wish the Censor Bureau could do the job by itself but they are limited by law. So you find literature on the newsstands that the Censor Bureau may object to but can't touch because there's no violation of the law. That's where we come in."[45]

Nevertheless, in time it became clear that the task of inspecting thousands of Detroit retailers was simply too large for the Catholic women volunteering for the job. And so, in September of 1954, efforts were made to establish a new organization that might more adequately handle the problem—the Detroit Committee for Better Literature for Youth (CBLY). The CBLY was imagined as nondenominational, attracting support from the Protestant-led Detroit Council of Churches, the Detroit PTA, the Jewish Community Council, and the Detroit Federation of Women's Clubs. Even so, the most active and vocal members of the CBLY were undoubtedly Catholic leaders, who fashioned the CBLY as their means of attracting the type of non-Catholic support for the cause of literary censorship that the Catholic-affiliated NODL never could. To kick-start the drive against indecent literature, when the CBLY was formed, leaders of the group quickly organized an Inter-Faith Rally Against Indecent Literature. Though the rally included some Protestant speakers, the bulk of the speakers were Catholic, with the planned principal speech (canceled at the last minute) being given by Edward Mooney, head of the Archdiocese of Detroit, who by that time was a cardinal. Newspaper accounts stated the rally had been sponsored jointly by the NODL and the National Council of Catholic Women.[46]

Within months of forming, representatives of the CBLY met with Herbert Case, who explained to them in detail the work of the Censor Bureau and how the CBLY might help. By early 1955, the CBLY had agreed upon a comprehensive strategy that included various efforts to raise awareness and promote "good" reading, as well as a plan to organize neighborhood teams to check retailers each week for any indecent literature on store shelves. The nearly two thousand retail outlets were coded by census tract through the tireless work of Protestant and Catholic volunteers, all of them women. The plan was to create one thousand neighborhood teams to visit one or two outlets each week, examining their shelves for inappropriate reading material. An issue that quickly emerged, though, was what list of objectionable titles to use. Catholic volunteer women had been checking the titles being offered by retailers against the NODL's list of objectionable publications, which was put out regularly by the national NODL in Chicago. The non-Catholic organizations in the CBLY, though, could hardly sign up to enforce a list that was prepared by Catholics and reflected Catholic morals. And so, by the spring of 1956, the CBLY decided they would use the Detroit Censor Bureau's list of "partially objectionable" publications. Doing so allowed the CBLY to pressure retailers to remove all publications on the list, thereby widening the Censor Bureau's influence beyond just the banned list (which never made it onto store shelves) and effectively making titles on the "partially objectionable" list inaccessible as well. In this way, the Censor Bureau relied on outside groups not only to make sure their edicts were being enforced but also to extend their reach beyond what the bureau believed they could legally ban. As Rusinack told a *Minneapolis Star* reporter, "Where we cannot act legally and we know a certain book should be off the stands, that's where a pressure group comes in handy."[47]

Soon, though, questions emerged about whether using the Censor Bureau's list was viable for all members of the CBLY. The issue arose over Evelyn Miller Duvall's book *Facts of Life and Love for Teenagers*, which was a sedate guide to topics like sex and marriage, geared toward teenage readers, that had frequently been used as an educational tool by Protestant church groups in Detroit. In September of 1956, though, when Reverend Donald Schroeder, a leader in the Protestant Detroit Council of Churches, tried to order three hundred copies of the paperback edition of the book, he was surprised to find out that the distributor would not fill the order because the book was on the Censor Bureau's banned list. This became the subject of much debate at a meeting held that month between prominent members of the CBLY, two representatives from the Censor Bureau, and two Wayne County assistant prosecutors, John Rusinack and Joseph Rashid. Of the fourteen members of the CBLY who attended the meeting, the majority, eight, were from the NODL or other Catholic groups, while the other attendees included three representatives from the Detroit Council of Churches, two from the Detroit Federation of Women's Clubs, and one from the Detroit Jewish Community Council. Latent tensions between Protestant and Catholic leaders over the issue of indecent literature were laid bare at the meeting. On the one hand, Catholic leaders at the meeting expressed anger that seven magazines that they considered indecent, and which had been found by Catholic women on newsstands, had not been already been banned by the Censor Bureau. On the other hand, Protestants, led by Pastor Sheldon Rahn and Rev. Schroeder, expressed confusion and frustration at the ban on *Facts of Life and Love for Teenagers*, demanding an explanation. Catholic reverend Paul J. Hickey, representing the NODL, replied that while he thought the book useful for guided educational purposes, it was inappropriate for general distribution on newsstands. Minutes from the meeting indicate that Hickey apparently went on to note that "he had a gentleman's agreement with Mr. Rahn that this would not be a point for discussion at the present meeting," further indicating the simmering Catholic-Protestant tensions. Assistant Prosecutor Rashid and Inspector Melville Bullach of the Censor Bureau promised to review both the ban on the book and the lack of a ban on the magazines in question and provide a more detailed answer on each when the group met again in a month's time.[48]

In October of 1956, representatives from the CBLY again met with officials from the Wayne County Prosecutor's Office and the Censor Bureau, this time along with multiple representatives from book distributors. At the meeting, as explained in a letter written shortly after by a Protestant representative of the Detroit Council of Churches, "Mr. Rashid emphasized that his 'Censorship List' was entirely extralegal and had no legal authority whatsoever. The preparation of the 'Censorship List,' and its voluntary acceptance by the Distributors had developed by agreement some years ago. Mr. Rashid said the only authority his office really had was to request a warrant from the Court to prosecute a publisher or distributor who made an illegal book available." Here, then, was an encapsulation of the extralegal approach to literary censorship taken by the Detroit Police Department with the aid of the Wayne County prosecutor. Rashid was arguing that the city's list of banned titles was not legally binding, since those titles were not in fact "banned" so much as distributors were warned that the circulation of those titles would result in their arrest and prosecution, and so distributors "voluntarily" agreed to withhold those titles. The way Rashid's argument amounted to a hollow attempt to make a distinction without a difference was made clear at the meeting by Protestant pastor Sheldon Rahn, who "pointed out that regardless of the legal authority of the censorship lists the fact was that the Council of Churches was still unable to buy a copy of Mrs. Duvall's book in Detroit." Whether he realized the full implication of this statement or not, Pastor Rahn, a professed ally of the Censor Bureau, succinctly pointed out here the obvious fallacy of Rashid and the Censor Bureau's claim that that they were not practicing censorship, which is that if a book was not available to purchase, then for all intents and purposes it was banned, even if those doing the banning wanted to deny it.[49]

The CBLY would continue to meet and cooperate with the Censor Bureau in the years ahead, but internal divides limited its effectiveness as a ground-level watchdog system for the Censor Bureau after 1956. After those two meetings of the CBLY, the Censor Bureau, and Wayne County prosecutors, Pastor Rahn recommended that the Council of Churches cease support for the CBLY's neighborhood visits to retailers. This recommendation came about because of a lack of confidence in the Censor Bureau's list of banned and partially objectionable books in the wake of *Facts of Life and Love for Teenagers* appearing on the former list and because the Detroit Council of Churches was unwilling to use the NODL list for retailer visits. Given this, wrote Rahn, "We cannot ask church women to go into outlets with no list at all since this would lead to the exercise of a wide variety of individual judgments by each woman."[50]

Even with the eventual decline of this Protestant-Catholic alliance on literary censorship in Detroit, the fact remains that for much of the 1950s, the Censor Bureau received aid in its mission from the two most prominent religious groups in Detroit, with particularly avid support from Catholics. Throughout the entirety of the decade, Catholic women organized to check retailers for indecent literature, first using the NODL list and later, with the support of Protestant women, the Censor Bureau's "partially objectionable" list. This watchdog system points to one of the defining features of Detroit censorship in the era—the degree to which it skirted the line between legal and extralegal. If the Censor Bureau was unable to check retailers to ensure compliance, they could simply enlist the help of volunteers to do the work for them. And, if the Censor Bureau felt certain titles did not qualify for banned status but were "partially objectionable," those same volunteers could simply do the work of keeping those books off store shelves just the same as if the books had been banned.

"THE NATION'S CAPITAL OF POLICE CENSORSHIP"[51]

Outside of sharing them with allied local organizations like Catholic groups and the PTA, the city's lists of banned and objectionable books were closely guarded by Case, who feared the attendant publicity for censored titles if the lists were leaked to the public. As Detroit's literary censorship regime grew, though, an issue arose that required the list to make its way outside the city's borders. As Case explained, "It became apparent that a man at the city limits on one side of the street could sell the material, and a man on the other side of the street, he could get away with it with no prosecution whatsoever."[52] This speaks to an issue identified by historian James Gilbert, who notes that as a result of the "mobility of modern Americans ... it becomes hard to employ censorship or other devices of self-isolation simply because a sustainable local community is so elusive." In light of this problem, the Censor Bureau began circulating the list to every chief of police across all of Wayne County (encompassing Detroit and its suburbs) so that they might enforce the banned book list in their areas as well and thereby prevent indecent books from making their way into Detroit. Beyond Wayne County, though, the banned book list soon came to be circulated to numerous cities and towns across the whole of Michigan. As Case said in testimony before Congress in 1952, "All this material and our information and things we make available to other law-enforcing agents and offices in the state of Michigan. There are about 17 or 18 other cities that are quite dependent on us, in this set-up." Among these was Saginaw, a city of about ninety-two thousand people roughly one hundred miles northwest of Detroit.[53]

In time, though, Detroit's list of banned books also made its way far beyond Michigan. As *Newsweek* columnist John Lardner put it in 1955: "When a police chief or city censor wants to know what books to ban, he sends for the 'Detroit Line'—which is the obscenity list compiled and rechecked from month to month by Inspector Herbert W. Case of the Detroit police license and censor bureau. ... The Detroit Line is now standard for local book-banners around the country. Censors in some 70 or 80 towns are said to have subscribed to the Line." Among those subscribers was Los Angeles, whose police department enforced Detroit's list of banned books. More often, though, the list was used by smaller towns and cities unable to afford the type of operation being run in Detroit—places like Youngstown, Ohio, which barred the sale of all the books on Detroit's banned and objectionable lists in 1953. As Lardner cheekily wrote, "[Case] and his team of twelve censors think of themselves as 'big brothers,' the inspector said one time, to smaller communities who don't have the time and money to find out for themselves that [Hans Christian] Andersen's fairy tales are obscene." Seemingly lost on Case was the irony of a literary censor proudly calling himself "big brother" just a few short years after the 1949 publication of George Orwell's *Nineteen Eighty-Four*.[54]

Detroit's censorial influence was also felt in a number of ways beyond just the circulation of its banned book list across the United States. In 1955, the *Detroit News* published an article with the title "Detroit Book Censorship a Model for Other Cities" that explained that other cities seeking to curb indecent literature had modeled their own censorship operations after Detroit's Censor Bureau. According to a *Minneapolis Star* article, "Case reported several men from the police departments of other cities have been sent to the censor bureau for a month of training." Meanwhile, when Minnesota was considering a new censorship law, the proposal was "patterned after the Detroit system."[55]

The federal government was also a major ally of Detroit's Censor Bureau. When the Select Committee on Current Pornographic Materials held congressional hearings in 1952, Case was called as a star witness, with committee chair E. C. Gathings fawningly saying at the close of Case's testimony, "As a matter of fact, we have a prohibition against the use of radio or television in the committee room, but I would like your testimony to have gone out over America." Case and the Censor Bureau regularly communicated with federal government officials, including postal authorities, the Department of Justice, and the Federal Bureau of Investigation. It was for this reason that the *Detroit Free Press* wrote in 1953 that "Detroit sets a pattern for national censorship," while *Newsweek* labeled Case "the country's leading handicapper of literature, or smut sleuth." Likewise, the trade journal *Publishers Weekly* called Detroit "the nation's capital of police censorship."[56]

The Censor Bureau's widespread influence led to another, perhaps unintended consequence that only further speaks to the city's outsized role in literary censorship of this era. Because Detroit's list of banned books circulated so widely, publishers were faced with a harsh economic reality. As Freeman Lewis, executive vice president of Pocket Books, Inc., put it, "A publishing company ... cannot afford to print a special Detroit edition and another for the rest of the country." Given this, it should perhaps come as no surprise that in 1953, it was reported that "one publisher now is sending the bureau his entire line in proofs," the idea being that the Detroit Censor Bureau would give their comments on an unpublished book, with the publisher then making those changes before the book went to press. A *Minneapolis Star* reporter who got access to Detroit's Censor Bureau described the scene thus: "In the office of the censor bureau a policeman sits at a desk reading the long proof sheets of a novel. This man is engaged in censoring a book before publication. He is censoring it for readers in Detroit. He also is censoring it, in effect, for thousands of other readers in all parts of the country." That the Censor Bureau not only reviewed published books but also proofs of unpublished ones is another indicator of the enormous power held by Case and the Detroit Police Department in this field of literary censorship. As the title of the aforementioned *Minneapolis Star* article succinctly put it, "What Detroit Censors May Affect All U.S."[57]

The key element that greased the wheels of this literary censorship machine was the cooperation of the industry, including the book dealers controlling the local sale of publications in the city. As Case said, "We find very rarely does a merchant who has a store in the neighborhood, where it is dependent upon the livelihood of the neighborhood, want to purvey smut. We find exceptions . . . but generally I think they are wholeheartedly in cooperation and sympathy with this program we have." Though the occasional arrest of a book dealer did occur during this era, uniform cooperation with Detroit's Censor Bureau was undoubtedly the norm. As Case summed up, "I'm happy to say that I've received the finest co-operation from Detroit book dealers."[58]

A level above dealers in the print industry food chain were local distributors, another key partner for Detroit's Censor Bureau. For the city's censorship machine to function, distributors needed to agree to submit their publications to the Censor Bureau before sending them to store owners. The importance of this step in the censorship process was not lost on Case, who said, "If we can keep that thing [indecent literature] out of circulation and it doesn't hit the streets, why, we are accomplishing a lot more than attempting to do something about it after it has gained its objective of being circulated." Case explained how he got the cooperation of local distributors:

> Now, in 1951 we called in—we have two distributors in Detroit. We called in the one independent distributor—the other is the American News Co.—and on one we had voluntary cooperation which, naturally, is the ideal method of suppression of this type of material, and the other was forced.
>
> We called them in, and we threatened prosecution in one instance, in view of the fact that we could not very well say to the one who was cooperating that he could put it out, and the other one can't. We had them in a conference with the Wayne County prosecuting attorney's office, and there they voluntarily agreed to submit to us for inspection the pocket-size magazines before distribution.

Regardless of whether the cooperation of local distributors was voluntary or forced, the result was the same, with both of Detroit's major distributors submitting their entire line of books for inspection before store owners, let alone the public, could get their hands on them.[59]

The protocol for censorial inspection once new titles arrived at distributors was regimented and systematic. As the manager of American News Co. said in 1954, "The Censor Bureau picks up all incoming publications as soon as they come in. If, within 72 hours, we don't hear from them (the Censor Bureau) we call them up. . . . We don't put out anything on the stands the Censor Bureau objects to." Likewise, the head of the other major distributor in the city, Ivan Ludington of Ludington News Co., said of titles found morally wanting by the Censor Bureau, "Those that don't get a clean bill of health we send right back to the publisher."[60]

Finally, the cooperation of publishers was also enlisted. By May 1952, as one article explained, "More than 50 publishers are co-operating now by sending advance copies of their lurid literature to [Detroit's] police censors." Beyond submitting their books in advance of publication, publishers also almost never put up a fight when the Censor Bureau banned one of their titles. As an employee at one distributor put it, "As far as the publisher—well, he knows that the Censor Bureau will not ban a publication unless there is a solid legal basis for it. We pass on all findings of the Censor Bureau to the publisher. They don't want trouble any more than we do." For publishers, the cost of a legal fight over any one banned book was simply not worth the time and effort. The same was true for why distributors and retailers uniformly cooperated with the Censor Bureau. As Rusinack said in a 1954 interview, "We cooperate closely with the distributor because we both know that by cooperating we can avoid trouble. Nobody wants trouble. What does the dealer or distributor lose by cooperating? Pennies. What does he gain? The continued support and patronage of his customers." As a result of this lack of incentive for causing any "trouble," publishers, distributors, and dealers almost always simply acceded to the Censor Bureau by withdrawing offending books from circulation in Detroit, which meant that it would be years before any entity took Detroit to court over the banning of a book.[61]

LAWS, SAUSAGES, AND CENSORSHIP

One of the defining features of the Detroit Police Department's Censor Bureau was the secrecy that surrounded it. Case figured out what so few censorial-minded individuals do, which is that to publicly ban a work is to publicize it.

As Walter Kendrick writes of the opponents of pornography throughout the nineteenth and twentieth centuries: "The real problem—though no one recognized this—was publicity itself, the permeation of the culture by images. Once the process was fully underway, as it was by the middle of the nineteenth century, any attempt to mark out a certain category of representations, to forbid them while permitting the rest, could only be futile. So it proved: 'pornography' spread irresistibly, flourishing in direct proportion to the energy of its combatants. It seemed, vampirelike, to batten on their strength, to rise up refreshed from each new campaign to put it down."[62]

Case was very much aware of this tendency of censors to inadvertently publicize the work they aimed to suppress. In 1947, Case criticized the Catholic Legion of Decency for this very reason, arguing that the result of their practice of publicly condemning particularly controversial films like *The Outlaw* (1943) had been "to obtain box office value for pictures instead of preventing their showing to the public." Given this, once he was head of the Censor Bureau, Case sought an approach that would minimize publicity through industry cooperation and secrecy. Case evidently reasoned that, like laws and sausages, the inner workings of the production of censorship were best hidden away from the public eye.[63]

Case and the Censor Bureau's avoidance of court cases through the solicitation of industry cooperation was a direct response to this perceived need for secrecy. As Case said in a 1954 interview, "We'd be in court every week if there was no cooperation. We cooperate with the distributors, newsstand dealers, and publishers."[64] On the rare occasions that publishers did push back on the banning of a particular book, the Censor Bureau would begin negotiations long before the disagreement made it to a courtroom. As Rusinack said, "If we get a whiff of it that there's going to be a [legal] challenge, then we start employing a little diplomacy." In this case, "diplomacy" meant negotiations happening outside the courtroom—and therefore outside the public eye. Indeed, Freeman Lewis, executive vice president of Pocket Books, Inc., explained that his firm had "gone to bat with the censors over more than one book" and that in each one of those cases, the Censor Bureau eventually backed down.[65] This willingness to back down was again based on Case's emphasis on avoiding court cases and publicity. As Case explained of this practice, "I don't like to go to court except as a last resort because usually the title is exploited, and it is given impetus toward sales in a great many parts of the country." The tremendous importance Case placed on avoiding court challenges is what made the cooperation of dealers, distributors, and publishers so critically important to the censorship operation.[66]

Another key source of cooperation came from Detroit's newspapers. As Case said in his 1952 congressional testimony, "The reaction of the press in Detroit has been the very best. I cannot speak too highly of the cooperation we have received." In his testimony, Case revealed that he met with local newspapers roughly every six months to discuss how they might cooperate and hash out any issues. What this "cooperation" meant was that the *Detroit Free Press* and the *Detroit News*, the city's two largest newspapers, tended to only cover the goings-on of the Censor Bureau in response to those rare times when the bureau made it into the national news. And when they did run stories, the two papers were uniformly supportive of Case, lavishing him and the Censor Bureau with praise. At the behest of Case, the local newspapers also took action against "risqué advertising of entertainments," meaning that, "at the sacrifice of financial losses on it," the *Free Press* and *News* had canceled ads for "salacious" shows and books. Most crucially of all, the newspapers helped Case keep quiet about which books had run afoul of the bureau by never publishing the banned or objectionable lists and only on the rarest of occasions mentioning specific banned titles.[67]

Comparing the coverage of the *Detroit Free Press* to that of the *Minneapolis Star* is illustrative in this regard. In February of 1953, the *Star* published a three-part exposé that, for the first time, publicly revealed the extent of Detroit's censorship practices. The articles were written by Leo Sonderegger, who was given access to the offices of the Censor Bureau; he interviewed Case, among others. The series of articles was harshly critical of Case and his team, and Sonderegger's reporting informed much of the news coverage of the Censor Bureau from the era. The articles were also read far beyond Minneapolis, moving out into the open what had, until then, largely been kept secret.[68]

Given all this, it became difficult for the *Free Press* to continue to remain silent on what was going on, and so one month after Sonderegger's articles, the newspaper published its own three-part series on censorship. On the surface, these articles seem to mirror the *Minneapolis Star*'s critical view of censorship. In the first piece, titled "Mental Cancer of Censorship Spreads in U.S.," writer Harold Tyler looks generally at censorship in the country, largely avoiding Detroit in particular. Early in the article, he insisted that "wherever practiced, censorship has high purpose and high principle for its beginning. Its ending is written in the bloody pages of history—Nazi Germany, Franco Spain, Red Russia, Peron's Argentina, the Japanese Empire and Mussolini's Italy." Such comparisons to the censorship of fascist and communist regimes were a common refrain during the era as a means of emphasizing the supposed superiority of American values and the importance of the First Amendment. Still, this general opposition to censorship was far from absolute. As Tyler went on to say, "Who can question that dirt—obscenities, smut—should not be thrust into the hands of our school children?" Such assertions were taken as givens. Instead, he argued, the problem with censorship lay in its targeting of works that fell outside this seemingly indefensible category of obscenity. Tyler continued, "Once censorship clears out the pornography, forces begin to work which want to clear out books which discuss opposing theological views, or varying educational opinions." This type of argumentation allowed critics of censorship to hold the seemingly contradictory positions that while censorship might be un-American in principle, censorship of pornography was warranted. Whitney Strub links this paradox to fears from the Cold War era, writing, "Allowing either communist speech or obscene materials was simply not included in what Americans meant when they expressed opposition to censorship."[69]

In that first of the three *Free Press* articles, Tyler leaves Detroit's censorship practices unmentioned until the end, at which point he writes, "In Detroit, censorship has been going on for 15 years, through the Detroit Police censor bureau. Here too, the purpose is high, the accomplishment good, and small complaint exists as to the operation of Inspector Herbert Case and his staff. But the cancer is there: Inspector Case will not live forever, and real danger lurks in the secrecy which shrouds this police activity." This was emblematic of one of the biggest differences between Sonderegger's and Tyler's respective takes on Detroit censorship. Whereas Sonderegger was openly critical of both Case and the Censor Bureau, every time Tyler put forward a critique of either, he almost immediately walked it back or tempered it with a compliment. In this case, the key problem with the Censor Bureau was that Case, who was seemingly above reproach in these articles, would eventually be replaced by someone not able to live up to the high bar set by him.[70]

The second article in the series more squarely dealt with Detroit's censorship practices (though, coincidentally or not, it appeared on page ten of the paper rather than the above-the-fold page-one placement of the first article). Tyler again went out of his way to flatter Detroit censorship, writing, "Inspector Herbert Case and his staff conduct the Police Censor Bureau within strict limitations, and with such integrity that the operation has been called the 'most brilliant and most intelligent argument there is on behalf of censorship.'" Case was given the chance to speak on the record extensively in Tyler's piece, responding to any and all criticisms. Regarding the critique leveled by Tyler in the first article that censorship invariably misses its target of pornography and hits "books which discuss opposing theological views, or varying educational opinions," Case was allowed to list what he claimed the Censor Bureau would not do:

1. Pass upon the literary merits or value of a book, nor upon the integrity and literary standing of an author or publisher.
2. Take a position in a theological dispute.
3. Attempt to pass on social standards.

No effort was made by Tyler to push back on any of these notions, and the article continues along these lines, told mostly through Case's own words interspersed with Tyler alternatingly raising objections to censorship in general and then flattering Case in particular. As previously, Case frequently emphasized what he and the Censor Bureau did not do so as to emphasize their supposedly restrained and deliberate approach. This continued in the third and final article in the series, in which Tyler writes, "Detroiters sometime write to Inspector Herbert Case, of the Police Censor Bureau, demanding that he ban this girlie book or that bosomy calendar. They appear quite pained when he explains that the objects of their wrath are not obscene within the legal definition." Tyler painted Case as reticent to use his authority, and indeed quite measured in responding to the complaints of citizens, rather than someone aggressively pushing for and enacting censorship.[71]

Perhaps the greatest difference between Sonderegger's and Tyler's respective series of articles is their diverging views when it came to the secrecy of the Censor Bureau. Sonderegger was critical of much of the bureau's censorial activity but reserved his harshest criticisms for Case's unwillingness to publish the list of banned books and simply tell Detroiters what books were unavailable to them, titling the second article in the series "Detroit Public Not Told What Is Censored." Case refused to give Sonderegger the list, but he did permit him to briefly look at it, which allowed Sonderegger to then publish the names of some dozen lofty and prestigious banned books on the list. By contrast, while Tyler did somewhat criticize the secrecy surrounding Detroit censorship, he conspicuously never mentions any books banned by the Censor Bureau, thereby abiding by Case's wish to not publicize any censored titles.

This secrecy about the banned books list points toward the complex relationship between the Censor Bureau and the people of Detroit. On the one hand, Case did all he could to keep the workings of his office secret so as to avoid giving free publicity to banned books. On the other hand, it was only with the tacit support of the general public that the Censor Bureau could function. Indeed, Case wanted, and claimed he had, the vocal support of the public.

In his 1952 appearance before Congress, Case expressed this viewpoint in an exchange with H. Ralph Burton, general counsel for the congressional Select Committee on Current Pornographic Materials:

> Mr. Burton: What would you say is the most essential single item in successfully prosecuting an effective campaign against obscene materials?
> Mr. Case: Without question that is militant public opinion.
> Mr. Burton: And the more that is done in the direction of arousing that public opinion, the better the results would be?
> Mr. Case: Unqualifiedly so; yes, sir.[72]

There is a clear disconnect between Case's view of the importance of "militant public opinion" and his concerted efforts to keep the public in the dark about Detroit's censorship operation. While the Censor Bureau did receive something akin to militant support from Catholic organizations, alongside a handful of other local groups, the wider public provided no such explicit backing. Rather than leading to "militant public opinion," the secrecy of the Censor Bureau and a lack of public knowledge could more accurately be said to have bred apathy and indifference among the general population of Detroit.

For his 1956 doctoral thesis on local literary censorship campaigns, Don Somerville wrote on the topic of public support for the Detroit Censor Bureau, saying, "Perhaps the best indication of community support for the existence and operation of the Censor Bureau lies in the absence of opposition to it." To back up this claim, Somerville drew on quotes from some of the numerous interviews he did for the project, like this one from a manager of a drugstore in Detroit: "If there has been opposition, I haven't heard of any." Likewise, one radio station manager told Somerville, "There has been little or no opposition to the activity of the Censor Bureau." But Somerville also included quotes that made clear exactly why the lack of vocal opposition to the work of the Censor Bureau did not equate with the bureau having real "community support." As the manager of another drugstore in the city put it, "I doubt if one in a thousand customers knows that the Censor and License Bureau exists." A staff person for the *Detroit News* similarly said of literary censorship in the city, "Most persons are not familiar with what is being done." Of course, one central reason for this was the lack of coverage in the *Detroit News* itself on what the Censor Bureau was doing. This point was made by a local representative of the American Legion, who said of the Censor Bureau, "All I know is what I read in the paper. And that's not very much."[73]

The lack of awareness mixed with indifference that characterized the stance of most Detroiters on the Censor Bureau was demonstrated in early 1955 when

Edward R. Murrow decided to focus an episode of his show *See It Now* on literary censorship. As part of the research for the program, Murrow sent a representative to Detroit to look into censorship there, thinking it might work as the central locale for the program to focus on. After a few days in the city, though, Murrow's staff person reported back, "I've never seen such enormous public apathy to what we supposed was a real menace to freedom." Murrow instead decided to focus his show on book censorship in Los Angeles.[74]

The reasons for this lack of outcry about literary censorship in Detroit went beyond the lack of public awareness in the city. As Walter Kendrick writes of the history of censorship and anti-porn politics, "Those who feel that no harm is being done [by pornography] are unlikely to form pressure groups in order to advance that view. Contentment and indifference are silent, while fear and outrage bellow; and in the pornography debate, hysteria on the part of a few has traditionally been given free rein by the obliviousness of the many." This apathy and obliviousness of the many, rather than the "militant public opinion" cited by Case, were the real reason the Censor Bureau was able to thrive. Crucial to fostering this public indifference was the secrecy of the censorship operation, in particular the refusal to publish or publicize the list of banned books. As one article stated, "There are regularly more than 300 books which Detroiters not only never have seen, but never have heard of, since the censorship list is censored, or, anyway, unannounced."[75]

BANNED AND OBJECTIONABLE

In 1954, Herbert Case said of the type of books the Censor Bureau did and did not ban, "From the beginning our attitude has been that of dealing only with obscene and indecent publications. We are not in the business of banning ideas from the political or aesthetic standpoints." Anti-porn advocates of the era often made similar claims, arguing that they sought to censor only "obscenity"—which amounted to "dirt for dirt's sake"—whereas works with artistic merit and carrying real ideas would never be targeted for censorship. This never aligned with the realities of censorship, where, in practice, works were banned precisely because of the ideas they contained—ideas that did not align with the values of the dominant powers in society who were the ones doing the censoring. Even so, for much of the 1950s, Case's claim that the Detroit Police Department was "not in the business of banning ideas" went unchallenged for the simple reason that Detroit's banned book list remained hidden away from the public, its contents unknown.[76]

That remained the case until 1957, when at last a sole copy of the Censor Bureau's list of banned books made its way to the public. In March of that year, the

Michigan Journalist, billing itself as the "Experimental Laboratory Newspaper of the Department of Journalism, University of Michigan," became the first and likely only newspaper to publish Detroit's list of banned books (though, notably, they only published the banned list, not the "partially objectionable" one, making it impossible to compare the two). The accompanying article only divulged that the newspaper had "obtained [the banned book list] from a reliable source who attests to its authenticity." The list published by the paper covers books banned from 1950 through March of 1955 and includes 276 specific titles. Most obviously pointing out the fallacy of Case's claim that the Censor Bureau was "not in the business of banning ideas from the political or aesthetic standpoints" were the celebrated works by prestigious authors dotting the list. This included books by Ernest Hemingway, James T. Farrell, John O'Hara, MacKinlay Kantor, John Dos Passos, and J. D. Salinger—works with obvious literary merit, many of which are still read and studied today. But the less lofty titles on the banned book list—the type of violent and erotic pulp novels that make up the bulk of the list—are no less noteworthy as examples of works bearing real ideas that were banned by the Censor Bureau because those ideas did not fall in line with the dominant values of the Detroit Police Department.[77]

Though the exact reason any individual book was banned may not be known, the recurrence of certain themes across different books points to the issues that most preoccupied the Censor Bureau. Among these were many works that were seemingly banned for their depictions of all manner of nonnormative forms of sexuality. Quite predictably, this included books discussing the topic of homosexuality or featuring any gay male characters. Among these were the gay coming-of-age story *Finistère* by Fritz Peters, the interracial gay romance *If This Be Sin* (originally published under the title *The Invisible Glass*) by Loren Wahl (pseudonym for Lorenzo Madalena), and *Bitter Love* by Taylor Dyson, which focuses on the story of a woman who marries a gay man. Also coming under fire were lesbian pulp novels, which emerged in the early 1950s and quickly became a target for censorship in Detroit and elsewhere. The first prominent example of the form, Tereska Torrès's *Women's Barracks*, was not only banned in Detroit but also helped spur the aforementioned 1952 congressional hearings into indecent literature. The book's popularity helped jump-start a wave of lesbian pulp novels, including *Spring Fire* by Vin Packer (a pseudonym for Marijane Meaker), a book that managed the rare feat of getting banned twice by Detroit, appearing on the list of prohibited books in both 1952 and in a new edition in 1954. Other lesbian pulp novels that followed would also be banned, including Nancy Morgan's *City of Women* and Wilene Shaw's *The Fear and the Guilt*.[78]

The inclusion of other forms of "deviant" sex-related behaviors, regardless of their presentation, also landed works on the banned book list. This included works dealing in any way with the topic of abortion, such as *The Flesh Baron* by P. J. Wolfson and *Waste No Tears* by Jarvis Warwick (pseudonym for Hugh Garner). That the latter work positioned itself as an exposé of the "abortion racket" and condemned abortion could not save it from censorship, as the topic itself was verboten. Numerous books in which characters engage in sex work also appeared on the banned list, including, to name just a few, Rae Loomis's *The Marina Street Girls*, Charles B. Philippe's *Bubu of Montparnasse*, and Doug Duperrault's *Red Light Babe*. Perhaps the form of illicit sex featured in the highest number of works on the banned book list was adultery, of which there are too many titles to list here. Finally, even paperback editions of scientific studies of sex occasionally ran afoul of the Censor Bureau, including *Sexual Practices of American Women* by Christopher Gerould, which drew off research by Alfred Kinsey, and the medical treatise *Psychology of Sex* by Havelock Ellis.

Given that it was police officers and prosecutors doing the censoring in Detroit, it was unsurprising that numerous books depicting crime could be found on the city's banned book list. This included multiple celebrated noir books that would be adapted into films by Hollywood, among them Jim Thompson's *Killer Inside Me* (film versions released in 1976 and 2010), Whitman Chambers's *The Come-On* (the basis of a 1956 film noir starring Sterling Hayden and Anne Baxter), and Harry Grey's *The Hoods* (adapted into the 1984 film *Once Upon a Time in America* by Sergio Leone). Critically lauded books dealing with the topics of drug use and addiction also frequently came into the Censor Bureau's crosshairs, including Jim Thompson's *The Alcoholics*, William S. Burroughs's *Junkie*, and George Mandel's *Flee the Angry Strangers*, the latter two being among the most prominent early Beat novels of the era.

Finally, in keeping with the 1944 ban on *Strange Fruit*, the leaked banned book list also included numerous titles that dealt, in one way or another, with the topic of race and racism. Books featuring interracial romance often were banned by the Censor Bureau, including *Stable Boy* by Adam Rebel, *Out of Bounds* by Ernest L. Matthews Jr., and *Trespass* by Eugene Brown, in addition to three separate banned books from African American writer Curtis Lucas that had interracial romances. Titles that acted as protest novels focusing on the African American experience also appeared on the banned book list. Among these was the paperback edition of Chester B. Himes's 1945 novel *If He Hollers Let Him Go*, which tells the story of a Black shipyard worker navigating racial discrimination and economic hardships. Also banned by the Censor Bureau was William Attaway's *Blood on the Forge*, a novel that focuses on three brothers who flee the inequality and racism of the South only to find inequality and racism waiting for them in the North. Such a story no doubt would have been of interest and relevance to many African American Detroiters, which is of course why the Censor Bureau chose to ban it.

All in all, the books banned by the Censor Bureau ran the gamut from lowbrow to highbrow, encompassing fictional novels, nonfiction, scientific treatises, and everything in between. In all these areas, decisions on what to censor reflected the biases and political predilections of the Detroit Police Department itself. That the Censor Bureau should choose to ban works tackling racism or depicting interracial romances fits squarely with the fact that the Detroit Police Department had frequently been accused of systemically racist practices and that in a city that was nearly 30 percent Black at that time, just 3 percent of police officers were African American. Likewise, the Censor Bureau's targeting of crime books was an inevitable result of the fact that it was police officers who were charged with censoring media for the city. Any sympathetic portrait of people struggling with addiction would naturally not sit well with a police department that, through its Narcotics Bureau, had made it a priority to arrest, prosecute, and incarcerate substance users. The conservative sexual politics of the Detroit Police Department were also reflected in which titles appeared on the banned book list. In the mid-1950s, the Detroit Police Department's Vice Bureau had sixty officers assigned to the task of arresting individuals on "morals charges." This included those engaged in sex work, helping explain why so many banned books featured characters having sex for money. Likewise, the ban on numerous gay and lesbian novels was part and parcel with the Detroit Police Department's efforts to criminalize homosexuality through Vice Bureau–led efforts to entrap suspected "sex deviates" in public spaces. Altogether, then, what the Censor Bureau chose to censor was a direct result of the fact that it was police officers who were determining what was and was not suitable reading material for the city of Detroit.[79]

"WHO BUYS AND READS THIS OUTPUT OF 'SMUT'?"[80]

Though it might be unclear what type of people actually made up the audience for paperback literature, the Censor Bureau had their own very clear conceptions of the would-be consumers of banned books, as well as the effect indecent literature could potentially have on them. As one 1952 *Detroit Free Press* article said of the Censor Bureau, "Authorities exercise constant vigil to keep pornographic pictures, magazines and books from the eager scrutiny of teenagers and mentally-warped adults." The focus, then, was both on youth—and, in particular, on teenagers, fitting with the era's dominant fears of juvenile delinquency—as well as a certain class of adults who were seen as being, in some way, defective or immature.[81]

Detroit's exclusive focus on paperbacks, with hardcover books only examined on complaint, speaks directly to the Censor Bureau's notions of who was consuming indecent literature and the supposed mental faculties of these readers. As a 1955 *Newsweek* article explained: "A feature of the Case handicapping service is that it censors nothing but paperback books. The buyer of hardback, $3.95 books is free to ruin his morals on his own time. Critics of the Detroit Line have called this rule undemocratic—the rich can have books, the poor can't. In short, let 'em eat newspapers. But Inspector Case does not think of buyers of paperback books as 'poor'; he thinks of them as 'the adolescent, the weak, and susceptible.' In other words, the whole concept of low-cost literature, of bringing reading to the masses, is unsound." Using the terms "weak and susceptible" may have allowed Case to sidestep criticism that the Censor Bureau's focus on cheap paperbacks was classist, but ultimately what made Case's imagined readers "weak and susceptible" was very much tied in with their inability to afford hardcover editions of books. In certain ways, Case anticipated a shift in understandings of the nature of the "poor" consumers of porn. Walter Kendrick writes that by the time of the 1986 Meese Commission Report on pornography, "the category of 'the poor' had definitively altered from those who lacked money to those who lacked enlightenment; the threat, however, was the same." For Case, even as the content of a book was obviously important, it was the condition of those who read the book that structured censorial practices. Thus, while enlightened individuals able to afford a hardcover copy of, say, J. D. Salinger's *Catcher in the Rye* were free to do so, the unenlightened, weak, and susceptible buyers of paperback books needed to be shielded from such indecent literature.[82]

This notion that working-class and poor readers in some sense lack "enlightenment" also contains implicit connotations as to the psychological state of these readers. Alex Canty, director of the Detroit Recorder's Court Psychiatric Clinic in 1953, made the case that the majority of readers of paperback "smut" were "young adults who have not matured." As he went on to say, "The regular reader of obscene literature is a person who receives some stimulation by it because he has not matured emotionally." This focus on "adults who never grew up mentally," as a 1953 *Free Press* article on Detroit censorship put it, tapped into what Kendrick identifies as the modern conception of the consumer of pornography as a "mentally defective adult—probably male, probably also of lower-class origin—who wallowed in infantile idiocy and wished to make others do the same." At times, the unsaid implication regarding the deviant sexuality of these maligned adult consumers of indecent literature in Detroit was made explicit, as when Inspector Bullach of the Censor Bureau stated that the goal of the bureau was to prevent illicit material "from falling into the hands of perverts."[83] For Case, pornographic literature could have a dire impact on these hypothetical developmentally stunted adults. Speaking before Congress in 1952, Case famously stated, "There has never been a sex murder in the history of the Detroit Police Department in which obscene literature hasn't played a part." In the decades since, this statement has been repeated ad nauseam by anti-porn advocates who have used it as evidence of the perceived link between criminality and the consumption of pornography.[84]

Paradoxically, on multiple occasions Case explicitly denied that he cared what adults read. As he said in one interview, "We are not interested too greatly in the welfare of the adult. We feel an adult's mental processes and ways of life are pretty well formed and we as police officers can't do much about it." Or, as one article put it, "The police censor bureau hopes to keep pornographic material out of the hands of Detroit's adolescents. They care little what the adult reads." This of course ignores the fact that the Censor Bureau very much cared about the reading habits of certain types of adults; in addition to the aforementioned quotes making that clear, there is the simple fact that they were censoring books for all residents of Detroit, not just children. Even so, the department's public comments greatly emphasized protecting children from indecent literature. Fears surrounding the corruption of youth particularly drove efforts to censor comic books, whose readers were always imagined as being exclusively children and teenagers. The bureau's focus on paperback rather than hardcover books, though, was also motivated by the same perceived threat to children, with Case saying, "Hard cover books have a limited circulation because of their price. All we try to do is to keep these low cost pocket-sized reprints with the sexy covers out of the hands of school kids."[85]

This focus on protecting youth stands in stark contrast to the views of one of Case's forebearers, the previously discussed Royal A. Baker. As Baker said in 1933, "The responsibility is clearly upon parents to see that their children are not allowed to see pictures they consider unfit for them. We cannot tie the standards of entertainment down to those of the child. The theater is for the intelligent adult." By contrast, Case was very much willing to tie the standards of literary entertainment down to those of the child by banning books for all of Detroit because they might fall into the hands of youth. While Baker was certainly much laxer in his role as Detroit police censor and friendlier with the industry, the marked difference between Baker's and Case's perspectives was more than just a matter of two individuals taking very different approaches to their jobs. Rather, the changing politics and growing fears of juvenile delinquency during the postwar era had shifted the terrain from which Baker and Case both operated.[86]

Fears surrounding the perceived connection between juvenile delinquency and the consumption of indecent literature were made plainly evident in the story of Robert Hearn. In March of 1952, sixteen-year-old Hearn and three friends were arrested on murder charges over the slaying of a gas station attendant in the Detroit suburb of Pontiac. That Hearn should have committed such a crime despite his upbringing—having grown up in a white middle-class family—led his parents, the community, and the press to all ponder where the boy had gone wrong and who was to blame. Drug use quickly emerged as the major perceived corrupting agent, with his father saying to the press, "If he did it, he must have been under the influence of dope." News reports detailed how Hearn and his compatriots drank alcohol and smoked marijuana before engaging in what the *Free Press* labeled "an orgy of crime."[87]

Over time, though, a different narrative began to emerge, one in which Hearn's mind had been warped by, in the words of his mother, Rose, "filthy magazines, comic books and horror movies." Rose Hearn emerged as an unlikely spokesman in the war against indecent literature, and she provided a statement in the same 1952 congressional hearings on objectionable literature in which Case had testified. Her statement is similar to many sympathetic stories of white teenagers of the era induced into a life of crime through exposure to drugs. First, Rose establishes the previous good nature of her son, saying, "Robert had always been a sweet boy. He was affectionate and kind. . . . Robert wouldn't hurt anyone or anything. He had cats and a dog, and loved them. He went out of his way to do things for people. . . . Everyone liked him." In time, though, according to her statement, Robert was corrupted—first by sexual and violent media and later by drugs. As Rose said of the time leading up to her son's arrest, "He was acting like a big shot and used the words that they use in the gangster movies and comic books. He would shut himself in his room with comic books. He didn't want to be around anyone or to be bothered. . . . We feel that reading the books started him off." In the end, marijuana use and then crime followed, with Rose blaming the pushers of drugs and indecent media for her son's crimes, stating, "Youngsters all over the country are using dope. They get it from older men and they commit crimes. They are really the killers when the children are under the influence of liquor, dope, and those books. The children wouldn't get the ideas if the older men hadn't sold these things."[88]

Rose's statement speaks to the way youth were imagined as being more akin to victims of indecent literature than willing consumers. The agency of those deciding to purchase such reading material was effectively stripped away in this formation, thereby reducing them to mere passive recipients of paperback pornography. Critically, this formulation drew on a similar one being developed during this same postwar moment regarding drug use. As Matthew Lassiter writes, "The ubiquitous discourse of 'dope peddlers' and 'narcotics pushers' animated the moral crusade for a supply-side war on drugs and transformed white teenage lawbreakers into the helpless victims of external villains who lured their prey into an urban dystopia of addiction, crime, and prostitution." Similarly, then, in the minds of those aligned with the work of the Censor Bureau, youth readers were not consenting consumers of indecent literature so much as unwitting dupes of their illicit pleasures. This in turn justified something akin to a supply-side war on indecent literature, one aimed at those publishing and distributing such material rather than those consuming it. And, as the case of Robert Hearn seemingly demonstrated to supporters of this campaign, if the Censor Bureau failed to keep salacious reading material out of the hands of the impressionable, the results for Detroit and society at large could be dire.[89]

CONCLUSION: BURN THE HOUSE TO ROAST THE PIG

This emphasis on protecting youth actually formed the basis of the legal ordinance underpinning literary censorship in Detroit. As section 343 of the Michigan Penal Code said at the time, "Any person who shall import, print, publish, sell ... any book, newspaper, writing ... containing obscene, immoral, lewd or lascivious language, tending to incite minors to violent or depraved or immoral acts, manifestly tending to the corruption of the morals of youth ... shall be guilty of a misdemeanor." The statute was over a century old in origin and had last been amended in 1953, when the clause "tending to incite minors to violent or depraved or immoral acts" was added, a reflection of the era's fears of juvenile delinquency. Though every state had its own laws against obscenity, Michigan's ordinance was unusual in that, even if a work was deemed morally permissible material for adults, it could still be banned for the entire population if it was determined to have undue influence on children. Ultimately, it was this emphasis on youth that would prove the undoing of Michigan's obscenity law and, with it, the Detroit's Police Department's literary censorship operation.[90]

The first test case of Detroit's censorship of literature was mounted in June of 1954, when Alfred E. Butler, Detroit district sales manager for distributor Pocket Books, Inc., was arrested for the sale of a paperback copy of John H. Griffin's *The Devil Rides Outside*. The book was the debut novel for Griffin— who would later go on to fame with his memoir, *Black Like Me*—and it was quickly banned by the city in paperback form, though it remained available in hardcover. At an agreed-upon time, Butler sold Case the book for its list price of fifty cents and was promptly arrested, setting up a challenge to Detroit censorship. As Case noted at the time, it marked the first censorship case in Detroit to reach the court system in ten years.[91]

The case first landed before recorder's court judge John A. Ricca, with Butler's attorneys arguing that the state obscenity law used by Detroit in banning the book was a violation of the First and Fourteenth Amendments. In particular, they singled out the Michigan obscenity statute's prohibition against works "containing" obscene content, arguing that this permitted the state to declare a work obscene based on isolated passages rather than the dominant theme of the book. Beyond this, Butler's team charged that Michigan's obscenity law was unconstitutional because it banned books for adults because of the impact they might have on children and therefore violated the First Amendment. Meanwhile, the opposing attorneys argued that shielding children from indecent literature was necessary to protect the general public welfare.

Judge Ricca sided with the state and against Butler, finding that the book was "obscene, immoral, lewd and lascivious" and that the state obscenity law was constitutional as a means of protecting against the corruption of youth. After a motion for a new trial in the recorder's court was denied by Judge W. McKay Skillman in early 1955, Butler's attorneys filed an appeal to the Michigan Supreme Court. After that appeal was denied, an appeal was then made to the United States Supreme Court, with the high court soon agreeing to hear the case, setting up a showdown on Detroit's literary censorship practices and the constitutionality of Michigan's obscenity statute.[92]

The case came at a significant moment in the history of censorship in the United States as, after years of studiously avoiding the topic, the United States Supreme Court was at last set to take on a number of cases involving obscenity law. Interested parties thus immediately understood that *Butler v. Michigan* could prove a major case in clarifying the legal tangle of obscenity law. Amicus briefs arguing that Michigan's obscenity law should be declared unconstitutional were therefore filed by the American Book Publishers Council, a trade organization representing the largest book publishers in the United States; the Authors League of America, representing thousands of authors and playwrights in the United States; and finally the Detroit branch of the American Civil Liberties Union (ACLU). Meanwhile, the attorney general for the state of Texas filed an amicus brief in support of Michigan's position owing to the similar obscenity statute Texas had on the books.

Figure 1.3. Comic after the *Butler v. Michigan* ruling. *Michigan Journalist*, March 27, 1957.

On February 25, 1957, in a unanimous decision, the Supreme Court declared that Michigan's obscenity statute was unconstitutional. As Justice Felix Frankfurter memorably explained in his majority opinion, "The State insists that, by thus quarantining the general reading public against books not too rugged for grown men and women in order to shield juvenile innocence, it is exercising its power to promote the general welfare. Surely, this is to burn the house to roast the pig." Justice Frankfurter went on to say, "The incidence of this enactment is to reduce the adult population of Michigan to reading only what is fit for children." Justice Frankfurter here neatly mirrored the words of Royal A. Baker when Baker said, "We cannot tie the standards of entertainment down to those of the child." Justice Frankfurter's criticism of censorship efforts that restrained the reading choices of adults in the defense of children was not without legal precedent. Most notably, Judge Learned Hand, in the 1913 literary obscenity case *United States v. Kennerley*, said in his opinion, "It seems hardly likely that we are even to-day so lukewarm in our interest in letters or serious discussion as to be content to reduce our treatment of sex to the standard of a child's library in the supposed interest of a salacious few."[93]

The court's decision was immediately hailed as a landmark victory in the struggle against media censorship, drawing front-page headlines in numerous newspapers around the country. Just a few months later, though, *Butler* would be eclipsed by the most famous obscenity ruling of this era, *Roth v. United States*, which gave the first new legal definition for "obscenity" at the federal level in eighty-nine years. This timing caused *Butler* to become largely overlooked by historians in favor of *Roth* and other splashier First Amendment cases from the period, despite *Butler*'s significant legacy in shaping censorship efforts in the years ahead. Soon after the ruling was handed down, the precedent it set was used to strike down a Washington State law forbidding the sale of objectionable comic books to both minors and adults as part of an effort to combat juvenile delinquency. In 1959, *Butler* was cited in a federal judge's decision against a Chicago ordinance banning certain films for those under age twenty-one so as to protect children. Meanwhile, the decision also prompted both Florida and Maine to amend their obscenity statutes, which were nearly identical to Michigan's now unconstitutional law. Rhode Island and Virginia were similarly forced to amend their Michigan-like obscenity statutes after adverse court decisions against each state.[94]

The precedent set in the case continued to influence the legal landscape for censorship in the decades that followed. Specifically, as media law scholar Stephen Bates writes in a 2010 *First Amendment Law Review* article, "*Butler* led to what came to be known as the 'variable obscenity' doctrine—the notion that materials may be obscene as to minors but not as to adults." The variable obscenity doctrine was put forward most clearly in the case of *Ginsberg v. New York* in 1968, but it was *Butler* that laid the groundwork for that ruling. As Jon Lewis argues, the variable obscenity doctrine became central to the movie ratings system that replaced the Production Code and still regulates film content in the United States to this day. *Butler* has also been at the heart of numerous significant free speech cases over the past half century. This includes *Butler* having been key to mitigating the free speech defeat in *FCC v. Pacifica Foundation* (1978), in which the Supreme Court ruled that the Federal Communications Commission (FCC) could set aside certain hours of the day during which indecency could not be broadcast, with *Butler* central to why the Supreme Court refused to allow the FCC to simply bar all indecent content from the airwaves. In *Reno v. ACLU* (1997), the first major case before the high court on First Amendment protections of speech online, the Supreme Court specifically cited

Butler in declaring two key provisions of the Communications Decency Act of 1996 unconstitutional for the way they limited the transmission of indecent material to adults in the name of protecting children. *Butler* has similarly been cited in a number of other rulings curtailing laws that have sought to protect children on the internet from indecency, including by Justice John Paul Stevens in his ruling on the constitutionality of the Child Online Protection Act and by a federal judge striking down an Alaska statute that sought to curtail the distribution of indecent materials to children online. All told, as a 2012 *Federal Communications Law Journal* by legal scholar Clay Calvert argues, while there are numerous better-known free speech cases from the era, "one of the most important free speech cases since 1950—an especially vital case today when considered within the context of the ongoing culture wars in which shielding minors from supposedly harmful content is an often-used government rationale, or perhaps excuse, for censorship—is the much less celebrated 1957 high court decision in *Butler v. Michigan*."[95]

While the Supreme Court's decision in *Butler v. Michigan* reverberated outward for years to come, its impact in Detroit was clearer and more direct. With Michigan's obscenity statute declared unconstitutional, literary censorship in Detroit died a quick death. The Detroit Police Department attempted to keep up their efforts, with police commissioner Edward Piggins in June of 1957 declaring a renewed war on obscene literature after "an influx of it" in the months following the *Butler* ruling. However, adverse court decisions kept going against the police, and so, by December of 1958, a *Detroit Free Press* headline declared that "Detroit's Censors Haven't Banned Book in 20 Months." By that point the Censor Bureau had ceased its practices of both screening paperbacks before release and keeping an updated list of banned books, while the preceding twenty months had also seen just one magazine peddler arrested for selling an obscene magazine—and only then after a complaint from a citizen. Inspector Bullach, Case's successor as head of the Censor Bureau, was none too happy at this development, mournfully telling the *Free Press*, "We hardly arrest anyone anymore." In the years ahead, despite pressure from Catholic organizations, the Detroit Police Department Censor Bureau never again made the censorship of literature the priority it had throughout much of the early to mid-1950s.[96]

This shift was emblematic of a broader decline in literary censorship occurring across the country at this point in time. In the face of the accelerating proliferation of moving-image pornography during the postwar era, lewd literature began to look relatively tame by comparison, and thus the printed word slowly grew to be seen as outside the scope of obscenity and not worthy of censorship. As Walter Kendrick laments, this shift largely resulted from a changing view of the power of books: "The liberation of writing from the shackles of moral censorship has proceeded apace with loss of the belief, all-powerful in the nineteenth century, that writing wields immediate force upon its reader. That belief remains as strong as ever when it comes to pictures, still or moving; but the peril of print has nearly vanished, perhaps because the Western world no longer attributes to words the quasi-magical aura that once invested them." This trend of devaluing the printed word meant that the urgency of literary censorship waned rapidly from the moment in the immediate postwar era when keeping indecent literature out of the hands of youth was a top priority in Detroit and across much of the United States. This decline of literary censorship was paired, though, with the perception of a renewed need for stringent censorship of motion pictures, which had been growing increasingly violent and sexually explicit throughout the postwar period. As explored more in chapter 2, this trend helped animate the shifting priorities of the Detroit Police Department's Censor Bureau, which began to focus more of its efforts on keeping Detroit free from immoral movies just as its literary censorship operation was in decline.[97]

NOTES

1. Rebecca Reed, "Regulating the Regulators: Ideology and Practice in the Policing of Detroit, 1880–1918" (PhD diss., University of Michigan, 1991), 97, 105; Robert Conot, *American Odyssey: A History of a Great City* (Detroit: Wayne State University Press, 1986), 189.

2. Lee Grieveson, *Policing Cinema: Movies and Censorship in Early-Twentieth-Century America* (Berkeley: University of California Press, 2004), 23.

3. "Smith Becomes Censor," *Detroit Free Press*, September 4, 1907, 12; "Censorship That Is Censorship," *Detroit Free Press*, October 5, 1903, 4; "Suggest It to Korte," *Detroit Free Press*, September 19, 1907, 5. For more on Chicago's censorship of movies, see Moya Luckett, *Cinema and Community: Progressivism, Exhibition, and Film Culture in Chicago, 1907–1917* (Detroit: Wayne State University Press, 2014).

4. "Detroit Police Make Rules," *Moving Picture World*, August 5, 1911, 279; "Need Permit to Show Each Film," *Detroit Free Press*, May 28, 1912, 9; "Putting the Ban on Lurid Movies," *Detroit Free Press*, February 23, 1913, sec. 5, 3.

5. "Are Detroiters 'Movie' Mad?," *Detroit Free Press*, October 5, 1913, G3; Reed, "Regulating the Regulators," 77–78, 232; David B. Wolcott, *Cops and Kids: Policing Juvenile Delinquency in Urban America, 1890–1940* (Columbus: Ohio State University Press, 2005), 30; "Detroit Lead in Popularity of the 'Movies,'" *Detroit Free Press*, June 15, 1913, 16. For more on cinema in Detroit during this era,

see Richard Abel, *Motor City Movie Culture, 1916–1925* (Bloomington: Indiana University Press, 2020).

6. "'Woman Censor of Films Would Be Big Moral Force,'" *Detroit Free Press*, June 29, 1913, 10; "'Movie' Managers Protest against Woman Censor," *Detroit Free Press*, August 14, 1913, 1.

7. "Do Exhibitors Want Censorship?," *Motion Picture News*, June 6, 1914, 33; L. W. Bailey, "Detroit Upholds National Censor Board," *Motion Picture News*, May 30, 1914, 31.

8. "Detroit Policeman Is Playwright," *Detroit Free Press*, February 4, 1912, sec. C, 3.

9. "Facts and Comments," *Moving Picture World*, June 21, 1913, 1227; "Detroit," *Moving Picture World*, August 22, 1914, 1116; Jacob Smith, "Detroit, Mich.," *Variety*, April 14, 1922, 34; "Censor Sells Scenario," *Variety*, January 19, 1923, 1; "It Gets 'Em All," *Variety*, August 25, 1931, 1; "Detroit Notes," *Film Daily*, December 7, 1934, 7; "Detroit Police Censor to Retire Next Month," *Billboard*, January 26, 1935, 19.

10. "Miles of Film Cut by Censor," *Detroit Free Press*, March 27, 1921, sec. 5, 3; "*Last of the Mohicans* Labeled Picture Classic by Police Censor," *Exhibitors Herald*, January 1, 1921, 63; "Censor Congratulates Paramount," *Moving Picture World*, January 21, 1922, 274; "Praise for *Great Expectations*," *Film Daily*, October 24, 1934, 7; "Geo. Trendle Agrees with Police Censor," *Variety*, November 7, 1933, 31; Harry E. Nichols, "With the Detroit Filmmen," *Exhibitors Herald*, June 12, 1920, 75.

11. "Detroit Censors Licked," *Billboard*, July 22, 1933, 4; "Detroit Man Fined on *Elysia* Stills," *Motion Picture Daily*, January 18, 1934, 10; "Setback for Detroit Censors," *Film Daily*, February 2, 1934, 1.

12. "350,000 Catholics Back Clean Films," *Detroit Free Press*, May 8, 1934, 9; "Detroit Censor Says Churches Unqualified to Pass on Films," *Billboard*, May 26, 1934, 20; "Detroit Churches Lineup Strong for Fight against Dirty Films," *Billboard*, June 16, 1934, 20; "Sneer at Decency Drive Denied by Police Censor," *Detroit News*, June 3, 1934, 14.

13. Whether intentional or not, Baker's comment here evoked a similar one made a decade prior by New York City mayor Jimmy Walker, who said, "I have never yet heard of a girl being ruined by a book." Thanks to Reader 1 for pointing out this similarity.

14. "Miles of Film Cut by Censor," 1; H. F. Reves, "Catholic Church's Film Drive Is Scored by Detroit Censor," *Film Daily*, May 25, 1934, 6; H. F. Reves, "Highlights in Film Censorship: The Career of Royal A. Baker, Former Detroit Censor," *Billboard*, April 13, 1935, 36.

15. "Lieut. Baker, a Liberal, Resigns as Det. Censor," *Variety*, February 5, 1935, 21.

16. Leslie Woodcock Tentler, *Seasons of Grace: A History of the Catholic Archdiocese of Detroit* (Detroit: Wayne State University Press, 1990), 298; Henry

J. Pratt, *Churches and Urban Government in Detroit and New York, 1895–1994* (Detroit: Wayne State University Press, 2004), 48, 57.

17. Thomas F. O'Connor, "The National Organization for Decent Literature: A Phase in American Catholic Censorship," *Library Quarterly* 65, no. 4 (1995): 395; Archbishop Edward Mooney, March 21, 1939, box 53, folder 20, Edward Mooney Papers, Archdiocese of Detroit Archives; *The Drive for Decency in Print: Report of the Bishops' Committee Sponsoring the National Organization for Decent Literature* (Huntington, IN: Our Sunday Visitor, 1939), 211.

18. Alban J. Norris to Anthony J. Beck, November 22, 1937, box 53, folder 20, Edward Mooney Papers, Archdiocese of Detroit Archives; O'Connor, "The National Organization for Decent Literature," 392; Anthony J. Beck to Adam Strohm, December 30, 1937, box 53, folder 20, Edward Mooney Papers, Archdiocese of Detroit Archives; Adam Strohm to Anthony J. Beck, January 3, 1938, box 53, folder 20, Edward Mooney Papers, Archdiocese of Detroit Archives.

19. "License Is Asked for Book Sellers," *Detroit Free Press*, June 6, 1936, 9; *The Drive for Decency in Print*, 104; O'Connor, "The National Organization for Decent Literature," 393–94.

20. "Asks Control of Magazines," *Detroit News*, February 10, 1938, 24.

21. "Hemingway's Novel Criticized by Paper," *Detroit News*, April 29, 1938, 9; "McCrea Bans Library Book," *Detroit News*, May 3, 1938, 1; Van Wyck Brooks, Archibald MacLeish, and Thornton Wilder, "Letters to the Editors: Question for Catholic Church Leaders," *Nation*, July 23, 1938, 96; Judge Ira W. Jayne, Alice C. Hamer, et al., v. Duncan McCrea, et al., No. 278-506 (Wayne Cty. Cir. Dec. 1939).

22. *McCrea*, No. 278-506; Mooney, March 21, 1939, Edward Mooney Papers.

23. Brooks, MacLeish, and Wilder, "Letters to the Editors."

24. "H. W. Case, Ex-Police Censor, Dies," *Detroit News*, April 29, 1971, sec. C, 13; James Rorty, "The Harassed Pocket-Book Publishers," *Antioch Review* 15, no. 4 (December 1955): 418.

25. "City's Censor Wants Ban on *Strange Fruit*," *Detroit Free Press*, May 18, 1954, 7.

26. "*Fruit* Sour in Michigan, Too," *Variety*, May 24, 1944, 39; "Book Ban Lifted," *Detroit Free Press*, May 26, 1944, 18; "*Strange Fruit* First Again," *Detroit Free Press*, May 28, 1944, 6.

27. "*Strange Fruit*," *Michigan Chronicle*, May 27, 1944, 6; Thomas J. Sugrue, *Sweet Land of Liberty: The Forgotten Struggle for Civil Rights in the North* (New York: Random House, 2008), xiv; Cyrus Durgin, "*Strange Fruit* Ban Here Surprised Lillian Smith," *Boston Globe*, November 7, 1945, 9.

28. "All Censorial Bodies in Detroit Merged: Pix, Stage, Cafes, Etc.," *Variety*, January 20, 1943, 7; "Ex-Censor Joins Allied," *Variety*, January 21, 1948, 16; "Toy Combines 2 Agencies into Unit," *Detroit Free Press*, September 23, 1948, 15.

29. David Hajdu, *The Ten-Cent Plague: The Great Comic-Book Scare and How It Changed America* (New York: Picador, 2009), 34, 47.

30. For more on Wertham, see Bart Beaty, *Fredric Wertham and the Critique of Mass Culture* (Jackson: University Press of Mississippi, 2005).

31. "Police Must Read Comics," *Charleroi Mail*, April 14, 1948, 1; "Are Comics Fascist?," *Time*, October 22, 1945, 67–68.

32. Jack Schermerhorn, "Juvenile Crime Fighters Join in Drive on Comics," *Detroit Free Press*, April 15, 1948, 1; "36 Comic Books Banned by Detroit's Censors," *Benton Harbor News Palladium*, April 29, 1948, 17; Jack Schermerhorn, "McNally Outlaws 64 Comic Books," *Detroit Free Press*, April 29, 1948.

33. "Comic Books Banned," *Holland Evening Sentinel*, May 17, 1948; "Three Cities Curb Comics," *New York Times*, May 25, 1948, 25; *Investigation of Literature Allegedly Containing Objectionable Material* (Washington, DC: United States Government Printing Office, December 1, 1952), 132.

34. Jack Schermerhorn, "Toy Wars on Comic Book Smut," *Detroit Free Press*, April 13, 1948, 1; Jack Schermerhorn, "Distributors Join in Drive on Comics," *Detroit Free Press*, April 16, 1948, 25; Jack Schermerhorn, "Parent-Teacher Groups Back Toy Comics Purge," *Detroit Free Press*, April 18, 1948, 8.

35. "Public and Dealers Asked to Censor Comic Books," *Detroit News*, September 18, 1948, 17. For more on the Comics Code, see Amy Kiste Nyberg, *Seal of Approval: The History of the Comics Code* (Jackson: University Press of Mississippi, 1998).

36. Michael Denning, *Mechanic Accents: Dime Novels and Working-Class Culture in America* (London: Verso, 1987), 47.

37. Kenneth C. Davis, *Two-Bit Culture: The Paperbacking of America* (Boston: Houghton Mifflin, 1984), 1, 4.

38. Leo Sonderegger, "Censors Guard Young Morals in Detroit," *Minneapolis Star*, February 9, 1953, 18.

39. "Detroit Witness Links Crime and Obscene Literature," *Detroit News*, December 3, 1952, 33.

40. John Lardner, "The Smut Detective—Part II," *Newsweek*, March 21, 1955, 95; Marjorie Elaine Porter, "PTA Opens Attack on Obscene Books," *Detroit News*, November 17, 1951, 8; Rorty, "The Harassed Pocket-Book Publishers," 418; *Investigation of Literature Allegedly Containing Objectionable Material*, 116; John Lardner, "Let 'em Eat Newspapers," *Newsweek*, March 14, 1955, 92.

41. Leo Sonderegger, "Detroit Public Not Told What Is Censored," *Minneapolis Star*, February 10, 1953, 18.

42. Sonderegger, 15, 18; Harold Tyler, "City Takes Lead in Smut War," *Detroit Free Press*, March 16, 1953, 18; Don Smith Somerville, "A Study of Local Regulations and Group Actions on the Circulation of Newsstand Publications"

(MA thesis, University of Illinois, 1956), 101; Louis Tendler, "Detroit Book Censorship a Model for Other Cities," *Detroit News*, May 5, 1955, 16.

43. Sonderegger, "Detroit Public Not Told What Is Censored," 15.

44. Sheldon Rahn, "Protestant Participation in Citizen's Committee for Better Youth Literature," October 24, 1956, box 12, folder 11, Metropolitan Detroit Council of Churches Records, Walter P. Reuther Library, Wayne State University; "Meeting in Prosecutor's Office of the Citizens Committee for Better Youth Literature," September 19, 1956, box 12, folder 11, Metropolitan Detroit Council of Churches Records, Walter P. Reuther Library, Wayne State University; Sonderegger, "Detroit Public Not Told What Is Censored," 18; "Druggists to Aid Drive on Indecent Literature," *Detroit News*, September 24, 1954, 41; Whitney Strub, *Perversion for Profit: The Politics of Pornography and the Rise of the New Right* (New York: Columbia University Press, 2011), 91.

45. Louis Tendler, "Vigilance Rids City News Racks of Objectionable Comic Books," *Detroit News*, April 26, 1954, 18; Somerville, "A Study of Local Regulations," 98.

46. "Crackdown Slated on Filthy Literature," *Detroit Free Press*, September 14, 1954, 31; "Bishop Asks Public War on Indecent Literature," *Detroit News*, September 22, 1954, 21.

47. Sonderegger, "Detroit Public Not Told What Is Censored," 18; Rahn, "Protestant Participation."

48. "Meeting in Prosecutor's Office," Metropolitan Detroit Council of Churches Records; Rahn, "Protestant Participation."

49. Rahn, "Protestant Participation."

50. Rahn.

51. James M. Haswell, "Is Dirty-Book Banning Legal?," *Detroit Free Press*, October 8, 1956, 7.

52. *Investigation of Literature Allegedly Containing Objectionable Material*, 116.

53. Sonderegger, "Censors Guard Young Morals in Detroit," 18; James Gilbert, *A Cycle of Outrage: America's Reaction to the Juvenile Delinquent in the 1950s* (New York: Oxford University Press, 1986), 8; "Maps Police Drive on Obscene Books," *Detroit News*, March 9, 1951, 12; *Investigation of Literature Allegedly Containing Objectionable Material*, 131; Louis A. Zurcher Jr. and R. George Kirkpatrick, *Citizens for Decency: Antipornography Crusades as Status Defense* (Austin: University of Texas Press, 1976), 40.

54. Lardner, "Let 'em Eat Newspapers," 92; Tendler, "Detroit Book Censorship a Model for Other Cities," 16; Rorty, "The Harassed Pocket-Book Publishers," 419–20; Lardner, "The Smut Detective—Part II," 95.

55. Leo Sonderegger, "What Detroit Censors May Affect All U.S.," *Minneapolis Star*, February 11, 1953, 46; Tendler, "Detroit Book Censorship a Model for Other Cities."

56. *Investigation of Literature Allegedly Containing Objectionable Material*, 126, 128, 132, 142; Tyler, "City Takes Lead in Smut War," 18; Lardner, "The Smut Detective—Part II," 95; Haswell, "Is Dirty-Book Banning Legal?," 7.

57. Sonderegger, "What Detroit Censors May Affect All U.S.," 33.

58. *Investigation of Literature Allegedly Containing Objectionable Material*, 130; Louis Tendler, "City Censor's Influence Felt over All U.S.," *Detroit News*, April 25, 1954, 21.

59. *Investigation of Literature Allegedly Containing Objectionable Material*, 116, 122.

60. Somerville, "A Study of Local Regulations," 97.

61. Leo Donovan, "Eight Police Censors Sift Literary Sewage," *Detroit Free Press*, May 18, 1952, 2; Somerville, "A Study of Local Regulations," 108–9.

62. Walter Kendrick, *The Secret Museum: Pornography in Modern Culture* (Berkeley: University of California Press, 1987), 238.

63. Kendrick, 238; "Legion of Decency Bans Movie of *Duel in the Sun*," *Detroit News*, January 21, 1947, 12.

64. Somerville, "A Study of Local Regulations," 107.

65. Sonderegger, "What Detroit Censors May Affect All U.S.," 33.

66. *Investigation of Literature Allegedly Containing Objectionable Material*, 117.

67. *Investigation of Literature Allegedly Containing Objectionable Material*, 127; "Detroit Witness Links Crime and Obscene Literature," 33.

68. In particular, Sonderegger's reporting was extensively cited in William B. Lockhart and Robert C. McClure's "Literature, the Law of Obscenity, and the Constitution," one of the most influential legal articles on obscenity from this period. See William B. Lockhart and Robert C. McClure, "Literature, the Law of Obscenity, and the Constitution," *Minnesota Law Review* 38, no. 4 (March 1954): 310–19.

69. Harold Tyler, "Mental Cancer of Censorship Spreads in U.S.," *Detroit Free Press*, March 15, 1953, 1; Whitney Strub, *Obscenity Rules: Roth v. United States and the Long Struggle over Sexual Expression* (Lawrence: University Press of Kansas, 2013), 106.

70. Tyler, "Mental Cancer of Censorship Spreads in U.S.," 8.

71. Tyler, "City Takes Lead in Smut War," 18; Harold Tyler, "'Idea' Censorship Seen as Peril to City, Nation," *Detroit Free Press*, March 17, 1953, 10.

72. *Investigation of Literature Allegedly Containing Objectionable Material*, 123–24.

73. Somerville, "A Study of Local Regulations," 110–12.

74. Tendler, "Detroit Book Censorship a Model for Other Cities," 16.

75. Kendrick, *The Secret Museum*, 226; Lardner, "Let 'em Eat Newspapers," 92.

76. Somerville, "A Study of Local Regulations," 106.

77. Dave Smith, "Detroit Renews Book Ban Despite Court's Decision," *Michigan Journalist*, March 27, 1957, 1.

78. For more on lesbian pulp novels, see Paula Rabinowitz, *American Pulp: How Paperbacks Brought Modernism to Main Street* (Princeton, NJ: Princeton University Press, 2014), 184–208.

79. Scott Kurashige, *The Fifty-Year Rebellion: How the U.S. Political Crisis Began in Detroit* (Oakland: University of California Press, 2017), 18; Anna Lvovsky, *Vice Patrol: Cops, Courts, and the Struggle over Urban Gay Life before Stonewall* (Chicago: University of Chicago Press, 2021), 102; Tim Retzloff, "City, Suburb, and the Changing Bounds of Lesbian and Gay Life and Politics in Metropolitan Detroit, 1945–1985" (PhD diss., Yale University, 2014).

80. Charles Manos, "5 More Face 'Smut' Charges," *Detroit Free Press*, February 16, 1953, 3.

81. Kenneth McCormick, "Here's How Detroit Is Winning the 'Dirty Book' War," *Detroit Free Press*, November 10, 1952, 19.

82. Sonderegger, "Censors Guard Young Morals in Detroit," 17; Lardner, "Let 'em Eat Newspapers," 92; Kendrick, *The Secret Museum*, 235.

83. Manos, "5 More Face 'Smut' Charges," 3; Kendrick, *The Secret Museum*, 208; Melville E. Bullach, "How Censor Bureau Works," *Detroit Times*, February 3, 1957, 3.

84. Strangely, the wording of this quote seemingly changes each time it is given, acting as something like a historical version of the children's game of telephone. See *Investigation of Literature Allegedly Containing Objectionable Material*, 140; Charles Manos, "6 Firms Are Indicted in Drive on Smut," *Detroit Free Press*, February 13, 1953, 3; Jack Harrison Pollack, "Newsstand Filth: A National Disgrace!," *Better Homes and Gardens*, September 1957, 10; *The Report of the Commission on Obscenity and Pornography* (Washington, DC: United States Government Printing Office, September 1970), 563.

85. Sonderegger, "Censors Guard Young Morals in Detroit," 17–18; Tyler, "City Takes Lead in Smut War," 18; Tendler, "Detroit Book Censorship a Model for Other Cities," 16.

86. "Detroit Censors Licked," 4.

87. Frank Beckman, "Slaying Confession Numbs Boy's Folks," *Detroit Free Press*, March 25, 1952, 21.

88. *Investigation of Literature Allegedly Containing Objectionable Material*, 370–71.

89. Matthew D. Lassiter, "Pushers, Victims, and the Lost Innocence of White Suburbia California's War on Narcotics during the 1950s," *Journal of Urban History* 41, no. 5 (2015): 788.

90. Butler v. Michigan, 352 U.S. 380 (1957).

91. "Publishers Test Ban on Books Here," *Detroit News*, June 16, 1954, 1.

92. "Convict Seller of Lewd Book," *Detroit Free Press*, July 14, 1954, 3.

93. *Butler*, 352 U.S. 380; "Detroit Censors Licked," 4; Kendrick, *The Secret Museum*, 176.

94. Clay Calvert, "Of Burning Houses and Roasting Pigs: Why Butler v. Michigan Remains a Key Free Speech Victory More Than a Half-Century Later," *Federal Communications Law Journal* 64, no. 2 (March 2012): 258; William B. Lockhart and Robert C. McClure, "Censorship of Obscenity: The Developing Constitutional Standards," *Minnesota Law Review* 45, no. 5 (November 1960): 17–18.

95. Stephen Bates, "Father Hill and Fanny Hill: An Activist Group's Crusade to Remake Obscenity Law," *First Amendment Law Review* 8, no. 2 (March 2010): 265; Donald W. Garner, "Fighting the Tobacco Wars on First Amendment Grounds," *Southwestern University Law Review* 27, no. 3 (1998): 394–95; Jon Lewis, "'American Morality Is Not to Be Trifled With': Content Regulation in Hollywood after 1968," in *Silencing Cinema: Film Censorship around the World*, ed. Daniel Biltereyst and Roel Vande Winkel (New York: Palgrave Macmillan, 2013), 33; Calvert, "Of Burning Houses and Roasting Pigs," 250, 257, 262–63, 266–70.

96. "Piggins Renews War on Obscenity," *Detroit Free Press*, June 22, 1957, 3; Tom Houston, "Detroit's Censors Haven't Banned Book in 20 Months," *Detroit Free Press*, December 7, 1958, sec. C, 2.

97. Kendrick, *The Secret Museum*, 178.

TWO

"WE'RE NOT REALLY CENSORS"
The (Il-)Legality of Detroit Police Movie Censorship

FOR OVER HALF A CENTURY, the premiere showing of every movie in Detroit occurred in a private screening room with just one or two audience members. A representative of the Detroit Police Department's Censor Bureau would watch every film intended for theatrical exhibition in the city, taking detailed notes while keeping an eye out for any indecent shots or scenes that should be cut out of the film. This censored print would then be the version of the film shown to the public in Detroit, with audiences typically none the wiser as to the missing content in the pictures they were watching. By the time this censorship operation was halted by court order in 1969, the Detroit Censor Bureau had, over the course of over a half century, inspected hundreds of millions of feet of film.

The legal backing for this system of film censorship was a city ordinance that required anyone operating a movie theater in Detroit to first present any motion picture they intended to exhibit to the police commissioner or superintendent for inspection, a duty that was, in practice, passed off to the Censor Bureau. If the police found the film to be "indecent or immoral," they were empowered to ban the film from being publicly exhibited in Detroit or require cuts to be made before exhibition. If no signs of indecency or immorality were found, they would issue a permit allowing the film to be screened publicly. Exhibitors showing a film without such a permit would face fines, the revocation of their theater license, and even a potential prison sentence.

Simultaneously, there was another form of movie censorship occurring in Detroit that was less systematic in its approach. In addition to its methodical censorship of movies intended for theatrical exhibition before their release, the Censor Bureau also used Michigan's obscenity law as part of its persistent yet uneven attempts to crack down on the nontheatrical circulation of pornographic films. The Censor Bureau frequently raided stag parties in search of obscene films and their suppliers, with those found to be exhibiting or distributing sex films typically arrested and prosecuted to the fullest extent of the law, with the very real possibility of prison time.

This chapter explores the legal history of movie censorship in Detroit, examining the laws the Detroit Censor Bureau used to regulate cinema and how these laws evolved over time. Just as importantly, though, this chapter points to what gets missed in studying only important judicial rulings when examining the history of movie censorship. As the history of film censorship in Detroit demonstrates, just because an existing law or even the United States Supreme Court declares that censorship can occur only within certain boundaries does not mean such strictures were actually abided by in practice. This chapter, then, while acting as a legal history of movie censorship and obscenity in the 1950s and 1960s, also points to the incompleteness of focusing only on the law. Therefore, I utilize a bottom-up approach to this legal history to show how judicial rulings were and were not followed at the local level by law enforcement and city officials. In so doing, this chapter tells the story of how the extralegal censorship of movies by the Censor Bureau was carried out under the guise of legal censorship.

Focusing on movie censorship in Detroit for this case study means centering the history of policing given the Detroit Police Department's role as censors. Though numerous cities in the United States had their own movie censorship boards during this era, Detroit was highly unusual for the way it empowered police officers, rather than political appointees or civilian boards, to censor movies. This led to certain particularities that were unique to a place where those in charge of censoring cinema were police officers whose expertise and experience were not in cinema or literary analysis but in the ordinary police work of walking a beat and handing out parking tickets. This chapter therefore places the Censor Bureau's regulation of movies within the broader context of the history of policing in Detroit, showing how the practices and malpractices of the Detroit Police Department were echoed in their movie censorship operation, which quite often either violated legal precedent or simply ignored the law entirely.

This chapter examines movie censorship in Detroit from the late 1940s through the end of the 1960s. During this time frame, the Detroit Police Department was forced to respond to a number of different challenges to its movie censorship regime, including numerous rulings by the United States Supreme Court that limited the constitutional scope of movie censorship and seemingly hemmed in the Detroit Censor Bureau. Another challenge over the course of this period came from the changing politics of media censorship, as society at large became increasingly suspicious of censorship and at least somewhat more tolerant of looser morals in film and media. Simultaneously, this era also saw Detroit as a whole dramatically change as the combined forces of white flight, systemic racism, and deindustrialization threw the city into steep economic decline. These trends, alongside rampant fears about rising crime rates in the city in the late 1960s, raised questions about whether it made sense for the Detroit Police Department to continue to devote so much manpower and resources to the task of censoring media for the city. In light of all this, over time the police officers who made up the Censor Bureau were forced to publicly change the tone and rhetoric they used to discuss their movie censorship operation so as to avoid looking out of step with the times, even as they simultaneously fought to maintain their power as the arbiter of what movies were and were not fit for exhibition in Detroit. In the end, a 1969 district court decision declared that Detroit's movie censorship law was unconstitutional, thus killing off what remained of the Censor Bureau. As this chapter shows, though, it was as much the changing political landscape as it was a solitary adverse legal ruling that ended the Detroit Police Department's movie censorship operation.

POSTWAR MOVIE CENSORSHIP BY PRIOR RESTRAINT

For nearly half a century, the headquarters for film distribution operations in Detroit was an eight-story office building at the intersection of Cass Avenue and Montcalm Street in the downtown area. There, beginning in early 1927, the Film Exchange Building operated as the entry point for nearly all films hoping to play in the region's movie theaters. Most of the major Hollywood studios had offices in the building out of which they ran film distribution exchanges that covered much of the state of Michigan. That nearly every film in the region made its way through this building before heading to movie theaters was particularly convenient for one lesser-known occupant of the building: the Detroit Police Department's head film censor. In the smoke-filled projection room on the seventh floor of the Film Exchange Building, for over four decades, a member of the Censor Bureau sat for up to eight hours a day watching film after film, checking for the type of cinematic indecency that would require the censor's shears.[1]

Much like the literary censorship practices cataloged in chapter 1, the film censorship operation of the Detroit Police Department was designed to work in secrecy. It involved the same emphasis on eliciting the cooperation of the industry so as to avoid court cases and publicity for censored works. For the

Figure 2.1. Sergeant John Brown of the Censor Bureau in the screening room of the Film Exchange Building. *Detroit Free Press*, March 27, 1955.

most part, the film industry agreed to work with the Censor Bureau in a friendly manner, preferring to simply edit out portions of their films as necessary rather than instigate a costly legal battle. Beyond this, the Censor Bureau also worked to remain secretive by trying to avoid banning movies outright. As Censor Bureau head Herbert Case said in 1952, "Generally objectionable scenes are cut. Very rarely do we ban the whole movie." Certainly, as we will see, there were exceptions to this, but the Censor Bureau generally tried to avoid complete bans on films, preferring to discreetly make cuts. With regards to these cuts, the bureau tried their best to make them as invisible as possible, with Case saying that his office "tried to make deletions in such a manner as not to mar the continuity of a story." In 1948, film censor Charles W. Snyder noted a case in which, to maintain continuity, his office cut out some 323 feet of film just to eliminate one use of the word *damn*. In a few instances, explained Sergeant John Brown of the Censor Bureau in 1955, "the censors' cuts are so severe that the continuity makes the movie impossible to show." Such cases were exceedingly rare, though, with Case explaining, "Most of the time the public never knows a film has been cut."[2]

Another parallel to the Censor Bureau's literary censorship operation was that, though technically the Detroit Police Department's edicts on movie morality only had a legal basis within the confines of the city of Detroit, in practice its influence as film censor extended beyond the city limits. In part this was because, as a 1948 article explained, an estimated "60 percent of Michigan communities have laws that no picture can be shown except as approved in Detroit." But even someone living in a part of Michigan that did not have a local law explicitly mandating adherence to the movie censorship decisions of the Detroit Censor Bureau in all likelihood was still watching the version of movies first censored in Detroit. That is because the Film Exchange Building operated as the starting point for film distribution not just for Detroit but for the rest of Michigan as well. Typically, this meant that a film print would first enter the Film Exchange Building, where it would be inspected by one or more members of the Detroit Police Department, after which it would play exclusively in a downtown Detroit movie theater before slowly making its way out into neighborhood and suburban theaters and eventually the whole of Michigan. But once a print was cut by the Censor Bureau, it almost always stayed cut, meaning that the version of a film censored in Detroit for Detroit became the version seen far outside the city's borders.[3]

In accordance with the language of the movie censorship ordinance first enacted in Detroit in 1907, the Detroit Police Department's Censor Bureau was tasked with identifying and excising film footage that was deemed "indecent or immoral." The Censor Bureau often tried to portray this task of judging the morals of films as work that was studious and bound by law rather than based on a police officer's subjective views. As the *Detroit News* explained of the work of the Censor Bureau in 1954, "They must be constantly on the alert to ensure the film conforms with all state, federal and city laws. Personal opinions are not adequate. After viewing the films they must make written and detailed reports as to deletions and recommendations." At other times, though, this veneer of staid legal evaluations fell away to reveal the arbitrary nature of the censorial decisions being made about films. As Inspector Snyder, the head film censor for Detroit, said in 1946, "We don't have any set rules. We just keep looking for signs of immorality, obscenity and indecency."[4]

Without ever establishing set rules, the officers of the Detroit Censor Bureau often interpreted the standards of "indecent or immoral" in ways that would fit with their own ideological views. At times, it was fear of stirring up racial unrest that precipitated the censoring of particular movies, as in October of 1947, when it was reported that the Censor Bureau had banned the film *The Burning Cross*. This low-budget movie, produced outside of Hollywood, was a retelling of the horrors of the vigilante violence enacted by the Ku Klux Klan against African Americans in the South during the Reconstruction era. The film had been banned in Virginia, fitting with the long history of southern cities and states censoring films that were seen as a threat to the racial status quo. But the film was also banned in Detroit, presumably for the purpose of shielding African

Americans in the city from seeing a film that might arouse their anger not just at the racial discrimination many of them had experienced in the South but at the discrimination they continued to face in Detroit after moving there during the Great Migration. Much like Detroit's banning of the book *Strange Fruit* just a few years prior, the ban on *The Burning Cross* reveals the myth of the notion of southern racist exceptionalism, with northern cities also enacting censorship to suppress works that sought to combat white supremacy.[5]

The ban on *The Burning Cross* in Detroit was protested by the film's producer, Walter Colmes, who referenced Detroit's recent history in saying, "It is inconceivable that Detroit, the arsenal of democracy in World War II, must be subjected to bigoted censorship that would withhold the exposé of the black deeds and un-Americanism of the Ku Klux Klan."[6] Colmes found a local ally on this issue in exhibitor Albert Dezel, who had been slated to play the film at one of his art-house theaters. Colmes and Dezel wrote to "the Governor of Michigan, Detroit officials and heads of local and national organizations, asking them to intercede in the film's behalf." Evidently the campaign worked, as in mid-December of 1947, the Censor Bureau quietly lifted its ban on the film.[7]

In June of 1947, Inspector Snyder gave a revealing interview to *Boxoffice* in which he discussed his views on Hollywood's self-censoring Production Code. In the interview, he suggested two specific changes to the Production Code, the first being a revision that would result in a "reduction of drinking scenes, because of the heavy and growing opposition to them on behalf of large sections of the public." This stance led Snyder to make "major cuts" to the MGM musical *Summer Holiday* (1948), with Snyder criticizing scenes "portraying Mickey Rooney as 17-year-old boy intoxicated in association with woman indicated as of easy virtue."[8]

The second change Snyder suggested to the Production Code in his interview with *Boxoffice* was an "avoidance of any scenes which tend to belittle police authority." Snyder expressed his anger at media "portraying the metropolitan police officer as a 'halfwit or screwball,' instead of maintaining the necessary respect for his role in protecting society." The article explained that Snyder was particularly frustrated with "the current vogue for [the] detective film, in which a private detective is brought in to solve problems that the police appear—on the screen—incompetent to handle." Snyder made similar comments in a speech that same month to the annual convention of the Michigan Association of Chiefs of Police, at which he connected a rise in juvenile delinquency to the belittling of the police in both film and comic books. In Snyder's view, media in which the police were portrayed as bumbling, or media "which had someone other than a member of the regular police bringing a criminal to justice," worked to denigrate the role of the police in upholding a safe and moral society.[9]

Snyder's hypersensitivity to fictional portrayals of the police was perhaps born out of the very real criticism that had repeatedly been leveled against the Detroit Police Department for its violations of civil liberties. As Joe T. Darden and Richard W. Thomas explore in their book, *Detroit: Race Riots, Racial Conflicts, and Efforts to Bridge the Racial Divide*, throughout the first half of the twentieth century, the African American community in the city repeatedly accused the Detroit Police Department of acts of police brutality. In 1953, local African American newspaper *Michigan Chronicle* reported that over the previous decade, "'police brutality' became a symbol of everything that was wrong with Detroit." It was not just African Americans charging the Detroit Police Department with acts of brutality, as labor organizers claimed routine harassment and violence at the hands of the police. The juvenile delinquency scare had also fueled this issue, as in a 1945 case in which five teenagers were forced into false confessions of murder after Detroit police officers had violently interrogated them. In that case, as was typical, the offending officers received no real discipline for their actions.[10]

It was within this context that Snyder criticized what he saw as the unjust portrayal of law enforcement officers in popular film and media, and it was this context that informed Snyder's decision in the summer of 1947 to ban the film *Brute Force*. The picture stars Burt Lancaster as a prisoner housed in a brutal penitentiary where the sadistic and nigh-fascist head prison guard delights in enacting violence against the incarcerated. The film was set to premiere in Detroit just weeks after Snyder's comments condemning negative portrayals of the police, but its portrayal of sympathetic incarcerated men in conflict with cruel prison guards evidently hit too close to home for Snyder, who announced plans to ban the film. Snyder wanted the film barred for "the alleged brutality shown in the film by police and prison employees," no doubt taking umbrage at one scene, in particular, in which the head prison guard violently interrogates a prisoner about his escape plans by handcuffing the man to a chair and beating him. That same head prison guard twice refers to himself as a policeman, which Snyder particularly objected to. Snyder further stated that "the film does not truly depict police conduct," while a *Newsweek* article quoted Snyder as saying that the film was a "direct slap at our penal institutions" and further claiming that "things like brutality to inmates and other scenes just don't go on in our prisons." Following Snyder's comments, two letters to the editor published in the *Detroit News* specifically noted the irony of Snyder opposing the film for supposedly unfairly depicting authority figures as perpetrators of violence when the Detroit Police Department had been enmeshed in multiple allegations of police brutality that year alone.[11]

The problem for Snyder, though, was that the ordinance used by the Detroit Police Department to censor movies only allowed the police to ban films if they were "indecent or immoral," which no one seemed to believe could rightly be applied to *Brute Force*. Indeed, even Snyder admitted that "there is no legal ground for banning the film." Instead, Snyder initially asked that the distributor, Universal Pictures, voluntarily withdraw the film from exhibition, with *Boxoffice* further explaining that he would "appeal to citizens to stop such showings." Weeks later, after Universal refused to voluntarily withhold the film from exhibition locally, the Censor Bureau banned the film in Detroit, despite the fact that they, by their own admission, had no legal basis for doing so. It was likely because of this questionable legality that the ban on *Brute Force* was quietly withdrawn in the months that followed, with the film ultimately premiering in Detroit in September of 1947 at the Fox Theater, where it raked in a huge box-office take in its opening week, no doubt aided by the notoriety surrounding the film.[12]

While the censorship of *The Burning Cross* and *Brute Force* in 1947 laid bare the political leanings of the Censor Bureau, the perhaps more paradigmatic case of movie censorship in Detroit that year came with the French film *The Well-Digger's Daughter* (1940). On September 16, 1947, just one day before it was set to open at the Cinema Theater in Detroit, *The Well-Digger's Daughter* was held up by the Censor Bureau for its "seduction theme," meaning its storyline in which a country girl sleeps with a pilot, resulting in a child being born out of wedlock. Snyder explained his rationale by saying, "The film is immoral because the heroine has an illegitimate baby and is thrown out of the house by her father and falls into the company of immoral women." Nevertheless, Snyder admitted he had not actually seen the film, instead basing his opinion on a synopsis of the picture. The manager of the theater threatened legal action if the film was banned entirely, which perhaps influenced the decision of the Censor Bureau to allow the film to open with a single word cut from the subtitles—*chippy*, in this case referring to a woman of loose morals. Numerous other foreign films that dealt with sex and sexuality similarly got snipped by the Censor Bureau during the postwar era. In 1950, the Italian film *The Bandit* (1946) ran into trouble for its love scenes, which, the *Detroit News* review of the film lamented, "you will not see, for the Detroit police censor, scissored out what he considered offending material." Meanwhile, the 1950 Detroit opening of the British comedy *The Facts of Love* (1945) was delayed a day so the Censor Bureau could trim some of the film's sexually suggestive dialogue.[13]

Another foreign picture targeted by the Censor Bureau was *La Ronde* (1950), a French film that centers on the interwoven love stories of five men and five women. The film had already attracted significant censorial attention in the United States by the time it came to Detroit in March of 1952, having previously been banned in New York. In advance of its opening at three art-house theaters in Detroit, *La Ronde* was screened in its complete uncut version for local critics, with the film receiving favorable reviews in both the *Detroit News* and the *Detroit Free Press*. When the film opened in theaters, though, it had been heavily censored by the Detroit police. Estimates varied as to exactly how much had been cut, with the *News* saying that three thousand feet had been cut from the film, amounting to around a half hour of the ninety-five-minute picture, while the *Free Press* pegged the cuts at sixteen minutes in length. Either way, the censorship of the film was substantial, and the film critics for both the *News* and *Free Press* expressed frustration that they had reviewed a version of the film that the public would not get to see.[14]

Even as the early 1950s saw the Detroit Police Department continue to try to keep the city free from indecent cinema, outside legal developments soon raised questions for the future of the Censor Bureau. In the 1952 case of *Burstyn v. Wilson*, the Supreme Court granted motion pictures First Amendment protections for the first time in what has come to be known as the Miracle Decision. The ruling also specifically declared that the New York State censorship board's use of "sacrilegious" as a standard for censorship was unconstitutional. However, the high court refused to rule out prior restraint of motion pictures entirely, only narrowing the standards by which a locality could legally censor films before their release. If the ruling was not quite a knockout blow leveled against movie censorship, then, it nevertheless augured ill tidings for local movie censors.

However, the Detroit Censor Bureau was quick to argue that the decision would not impact their work, with the *Detroit News* publishing an article titled "No Shift Here in Censorship" just a day after the *Burstyn* ruling. In the article, Lieutenant Howard M. Stewart of the Censor Bureau noted that the city's movie censorship ordinance only allowed for the censorship of films that were "indecent or immoral," with Stewart declaring, "We have no right to censor them for any other reason." By this reasoning, the Censor Bureau would be unaffected by the ruling because the Supreme Court had only explicitly thrown out movie censorship based on the standard of a film being "sacrilegious." Of course, this ignored the fact that the ruling had granted movies First Amendment protections for the first time, a monumental shift that would inevitably have repercussions for every effort by local governments to censor the cinema.[15]

Just two years later, in 1954, a ruling that seemingly more directly implicated the Censor Bureau came up before the Supreme Court, with the case centered on New York's ban on *La Ronde* due to it being "immoral." The high court issued a unanimous decision in the case that overturned the film's ban in New York, citing the *Burstyn* ruling while offering little else on the broader issue of the constitutionality of movie censorship. As Laura Wittern-Keller and Raymond J. Haberski Jr. explained of the ruling, "The only thing that was clear was that New York could no longer censor on the ambiguous grounds of immorality."[16]

Once again, the Censor Bureau was quick to argue that the ruling would have no impact on them, seemingly a tough sell given that the ordinance used to censor movies in Detroit expressly invoked "immorality" as grounds for censorship. Even so, Inspector Case told the *Free Press* that "Detroit censorship is limited to obscenity grounds." Put simply, this statement is categorically false. While the Censor Bureau did (as we will see shortly) go after pornographic stag films using obscenity law, the licensing ordinance that the city used to censor movies before their release allowed the Detroit Police Department to censor films only if they were "indecent or immoral." By contrast, the ordinance made no reference whatsoever to obscenity. Case's statement also directly contradicted the one given by one of his lieutenants less than two years prior in which the officer claimed that the Supreme Court ruling out censorship based on a film being "sacrilegious" would have no impact on the Censor Bureau because it relied on the standards of "indecent or immoral." It was no coincidence that Case falsely indicated that obscenity was the supposed standard used by the Censor Bureau, as by that time obscenity was increasingly looking to be the only stable ground from which movie censors could operate.[17]

Seemingly no one realized that Case was not being forthright, with the *Free Press* giving no pushback in that article. The following day, both the *News* and *Free Press* printed editorials hailing the Supreme Court's decision as a victory for freedom of speech. Neither made any mention of the fact that the ruling might impact movie censorship in Detroit.[18]

Therefore, despite the highly questionable legality of the ordinance it was using, the Censor Bureau simply continued on with its work of keeping movie theater screens in Detroit free from material they deemed indecent or immoral. And so, when the Swedish film *One Summer of Happiness* (1951) made it to Detroit in late 1954, audiences did not see the nude bathing scene that had been cut out by the Censor Bureau. Nudity in documentary form was also out, as happened with the film *Latuko*, which had been sponsored by the American Museum of Natural History with the purpose of documenting a remote

Sudanese tribe but had also gained notoriety for its display of nude bodies. *Variety* reported that "the Censor Bureau of the Police Department had 'suggested' so many deletions of the ungirdled natives that there weren't any Latukos left." The demanded cuts were so extensive that the organizers of the film series at Wayne State University that had been planning to show *Latuko* ultimately decided to substitute in a Greta Garbo movie instead.[19]

Even as the Censor Bureau continued to cut salacious cinema into the mid-1950s, challenges emanating from outside the city emerged from not only the legal arena but the cultural one as well, as this era saw the early rumblings of what would come to be known as the sexual revolution. Running parallel to this was a push to loosen the restrictions on what was permissible to show in the movies to meet audience demand for more adult-oriented films. In light of the changing times, the strictures of the Production Code had begun to seem outmoded, eventually leading, in 1956, to the first major revisions of the code in over two decades. Inspector Melville E. Bullach, head of the Censor Bureau at that time, was quick to promise to the *Detroit News* that "the new code made no difference to him," saying, "When we find something offensive, it goes out, no matter whether it has a code approval or a good or bad rating." In truth, though, as the industry's self-censoring Production Code declined, more pressure was placed on local censors to deal with Hollywood films that were increasingly pushing the norms of acceptable violent and sexual content.[20]

The problem for the Censor Bureau was not only the progressively more graphic nature of the films entering Detroit but also, just as significantly, an industry that was increasingly unwilling to blindly kowtow to the Censor Bureau's rulings. This was often the case with highbrow art cinema, such as the documentary *The Naked Eye* (1956), which examines the history of photography and had been nominated for an Academy Award for Best Documentary. With the film set to play at two art-house venues in the city in September of 1957, the Censor Bureau demanded that three scenes be cut from the film because they depicted nude bodies. However, rather than simply accept the cuts, the director and producer of the film, Louis Clyde Stoumen, outright refused to make them. In the face of this heretofore unusual intransigence, the Censor Bureau backed down, allowing the film to play in its uncensored form.[21]

At other times, it was major Hollywood players who stood up to the Censor Bureau. Though for the most part the Censor Bureau typically allowed mainstream Hollywood cinema to play in Detroit without issue during the 1950s, a major exception to this was *The Moon Is Blue* (1953). The film was the rare major Hollywood picture to be released without a Production Code seal during this era—a fact that, along with its risqué dialogue and condemnation by the Legion of Decency, led to it being banned by state censorship boards in Kansas, Ohio, and Maryland. In Detroit, the Censor Bureau was reportedly hesitant to ban the picture given that the film was based on a stage production that had played in Detroit on three occasions, meaning that the same Censor Bureau had given their stamp of approval to the play as part of their censorship of live theater. Because of this, rather than ban the film, in July of 1953, Censor Bureau head Herbert Case announced that the film would be allowed to play in the city once two cuts to the dialogue had been made, removing the words *virgin* and *seduce*. As to why the film was in need of these cuts when its screenplay hewed closely to the stage production once approved by the Censor Bureau, police commissioner Donald Leonard explained that the motion picture audience "is considered much less sophisticated because it customarily includes many children." Newspaper accounts at that time specified that there were no scheduled dates yet for the picture to open in Detroit but it was expected the film would come to the city soon once those required deletions were made.[22]

As it turned out, it would be some time before *The Moon Is Blue* premiered in Detroit. Whereas the vast majority of filmmakers and distributors acceded to any necessary cuts to get their film passed by the Detroit Censor Bureau, *The Moon Is Blue* producer-director Otto Preminger refused entirely, declaring he would not "delete a single word or line" from the film. And so, months passed with this stalemate of the Censor Bureau demanding cuts and Preminger declining to make them. In the meanwhile, the film grossed millions of dollars across the United States and garnered three Academy Award nominations. These months also saw the Supreme Court hand down its ruling against New York for its ban on *La Ronde* while simultaneously ruling against Ohio for its ban on the film *M* (1951). Following these rulings, which had further put movie censors on their heels, in March of 1954, *Variety* reported that there was pending litigation against Detroit for its censorship of *The Moon Is Blue*. In light of all this, Case solicited the advice of the city's legal counsel, who reportedly told him that "it would be futile to retain the city censorship [of *The Moon Is Blue*] in the face of the high court's action." Therefore, in April of 1954, just under nine months after first demanding cuts on *The Moon Is Blue*, the Detroit Censor Bureau backed down, granting the film a permit for exhibition without cuts.[23]

The Censor Bureau also continued its focus on foreign art cinema throughout the mid- to late 1950s, though again, challenges soon emerged. When the adultery-themed French film *Lady Chatterley's Lover* (1955) first made it to Detroit, the Censor Bureau ordered that some eight hundred feet, or roughly 8 minutes of the film's 101-minute run time, be cut out from the picture. Meanwhile, the film had been banned entirely in New York due to its subject matter of adultery, with a legal challenge to that decision eventually making its way up to the Supreme Court. In yet another defeat for movie censorship at the high court during this era, in June of 1959, the Supreme Court struck down New York's ban on *Lady Chatterley's Lover*, with the court reiterating that a film could not be banned for presenting "immoral" ideas. In light of this, Albert Dezel, who owned multiple art-house cinemas in Detroit, announced that he would screen an uncut version of the film in defiance of the Censor Bureau since he "believed the Supreme Court decision overruled any local police censor action." The Censor Bureau apparently stood down, and the film soon opened at Dezel's Surf Theater and Coronet Theater, with newspaper advertisements crowing that the film was "Showing Now in Its Entirety!"[24]

Finally, in the latter half of the 1950s, the Censor Bureau also began to receive pushback from perhaps the most maligned and marginalized form of movies intended for theatrical exhibition: exploitation films. For decades, the Censor Bureau had repeatedly cut and banned particularly scandalous exploitation pictures, including the nudist film *This Naked Age* (1932), the venereal disease–themed film *Damaged Lives* (1933), and the pregnancy-themed film *Child Birth* (1938) in the 1930s. In the 1940s, the hugely popular sex-hygiene film *Mom and Dad* (1945) was given a complete ban in Detroit by the Censor Bureau. Typically, the Censor Bureau received little pushback when it cut or banned exploitation films owing to the genre's low cultural status. This explains why there are few newspaper accounts documenting the censorship of exploitation films in Detroit when it is likely that numerous other films of this ilk also ran into trouble with the Censor Bureau.[25]

In the latter half of the 1950s, though, the censoring of the film *Garden of Eden* (1954) did provoke a response from the film's distributor, Excelsior Pictures. The film was one of a number of nudist films of the era that focused their attention on the sight of bare bodies in a nudist colony. After previewing the film, the Detroit Censor Bureau demanded that all nude scenes be eliminated from *Garden of Eden* for a permit to be issued. The producers refused to do so, and the film was initially relegated to playing at drive-in theaters in suburbs outside Detroit that were laxer with their enforcement of movie morality than Detroit itself.[26]

Once again, though, outside legal decisions hemmed in the Censor Bureau's position. In 1957, the New York Court of Appeals declared that *Garden of Eden* was not obscene, and thus New York's ban on the film was overturned. Then, on September 10, 1958, the Michigan Supreme Court overturned the convictions of four people who had been arrested at a nudist camp near Battle Creek on charges of indecent exposure. Though this latter case did not directly implicate the censorship of *Garden of Eden*, it was further evidence that nudity did not, on its own, violate the law. And so, a day after this decision was handed down by the Michigan Supreme Court, the distributor of *Garden of Eden*, Excelsior Pictures, wrote to the Detroit branch of the ACLU, explaining the situation and "asking for your advise [sic] and guidance in getting a censor permit for the showing of our picture without any cuts and eliminations." The letter further noted that another nudist film, *Adam and Eve* (1956), had been allowed to play in Detroit despite showing "more nudety [sic] than our picture." Ernest Mazey, an attorney and member of the executive board of the Detroit ACLU, replied to the letter; he expressed that his organization was "definitely interested" in helping overturn the Censor Bureau's decision on the film and suggested legal counsel the distributor might employ. A year later, *Variety* reported that Excelsior was in the midst of challenging the ban on the film in Detroit, among other places.[27]

The cases of *Garden of Eden*, *Lady Chatterley's Lover*, *The Naked Eye*, and *The Moon Is Blue* make clear that as the 1950s progressed, an increasing number of film exhibitors and distributors were unwilling to quietly accede to any and all proclamations made by the Censor Bureau. The cooperation of the industry was not only central to the Censor Bureau's hope to continue to operate in secrecy but also increasingly essential given that rulings by the Supreme Court during the 1950s had made the movie censorship ordinance used by the Censor Bureau appear increasingly legally dubious. Even so, no legal action to directly challenge the ordinance Detroit used to censor movies before their release was mounted during the 1950s. As it turned out, the same could not be said for the Michigan obscenity ordinance that the Censor Bureau relied on as the legal basis for a very different form of movie censorship.

OF SMOKERS, STAG FILMS, AND OBSCENITY LAW

While the bulk of the Censor Bureau's work regulating movie morality was based around a systematized approach to film censorship, with movies inspected before their theatrical release, there also existed a more covert and haphazard type of movie censorship in Detroit. Namely, in addition to monitoring films intended for movie theater screens in the city, the Censor Bureau was simultaneously engaged in an effort to crack down on sexually explicit films that were never intended to play in a traditional theater space. Instead, these sex films—often existing on smaller-gauge formats like 8mm and 16mm film rather than the Hollywood standard of 35mm—circulated through informal networks and were exhibited in a variety of nontheatrical settings, with the Censor Bureau always hot on their trail.

One of the primary forms of illicit sexually explicit cinema pursued by the Censor Bureau was motion pictures intended for what were called stag parties or smokers. These types of gatherings were typically organized by civic or social organizations and featured an all-male audience watching scantily clad or fully nude female bodies—whether in the form of actual dancers onstage or represented in films—in a rented-out hall or home. Stag parties and smokers were a common phenomenon in American cities starting in the early twentieth century and continuing through the 1960s, and so the Censor Bureau made it their mission to crack down on these affairs with targeted raids and arrests.

In the early decades of the century, the Censor Bureau often broke up stag parties that featured exotic female dancers performing live onstage for patrons. In January 1924, it was reported that the Detroit police, headed by Lieutenant Lester Potter of the Censor Bureau, had raided a number of "smokers," where "undressed girls, as dancers, have been the principal attraction." These parties were said to have a price tag of between $1.50 and $3 a ticket, with one or two dances given and an average of one thousand men in attendance. When police did raid these smokers, the organizers and dancers were typically brought up on charges.[28]

Exactly when films began to appear as attractions at stag parties in Detroit is not entirely clear, though there are newspaper accounts at least as early as 1922 of the police finding obscene films at smokers. In February of that year, some twenty-five police officers, acting under the command of Lieutenant Potter, raided the Plaza Theater on the east side of Detroit at around one in the morning. There they discovered an audience of some 1,500 men watching a show that featured an "Oriental dancer," as well as around 2,500 feet of "indecent" film. The owner of the theater was arrested, as were the organizers of the event, which was said to have been arranged by a local fraternal organization. Just months later, in June of 1922, Royal A. Baker of the Censor Bureau, along with three assistants, raided a smoker in which approximately eight hundred men were caught watching an "immoral film." In addition to confiscating the three reels of film, the police also arrested four men who had allegedly either organized the event or were found to be operating the projector. In April of 1927, the Detroit police, led by Lieutenant Potter, raided a smoker organized by the Detroit American Soccer League. Upon entering the hall, the police apparently found about four hundred people "viewing a motion picture and watching the young women dance." As was typical in newspaper accounts of raids like this, the exact nature of the film was not specified, meaning it may have been a stag film (i.e., a short hard-core pornographic film) or just as easily a less salacious cousin of the stag film, with a nude or near-nude woman dancing before the camera but no sex occurring.[29]

In the years ahead, the Censor Bureau continued to try to crack down on smoker parties and obscene films, with mixed success. In September of 1940, a stag party held at the Barlum Hotel was raided by the police, resulting in the arrest of four men and seven women as well as the seizure of six reels of film. The 125 patrons in attendance—most of whom were employees in an automobile factory and had paid admission of two dollars for the event—were allowed to go home. Unusually, though, for cases like this, the four men were acquitted on the charges because the judge found that the police "had made their entrance through coercion." Because of this, while the films remained in police possession, presumably to be destroyed, the projector was returned to its owner. The seven arrested women, meanwhile, were held under investigation.[30]

Sloppy police work also doomed a case against the organizers of a March 1947 smoker held at the Paul Revere Athletic Club in Detroit. A police raid on the event led to 254 men being taken down to the police station and questioned, with four reels of "lewd film and motion picture projection equipment" also seized.[31] Of those who were brought in, 251 were released, while the three alleged organizers of the event were arrested and charged with possession and display of obscene films. The case received added attention from local newspapers because one of the three men charged was the son of prominent local labor organizer Frank X. Martel. This media spotlight made it all the more embarrassing once the case fell apart for the Censor Bureau. The problem was that the films in question were not being shown at the time of the arrest and were not found in the possession of the men arrested; rather, the reels were apparently found tucked away under a radiator. The judge therefore acquitted the defendants, finding "no police evidence linking the three defendants directly with the crimes charged."[32] This ruling, in turn, prompted the police deputy superintendent to launch an investigation into whether "the case had been carried on conscientiously by police officers." In the end, the Censor Bureau and its head at the time, Herbert Case, were cleared of any wrongdoing in the internal investigation, though the publicity garnered by the whole affair was a black mark for all involved.[33]

In the vast majority of cases, though, those who organized the smoker, any dancers present, and those found to be in possession of obscene films were all prosecuted and found guilty. A typical case was the police raid on a smoker in May of 1944 that resulted in two men being found guilty of exhibiting obscene motion pictures. One defendant was fined one hundred dollars, while the other was sentenced to ninety days in the Detroit House of Correction. Just a few months later, a smoker at Hotel Webster Hall was raided, resulting in two men being convicted of possession of obscene motion pictures while two dancers were found guilty of indecent exposure.[34]

Beyond the arrest and prosecution of those found displaying obscene cinema, the Censor Bureau also frequently sought to discipline those caught attending stag parties by publicly shaming them. In a 1948 interview, Inspector Snyder discussed a time when he brought ten men caught at a smoker down to the police station and told them, "I'm not taking you to court. But there's a phone over there and I've got plenty of nickels. You're not going home until you call up your wives and they come and get you." According to Snyder, none of them called, and so they were kept overnight at the police station before being let go, as Snyder "figured they would have a hard enough time explaining where they had been all night to teach them a lesson."[35]

A similar tactic of shaming those who attended a smoker was utilized by recorder's court judge Paul E. Krause, who in March of 1952 admonished sixty-eight men for having been caught at a smoker, telling them in court, "You men ought to be ashamed of yourselves. I'll bet your wives and families are proud of you." After convicting them on the misdemeanor charge of loitering, Judge Krause told the men, "You may go home now. Your convictions are on police records. I hope you can explain things to your wives." Such rhetoric made clear the moralizing that was always at the center of these efforts to clamp down on indecent cinema.[36]

When it came to those organizing smokers, though, these shaming tactics were seen as insufficient. Instead, a guilty verdict resulting in incarceration was perceived as a necessary suitable punishment. In March of 1952, just weeks after the case in which he had shamed the attendees of one stag party, another case resulting from a police raid on a smoker came before Judge Krause. In that case, Arthur Tarnapol was convicted of possession and exhibition of an obscene film and sentenced to ninety days of jail time. Judge Krause lamented that "90 days are not enough but that is all I can give you."[37]

Even as the Detroit Police Department, led by the Censor Bureau, spent decades chasing after any and all illicit smokers it heard about, their real targets were not those attending or even organizing smoker parties but rather the suppliers of the indecent films. At times this meant going undercover to try to buy obscene material kept under the table or in the back rooms of bookstores and novelty shops. This was the case in 1951 when Patrolman Stanley Rekiel walked into a novelty shop in downtown Detroit and bought $82.50 worth of obscene material, including indecent comic books, playing cards, and eight reels of film. The man convicted of selling the obscene material, Haskell Berg, was sentenced by the same Judge Krause to the maximum penalty of ninety days in the Detroit House of Correction. Just over a year later, he was arrested again on charges of distributing obscene materials and given another ninety-day sentence.[38]

At other times, members of the Censor Bureau used more circuitous methods for uncovering distributors in the city. As the *Free Press* reported in March of 1953: "Going about his duties as a member of the police censor bureau, Sgt. Richard Loftus spotted a 31-year-old woman in the Loop area whom he recognized as an actress in smoker movies recently confiscated by police. Taken to headquarters, the woman was highly indignant when told that the movies had been used commercially. She said the man who took them paid her $200, claiming it was his 'hobby.'" This interrogation led the police to raid the house of Paul Patterson, in whose basement were reportedly found some "2,100 feet of obscene movies" as well as what the newspapers described as "an elaborately-equipped studio" complete with "$1,200 worth of movie equipment." The Federal Bureau of Investigation (FBI) was also present when the police raided the house, with FBI agents hoping to "determine if Patterson is the source of numbers [sic] of films seized in raids on smokers outside of Michigan." Patterson was subsequently fined $105, with the *Free Press* reporting that the confiscated films would be burned "in Judge Mokersky's court in Patterson's presence as required by law." At the time of his arrest, Patterson refused to comment on the seized films to local newspapers, saying only that he had been making "legitimate movies" for years. Few others at that time were willing to side with Patterson's contention that sexually explicit stag films might, in fact, be legitimate movies not requiring arrests and court cases.[39]

The case of Meyer Rogow points to the way the Censor Bureau went about its task of cracking down on the distributors of obscene cinema. In 1951, the Detroit police searched Rogow's home, seizing a collection of indecent films, phonograph records, and literature that they valued at over $4,000. Censor Bureau head Herbert Case said that the "lewd material was being sold in factories and gas stations" and that he would be seeking a warrant for Rogow's arrest in the coming days. Left unclear in newspaper accounts was whether the police had possessed a warrant to search Rogow's home in the first place—something the Detroit Police Department had often been accused of not bothering with. Regardless, it was later reported that Rogow was fined one hundred dollars in this case.[40]

Two years later, Rogow was again in trouble with the Detroit police. In late September of 1953, the police, acting on a tip, raided a storeroom just down the street from Rogow's house. There the police seized indecent materials that they valued between $15,000 and $20,000, including ninety reels of motion pictures and thousands of photos and booklets. Soon after that the police arrested Rogow, claiming the storeroom was his. As it turned out, though, the police lacked the evidence to back up this claim. The storeroom had been sublet from a grocery store, but in court, the owner of the grocery said he could not say whether he had ever seen Rogow enter or leave the storeroom and did not know whose storeroom it was. The same Judge Krause was therefore forced to find Rogow not guilty, though he also made sure to say, "I will find you not guilty, but very reluctantly."[41]

Rogow's luck began to run out in 1954 due to the persistent efforts of the Censor Bureau. In February of that year, Patrolman Stanley Russell of the Censor Bureau witnessed Rogow selling obscene playing cards, and subsequently "a quantity of lewd literature and devices was found in Rogow's home."[42] In the resulting court case, Rogow was found guilty of possessing obscene literature and movies and fined one hundred dollars. Less than three months later, the Censor Bureau executed a search warrant of Rogow's home, finding some "$2,500 worth of obscene literature and film" reportedly hidden throughout the house. The police described Rogow at that time as Detroit's "principal distributor of obscene material." At trial in August of 1954, Rogow admitted to operating a false clothing business meant to conceal a salesroom out of which he distributed indecent materials. Given that it was a second conviction on obscenity charges, Rogow was given a ten-month prison sentence.[43]

Rogow did not serve out his full term but was granted parole at some point during his sentence. In April of 1955, though, he was back in court on obscenity charges. That month, an undercover police officer in the Censor Bureau bought thirty dollars of obscene pictures and literature from Rogow, ultimately leading to Rogow being sent back to prison on a ten-month sentence for violating the terms of his parole and facing new obscenity charges that, as a third-time offender, were bumped up to felony status. Rogow was allowed to serve the sentence for that felony conviction concurrently with his sentence for parole violation and was also put on probation for three years. Meanwhile, in May of 1955, David Rosen, a friend of Rogow's, was arrested for possession of some $20,000 worth of obscene material found in his house by the Detroit police. Though Rosen claimed the material had been left there without his knowledge by Rogow, he was given a thirty-day sentence in the Detroit House of Correction.[44]

Rogow's story points to the dogged way the Censor Bureau pursued suspected distributors of obscenity, with the aim of not only confiscating material intended for distribution but also locking up those found responsible. The hope evidently was that in doing so, they might cut off the supply of indecent films clandestinely circulating throughout the city and being exhibited at stag parties. In reality, there is little to indicate that the arrest or imprisonment of Rogow or any dealer during the 1950s accomplished this goal of diminishing the supply of indecent movies in Detroit.

The Censor Bureau's efforts to capture and prosecute those responsible for disseminating obscene cinema were one part of a broader story of policing and mass incarceration in Michigan. Throughout the mid-twentieth century, Michigan had one of the highest rates of incarceration in the country. In 1951, Michigan incarcerated 143 out of every 100,000 of its citizens, a mark topped by only four states at that time and far outweighing the incarceration rates of nearby Ohio (115) and Illinois (85). Though, to be sure, the Detroit Censor Bureau was by no means a primary driver of those numbers, their work did result in a steady flow of men (and, more rarely, women) sent behind bars. Between 1942 and 1950, according to annual reports put out by the Detroit Police Department, the Censor Bureau, on average, was responsible for just under 22 arrests each year. Between 1951 and 1953—after which the police annual reports were more scattershot in their reporting of Censor Bureau arrests—the average number of arrests made by the Censor Bureau each year shot up to nearly 114. In 1954, pondering the reasons behind Michigan's sky-high incarceration rate, state senator Robert E. Faulkner said, "It just can't be that Michigan people break that many more laws and get caught at it than the people of neighboring and comparable states." Seemingly no one at that time wanted to consider that the answer to the question might have something to do with the type of overpolicing by the Detroit Police Department that resulted in hundreds of people being arrested and incarcerated for distributing or displaying sexually explicit media.[45]

In a 2017 essay, scholar Roger N. Lancaster argues, "Harsher sex crime laws contributed to the rise of the mass incarceration more than is usually acknowledged." Lancaster usefully traces how the alliance of white feminist groups and law-and-order conservatives fed the massive growth in incarceration rates in the United States and, in turn, how all manner of sex crimes contributed to the rise of mass incarceration. While Lancaster focuses primarily on the period of the 1990s onward, the history of the Detroit Censor Bureau seeking prison time for obscenity offenses points to a longer trajectory of nonviolent sex crimes fueling incarceration rates.[46]

When it came to its decades-long crusade against indecent films exhibited at smokers, the Censor Bureau did not use the same city ordinance barring "indecent or immoral" pictures that it used to censor films intended for theatrical exhibition. Rather, because these stag films were never intended to play in theaters, the Censor Bureau relied upon obscenity law. The city itself had an obscenity ordinance on the books, but as its legal basis for censoring stag films, the Censor Bureau instead turned to the same Michigan obscenity law that it used to censor literature, as discussed in chapter 1. Michigan's obscenity statute dated back to 1837, with the law making it illegal to distribute any printed material containing obscene language "manifestly tending to the corruption of the morals of youth." The ordinance had been revised a handful of times in its more than century-long existence, including notably in the 1940s due to the efforts of Inspector Case, who appeared before the state legislature to argue for adding a section to Michigan's obscenity law that upped the penalties for successive obscenity convictions such that the potential sentences for second and third offenses would be much harsher. Case argued that the change in the ordinance "was passed for the simple reason that in many instances in Detroit we would have the same operator charged over and over again." For Case, then, harsher sentencing was needed to more severely punish those repeatedly violating obscenity law. It was under this provision that Meyer Rogow was given a longer prison sentence than the first-time obscenity conviction maximum of ninety days and was charged with a felony on his third offense.[47]

However, as discussed in chapter 1, Michigan's obscenity statute was ruled unconstitutional in February of 1957 by the United States Supreme Court. On the same day the ruling was handed down in *Butler v. Michigan*, the *Detroit News* reported that work "was started immediately in Lansing to get a new state law on the books to replace the one which was declared unconstitutional."[48] Though numerous components would be debated about the makeup of this new obscenity law, the most central and contentious issue was whether a judicial ruling would be required to determine whether a work was obscene or whether the police could be allowed to do so on their own. Among those favoring the former approach was the *Detroit Free Press*. In an editorial titled "Safe and Sane Censorship" published two days after the Supreme Court's ruling, the paper expressed "doubt that a hard and fast definition of what is obscene can be written." The editorial therefore suggested that each book, movie, photograph, and magazine be judged on its individual merits, with the question then being "whom we are to rely on for such judgment." The editorial answered this by stating, "It is the firm opinion of this newspaper that the task is not one for a police censor. No matter how well intentioned a police officer may be, regardless of how erudite he is in matters of art and literature, he should not be given the responsibility of having to rely on his best judgment." Many members of the state legislature who hailed from outside Detroit felt similarly. In January of 1957, a month before *Butler* was handed down, the *Free*

Press reported, "If the Supreme Court declares Michigan's obscenity code unconstitutional, critics of Detroit censorship plan to sponsor a new bill in the 1957 Legislature." The ordinance that these critics were proposing was modeled on Minnesota's obscenity statute and would have required prompt judicial hearings, after a work had already been disseminated, to determine whether it was obscene or not.[49]

On the other side of this debate, the Detroit Police Department was not keen on giving up the power to use their own discretion in determining obscenity for publications prior to their release and to do so without a judicial ruling. Leading the charge on behalf of the Detroit police was Harold M. Ryan, who represented Detroit in the state senate. Ryan had been a frequent spokesman in the state senate on behalf of the interests of the Detroit Police Department on issues like state funding for the police and revisions to the state's drug laws. He also had particular experience in advocating on behalf of the Detroit Censor Bureau as he had successfully spearheaded an effort to alter the state's obscenity law in 1953 to add a section banning comic books "glamorizing crime, lust and heinous acts." And so, unsurprisingly, Ryan was the most vocal proponent in 1957 of a new state obscenity law that would allow for the maximum level of police discretion. In January of 1957, a month before the Supreme Court's ruling was handed down, Ryan announced that he had prepared a new obscenity ordinance in case the state's current one was ruled unconstitutional. His bill was modeled after Maryland's obscenity ordinance and allowed the police to ban works as obscene without first requiring a judicial hearing.[50]

While Ryan was leading the charge in the Michigan Senate for a new obscenity ordinance that would empower Detroit police censorship, the Michigan House of Representatives had other ideas. In late March, Representative Theodore F. Hughes—an attorney who represented part of suburban Oakland County, just north of Detroit—proposed legislation that would require a judicial hearing to "determine if the publication is obscene for the class of readers to whom it is directed." The focus on the class of readers a work was intended for was a response to the Supreme Court's ruling in *Butler* that you could not ban a work for adults because of its supposed effect on children. The legislation was also specifically designed as a reaction against the police censorship practiced in Detroit, with one legislator saying, "All the suggested procedure is through the courts. We have attempted to avoid any recourse to actions of a police censor or some other nonjudicial officer." Under this proposed legislation, no work could be banned prior to an adversarial hearing in which a circuit court judge formally ruled a work obscene. On April 12, the state house passed the ordinance unanimously.[51]

Opposition to the house's proposal was immediately evident in the state senate, with Senator Ryan pushing back by saying that the house bill "would make the situation far worse than the technical difficulties it is trying to correct.... Instead of an effective process to halt the dissemination of obscene material, it would invite dilatory legal tactics that might hold up any real action for months." In particular, Ryan stressed that a work would be able to be distributed widely before a judicial ruling could be secured and that a court case would spur publicity and demand for a work before it could be deemed legally obscene. The *Detroit News* reported that it was "Detroit law enforcement officials" who were driving the push against the house bill, with those unnamed officials calling the bill "a procedural monstrosity... worse than nothing at all." The *News* article specifically noted that those voicing opposition to the house bill included Inspector Bullach, the head of the Censor Bureau at the time, who had also corresponded with Ryan on the issue.[52] Meanwhile, an assistant Wayne County prosecutor, whose office was tasked with handling obscenity prosecutions for the Detroit Police Department, harshly criticized the house bill, saying it "would hinder law enforcement rather than aid it."[53]

Beyond keeping control in the hands of the police, Senator Ryan's plan also included stiff penalties for the distribution of obscene material, with those convicted facing up to a year in jail and a fine of $1,000. In mid-May, the bill was unanimously passed by the state senate, setting up a tough negotiation with the house to merge their respective obscenity bills. Members of the house declared that the senate law was too similar to the one just declared unconstitutional by the Supreme Court and would likely be held invalid as well. Nevertheless, the state senate, led by Ryan, would not take no for an answer, and so the house ultimately agreed to pass the senate's version of the bill without any significant changes.[54] As Representative Hughes said, "It won't be good law but the Senate would take no other version." With that, Michigan's obscenity law was restored, with the Detroit Police Department retaining their primary role as the arbiters of obscenity.[55]

Through all this, state legislators were working largely in the dark as to how to define obscenity because the United States Supreme Court had for years sought to avoid the subject. *Butler* had marked the high court's reentrance into the issue of obscenity after a decades-long absence, but the narrow ruling in the case had only struck down Michigan's obscenity ordinance, not provided much in the way of guidance as to what would be a constitutionally acceptable obscenity law. This remained the case when Michigan's governor signed into law the state's new obscenity ordinance on June 14, 1957. Just ten days later, though, some measure of clarity was given when the Supreme Court handed down its landmark ruling in the case of *Roth v. United States*. In a six-to-three decision, the court declared that obscenity was not protected by the First Amendment and gave as its test for obscenity "whether, to the average person, applying contemporary community standards, the dominant theme of the material, taken as a whole, appeals to the prurient interest." Therefore, in 1958, the Michigan legislature revised the state's obscenity statute once more, this time by bringing in line its test for obscenity with the one used in the *Roth* decision. Once again, legislators from Detroit led the charge in the state legislature to reform the state's obscenity law.[56]

With Michigan's obscenity statute restored—and with it the broad discretion of the police to act as censors—the Detroit Censor Bureau redoubled its efforts to stamp out obscene materials. The police continued to raid smoker parties, including at least two in 1959, though the dealers of sex films continued to be the main target for the Censor Bureau.[57] In September of 1958, Patrolman John McClain of the Censor Bureau entered an east side camera shop and bought four two-hundred-foot reels of obscene film with seventy-two dollars in marked bills. The owner of the shop, Theodore Wichman, was subsequently arrested, after which, reported the *Detroit News*, "Censor Bureau officers found another seven reels of film, 10 obscene booklets and 124 photographs in his shop."[58] Wichman pleaded guilty to the sale of obscene materials and was sentenced to a year in the Detroit House of Correction, with his lengthy prison term a product of the harsher sentencing rules for first-time offenders under the new obscenity law.[59]

As the decade came to a close, the officers of the Detroit Censor Bureau boasted of their success in stamping out the circulation of smut in the city. In 1959, Senior Inspector William J. Bourke exclaimed, "Locally, this situation has been dried up to a trickle. Detroit is very clean in this respect.... Years ago, any factory, poolroom or alley had pornography available. This is not true anymore." In explaining this, Bourke credited Detroit's courts "for giving jail sentences, rather than fines, to smut peddlers." And so, as the 1960s began, the Censor Bureau continued to prioritize the arrest, conviction, and incarceration of those found to be distributing sexually explicit media.[60]

THE CENSOR BUREAU AT WORK, 1960–1964

At the outset of the 1960s, the Detroit Censor Bureau could, at least nominally, claim to be operating at full strength. Though the Supreme Court's decision in *Butler* had been a blow, the state's obscenity ordinance had quickly been reinstated and even strengthened. Meanwhile, even as numerous other local movie censorship boards had faced direct legal challenges during the 1950s, Detroit's movie censorship ordinance had emerged from the era unscathed. And yet, the Censor Bureau was undoubtedly in a vulnerable position, as the Detroit ordinance it used to censor movies was almost certainly unconstitutional given the Supreme Court's repeated rulings against censoring movies based on "immorality."

In 1961, though, the Censor Bureau got a temporary boost from an unlikely source: the Supreme Court. After repeatedly losing before the high court throughout the 1950s, movie censors finally pulled out a victory in the case of *Times Film Corp. v. Chicago*. Though free speech advocates had hoped the Supreme Court might at last follow through on what it had started with the Miracle Decision by rendering prior restraint of the movies unconstitutional, the court instead ruled in favor of Chicago's censors in a narrow five-to-four decision. Though it was a setback for those hoping to end film censorship, it was nevertheless notable that four justices vehemently dissented in the case, with the minority opinion offering a strong argument that movies should not be singled out for levels of censorship not suffered by other forms of constitutionally protected media.

In the days following the Supreme Court's ruling, as had been the case after previous significant Supreme Court rulings in the 1950s, Inspector Bullach spoke to both the *Detroit Free Press* and the *Detroit News* to assure the readers of both papers that the Censor Bureau's work would continue unabated. When it came to the city's movie censorship law, wrote the *Free Press*, "the ordinance, as interpreted by police, gives authority to ban obscenity, so they watch for nudity and obscene poses." Of course, the ordinance did not, in fact, mention obscenity at all. That the head of the Censor Bureau was indicating otherwise, and not for the first time, was the result of the legal trend noted by Wittern-Keller and Haberski: "By 1960, court challenges had lopped off every censoring standard but obscenity." Because of this, the Censor Bureau often took to claiming that obscenity was the basis for their work censoring movies before their release. In reality, it was only through the continued cooperation of the industry that their work could continue, with Inspector Bullach bragging at that time, "There has been no difficulty locally for several years because exhibitors have co-operated fully with the bureau in following recommendations for deletions. We expect these good relations to continue." This emphasis on cooperation pointed to the slippery line between legal censorship and the extralegal version of censorship that was being practiced by the Censor Bureau. Legally, the Censor Bureau was on increasingly shaky ground given the high court's rulings throughout the 1950s, but so long as they were by and large receiving the cooperation of the industry, they could continue on with their work largely unaffected by outside legal decisions. Of course, Bullach's statement left out the fact that the bureau's vaunted success in gaining the cooperation of the industry had already begun to fray in the late 1950s with the aforementioned challenges to the proposed censorship of films like *Garden of Eden*, *The Moon Is Blue*, *The Naked Eye*, and *Lady Chatterley's Lover*.[61]

Further challenges to Censor Bureau rulings emerged in the early 1960s, including with the Vittorio De Sica–directed Italian film *Two Women* (1960), which ran into trouble in Detroit over its depiction of adultery and rape. As *Free Press* film critic Louis Cook wrote in his review of the film, "*Two Women* was originally scheduled to be shown in Downtown Detroit but the changes requested by the censors would have made it meaningless." Therefore, the film instead opened in its uncut form in November 1961 at the Studio North Theater in Ferndale, a suburb just north of Detroit. The tussle between the distributors of the film and the Censor Bureau was given a further spotlight in April 1962 when Sophia Loren won an Academy Award for her performance in *Two Women*. Afterward, local newspapers noted that the film still had not played in Detroit proper because of the Censor Bureau. It was clarified at this time that the Censor Bureau had initially demanded five cuts to the film before eventually backing down to just two cuts, which the film's distributors had still rejected. Weeks later, a compromise was finally reached whereby one cut was made to a scene depicting rape while the rest of the film was left untouched, after which it was allowed to play in Detroit.[62]

Another challenge to the Censor Bureau came over the film *The Sky Above, the Mud Below* (1961), which, like *Latuko*, was an expeditionary documentary that depicted some nudity among the Indigenous people featured in the film.[63] Rather than outright censoring the film, the Censor Bureau tried to have it both ways by allowing the film to play uncut in the city but only in art-house theaters restricting admission to adults only. According to Bullach, "If it is to be shown for general patronage, it will have to be submitted for additional censorship, and probably some scenes of unclad natives would have to be deleted."[64] This new system proposed by the Censor Bureau prompted some confusion. Said one local film exhibitor, "I do not understand the situation as reported. Detroit censorship does not make any provision for classification. Aside from the content of the picture—it is either good enough to show to all or bad enough not to be shown at all."[65]

The distributor of the film, Joseph Levine, was evidently not satisfied with this proposed arrangement or with the Chicago censor board's decision to ban the film entirely unless the nudity was cut from the picture. And so, to challenge this censorship, Levine hired famed New York–based attorney Ephraim S. London, who had made a name for himself in the 1950s as one of the most prominent and successful opponents of movie censorship. London's public comments made clear the two main issues he saw with the Detroit Censor Bureau's ruling on the film. The first was the notion of cutting out scenes featuring nudity from the film to make it acceptable for general audiences, of which London said, "I don't see how we could very well put clothes on aborigines in this sort of film. The New York Board of Education has urged that its teachers see the movie and I think it was recommended by the Boy Scouts." [66] Here, then, London sought to distance the film from the more prurient nudity offered up in exploitation cinema by emphasizing the film's educational bona fides. Beyond just rejecting the suggestion that the distributor cut the nudity out of the film, London also specifically attacked the Detroit Censor Bureau's position that the film could be screened uncut at art houses in the city but not in general movie theaters. As he rhetorically asked, "Is a man more adult when he sees a film in an art theater than when he views it at a neighborhood movie house?" His comments made clear that he was raring for a fight; as he told the *New York Times*, "I think that Detroit's position is particularly silly. It is a position I have always wanted to test in the courts."[67] He would not get the chance. Facing a court challenge from one of the most renowned free speech attorneys of the era, the Censor Bureau stood down, and the film was allowed to play unrestrained in the city.[68]

Even so, the possibility of a direct legal challenge to movie censorship in Detroit continued to linger. In a 1963 letter discussing the Censor Bureau withdrawing its interference on *The Sky Above, the Mud Below*, Ernest Mazey, executive director of the Michigan chapter of the ACLU, wrote of the Censor Bureau, "We continue to be concerned with this operation and will undoubtedly have an issue next time which will permit us to come to grips with this problem." A year later, Mazey wrote famed First Amendment and civil rights attorney Ernest Goodman to "inquire if you would consider initiating a taxpayer's suit against the City of Detroit . . . in an effort to eliminate the Police Censor Bureau." For reasons that are not entirely clear, such a lawsuit did not emerge at that time, but nevertheless it was evident that free speech advocates were hoping to soon strike a blow that would kill off the Censor Bureau entirely.[69]

It was perhaps because of the ever-present threat of a legal challenge that, in 1962, the city's movie censorship ordinance was given its first significant update since it was first passed over a half century prior. That year, the ordinance was revised by the city council such that it now read that if the police found that "the motion picture *or any part thereof* is indecent or immoral, he shall reject that motion picture *or part thereof*." The change thereby reaffirmed the power of the Censor Bureau to cut films rather than just ban them outright. Of course, the Censor Bureau had, in fact, already been operating this way for decades; although they had occasionally banned a film in its entirety, much more often they simply required that certain cuts be made to a picture. The fact is, then, that this 1962 change to the ordinance was seemingly designed to retroactively justify a long-standing Censor Bureau practice. In any case, though the exact impetus for the change is not clear, undoubtedly it was an attempt to bolster the case for the legality of the city's movie censorship regime moving forward.[70]

Throughout the early part of the 1960s, the Censor Bureau was highly active in their role censoring movies. According to Detroit Police Department annual reports between 1950 and 1955 (with similar data not available in the later years of the decade), the Censor Bureau on average was annually inspecting just over 5.3 million feet of film and eliminating 28,245 feet of indecent material. Between 1960 and 1964, the total feet of film inspected annually dropped slightly, to just under 4.8 million, but the amount rejected went up to 49,995 feet. All told, the percentage of film eliminated by the Censor Bureau nearly doubled from 0.55 to 1.04 between these time frames. Of course, even as the amount of material cut by the Censor Bureau went up dramatically during the early 1960s, they continued their policy of trying to avoid publicity, meaning we do not know about most cases of films being censored in Detroit during this period.[71]

―m―

One unique element of the Detroit Censor Bureau was that, unlike nearly every other local movie censor board of the era, it was responsible for upholding the moral standards not just for movies but for all manner of public entertainment in Detroit. Given this, it is worth briefly pivoting here to discuss some of the other work being done by the Censor Bureau during this era. As discussed further in chapter 4, throughout this time, the Censor Bureau regularly inspected any entertainment venues that offered up dancing female bodies. According to annual reports put out by the Detroit Police Department, between 1960 and 1964, the officers of the Censor Bureau on average made 2,743 visits to cabaret performances each year to make sure nothing was too risqué. For burlesque shows, the number of inspections by the Censor Bureau in 1960 totaled 360, which was roughly in line with the number of visits to burlesque houses it annually made throughout the 1950s. The following year saw a jump, though, and between 1961 and 1964, the Censor Bureau made an average of 1,334 annual visits to burlesque shows. Though the annual reports as a whole typically did not specify the number or nature of what the Censor Bureau termed "corrections" to cabaret and burlesque shows, a more detailed report on their activities from 1962 does provide further information. That year, the bureau's 2,473 inspections of cabarets resulted in 119 "eliminations" in the areas of "costume, dialogue, [and] conduct," while 5 cabaret shows were closed entirely for being "indecent." For burlesque shows, the bureau's 1,275 visits resulted in 68 eliminations, with 2 shows closed entirely. All told, as was the case when inspecting movies, the sight of seminude female bodies often provoked action by the Censor Bureau.[72]

Beyond its ever-present surveillance of female performers, the Censor Bureau also went after the burgeoning youth culture in the city in the form of beatnik poets. In August of 1959, local poet and playwright Win Wells was arrested after a reading at the Hungry Eye café of his thirteen-page poem, "A Gypsy in Asphalt," which the police claimed contained "indecent language." Wells was found guilty of "indecent conduct" and sentenced to ninety days in jail or a fine of one hundred dollars. Wells attempted to appeal his conviction but had the misfortune of winding up before Judge Paul Krause, whose harsh stance on obscenity was discussed earlier. When Wells's attorney argued that it was unfair that only the most explicit lines from the poem had been read to the jury at trial rather than the poem as a whole, Judge Krause proceeded to read the same excerpts aloud before telling the court, "If this isn't indecent, I give up."[73]

The case marked the beginning of a years-long scrutiny of beatnik cafés and poetry by the Censor Bureau. Between 1960 and 1964, the Censor Bureau made an average of fifty-eight inspections of "beatnik establishments" each year. Beatnik establishments were also often targeted for further surveillance and harassment by the Detroit Police Department. One beatnik café received twenty-four tickets from the police for all manner of offenses in the ten months following its opening. The attorney for that café pointedly claimed, "There are more policemen there at night than at Central Station." At times these police inspections resulted in prosecutions, as in March 1960, when Patrolman Howard Gaide of the Censor Bureau arrested Jau Billera after he read "suggestive poems" at a beatnik coffeehouse. Billera claimed that he was the victim of repeated police harassment and that his words had been taken out of context in arresting and prosecuting him. He was soon convicted of "indecent and obscene conduct," with the *Detroit News*—which referred to Billera as a "smut bard"—reporting that he had been fined twenty-five dollars and placed on probation for eighteen months. This work monitoring beatnik culture in the city was an extension of the Censor Bureau's literary censorship operation, which, as discussed in chapter 1, had banned numerous important beat novels of the era.[74]

Throughout these years, the Censor Bureau also inspected legitimate theater for any signs of indecency, as it had been doing for decades. In 1960, the *Free Press* explained that two officers of the Censor Bureau attended "the opening performance of every legitimate theater show that comes into Detroit." As Patrolman Edward Marks explained, "If something seems in bad taste, we suggest to the managers that it be changed. We always get wonderful cooperation."[75] They got somewhat less than "wonderful cooperation" in 1965 when the Censor Bureau decided to go after Concept East, a small African American–run independent theater in Detroit. That summer Concept East put on a production of two plays by LeRoi Jones (who would later change his name to Amiri Baraka) titled *The Toilet* and *The Slave*, each dealing with issues of race and Black nationalism, while the former also dealt with queer desire and antigay violence. After just a few short weeks, though—and after earning a positive review from the *Free Press*—the theater was ticketed two nights in a row on obscenity charges. Though these were dismissed in court due to the police mistakenly listing the wrong person on the charges, that did not stop the police from effectively shutting the theater down by refusing to grant them a theatrical license, without which they could not operate.[76] The theater appealed to the mayor, who eventually overruled the police by granting Concept East their license nearly four months after the whole affair began. In his statement, the mayor was nevertheless careful to say of the theater, "They still, of course, will be subject to review by the police censors."[77]

Finally, throughout the first half of the 1960s, the Censor Bureau continued to arrest and seek the prosecution of those found to be organizing stag parties or distributing sexually explicit media. A 1962 letter sent by Censor Bureau head Melville Bullach to Reverend Donald Schroeder of the Detroit Council of Churches detailed the activity on this front by the Censor Bureau over the course of 1960 and 1961. During that time frame, the Censor Bureau arrested seventy-one people for various violations of obscenity law. Over half of these came from a December 1961 raid on a smoker party that resulted in seven people being convicted of gross indecency while a further thirty-nine people were convicted of "frequenting [an] obscene smoker." Of the remaining twenty-five people brought up on obscenity charges over the course of this two-year period, most involved the possession or display of obscene film or literature. The majority of these cases resulted in a fine and probation, though at least three people were sentenced to prison time. Eleven of the cases, though, were lost in court by the Censor Bureau—most for, in Bullach's words, "insufficient evidence," though an illegal search also killed one case while two others resulted in not guilty rulings.[78]

One of the cases in which a defendant was found not guilty came on the charge of selling obscene phonograph records and was illustrative of a flaw in Michigan's obscenity ordinance. This issue became evident following the 1959 case of *Smith v. California*, in which the United States Supreme Court had reversed the obscenity conviction of a bookstore owner because the Los Angeles obscenity ordinance under which he was convicted "did not require a showing that the appellant had knowledge of the contents of the book." The ordinance was therefore ruled unconstitutional, with the court making clear the necessity of *scienter*, a legal term meaning that one had knowledge of wrongdoing. Michigan's obscenity statute, as enacted in 1957, did not make knowledge of a work's illicit nature a necessary component for prosecution. This problem was pointed out in a 1960 letter sent by Michigan attorney general Paul L. Adams to prosecutors throughout the state in which he discussed the state of obscenity law in Michigan. As Adams noted, the *Smith v. California* ruling "raises additional problems in the prosecution of cases under the Michigan statute and indeed casts some doubt upon the constitutionality of the present state statute." It was this *scienter* issue that doomed one prosecution by the Censor Bureau dated March 7, 1961. Another conviction from that same year was later overturned by the Michigan Supreme Court specifically because the state's obscenity ordinance at that time did not require knowledge on the part of the accused.[79]

Because of this problem with the law, the state legislature once again went to work revising Michigan's obscenity ordinance with the prodding of the Detroit Censor Bureau. In November 1960, Bullach appeared before a Michigan House Sub-Committee on Obscenity. Bullach told the committee that he wanted to see the penalties for obscenity convictions stiffened with longer prison sentences for repeat offenses, including up to two years in prison for third-time violators. He also argued that "possession alone should be made a crime in the case of hard core pornography," rather than the current standard in the law by which a person could only be charged for either displaying or distributing obscene material. Finally, the issue of indecent vinyl records came up in regard to bawdy comedian Rusty Warren. Bullach lamented that the Censor Bureau had been unable to act because records were not specifically mentioned in the state's obscenity statute, though he was quick to note, as well, that they had made sure Warren's live performances in Detroit were free from her most obscene material.[80]

In early 1961, the state legislature moved to correct the *scienter* problem with Michigan's obscenity law as well as address the recommendations suggested by Bullach. In February, the Censor Bureau's longtime ally Senator

Ryan introduced a bill to "make possession of two or more pieces of obscene materials a misdemeanor ranking with their sale." Ryan specifically explained the need for the bill by saying, "Our present law allows a one-year prison term and/or a $1,000 fine for selling obscene materials, but Detroit police are having trouble proving the sales." After the Michigan Senate passed Ryan's bill, in mid-April, Bullach appeared before the Judiciary Committee of the Michigan House of Representatives to urge the passage of the bill. To illustrate what he saw as the grave nature of the threat posed by obscene media, Bullach showed lawmakers "a variety of pornographic pictures or cartoons" at the hearing, telling lawmakers, "Often I'll find a man with 75 to 100 copies of this type of pornography. I have no case against him unless I can prove intent to sell. Yet he can be operating in an area where five schools are within blocks." A month later, the Michigan House and Senate agreed on a bill that revised the state's obscenity ordinance to both add a *scienter* clause and make possession of six or more copies of obscene materials "evidence of intent to sell or distribute the materials."[81]

With this change to the state obscenity ordinance in place, the Detroit Censor Bureau went after pornographic material with renewed vigor. In 1962, the Censor Bureau made seventy-four arrests on misdemeanor charges and a further six arrests on felony charges, a significant spike from previous years. These arrests led to fifty-five misdemeanor court cases and three felony court cases, resulting in forty-four misdemeanor convictions and two felony convictions. A further twenty-eight federal cases involving obscene mail were referred to the United States Postal Inspector. All in all, with the revised Michigan obscenity ordinance in place, both arrests and convictions shot up tremendously as the Censor Bureau wielded its new legal tools against those distributing, displaying, or, under the new law, even just possessing obscene material.[82]

THE DEATH OF THE CENSOR BUREAU

As the 1960s progressed, the Censor Bureau's position was increasingly precarious as it dealt with threats emanating from both within the city and outside it. Internally, it was clear that, if public sentiment had not entirely turned against the Censor Bureau (to the extent that the public was even aware of its work), certainly its support among the general populace had eroded. This was in line with broader nationwide trends that had put those who sought to censor on the defensive. This shift was reflected in the comments made by the officers of the Censor Bureau in the early part of the decade, as in 1960, when Bullach told the *Free Press*, "Censor Bureau is really a misnomer. We are not censors, but a review board. Our main job is to keep obscenity out of the reach of youngsters." Later in the same article, Bullach reiterated the point, saying again, "We're not really censors." Bullach clearly doth protest too much here, and his insistence that they were not acting as censors only makes it clear that censorship was precisely the task of the Censor Bureau, which is why it was so important to deny they were censors in the midst of changing public sentiment on the issue. In 1964, Patrolman Marks of the Censor Bureau similarly said, "The police are anticensor, but we do carry out the rulings of the Supreme Court." This statement was wrong on two counts. First, put simply, if the Detroit Police Department was in fact "anti-censor," they would not have had fifteen police officers devoted to the task of censorship. Second, as noted previously, the Censor Bureau quite often ignored the Supreme Court entirely when it came to censoring movies.[83]

The growing public opposition to censorship was also evident in the lack of support for the work of the Censor Bureau from Detroit mayor Jerome Cavanagh. In 1961, Cavanagh had shockingly won the position of mayor despite the fact that he was a thirty-three-year-old political neophyte who had never held or even run for elected office and had little name recognition citywide. Cavanagh upset the incumbent, Louis Miriani, by running to the left of him, in particular by tapping into the African American community's frustration over the state of policing and race relations in Detroit.

After taking office, Cavanagh showed little interest in engaging in anti-porn politics or furthering the city's media censorship practices. He laid out his views on pornography and censorship most clearly in a November 1963 speech before the Detroit Committee for Better Literature for Youth, the same group discussed in chapter 1 that had sought to monitor newsstands for literary indecency in the mid-1950s. In his talk, Cavanagh did express concern over the "profusion of suggestive, lurid, and sometimes downright filthy books." Still, he reserved most of the criticism in his speech for efforts to censor media, saying, "It seems to me that extreme care must be exercised when setting up any screening system whether it be private or public.... Shall we attempt to read every book, examine every magazine, review every movie? Is the answer in banning books or is the responsibility one which can be met in other ways?" For Cavanagh, the answer to that last question was clearly the latter approach, as his speech went on to call for a "campaign for the classics" and stipulate that "parents assume their proper responsibility in regard to the reading matter to which their children are exposed." Cavanagh's remarks made clear not only his own feelings on the matter but also that he seemed to have learned important lessons from the failures of earlier censorship campaigns. He specifically alluded to the Supreme Court's ruling in *Butler* as evidence to back up his assertion that any effort at censorship must be moderated by constitutional norms. He also drew on the notion that censoring a work tends to publicize it, arguing, "Instead of giving free advertising by banning a book or thundering against a movie or magazine, let us proclaim the merits of good books and good movies." In keeping with this, Cavanagh created a Good Literature Week for Detroit and further used his speech to champion the Sidney Poitier film *Lillies of the Field* (1963), saying it "should be playing to standing room only." These views on censorship no doubt informed the fact that, during his two terms in office, Cavanagh made no moves to either praise or prioritize the work of the Censor Bureau.[84]

Still, even with the public and the mayor turning against censorship, the Detroit Censor Bureau may have continued on its mission unabated were it not for the Supreme Court's momentous 1965 decision in *Freedman v. Maryland*. While the high court's unanimous opinion refused to declare all forms of prior restraint on the movies unconstitutional, they nevertheless made this type of censorship nearly impossible to pull off in practice. In particular, the Supreme Court ruled that for a censorship board to ban a work, they would have to institute a judicial hearing that would need to occur hastily and without delay, meaning they could no longer simply ban a work without a judicial ruling. The Supreme Court also shifted the burden of proof in censorship cases, as now censors would have to conclusively prove to a judge that a film was a danger to the public rather than distributors having to demonstrate a film to be harmless in nature.[85]

The ruling sounded the death knell for movie censorship boards across the country, finishing off what the Miracle Decision had started in 1952. In the intervening years between the two rulings, state censorship boards in Ohio and Pennsylvania had closed up shop, and by 1964, according to an amicus brief by the ACLU in the *Freedman* case, only four states (Maryland, New York, Virginia, and Kansas) and two cities (Chicago and Detroit) were still practicing a systematic prior restraint on movies. Following the *Freedman* ruling, New York soon shuttered its state censorship board, with Kansas and Virginia following in 1966, leaving Maryland the lone holdout. Chicago's censorship board would be killed off in the years ahead as well.[86]

The *Freedman* ruling was an obvious threat to the Censor Bureau. Most centrally, abiding by the ruling would force the Censor Bureau to do what it had always tried to avoid, which was to appear before a judge to determine whether they could censor a film. Nevertheless, when the ruling was announced in March of 1965, the *Detroit News* was quick with an article optimistically titled "Film Ruling Won't Affect City Setup," with the article offering assurances that the Supreme Court's decision "will have no immediate effect on practices of the Detroit police censor bureau." The article stated that "the definitions of obscenity are so vague" that, in the words of Inspector Robert S. Quaid, the Censor Bureau operated "in a rather informal manner." Of course, the movie censorship ordinance used by the Censor Bureau made no mention of obscenity, a fact that the article and Quaid neglected to mention. Quaid claimed the Censor Bureau would "recommend to the movie people that certain cuts be made, in the interest of good taste, if we feel it advisable. We aren't adamant." As we will see, this would become their oft-stated position in the years ahead, though here again it is important to point out that this simply was not true, as the Censor Bureau absolutely did require cuts to indecent films before a permit would be issued. In fact, in 1965 the Censor Bureau required 1.78 percent of all film footage reviewed to be eliminated, a record high.[87]

Despite the assurances that movie censorship would not be altered by the *Freedman* ruling, just over two months later, police commissioner Ray Girardin made significant changes to the Censor Bureau. Five of the fourteen police officers then in the Censor Bureau were reassigned to other departments, while the bureau itself was placed under the direction of the Vice Bureau. Commissioner Girardin explained that the move came due to "the complete confusion in the field of obscenity enforcement. . . . Things have gotten to the point that no one can define obscenity. As such, it doesn't make sense to have a squad of police officers ruling on what is or is not obscene, when there is no definition to test." Nevertheless, Girardin was quick to promise that the change "doesn't mean a permissive breakdown in morality." Initially, the *Detroit News* article on the move indicated that the change "is expected to reduce the examination of motion pictures and printed matter." However, deputy police commissioner James Lupton later clarified that the reduction in staff for the Censor Bureau would not impact movie censorship, with *Boxoffice* explaining, "Films will be reviewed, as in the past, by essentially the same personnel, and no change in operation is contemplated in this area, Lupton said." Nevertheless, changes were clearly afoot for the Censor Bureau in the wake of the *Freedman* ruling.[88]

The Censor Bureau also closed ranks during this time, a fact detailed in Ira Carmen's 1966 book, *Movies, Censorship, and the Law*. As part of his research for the dissertation the book was based on, Carmen sat down for an interview with three members of the Censor Bureau in December of 1962, with Carmen writing that the "tenor of the discussion was one of conviviality" and that all his questions were answered directly, with the officers "pulling no punches about how the Bureau functions as a censorship unit." Notably, Carmen's dissertation includes the full transcript of the interview. In November of 1965, though, Carmen approached the Detroit Police Department again to "gain their approval so that the facts of this interview could be published" as part of Carmen's book, only to find that "an iron curtain had descended over film censorship activities in the Motor City." Carmen was told at that time that the facts presented in the 1962 interview were now "outdated" and that "no public statements on censorship policies might be released unless the Commissioner himself approved." Even worse, Carmen was informed that permission to "publicize the interview," including permission to allow it to be printed in full or even simply quoted from in the book, would only be given if the entire book was scrutinized by the police. As Carmen wrote of his response, "Having no intention of submitting my manuscript to the well-honed hatchet of Detroit prior restraint, I refused to comply with this request." The Censor Bureau's change in attitude, Carmen explained, was the result of "pressure from various sources," in particular from those with a "libertarian" ideology who were opposed to the work of the Censor Bureau. Not coincidentally, then, Carmen found the Censor Bureau far less open to dialogue just months after the *Freedman* decision, when the bureau was on the defensive, its survival seemingly in jeopardy.[89]

The changes made by the Detroit Police Department to the Censor Bureau in 1965 did not go unnoticed by nationally prominent anti-porn crusaders. Just weeks after the move was announced, Charles H. Keating, the founder of the era's most influential anti-porn group, Citizens for Decent Literature, wrote a letter to the *Free Press* expressing his disapproval of the move, saying, "At a time when judicial opinions more and more recognize and support 'obscenity enforcement' I was sorry to see Detroit Police Commissioner Ray Girardin's comment that there was 'complete confusion' in this field of law enforcement." Keating went on to quote from Chief Justice Earl Warren's opinion advocating for greater obscenity enforcement in the 1964 Supreme Court case of *Jacobellis v. Ohio*, though he neglected to mention that Warren's opinion was the minority one, as the majority of the Supreme Court had actually overturned an obscenity conviction in that case.[90]

The Detroit Censor Bureau also was given a new name in the year following the *Freedman* ruling, rebranded as the Obscenity Detail. This name change obviously put the focus on obscenity, thereby downplaying the way the movie censorship law the police were using relied on concepts like "indecent or immoral" rather than obscenity. Just as importantly, though, the move was designed to distance the police from the increasingly unpopular idea of censorship. When Ira Carmen spoke to the Detroit police in late 1965, he wrote that "it was made clear to him that the agency was in no sense a censorship tribunal."

As Patrolman Marks of the Obscenity Detail explained in a 1966 talk, the "new job is to act as a protective force rather than a censorship board."[91]

In a 1967 series of five *Detroit Free Press* articles on the state of movie censorship in Detroit, the officers of the Obscenity Detail were quick to distance themselves from censorship, with one article stating, "What they do, they say, is not censorship." This claim referred to a tactical shift on the part of the Obscenity Detail. To be sure, the police still utilized the screening room in the Film Exchange Building to review films intended for theatrical exhibition before their release and still gave notes as to what they thought should be cut. The Obscenity Detail claimed the difference was that they were no longer requiring cuts to be made before granting a permit for a film's exhibition. Because the Detroit police had no interest in securing a prompt judicial review of their censorship decisions, as necessitated by the *Freedman* ruling, the Obscenity Detail simply provided a set of recommendations for what theater owners should cut from offending films to ensure they followed the law. The *Free Press* wrote, "What the police are doing, in effect, is this: They are telling the motion-picture exhibitor that they believe such-and-such scenes are subject to prosecution under Michigan's obscenity law and under the guidelines set down by the U.S. Supreme Court." Thus, if an exhibitor failed to comply with the suggested cuts, they would risk prosecution for violating obscenity law. As was typical of the long history of the Censor Bureau, though, it never came to this, with one officer boasting, "We get 100 percent co-operation."[92]

In a *Detroit News* article from the same year, Inspector James Cole of the Obscenity Detail explained of this setup, "Actually what we do is advise the exhibitors as to what the courts have passed as being acceptable. If they wish not to comply, and a complaint is received by police from a citizen, they have been warned and a court case may be involved." This was part of the Obscenity Detail's effort to distance their work from that of censorship, with Cole saying, "The bureau used to be called the license and censor bureau. But censor has been taken out since we act in an advisory capacity to exhibitors and issue permits."[93]

Once again, though, the Detroit Police Department's statements were more than a bit misleading. The rebranded Obscenity Detail absolutely continued to censor films before release, and every film hoping to be publicly exhibited in the city still had to get a permit first from the Detroit Police Department. Because of the willing industry cooperation that they, for the most part, received, the police claimed that exhibitors and distributors voluntarily cut films on their own rather than due to police censorship, but in reality, the industry made those cuts because the Detroit Police Department expressly warned them that if they did not, they could be prosecuted and subject to fines and incarceration under the state obscenity law. Moreover, the police wielded their power to prevent any film from being exhibited without a license as a weapon to try to force exhibitors to acquiesce to their censorial demands. In September of 1966, the Obscenity Detail "requested" cuts to the French film *Le Bonheur* (1965). When the Studio One Theater in Detroit refused to make the cuts, it did not simply play the film unencumbered; rather, the film was delayed for six weeks until the Obscenity Detail finally backed down and let the film play in its uncut version. The Obscenity Detail no doubt would have claimed they did not practice censorship in this case given that the film was eventually allowed to play in its original form. However, the fact that the film had its premiere delayed altogether was the direct result of the Obscenity Detail's threat of censorship and demand for cuts to the film. Further cases of censorship by the Detroit Police Department emerged in the years ahead. In 1969, the Obscenity Detail told director Robert Aldrich that his film *The Killing of Sister George* (1968) would need to cut out five minutes from its run time to gain a permit for exhibition. When the film eventually played in Detroit, negotiations had reduced that to some 120 feet of the film, amounting to just over one minute, which was excised by the Obscenity Detail because it depicted a lesbian sexual encounter. All told, for all the claims that it was no longer acting as censor, there were far more similarities between the movie censorship operations practiced by the Censor Bureau and its successor, the Obscenity Detail, than there were divergences.[94]

During this period, the Obscenity Detail repeatedly claimed that their movie censorship practices were based on the state's obscenity law. In 1966, *Boxoffice* reported on a speech given by Patrolman Marks and detailed how Marks explained the work of the Obscenity Detail: "The members work strictly within the jurisdiction of the [state] obscenity law, and it is their job to view questionable films, take notes of obscene sections and to make suggestions that certain scenes be cut from the film." A 1967 *Detroit News* article reported that, when it came to "previewing movies" before their release, the Obscenity Detail was "relying entirely on the state obscenity laws for whatever legal backing it needs." Ira Carmen, noting this rhetoric, correctly stated, "This is indeed a curious phenomenon given the fact that the word 'obscene' is not even mentioned in the licensing law," writing further, "It may well be that the words 'indecent' and 'immoral' are dead letters in the Motor City."[95]

The police were claiming to be using obscenity law because, as previously discussed, the licensing law used by the city to inspect and censor movies before their release was plainly unconstitutional. And the Detroit Police Department knew it too. In 1967, the *Free Press* reported that, according to the officers of the Obscenity Detail themselves, "the city ordinance under which they operate is considered unconstitutional." And so, the Obscenity Detail simply ignored what the law actually said and continued on censoring movies long after the law they were using to do so was clearly invalid. At times they admitted this, and at other times they gave statements that had a more tenuous relationship with the truth. In 1967, Inspector Cole said of the city's movie censorship operation at that time, "Our main job is to make sure that anything that needs a permit under the city's ordinances adheres to standards set by the ordinance." This was simply not the case, as the police were ignoring the strictures of the city's licensing ordinance as well as established law to instead censor movies according to their own whims. Moreover, even if one were to take the Obscenity Detail's assertion that they were using the state's obscenity ordinance to censor movies at face value, there is still the obvious problem that Michigan obscenity law made no provision for the licensing procedure that was the entire basis for how Detroit's movie censorship operation worked.[96]

As to what movies were being censored in Detroit during the late 1960s, the Detroit police publicly claimed that foreign art films were now allowed to play unhindered, though, in truth, a number of foreign films ran into trouble in Detroit during this era, including the aforementioned case of *Le Bonheur*. Nevertheless, it is true that foreign art cinema was not as central a focus as it had been during the 1950s. Instead, as Carmen explains, "The type of movie that causes the most trouble is the American 'quickie nudie' commodity that is produced by various 'fly-by-night' companies." Such films were part of the sexploitation genre, which focused on nudity and nonexplicit sex and often came under scrutiny by the Obscenity Detail. In his 1968 book, *Censorship of the Movies*, Richard S. Randall provides the following notes taken by a member of the Obscenity Detail during an examination of a sexploitation film he refers to as *The Phantom Peeper*:

- 10:55—start of movie.
- 11:08—girl at dressing table, cut bare breast.
- 11:24—girls with nude breasts in dressing rooms.
- 11:26—scene in nudist camp, cut all shots of bare breast.
- 11:33—cut all closeups of girl undressing in office.
- 11:34—cut all pool scenes showing bare breasts.
- 11:42—cut scene of girl in dressing room—bare breast.
- 11:50—girl in bathtub, cut shot of bare breasts.

The officer's notes are indicative of the way nudity was often the focus of Detroit movie censorship. In the end, this film was passed after seven deletions to the film amounting to four hundred feet out of a film five thousand feet in length.[97]

Though the Obscenity Detail generally tried to avoid having its censorial policies pinned down too clearly, in one interview, officers made clear that language was important to what the Detroit police were cutting, as a stray *goddamn, bitch,* or *whore* might land a film in hot water.[98] In 1967, after interviewing police officers and reviewing exhibition permits, the *Free Press* explained that "they generally draw the line at scenes showing a fraction too much nudity below the waist, a nude woman in contact with a man, burlesque-type 'bumping and grinding' or excited writhing, any kind of preliminary sex play, and unmistakable signs that 'perversion' or other unreserved erotic activity is going on." The allusion to "perversion" was an indication of the fact that the Obscenity Detail frequently went after films with gay content, as was the case with the low-budget noir film *Aroused* (1966), which was forced to cut out "some 20 minutes of film which police considered obscene" due to the lesbian storyline in the picture. *The Killing of Sister George* was similarly forced to make cuts due to its depiction of lesbian sex.[99]

When it came to censoring films for exhibition, the Obscenity Detail generally stuck to a policy of cutting films rather than banning them outright. As Carmen writes, "Detroit stands alone among censorship communities" for its policy by which "no film is ever proscribed in this city." Randall notes a case in which the Censor Bureau "once required 6,000 feet of deletions in a film 8,000 feet long. Needless to say, the film was not shown." This policy was often centered on what could sustain industry cooperation, with the *Free Press* writing in 1967, "In practice, this also means cuts are made according to what exhibitors are not likely to fight. And they've fought hardly anything at all so far. It's the voluntary co-operation and submission to the system by movie exhibitors, in fact, that enables Detroit police to operate their not-really-censorship brand of censorship."[100]

This policy of cutting films rather than banning them was evidently an attempt by the Obscenity Detail to take a more lenient stance, with the aim being to both prevent public accusations that they were in the business of hard censorship while also helping stave off a potential court case that might bring down the whole system. The problem with this policy, though, one that few seemed to realize at the time, was that this stance of cutting rather than banning films actually made what the Detroit police were doing even more unconstitutional. The 1957 Supreme Court ruling in *Roth v. United States* made it clear that the test for obscenity involved whether a "dominant theme taken as a whole appeals to the prurient interest." The "taken as a whole" portion meant that a work could not be judged obscene because of stray passages, and the court further clarified that the work as a whole must be "utterly without redeeming social importance." If the Detroit police were, as they claimed, using obscenity law to censor movies before their release, then they could only ban an entire movie if the whole of it was deemed (by a judge) to be obscene and without redeeming social importance. By contrast, they had absolutely no right to cut out an "obscene section" of a work, as the work needed to be judged as a whole. This issue was laid bare in a 1962 interview by Ira Carmen in which a member of the Censor Bureau stated, "We never ban a movie. No picture is obscene throughout." This statement betrays a complete lack of understanding of obscenity law by this police officer. If this officer indeed held the view that "no picture is obscene throughout," then, legally speaking, this would mean that no movie would be obscene according to Supreme Court guidelines, as obscenity law does not provide for labeling only certain sections of a work obscene. As Carmen succinctly writes, "The [Detroit Censor] Bureau delivers the coup de grace to [the test for obscenity under] *Roth-Alberts* by admitting that it deletes nudity, rape scenes, and profanity irrespective of the context of the movie itself."[101]

A final key characteristic of film censorship in Detroit during the latter half of the 1960s was the expansion and systematization of the policy of granting greater leeway to films playing to adults-only audiences in art-house theaters. Throughout the late 1960s, the Obscenity Detail distinguished between general movie theaters and art-house theaters, with the latter allowed to play relatively uncensored sexually explicit art films in exchange for their enforcement of an adults-only policy. Patrolman Marks explained in a 1962 interview with Ira Carmen what would happen if an exhibitor refused to bar those under eighteen years of age from entrance, saying, "If they refuse we will cut such pictures to pieces." Under this policy, foreign films like *Le Bonheur*, *Knife in the Water*, *Dear John*, and *Loving Couples* were allowed to play uncut in Detroit but were restricted to art houses. Thus, a distributor might be presented with the option of either cutting a film to qualify for general release in Detroit or sequestering the film's release to the small handful of art houses in the city. If they chose the latter, the film's permit for exhibition would stipulate that it could only be shown at art-house theaters with an age restriction in place. Beyond just the age minimum, though, the appeal of restricting films to art houses was that they were presumed to draw the "right type" of audience, meaning upstanding middle- and upper-class adults. As Patrolman Marks, in the same 1962 interview with Carmen, said of this policy, "For one thing, the price of admission is usually higher for the movies they show—about $1.50—so that the audience will be more of a select group." The elitism of this policy and the Censor Bureau's work as a whole was laid bare throughout this interview, with Patrolman Marks later saying that movie censorship was needed "for the protection of children and immature adults." With this policy of sequestering certain films to higher-priced art theaters, then, the Detroit Police Department sought to shield "immature adults," in their classist terminology, from indecent cinema.[102]

This policy was an attempt to try to skirt the challenges Detroit faced in the wake of the Supreme Court's decision in *Butler v. Michigan*. Where that decision had declared that you could not censor a work for adults solely because it might corrupt the morals of youth, the policy on art houses seemingly allowed films to play to adult audiences while keeping youth out. In creating a de facto age-classification system through art-house theaters, the city was attempting to, in the words of the *Free Press*, "have its cake and eat it too. Protection for young innocence, yet more freedom for adults." Here again, though, this censorship policy adopted by the Detroit Police Department was, at best, of questionable legality. What the Detroit Police Department used as justification for this policy was a particular section of Michigan's obscenity statute that made it a crime to show "any obscene, lewd, lascivious, filthy or indecent motion picture film manifestly tending to corrupt the morals of youth" to those under the age of eighteen. However, the Supreme Court in *Butler* had already made clear that the test of obscenity did not rest on its supposed impact on youth in particular but rather upon society as a whole, meaning a work could not be declared obscene only for children. If a work was declared obscene, it was obscene to everyone and thus could not be shown to adults either. The same point had been made in a 1959 United States District Court decision striking down Chicago's similar movie censorship age-classification system, with the judge writing, "A picture is either 'obscene' . . . or it is not."[103]

On top of the dubious legality of Detroit's age-classification system is the fact that the actual city law that was the basis for censoring movies before their release made no mention whatsoever of age restrictions for movies. Indeed, previously the city had made clear that it had no power to classify films as suitable for certain age groups only. In 1953, in the midst of the debate over whether *The Moon Is Blue* should be allowed to play in the city, Nathaniel Goldstick, part of the attorney's office for the city, noted that "Detroit has no law under which certain films can be classified as fit for viewing by adults only. The content of all must be judged on whether it is immoral, indecent or obscene." Given that, and given the major financial implications of restricting certain films to only a small handful of art-house theaters in the city, this policy was unlikely to stand up to a legal challenge. As Carmen wrote at that time, "The law of the city uses these terms [indecent and immoral] only as absolutes without regard to the age level of the viewer. It is hard to believe, therefore, that these censors have a legal right to hobble films financially that could have a deleterious effect only on the younger set."[104]

Overall, what the Detroit Police Department was doing was unquestionably unconstitutional on numerous fronts. The city ordinance they used to censor movies before release was plainly invalid due to its reliance on the concept of "indecent or immoral" as the basis for censorship. Because of this, the police then ignored what the law said and instead claimed they were censoring movies based on the standard of obscenity. However, they also did not actually abide by obscenity law because they did not judge works as a whole and did not hold to the notion that a work must be judged by its impact on the average person, not on children. In addition, Michigan's obscenity law did not even allow for the type of prior restraint licensing that the police were doing. All this was in addition to the most flagrant way the Detroit Police Department was violating the law, which is that they were making no effort to get a judicial determination on whether a work was obscene. Both obscenity law in general and movie censorship in particular after the *Freedman* ruling made clear that it was the courts, not the police, who had the power to declare a work obscene. As the *Free Press* wrote in 1967, "Although the courts have ruled that they, themselves, are the final arbiters [of obscenity], in practice it's really the police—especially in Detroit, the only big city besides Chicago that still has a movie censorship setup." The courts were, under clearly established law, necessary for determining whether a work was obscene due to it violating a community's standards. In the absence of this judicial determination, the Detroit Police Department simply made up and enforced their own standards as they saw fit.[105]

In the end, the lack of judicial determination would doom the Detroit Police Department's movie censorship operation. In 1969, the Obscenity Detail attempted to censor the sexploitation film *Vixen*, which was directed by Russ Meyer, known colloquially as the "king of the nudies." Meyer was no stranger to the Detroit police, as in a 1962 interview, Patrolman Roy Gutch of the Censor Bureau responded to a question about the types of films coming in for censorship by saying, "The most common type of movie we cut is the 'quickie nude film.' It is a cheaply made product put out by small companies and it emphasizes nudity. For example, there is this fellow Russ Meyers [sic] who specializes in these. We cut two-thirds of his movies." It is perhaps fitting, then, that it was Meyer who wound up bringing down the Detroit Police Department's system of prior restraint on movies. After a private screening of *Vixen* in March of 1969 in the Film Exchange Building, Patrolman Marks of the Obscenity Detail issued a permit for the film on the condition that cuts be made to five soft-core sex scenes amounting to 1,200 feet of film, or nearly 20 percent of the complete picture. The permit also stipulated that even with those cuts, the film would still be restricted to those eighteen years of age and above, which went beyond the minimum age of sixteen as stipulated by the film's X rating, self-applied under the new Motion Picture Association of America ratings system. Rather than simply agreeing to these terms, Meyer's production company sued the city, claiming that it had unfairly threatened "criminal prosecution under the state and municipal obscenity laws" if the film was exhibited publicly and that the city had violated the First Amendment in threatening this "prior to a judicial determination of obscenity." In his decision, district court judge Fred W. Kaess killed off Detroit's movie censorship law, writing, "There is no dispute, and this court so holds, that Section 5-2-7 of the Detroit Municipal Ordinances entitled 'Censorship of moving pictures' is unconstitutional." Judge Kaess cited only *Freedman v. Maryland* on this point, though, as discussed earlier, the constitutionality of the ordinance had been in doubt long before that 1965 decision. In any case, the mention of a lack of dispute about the constitutionality of the ordinance indicates that the city's attorneys likely did not even bother to argue the point, knowing it was a losing battle. Though the court refused to declare Michigan's obscenity law unconstitutional as well, it was nevertheless a major victory for Meyer and free speech advocates.[106]

With that ruling, movie censorship as it had been practiced by the Detroit Police Department for over sixty years was at an end. No longer did the police have a mechanism for enacting prior restraint of the movies, and a determination of obscenity would need to be made by a judge rather than a police officer. Following this, the police still attempted to suppress indecent media and public entertainment using obscenity law, but with limited success. In early 1970, a series of lithograph drawings by John Lennon depicting his sex life with wife Yoko Ono came under police scrutiny when they were exhibited in a Detroit art gallery. The Obscenity Detail came to the exhibit to take photographs of the lithographs, which they, in turn, showed to the Wayne County prosecutor, who declared that the drawings were not obscene, leaving the police with no ability to stop the exhibition.[107] Meanwhile, the police were similarly feckless in their attempts to regulate the morality of stage plays in the city. In the weeks leading up to its Detroit premiere in June 1970, much was made over whether the police would shut down the rock musical *Hair*, which had a brief scene featuring dimly lit actors nude onstage. In advance of the play's public opening at the Vest Pocket Theatre, a delegation of seven law enforcement officers sat through a private showing to determine whether it was obscene. Lieutenant Joseph Areeda of the Obscenity Detail subsequently denounced the play, calling it "anti-religion, anti-family, anti-flag, anti-war, anti-Establishment in general; pro-free sex and pro-pot."[108] Nevertheless, James Lacey, assistant Wayne County prosecutor, found that there was nothing the police could do to stop the play from going on, declaring that because it "espouses social relevancy," it is therefore "protected under the First Amendment." Lacey regretfully noted the dramatic shift that had occurred in short order to police censorship by saying, "If this show had appeared in Detroit five years ago, it would never have gotten beyond opening night."[109]

The one area where the Detroit Police Department found at least some measure of success in their use of obscenity law was in their continued pursuit of those distributing hard-core pornography. In 1970, in the midst of rapid growth in the number of adult bookstores and movie theaters in the city, the Obscenity Detail attempted to crack down with targeted raids and obscenity prosecutions. On July 17, the police arrested the owner and salesman at an adult bookstore on charges of possession and sale of obscene motion pictures. Four days later, the Obscenity Detail raided an adult bookstore, confiscating three peep show machines and promising that arrest warrants on obscenity charges would soon be issued. Just weeks after that, on August 7, the police raided six adult bookstores in what was hailed as "the biggest anti-pornography strike ever conducted in Detroit." Very quickly, though, a lawsuit was filed challenging this last raid, arguing that the state's obscenity law was unconstitutional. In some of these cases, the police were successful in prosecuting individuals for obscenity, but those instances were greatly outnumbered by the court decisions going against attempts at enforcing obscenity law. As Lieutenant Areeda mournfully put it in 1970, "You can't hardly get a conviction on any form of obscenity anymore."[110]

POLICING AND THE ILLEGALITY OF DETROIT MOVIE CENSORSHIP

As this chapter outlined, over the course of decades, the law enforcement officers who made up the Detroit Censor Bureau and later the Obscenity Detail systematically ignored and violated the law in their censorship of movies. And so, when the film *Brute Force* was seen by Detroit's head movie censor as demeaning to law enforcement, he tried to outlaw it despite fully admitting that "there is no legal ground for banning the film." When the city's censorship ordinance was put in jeopardy by Supreme Court decisions barring censorship based on "immorality," the Censor Bureau simply ignored the standards for censorship set out by the city's own law and instead substituted in the standard of obscenity. And yet, even as the police suggested in interviews that they were now examining movies to look for obscene material, they did not actually abide by obscenity law. They refused to follow legal precedent that made it clear that it was the courts, and not the police, who had the power to determine whether a work was obscene, and they cut out "obscene sections" of works in clear violation of the Supreme Court's ruling that a work must be judged as a whole. At other times, the Censor Bureau simply made up law that did not exist when it suited their interests, as when they created a two-tier system of censorship for adults-only art houses and general movie theaters.

When the Detroit Police Department was not ignoring the law in their censorship of movies, they were shaping it, as the Censor Bureau repeatedly enlisted its allies in the state legislature to make sure the state's obscenity laws were tailored to meet their preferred mode of censorship. This included strengthening the penalties for violating obscenity law so the police could give longer prison sentences for offenders. After the state's obscenity law was struck down by the Supreme Court in 1957, it also meant shaping the replacement obscenity ordinance so it would be the police, rather than the courts, who wielded the power to determine obscenity.

All this added up to the police officers of the Detroit Censor Bureau having enormous power and latitude in their decision-making. In its empowerment of the police to act as censors, Detroit's movie censorship operation was unique in this era. In his examination of film censorship boards of the 1960s, Ira Carmen explains how unusual Detroit's setup was in comparison with other local boards. In Memphis, the mayor was responsible for appointing a civilian board of film censors, while in Atlanta, the mayor appointed a chief film censor, and members of the public library board were responsible for hearing any appeals. State censorship boards had similar systems, with New York's board housed in the State Department of Education and civilian and political appointees making up the movie censorship boards in Kansas, Maryland, and Virginia. The only other system of prior restraint of the movies that was run by the police was in Chicago, where the city's censorship ordinance empowered the superintendent of police to review all films intended for exhibition. And yet, in practice, Chicago's system was actually quite distinct from Detroit's. In Chicago, a six-person Film Review Section was responsible for initially reviewing films and presenting the police superintendent with their recommendation about whether a permit should be granted. This panel was not made up of police officers but rather was appointed by the mayor, and in 1962, all six members were civilian women, with police officers then reviewing their work. Appeals of their censorial decisions went either to the mayor or to an appeals board appointed by the mayor. Therefore, while movie censorship in Chicago was based in the police department, much of the ground-level work was done by civilians, with the mayor the final arbiter before the courts.[111]

By contrast, movie censorship in Detroit was a police-run operation through and through. It was typically a single police officer of the Censor Bureau who inspected every film, and if a distributor or exhibitor pushed back against a decision, a second screening would be held with the head of the Censor Bureau. A further appeal would then wind up in the hands of the police commissioner, who had final say on the matter, after which the only recourse was to the courts. No other movie censorship board was arranged in such a manner as to put power solely in the hands of police officers. As Carmen writes, "The most striking feature of the work of the Detroit License and Censor Bureau (or, if you will, the Obscenity Enforcement Bureau) is that it is under the exclusive management of policemen."[112]

That the Detroit Police Department, in its efforts to censor cinema, should have so consistently both violated and ignored the law is part and parcel of a broader history of police malfeasance in Detroit. Police brutality and harassment targeted at African Americans were rampant in Detroit throughout this era, ultimately acting as the kindling for the fires and violence that swept through the city in the summer of 1967. There was also a long history of the Detroit Police Department systematically violating the law when it came to searches, seizures, and arrests. In 1948, the State Bar of Michigan found that "it is settled policy of the Police Department for the City of Detroit to make arrests and detain citizens 'for investigation' without warrants," a practice that in most cases violated habeas corpus. A 1958 study by the Detroit Bar Association found that out of 63,301 arrests made by Detroit police in 1956, some 26,696 were made without a warrant. In 1958, attorney Harold Norris wrote of this policy, "What makes this deprivation of fundamental liberty the more insidious is that it seems to have no basis in law; in fact, [it] is in direct contravention to both the letter and the spirit of the law." No doubt a number of these illegal warrantless arrests by the Detroit Police Department were targeted at those suspected of violating obscenity law.[113]

Beyond fitting into this broader history of illegal practices carried out by the Detroit Police Department, the illegality of movie censorship in Detroit is also a product of the fact that it was police officers who were put in charge of an operation that required significant legal expertise. The repeated actions and statements of the officers of the Censor Bureau make clear that many of them lacked even a basic understanding of the laws regarding censorship and obscenity. As already discussed, in a 1962 interview with Ira Carmen, three police officers of the Censor Bureau made numerous statements that were flat-out incorrect. Patrolman Marks, whom Carmen called the Censor Bureau's unofficial "legal consultant" due to his "cursory knowledge of Supreme Court decisions," told Carmen in this interview: "As for the term 'immorality,' the Supreme Court has approved banning such behavior on many occasions." Exactly what type of "behavior" he was referring to is unclear given that the Supreme Court in 1954 and again in 1959 had made it perfectly clear that it was unconstitutional to ban movies based on the standard of "immorality."[114]

This lack of legal expertise colored everything the Censor Bureau did and was the inevitable by-product of entrusting enormous amounts of power to a few ill-equipped police officers. Inspector Bullach, who took over from Herbert Case as head of the Censor Bureau in 1954 and continued in the post until his retirement in 1963, explained in an interview the qualification necessary to be part of the Censor Bureau, saying, "We prefer married men." Apart from one's married status—which seemingly made a person more morally righteous in the eyes of the police—Bullach's statement also, perhaps inadvertently, made clear another preferred qualification, which was being a man. To my knowledge, there were never any female police officers assigned to the Censor Bureau over the course of its decades of existence, a fact that fits with the overwhelmingly male makeup of the Detroit Police Department as a whole during this time frame. As to the other qualifications to be part of the Censor Bureau, police officers were required to "have two years of college or its equivalent." For Inspector Bullach, this meant that he had a degree in forestry from Michigan State University. Before joining the Censor Bureau and being charged with censoring media and entertainment for the more than one and a half million citizens living in Detroit at that time, officers would have spent years doing the routine work of being police officers.[115] As Carmen put it, "The fact is that these are men, though undoubtedly highly competent in their traditional law enforcement tasks, who worked their way up the police ladder by walking a beat, doing patrol duty, and by serving in accident investigation. It is not surprising, then, that the sophistication needed to enforce Supreme Court guidelines properly is woefully lacking."[116]

CONCLUSION: THE DEATH OF THE BLUENOSE CENSOR

In the end, what killed off Detroit's system of censorship of movies before their public exhibition was as much the changing times as the 1969 ruling by Judge Kaess. By the end of the 1960s, the political climate underlying the work of the Censor Bureau had been altered irrevocably as American society turned against morality-based censorship campaigns and their associations with Catholic-led prudery and puritanism. These changes were indicated in a speech given by Methodist reverend James M. Wall at the 1969 convention of the Michigan branch of the National Association of Theater Owners, a film exhibitor trade group. In his talk, Reverend Wall discussed what he called the "new breed minister," who was far removed from what he saw as the older image of the clergyman as "a beady-eyed little man who sees sex in every piece of celluloid." By contrast, promised Wall, the clergy of today and movie theater owners had two things in common: "A growing conviction that the film is an art form which has enormous potential to be redemptive; and an intense dislike for anything smacking of censorship." Whereas once Protestant groups had been largely willing to ally with Catholic-led censorship campaigns, or at the very least permit them to flourish through their silence, by the close of the 1960s, it was clear that the politics of movie censorship had shifted.[117]

In 1967, the *Detroit Free Press* captured these changes by writing, "Since the entire public attitude has shifted to more permissiveness, the conservative segment has also been dragged into a less suppressive position. Even the 'censor-minded' reluctantly at first and then often with surprising adaptability, have become more liberal—from the Catholic church to the Detroit Police Department obscenity detail that screens every film before it is shown in Detroit." The same article went on to describe the police officers of the Obscenity Detail as "surprisingly broad-minded." Importantly, the reason the *Free Press* was calling police officers who were responsible for movie censorship "broad-minded" was because that is exactly the image the Censor Bureau had been trying to cultivate for nearly a decade in response to the changing mores in society. In 1959, Inspector Bullach said of the Censor Bureau, "We're not prudish." Three years later, Bullach echoed these comments by saying, "People have the idea we're some kind of prissy characters imposing our own backwoods morality on the public. We're not. We're following legal rules about what is acceptable and what is lewd, lascivious and designed to arouse a prurient response." This attempt at distancing the Censor Bureau from "prudes" and "prissy characters" was part of a sustained effort to dissociate the Censor Bureau from negative associations with censorship. Such efforts also led to Bullach saying in 1960 that "we're not really censors," Patrolman Marks saying in 1964 that "the police are anticensor," and, of course, the rebranding of the Censor Bureau as the Obscenity Detail.[118]

As head of the Obscenity Detail in the late 1960s, Sergeant Joseph Joabar was similarly quick to position himself as "broad-minded." This led the *Detroit News* in 1968 to declare that "Joabar himself is nothing like the classic stereotype of the censor" and that he was "no prude." Likewise, in 1967 the *Free Press*

Figure 2.2. Comic in the *National Decency Reporter*, May–July 1971.

wrote, "Sgt. Joabar says he enjoys foreign films such as *Alfie, Georgy Girl* and the controversial Swedish film, *Dear John.*" In publicly embracing foreign films such as these, Joabar sought to portray himself as worldly and cultured, nothing like the imagined puritanical censor. Ultimately, though, these efforts to position the Censor Bureau/Obscenity Detail and its officers as open minded and in step with the times would prove futile, as no amount of rebranding and espousal of a love for foreign films could cover up the fact that these police officers were, first and foremost, engaged in censorship. Indeed, the contradiction inherent in the notion of a "broad-minded censor" is indicated by the fact that both *Georgy Girl* and *Dear John* had previously run afoul of the Obscenity Detail, which had limited their exhibition to art-house theaters in Detroit.[119]

While the changing politics of censorship along with attendant permissive legal decisions by the Supreme Court had worked to kill off nearly every movie censorship board by the end of the 1960s, there were also local factors working against the Censor Bureau. Namely, by the end of the 1960s, Detroit

Figure 2.3. Sergeant Joseph Joabar of the Obscenity Detail screening a film. *Detroit Free Press*, December 15, 1968.

was a city visibly in a state of crisis. In the early 1960s, even as whites fled to the suburbs in increasing numbers and African Americans grew increasingly frustrated with the stark racial inequities in the city, Detroit still cultivated an image as a city that was both economically prosperous and racially harmonious. This image was shattered, though, with the violence that shook the city in the summer of 1967. The civil disorder started when the police tried to shut down an after-hours drinking establishment in a predominantly African American neighborhood and eventually expanded to one of the deadliest "riots"—or "rebellions," in the preferred parlance of many Black Detroiters—in the history of the United States. At the end of five days of turmoil that saw fires rage and the National Guard patrolling the streets of Detroit, 43 people were dead and 1,189 injured. Numerous complaints of unprovoked police aggression emerged during this period, including the infamous execution-like killing of three unarmed African American men at the hands of police in the Algiers Motel. In the wake of this, Detroit's many long-festering problems were made evident to the world, only hastening Detroit's economic decline. By the decade's close, the twin issues of crime and Detroit's ailing economy had come to dominate Detroit politics.

Given all this, police officers would soon be shifted from the task of censorship in order to deal with more urgent problems. In November of 1967, with the city still reeling from that summer's violence, Mayor Cavanagh called on Police Commissioner Girardin to put more than four hundred police officers on the streets as part of a "'no-holds-barred' battle against crime." To do so, Cavanagh suggested that civilians take on tasks being done by police officers in numerous departments, including the Obscenity Detail, thereby freeing up police to be reassigned into roles fighting street crime. At that time, the Obscenity Detail had seven full-time police officers assigned to it, already less than half the number who had worked in the Censor Bureau at its peak. This number was reduced further after Cavanagh's order was carried out and hundreds of officers were shifted from various departments, including the Obscenity Detail, to patrol high-crime areas. By 1970, the *Detroit News* reported that "the obscenity detail, which had 15 members about five years ago, is down to two staffers who are mainly concerned with checking bookstores and stage productions, including burlesk houses."[120]

It was not just that the police officers once assigned the task of censoring film and media in Detroit were now needed elsewhere but rather that the city's litany of pressing problems made the issue of upholding the morals of public amusement in Detroit seem rather less urgent by comparison. This was the point made by David A. Uskali, whose letter to the editor was published in the *Detroit Free Press* in February of 1969. In his letter, Uskali called out the police for making cuts to the film *The Killing of Sister George*, writing, "This is only the latest in a long line of episodes devoted to supposedly upholding the morals of some three million people, while the city goes to pot." The letter went on to discuss an incident in which "the police stationed themselves at a performance of a group called 'Dionysus in '69,' ready to pounce on any performer who dared remove their clothes. Outside this particular theater, there exists one of the city's highest crime rates, yet more pressing business inside required the presence of police to again protect the public." As this letter argued, in the context of a city in the midst of rapid economic decline and growing public concern over crime, the notion of police officers acting as censors seemed more than a bit absurd. Given this, for censorship to survive in this new era, a new form of media censorship politics was needed, one that could successfully distance itself from the bluenose prudish censors of old while simultaneously responding to the urgent concerns surrounding urban decline in Detroit at this time. In the chapter that follows, I examine the formation of just such a new form of procensorship politics in one Detroit neighborhood in the early 1970s.[121]

NOTES

1. "Film Exchange Building Is Formally Opened," *Detroit News*, January 30, 1927, 5; "Detroit's Film Capitol," *Detroit Free Press*, March 27, 1955, sec. Roto, 4.

2. Joseph N. Hartmann, "Pocket-Size Books Give Police Censors Biggest Headache," *Detroit News*, December 29, 1952, 12; John Finlayson, "City's Censor Gives Movies a Good Word," *Detroit News*, July 19, 1953, 18; "Detroit Film Inspector Quits after 15 Years," *Winona Republican-Herald*, May 4, 1948, 13; "Detroit's Film Capitol," 4.

3. "Detroit Film Inspector Quits after 15 Years," 13.

4. Armand Gebert, "Soft Job Proves Tough to Find," *Detroit News*, August 29, 1954, 18; Arthur Juntunen, "He's Paid to See What You Can't," *Detroit Free Press*, June 9, 1946, sec. 2, 1.

5. For more on the banning of *The Burning Cross* in Virginia, see Melissa Ooten, "Censorship in Black and White: *The Burning Cross* (1947), *Band of Angels* (1957) and the Politics of Film Censorship in the American South after World War II," *Historical Journal of Film, Radio and Television* 33, no. 1 (March 2013): 77–98.

6. Mark Beltaire, "Wake Up, Beltaire, You Gotta Eat," *Detroit Free Press*, November 11, 1947, 24.

7. "Dezel to Fight Banning of 'The Burning Cross,'" *Film Daily*, November 5, 1947, 12; "Detroit Lifts 'Cross' Ban," *Variety*, December 17, 1947, 9.

8. "Local Censors Urged to Meet on Program," *Boxoffice*, June 28, 1947, 21; "Detroit Police Censor Cuts 'Summer Holiday,'" *Film Daily*, January 8, 1948, 1.

9. "Local Censors Urged to Meet on Program," 21; "Censor Head Criticizes Yarns Belittling Police," *Boxoffice*, July 5, 1947, 80; Harry Sahs, "Comics Draw Police Frown," *Detroit News*, June 19, 1947, 30.

10. Joe T. Darden and Richard W. Thomas, *Detroit: Race Riots, Racial Conflicts, and Efforts to Bridge the Racial Divide* (East Lansing: Michigan State University Press, 2013), 29–66; Charles J. Wartman, "Police Relationship with Negroes Still Detroit's Sore Spot," *Michigan Chronicle*, March 21, 1953, 6; "Police Brutality Draws Reprimand," *Detroit Free Press*, May 22, 1945, 3.

11. "Police Official Protests 'Brutality' in U-I Film," *Boxoffice*, July 12, 1947, 86; "Big House Roughhouse," *Newsweek*, July 28, 1947, 84; "Censor Seeks Ban on Movie *Brute Force*," *Detroit Times*, July 5, 1947; Andy Coffey, letter to the editor, "Wants to See It," *Detroit News*, July 9, 1947, 22; J.M.A., letter to the editor, "Too Brutal?," *Detroit News*, July 10, 1947, 26.

12. "Police Official Protests 'Brutality' in U-I Film," 86; "Detroit Police Ban 'Brute' as Too Rough," *Hollywood Reporter*, July 22, 1947, 3; "'Brute Force' Bags 45G in Detroit; 'Father' Does 32G," *Hollywood Reporter*, September 23, 1947, 10.

13. "Police Ban Movie Scheduled at Cinema," *Detroit News*, September 17, 1947, 32; "Showing Approved," *Detroit News*, September 18, 1947, 33; "Censor

Bans French Film Scheduled for Cinema," *Detroit Times*, September 17, 1947, 28-C; "Police Purify Film by One Deletion," *Detroit Times*, September 18, 1947, 43-C; John Finlayson, "Magnani Sultry Gang Girl in Italian Film, 'The Bandit,'" *Detroit News*, January 26, 1950, 24; "Young Love Gets Ideas," *Detroit News*, May 27, 1950, 15.

14. Helen Bower, "Love Makes Its Round in 'La Ronde' Fantasy," *Detroit Free Press*, March 20, 1952, 10; John Finlayson, "French Film, 'La Ronde' Laundered for Showing," *Detroit News*, March 21, 1952, 26; Helen Bower, "Public Saw Censored Version of 'La Ronde,'" *Detroit Free Press*, April 9, 1952, 21.

15. "No Shift Here in Censorship," *Detroit News*, May 27, 1952, 6.

16. Laura Wittern-Keller and Raymond J. Haberski Jr., *The Miracle Case: Film Censorship and the Supreme Court* (Lawrence: University Press of Kansas, 2008), 128.

17. "Ruling Won't Affect City Police Censors," *Detroit Free Press*, January 19, 1954, 13.

18. "Another Affirmation for Free Speech," *Detroit Free Press*, January 20, 1954, 8; "Charter of Freedom," *Detroit News*, January 20, 1954, 30.

19. Walter Stevenson, "Realistic Romance at Krim," *Detroit News*, December 14, 1954, 14; "'Latuko' Shocks Detroit," *Variety*, March 9, 1955, 7.

20. "Relaxed Film Code Hit by Church, PTA," *Detroit News*, December 13, 1956, 75.

21. Ernest R. Tidyman, "Detroit Gets to Peer Into the 'Naked Eye,'" *Detroit News*, September 15, 1957, 16-G.

22. "Disputed Movie OK'd for Detroit Showing," *Detroit Free Press*, July 23, 1953, 32; "'Moon' OK'd Dialog Cut," *Detroit News*, July 23, 1953, 29; Harvey Taylor, "Detroit Stage: Playwright Herbert's Aim Is to Get Laughs," *Detroit Times*, October 11, 1953, sec. 4, 10; "Leonard OKs *Moon Is Blue*," *Detroit Times*, July 22, 1953, 1.

23. "Detroit," *Exhibitor*, August 5, 1953, NT-2; "'Moon' Comes Over the Moralist," *Variety*, March 17, 1954, 5; "'Moon Is Blue' Licensed," *Variety*, April 21, 1954, 13.

24. "'You're Just Local Yokels,'" *Variety*, July 22, 1959, 20; "Now Showing at Your Neighborhood Movie Theater," *Detroit Free Press*, July 25, 1959, 12.

25. "Sponsor of Nudist Movie Fights Ban," *Detroit Free Press*, November 8, 1933, 5; "Police Censors Enjoined from Halting Film Show," *Detroit Free Press*, September 4, 1937, 5; "Ban by Police Is Upheld on Picture, 'Motherhood,'" *Detroit Free Press*, May 17, 1938, 4; "Showing of Sex Film Stirs Dearborn Trial," *Detroit Free Press*, November 4, 1949, 3.

26. Walter Bibo to Ernest Mazey, September 11, 1958, box 10, folder Censorship 1958–59, American Civil Liberties Union of Michigan/Metropolitan Detroit Branch Collection, Walter P. Reuther Library, Wayne State University.

27. "Nudist Film Gains in Censor Battle," *New York Times*, July 4, 1957, 16; Carl B. Rudow, "Court Voids Convictions of 4 Nudists," *Detroit News*, September 10, 1958, 1; Ernest Mazey to Jack Zide, October 15, 1958, box 10, folder Censorship 1958–59, American Civil Liberties Union of Michigan/Metropolitan Detroit Branch Collection, Walter P. Reuther Library, Wayne State University; "Bibo Girds to Push 'Eden' Past Censors," *Variety*, November 18, 1959, 17.

28. "Detroit Police Raid Raw Stag Dances," *Variety*, January 3, 1924, 16; "Detroit Police after 'Smoker' Gatherings," *Billboard*, January 5, 1924, 21.

29. "1,500 in Panic, as Police Raid Movie Theater," *Detroit Free Press*, February 25, 1922, 1; "Police Seize Films in Raid on 'Smoker,'" *Detroit Free Press*, June 11, 1922, 9; "4 Dancers Arrested in Raid on Smoker," *Detroit News*, April 23, 1927, 2.

30. "11 Seized in Raid at Barlum Hotel," *Detroit Free Press*, September 28, 1940, 3; "Police Seize Film, Arrest 11 at Hotel," *Detroit News*, September 28, 1940, 1; "4 Freed in Seizure of Obscene Films," *Detroit News*, October 3, 1940, 14.

31. "Police Raid Stag Smoker," *Detroit News*, March 6, 1947, 1.

32. "Martel Case Brings Quiz," *Detroit News*, April 5, 1947, 13.

33. "Backs Police in Martel Sift," *Detroit News*, April 13, 1947, 6; "Martel's Son, 2 Others Deny 'Smoker' Count," *Detroit Free Press*, March 7, 1947, 14.

34. "Obscene Movie Show Brings Jail Term, Fine," *Detroit News*, May 24, 1944, 7; "Smoker Raid Convicts Four," *Detroit Free Press*, October 5, 1944, 10; "2 Smoker Dancers Guilty of Indecency," *Detroit News*, October 31, 1944, 16.

35. "Detroit Film Inspector Quits after 15 Years," 13.

36. "Smoker Fans Land in Jail," *Detroit News*, March 16, 1952, sec. 2, 15.

37. "7 Given Jail after Smoker," *Detroit News*, March 30, 1952, 19.

38. "Shopkeeper Jailed for Obscene Sales," *Detroit News*, March 24, 1951, 14; "2 to Be Sentenced on Obscenity Charge," *Detroit News*, June 28, 1952, 14; "Obscene Literature Sellers Are Jailed," *Detroit News*, July 12, 1952, 13.

39. "Policeman Halts Smut Film Racket," *Detroit Free Press*, March 11, 1953, 3; "Raid Causes Mental Test," *Detroit News*, March 11, 1953, 16; "Filthy Films Cost Him $105," *Detroit Free Press*, March 18, 1953, 7.

40. "Obscene Literature, Films Are Seized," *Detroit News*, June 17, 1951, 2; "Arrested 3rd Time for Obscene Books," *Detroit News*, May 9, 1954, sec. D, 20.

41. "Police Seize Lewd Films, Literature," *Detroit Free Press*, October 1, 1953, 5; "Obscene Literature Seized at Grocery," *Detroit News*, October 1, 1953, 26; "Trial Scheduled in Obscenity Raid," *Detroit News*, October 2, 1953, 8; "Suspect Cleared of Owning Cache of Obscene Films," *Detroit News*, October 16, 1953, 15.

42. "Smut Sales Bring Fine," *Detroit Free Press*, February 28, 1954, 3; "Smut Seller Fined," *Detroit News*, February 27, 1954, 17.

43. "$2,500 in Obscene Material Seized, Distributor Held," *Detroit News*, May 8, 1954, 20; "Obscene Photos Bring Salesman 10-Month Term," *Detroit News*, August 24, 1954, 19.

44. "Parolee Back for 10 Months," *Detroit News*, April 23, 1955, 2; "Obscenity Dealer Gets 60-Day Term," *Detroit News*, November 8, 1955, 13; "Obscene Cache Costs 30 Days," *Detroit News*, May 26, 1955, 23.

45. Owen C. Deatrick, "Why Do We Jail So Many Men?," *Detroit Free Press*, August 22, 1954, 11; Detroit Police Department, *Annual Reports* (Detroit: Detroit Police Department, 1942–53).

46. Roger N. Lancaster, "The New Pariahs: Sex, Crime, and Punishment in America," in *The War on Sex*, ed. David M. Halperin and Trevor Hoppe (Durham, NC: Duke University Press, 2017), 83.

47. *Investigation of Literature Allegedly Containing Objectionable Material* (Washington, DC: United States Government Printing Office, December 1, 1952), 113.

48. "Police Censors of Books to Stay," *Detroit News*, February 26, 1957, 1.

49. "Safe and Sane Censorship," *Detroit Free Press*, February 27, 1957, 8; Evelyn S. Stewart, "Censorship Assailed, Upheld," *Detroit Free Press*, January 18, 1957, 11.

50. Don Hoenshell, "Liquor Fund Cut Rejected," *Detroit News*, February 19, 1952, 23; M. M. Hollingsworth, "Bill Would Hospitalize Dope Addicts," *Detroit Free Press*, February 9, 1954, 1; "Comic Book Ban Studied," *Detroit News*, December 14, 1952, 3; "Bill Calls for Ban on Sale of Lewd Books to Juveniles," *Detroit News*, January 24, 1957, 8.

51. Carl B. Rudow, "Offer Bill to Restore Censorship in State," *Detroit News*, March 29, 1957, 8; "Mandatory TB Treatment Bill Backed by Doctors at Hearing," *Detroit News*, April 12, 1957, 58.

52. "2 State Senators Drafting 'Tougher' Obscenity Bill," *Detroit News*, April 18, 1957, 6; "Cites Need for Smut Controls," *Lansing State Journal*, April 30, 1957, 10.

53. "House Anti-Smut Bill Called a 'Monstrosity,'" *Lansing State Journal*, May 1, 1957, 3.

54. "University and Road Patrol Budget Issues Left in Doubt," *Detroit News*, May 18, 1957, 12; "Senate GOP Backs Compromise on Road Fund Distribution," *Detroit News*, May 21, 1957, 21.

55. "'Tough' Anti-Obscenity Bill Agreed Upon in Conference," *Detroit News*, May 23, 1957, 35.

56. Richard L. Milliman, "Legislators Are Working Overtime," *Lansing State Journal*, March 12, 1958, 43. For a detailed history of *Roth v. United States* and its legacy, see Whitney Strub, *Obscenity Rules: Roth v. United States and the Long Struggle over Sexual Expression* (Lawrence: University Press of Kansas, 2013).

57. "Raid Movie, Arrests 49 Deaf Mutes," *Detroit News*, February 15, 1959, sec. B, 2; Robert DeWolfe, "56 Youths Caught with Smut Films," *Detroit Free Press*, April 27, 1959, 1, 10.

58. "Pleads Innocent to Possession of Obscene Film," *Detroit News*, September 28, 1958, sec. C, 22.

59. "Sentence Seller of Obscene Films," *Detroit News*, December 5, 1958, 51.

60. "Smut Pouring into City, but Crackdown Is Due," *Detroit Free Press*, April 29, 1959, 10.

61. "Ruling Has No Effect on Censorship Here," *Detroit News*, January 24, 1961, 10; "Movie Men, Censor Live in Harmony," *Detroit Free Press*, January 25, 1961, 3; Wittern-Keller and Haberski Jr., *The Miracle Case*, 133.

62. Louis Cook, "Sophia Loren Can Act," *Detroit Free Press*, November 3, 1961, 42; "Loren Film Hits Censor Snag Here," *Detroit News*, April 10, 1962, 8; Louis Cook, "Sophia's Oscar Adds to Detroit Film Fuss," *Detroit Free Press*, April 11, 1962, sec. B, 6; "'Two Women' to Detroit with One Scene Cut Out," *Boxoffice*, May 7, 1962, ME-1.

Two Women was only the latest film to be held up by the Censor Bureau over its representation of sexual assault, as just a few years prior, the Censor Bureau had cut a scene depicting rape from the Ingmar Bergman picture *The Virgin Spring* (1960). See Ira Harris Carmen, "State and Local Motion Picture Censorship and Constitutional Liberties with Special Emphasis on the Communal Acceptance of Supreme Court Decision-Making" (PhD diss., University of Michigan, 1964), 418–19.

63. Louis Cook, "A Documentary with Some Ham," *Detroit Free Press*, July 2, 1962, sec. C, 8.

64. "Censor Ruling Faces Court Test," *Detroit News*, August 3, 1962, 3.

65. "Detroiters Puzzled by 'Sky' Situation," *Boxoffice*, August 20, 1962, ME-1.

66. Murray Schumach, "Two Cities Face Film Censor Test," *New York Times*, August 2, 1962, 16.

67. "Censor Ruling Faces Court Test," 3.

68. Ernest Mazey to Spencer Kimball, May 20, 1963, box 10, folder Censorship 1963, American Civil Liberties Union of Michigan/Metropolitan Detroit Branch Collection, Walter P. Reuther Library, Wayne State University.

69. Mazey to Kimball, May 20, 1963, American Civil Liberties Union of Michigan/Metropolitan Detroit Branch Collection; Ernest Mazey to Ernest Goodman, February 13, 1964, box 10, folder Censorship 1964, American Civil Liberties Union of Michigan/Metropolitan Detroit Branch Collection, Walter P. Reuther Library, Wayne State University.

70. Ira H. Carmen, *Movies, Censorship, and the Law* (Ann Arbor: University of Michigan Press, 1966), 200–201. Emphasis added.

71. Detroit Police Department, *Annual Reports*, 1950–55, 1960–64.

72. Detroit Police Department, *Annual Reports*, 1960–64; *Annual Report of Activities of Censor Bureau for the Year 1962*, January 4, 1963, box 65, folder 6, Ernest Goodman Collection, Walter P. Reuther Library, Wayne State University.

73. "Like Cool It Man, It's Just a Raid," *Detroit Free Press*, August 8, 1959, 3; "Jury Finds Beat Poet Indecent," *Detroit Free Press*, September 18, 1959, 3;

"'Beatnik' Poet Challenges Legality of 6-Man Jury," *Detroit News*, October 3, 1959, 6.

74. "Tantrum Cafe Sues for License in U.S. Court," *Detroit News*, October 4, 1960, 7-B; "Indecency Trial Set for Beatnik Poet," *Detroit News*, March 12, 1960, 6; "Jurors Weigh Whether Poet Recited Obscenity," *Detroit News*, March 25, 1960, 16-C; Detroit Police Department, *Annual Reports*, 1960–64.

75. Arthur O'Shea, "Paid to Go to Shows," *Detroit Free Press*, July 3, 1960, sec. Roto, 6.

76. Louis Cook, "A Look at Two Leroi Jones Plays: 'Acting Out What Can't Be Said,'" *Detroit Free Press*, August 2, 1965, 8-B; "Future of 2 Theaters Periled by City Tickets," *Detroit News*, August 19, 1965, 9-B; "Legal Woes Hit 2 Theaters," *Detroit Free Press*, August 20, 1965, 3-B; "Obscenity, License Suits against 2 Theaters Fail," *Detroit News*, August 20, 1965, 6-D. For more on the queer politics of *The Toilet*, see José Esteban Muñoz, "Cruising the Toilet: LeRoi Jones/Amiri Baraka, Radical Black Traditions, and Queer Futurity," *GLQ: A Journal of Lesbian and Gay Studies* 13, no. 2–3 (June 2007): 353–67. My thanks to reader 1 for pointing me toward this source.

77. "Censored Theater to Reopen," *Detroit Free Press*, December 9, 1965, 10-C.

78. Melville E. Bullach to Reverend Donald Schroeder, May 24, 1962, box 12, folder 11, Metropolitan Detroit Council of Churches Records, Walter P. Reuther Library, Wayne State University.

79. Paul L. Adams to Michigan Prosecuting Attorneys, June 27, 1960, box 10, folder Censorship 1962, American Civil Liberties Union of Michigan/Metropolitan Detroit Branch Collection, Walter P. Reuther Library, Wayne State University; People v. Villano, 369 Mich. 428 (1963).

80. Carl B. Rudow, "Police, Clergy Ask War on Obscenity," *Detroit News*, November 4, 1960, 4; "Memorandum on Hearings before the House Sub-Committee on Obscenity," November 3, 1960, 2–3, box 10, folder Censorship 1960, American Civil Liberties Union of Michigan/Metropolitan Detroit Branch Collection, Walter P. Reuther Library, Wayne State University.

81. "Democrats Ask Changes in Jobless Benefits Law," *Detroit News*, February 10, 1961, 13-B; "Censor Supports Curb on Filthy Literature," *Detroit News*, April 19, 1961, 12; "New Law on Obscenity Approved," *Detroit News*, June 8, 1961, 12-B.

82. *Annual Report of Activities of Censor Bureau for the Year 1962*, Ernest Goodman Collection.

83. O'Shea, "Paid to Go to Shows," 6; Jackie Korona, "Thumbs Down on Book Banning," *Detroit News*, May 13, 1964, 8-C.

84. "Remarks by Mayor Jerome P. Cavanagh before the Metropolitan Detroit Council on Better Literature for Youth," November 13, 1963, box 108, folder 17, Jerome P. Cavanagh Collection, Walter P. Reuther Library, Wayne State University.

85. Freedman v. Maryland, 380 U.S. 51 (1965).

86. Brief of Amici Curiae American Civil Liberties Union and Maryland Branch, *Freedman v. Maryland*, 380 U.S. 51 (filed October 1964); Wittern-Keller and Haberski Jr., *The Miracle Case*, 200.

87. "Film Ruling Won't Affect City Setup," *Detroit News*, March 2, 1965, 6; Detroit Police Department, *Annual Report*, 1965.

88. "Police Censor Bureau Staff Cut; Duties Assigned to Vice Bureau," *Detroit News*, May 22, 1965, 3; "Detroit Police Commissioner Says Film Censorship Will Continue," *Boxoffice*, June 7, 1965, ME-1.

89. Carmen, *Movies, Censorship, and the Law*, 201.

90. Charles H. Keating Jr., letter to the editor, "Case against Obscenity," *Detroit Free Press*, June 15, 1965, 6.

91. Carmen, *Movies, Censorship, and the Law*, 202; "Detroit Patrolman Speaks on Censorship of Films," *Boxoffice*, January 17, 1966, ME-2.

92. James H. Dygert, "Police Exercise Subtle Control over Films," *Detroit Free Press*, August 15, 1967.

93. Paul Neal Jr., "Censor by Any Other Name...," *Detroit News*, January 29, 1967, sec. E, 5, 7.

94. "Censor Delays 'Le Bonheur,'" *Detroit News*, September 9, 1966, 13-B; Arnold S. Hirsch, "Uncut 'Le Bonheur' OK'd," *Detroit News*, October 20, 1966, 9-E; James H. Dygert, "The Standards—And the Times That Hold Sway over Movies," *Detroit Free Press*, August 13, 1967, sec. B, 1; "Curb on Ads for X-Pix Cues 'Sis' Suit by Aldrich," *Variety*, February 5, 1969, 70; Ken Barnard, "Who Killed 'Sister George?,'" *Detroit News*, February 14, 1969, 11-C.

95. "Detroit Patrolman Speaks on Censorship of Films," ME-2; John Finlayson, "'Ulysses' Unchained in Suburban Opening," *Detroit News*, March 12, 1967, sec. E, 20; Carmen, *Movies, Censorship, and the Law*, 203.

96. Dygert, "The Standards," 1; Neal Jr., "Censor by Any Other Name...," 7.

97. Richard S. Randall, *Censorship of the Movies: The Social and Political Control of a Mass Medium* (Madison: University of Wisconsin Press, 1968), 94–95. It is worth mentioning that while Randall says the title to the film was *The Phantom Peeper*, there is no indication that a film by this title was ever released in Detroit, and I have not found evidence of an exploitation film with this title. The actual title of the film that was commented upon by the police here remains unknown to me.

98. Carmen, *Movies, Censorship, and the Law*, 202; Randall, *Censorship of the Movies*, 98–99.

99. Dygert, "The Standards," 4.

100. Carmen, *Movies, Censorship, and the Law*, 202; Randall, *Censorship of the Movies*, 93; Dygert, "Police Exercise Subtle Control over Films," 10.

101. Carmen, *Movies, Censorship, and the Law*, 234; Carmen, "State and Local Motion Picture Censorship," 417.

102. Carmen, "State and Local Motion Picture Censorship," 418, 420; Neal Jr., "Censor by Any Other Name . . . ," 5, 7; Dygert, "The Standards," 1; Carmen, *Movies, Censorship, and the Law*, 202.

103. James H. Dygert, "Adults Only: Handy Device to Silence Film Censors," *Detroit Free Press*, August 16, 1967, 4; Carmen, *Movies, Censorship, and the Law*, 192–93.

104. John F. Griffith, "'Jury' Split on Film Tagged as Naughty," *Detroit Free Press*, July 21, 1953, 12; Carmen, *Movies, Censorship, and the Law*, 204.

105. Dygert, "The Standards," 1.

106. Carmen, "State and Local Motion Picture Censorship," 418; Ken Barnard, "Film Raids Go Way of All Flesh," *Detroit News*, September 20, 1970, sec. H, 11; Eve Productions, Inc. v. Detroit, No. 33261 (E.D. Mich. S. Div. 1969).

107. Stephen Cain, "Lennon's Curious Art Bugs Detroit Police," *Detroit News*, January 21, 1970, 11-B; Joy Hakanson, "Lennon's Sex Art Isn't . . . ," *Detroit News*, January 22, 1970, 2-B.

108. "'Hair' Here to Stay Despite Police Frowns," *Detroit Free Press*, June 18, 1970, sec. B, 4.

109. Robert M. Pavich, "'Hair' Passes Its Short Brush with the Law," *Detroit News*, June 17, 1970, 3.

110. "Police Charge 2 with Smut Sale," *Detroit Free Press*, July 19, 1970, 13; "Police Hit Peep Show in Raid," *Detroit Free Press*, July 22, 1970, 3; "Smut Raids Hit 6 Bookstores," *Detroit News*, August 8, 1970, 6; Ron Landsman, "Suit Challenges Michigan Obscenity, Seizure Laws," *Detroit Free Press*, August 22, 1970, 5; Tom Pawlick, "Underground Sex Ads: They're 'Healthy,' Says a Sociologist; They're 'Degenerate,' Says a Minister," *Detroit News*, August 20, 1970, sec. The Other Section, 10.

111. Carmen, *Movies, Censorship, and the Law*, 141–42, 153–54, 176–77, 186–99, 206–14, 244.

112. Dygert, "Police Exercise Subtle Control over Films," 10; Carmen, 205.

113. "Committee on Civil Liberties," *Michigan State Bar Journal*, September 1949, 19; Harold Norris, "Arrests without Warrant," *Crisis*, October 1958, 481–82.

114. Carmen, "State and Local Motion Picture Censorship," 417, 419; Carmen, *Movies, Censorship, and the Law*, 205.

115. Nancy Masterton, "Censorship Confab Kicks Off Series," *Detroit News*, November 23, 1957, 22; Carmen, "State and Local Motion Picture Censorship," 423.

116. Carmen, *Movies, Censorship, and the Law*, 205.

117. Hiley Ward, "Churchman Urges Theater Owner-Clergy Truce," *Detroit Free Press*, April 5, 1969, 8.

118. James H. Dygert, "How Parent Groups Seek Cleaner Movies," *Detroit Free Press*, August 17, 1967, 10; Ralph Nelson, "It's Girlie Era, but Police Watch for Error," *Detroit Free Press*, June 8, 1959, 10; John Millhone, "Censor's Job Is All Work...," *Detroit Free Press*, September 16, 1962, 3; O'Shea, "Paid to Go to Shows," 6; Korona, "Thumbs Down on Book Banning," 8-C.

119. Lee Winfrey, "Our Over-18 Reporter Enters the Peculiar World of the Peep Show," *Detroit Free Press*, December 15, 1968, sec. Magazine, 24, 31; Dygert, "How Parent Groups Seek Cleaner Movies," 10.

120. Robert L. Wells, "'Put 400 More Police on Street!': Cavanagh," *Detroit News*, November 7, 1967, 1; Neal Jr., "Censor by Any Other Name...," 5; Robert DeWolfe, "High-Crime Areas Get Additional Police Protection," *Detroit Daily Dispatch*, November 24, 1967, 3; Barnard, "Film Raids Go Way of All Flesh," 11.

121. David A. Uskali, letter to the editor, *Detroit News*, February 21, 1969, 22.

THREE

"THE BLIGHT OF INDECENCY"

Anti-Porn Politics and the Urban Crisis in Detroit

LATE IN THE SUMMER OF 1972, the Adult World bookstore opened its doors in the neighborhood of Redford, a residential community in northwest Detroit. The bookstore—and the pornographic material it housed—quickly caught the attention of Pastor James O. Banks of the Redford Presbyterian Church, who used his weekly sermon to discuss Adult World on September 17. In his sermon, the pastor condemned the bookstore, bemoaning what its opening symbolized both for the Redford neighborhood and more broadly for Christian values. He sought to draw distinctions between normative sexuality (practiced within the bounds of heterosexual marriage) and commercial sex as represented by the goods on offer at Adult World: "It is cheap. It is raw sex. It is crude. It is degrading. It is sex separated from sexuality. It is sex pictures and symbols being sold. It is wrong. It represents a way of life in total contradiction to the Christian." The pastor used his sermon to reiterate the importance of Christian norms on sex, which had been central to anti-porn politics for decades. Banks ended his speech by calling on his congregation to reject apathy and take action against the bookstore.[1]

And take action they did. Letters protesting Adult World soon began arriving in the mailboxes of major city officials. What started as a slow stream of letters soon became a flood, with not only church members but also many neighborhood residents and organizations writing to express their consternation. Their letters, however, quite often emphasized concerns very different from those highlighted by Pastor Banks: fears that the bookstore would lead to an "invasion" of unwanted outsiders, the perceived need to protect children from the excesses of commercial sex, the right of homeowners to decide the character of their neighborhoods, and the belief that Adult World would cause the economic decline of Redford and Detroit. Together, these letters helped form a potent new anti-porn discourse that eschewed the overt moralizing of previous anti-porn efforts in favor of economic- and rights-based arguments rooted in concerns about urban decay.

This shift away from moral rhetoric reflected broader changes in society that had put the anti-porn movement on the defensive in recent years. Throughout the 1950s and 1960s, the United States Supreme Court repeatedly issued rulings that narrowed the scope of obscenity law and provided greater free speech protections for film and media. This forced nearly every state and city movie censorship board to close by the end of the 1960s. Meanwhile, the Production Code—the document that had regulated what Hollywood could and could not depict in its films for over three decades—also met its inglorious end in the 1960s, replaced by the more permissive ratings system. This decline in the prevalence of film and media censorship was the result of not just legal decisions but changes in public opinion as well, which had increasingly turned against censorship efforts. The sexual revolution led to what conservative critics derisively labeled "the permissive society" of the late 1960s and early 1970s, and within this context, anti-porn efforts and media censorship based on Christian norms of propriety and decency looked increasingly out of step with the times. As Whitney Strub writes of this era: "Government commissions, courts, social scientists, and the general public alike reached a consensus that, if pornography might not be something to celebrate, it nonetheless posed no threat to the perpetuation of the republic."[2]

Due to the confluence of these factors, in the early 1970s, pornography achieved a level of mainstream visibility and respectability that it never had before (and arguably has not had since). This was the time of "porno chic," when feature-length adult films racked up box-office numbers rivaling those of the era's biggest Hollywood blockbusters. Contrary to the old stereotype of dirty old men in raincoats as the audience for adult movies, the hipness of adult films like *Deep Throat* (1972) and *The Devil in Miss Jones* (1973) attracted audiences of young people, well-to-do couples, and even major celebrities. Pornography was paid serious attention by critics and journalists of the era, with outlets like the *New York Times* and *Esquire* reviewing major adult film releases and publishing think pieces on the new cultural phenomenon. All this meant that, seemingly overnight, pornography became a ubiquitous part of the urban landscape, rapidly moving from being sold clandestinely under the counter to being advertised in major newspapers and offered in the hundreds of adult businesses now located in the downtowns and neighborhoods of cities across the country.[3]

In light of all this, anti-porn activists were forced to develop new forms of morality-neutral arguments against pornography—ones that could create distance from the now-unpopular overt moralizing of the anti-porn campaigns of old while maintaining the goal of curbing the spread of adult media. The new form of anti-porn politics that emerged in the early 1970s in grassroots campaigns like in Redford was shaped by concerns about broader social trends. As Gayle Rubin writes, "Disputes over sexual behavior often become the vehicles for displacing social anxieties, and discharging their attendant emotional intensity." With this in mind, I argue that the anti-porn politics and activism of this era, exemplified in Redford's letter-writing campaign, need to be understood within the context of contemporaneous white racial politics and debates over the urban crisis. This period saw a growing panic over the state of American cities, which had been ravaged by structural forces like white flight and deindustrialization, leaving urban centers both economically struggling and, at the very least in the minds of white observers, crime ridden. The anti-porn rhetoric that emerged in the early 1970s therefore drew upon the rampant racialized anxieties surrounding the present and future of American cities. Here I draw on an argument put forward by Robert Self, who writes, "Rather than seeing race on one hand and gender, sex, and family on the other as distinct crucibles of political contest, we might find it more profitable to conceive of them as intertwined." This insight helps us better understand why the grassroots anti-porn politics of the early 1970s started to avoid the religion-infused moralizing that had long typified anti-porn political discourse and instead began to emphasize seemingly more mundane concerns surrounding property values, neighborhood deterioration, and white flight. In the process, anti-porn advocates also managed to adopt and adapt the color-blind rhetoric that had become central to white racial politics in fights over issues like school-desegregation busing.[4]

This chapter examines anti-porn politics during the early 1970s, exploring how the rhetoric used by anti-porn advocates evolved in the face of the era's massive proliferation of pornography, as well as how this rhetoric was shaped by broader social and political contexts. I begin by examining the history and demographics of Redford, using digital mapping to argue that the neighborhood was perched uneasily between poor Black inner city and rich white suburb. I then move to an overview of anti-porn politics and the letters sent by Redford's protesting residents, using maps showing where the letters were coming from to speak to the racial and gender makeup of Redford's anti-porn activists. Looking at the content of the letters themselves, I next examine the major themes running throughout them—in particular, pornography's perceived threat to children, the rampant fears that Adult World would attract "undesirable" individuals, and concerns over property values and white flight. Finally, I conclude by looking at the results of Redford's fight against Adult World as well as what happened to the neighborhood itself.

THE POLITICS AND DEMOGRAPHICS OF REDFORD

By the early 1970s, Detroit was a city in a visible and rapidly accelerating state of economic decline. The postwar era had seen middle-class whites flee Detroit in droves for racially segregated suburbs. Meanwhile, the process of deindustrialization, whereby automobile and other industry jobs moved elsewhere, only further hollowed out the city's tax coffers. These forces had already done major damage to the economy of the city by the time the riots or rebellion shook Detroit in the summer of 1967, causing destruction to the city itself while simultaneously making the city a national symbol of racial turmoil. This violence only accelerated white flight from the city, and by the early 1970s Detroit was close to becoming a majority Black city. One decided exception to this, though, was the neighborhood of Redford, which, even in the face of white flight and the growing African American population of Detroit, remained one of the last bastions of whiteness in the city at that time.[5]

Not to be confused with Redford Township, the suburb located just outside Detroit's borders, the neighborhood of Redford (sometimes called Old Redford) was annexed by Detroit in 1926, making it one of the last major additions to the city. The neighborhood lies in the northwest corner of Detroit, near the border between the city and the surrounding suburbs of Livonia, Farmington Hills, and Southfield. This location meant that, in many ways, the Redford of the early 1970s more closely resembled the neighboring suburbs than it did the rest of Detroit. Because of the massive size of the city—the combined areas of Manhattan, Boston, and San Francisco can fit snugly within the boundaries of Detroit—neighborhood residents could claim to be closer to and share more in common with the white suburbs than with the rest of the increasingly Black city. This was particularly the case given that Redford, like most of northwest Detroit, was almost uniformly white, with whites representing upward of 90 percent of the population (see fig. 3.1).[6]

Still, even as Redford's racial composition resembled that of the suburbs, its economic status was more mixed, with many families in the area making less than $8,000 a year, roughly the median national family income in 1970 (see fig. 3.2). While the area was certainly more well off than much of the rest of Detroit, the spending power of its residents nevertheless paled in comparison to the wealth of the surrounding suburbs. This meant that Redford acted as

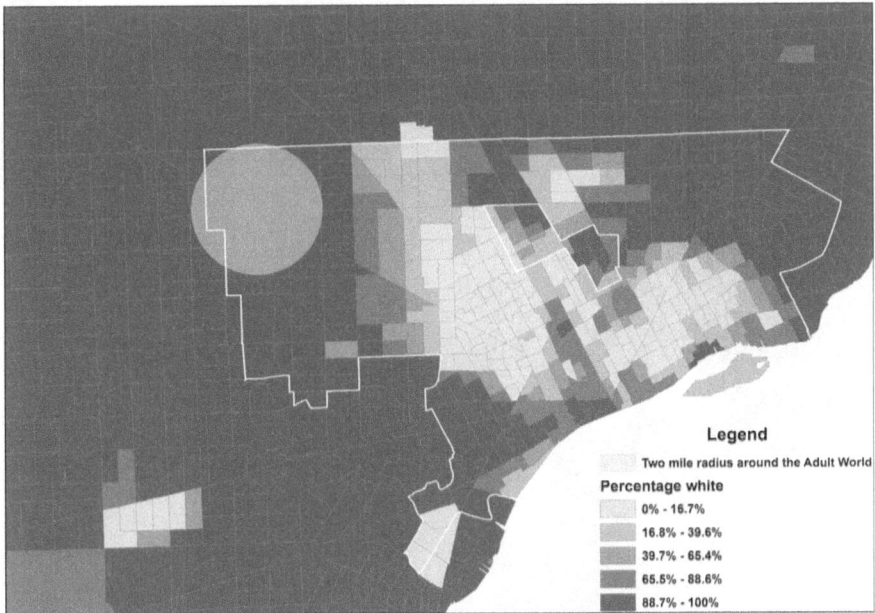

Figure 3.1. Percentage of white residents in the Detroit metropolitan area, 1970 United States Census.

something of a frontier between the poor Black inner city and the wealthy white suburbs, with its racial makeup more like the latter even as its economic status fell somewhere between the two.

This in-between status explains why Redford and much of northwest Detroit had long been a hub of white resistance to racial integration. As Joe T. Darden, Richard Child Hill, June Thomas, and Richard Thomas argue in their book, *Detroit: Race and Uneven Development*, in the 1950s, "the most hard-core resistance to the 'Negro tide' centered in the far northwest section of the city." This meant that area residents of the era organized to keep their neighborhoods racially segregated by attempting to block the sale of houses to African Americans and protesting proposed public housing projects. In 1960, an effort to bus students from overcrowded inner-city schools to more prosperous nearby neighborhoods was met with fierce resistance from the white residents of Redford and northwest Detroit. By the 1970s, area residents were keenly aware of their growing isolation in a changing Detroit, which only gave their repeated fights with the rest of the city over racial issues an added urgency. Critically, too, while whites in suburbs like Grosse Pointe and Bloomfield Hills were engaging in

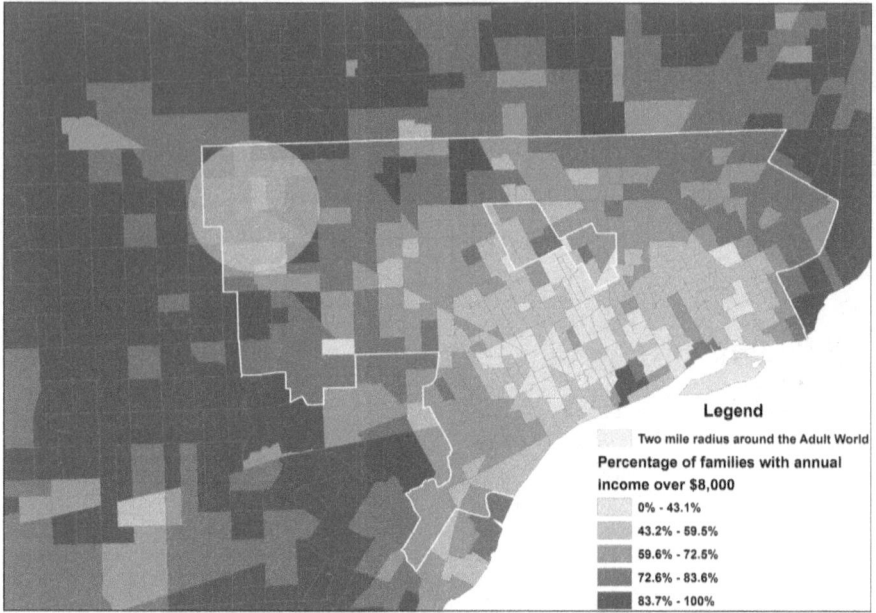

Figure 3.2. Percentage of households with yearly income over $8,000, 1970 United States Census.

their own battles over racial issues, they had less to lose economically, being firmly entrenched within the middle and upper classes. Many of these same suburbs also used zoning laws to keep "incompatible" populations from moving into their communities, which often amounted to little more than thinly veiled racial segregation by zoning. By contrast, as evidenced by their staunch opposition to racial desegregation efforts throughout the postwar era, whites in Redford felt themselves to be more vulnerable to the impact of urban decay, believing that the spread of the impoverished inner city was a direct threat to their increasingly tenuous hold on middle-class status.[7]

In the summer of 1972, amid this turmoil, the Adult World bookstore quietly opened its doors in the heart of Redford. The bookstore was tucked between the Redford Presbyterian Church and Redford High School, which were located just a few hundred yards to either side (see fig. 3.3). Linking the church, bookstore, and school was the major thoroughfare of Grand River Avenue, one of Detroit's five main spokes, which acted as something of a commercial strip in Redford with numerous small businesses and retail outlets. Given its proximity to the suburbs and the class and racial makeup of the surrounding

"THE BLIGHT OF INDECENCY" 141

Figure 3.3. Key locales in Redford mapped onto 1973 aerial photograph of Detroit. Aerial image courtesy of the United States Geological Survey.

neighborhood, it is no surprise that this section of Grand River in northwest Detroit was a popular destination for suburbanites doing their shopping in the city. The proprietors of Adult World no doubt were attracted to this prime commercial location on a major thoroughfare, but this visibility also fueled the ire of many residents in Redford who saw the new business as a threat to the community.

AN OVERVIEW OF THE LETTERS OF PROTEST

The campaign against the Adult World bookstore was kick-started when Pastor Banks of the Redford Presbyterian Church used his weekly sermon to call on his parishioners to not go into the recently opened bookstore and to instead fight back against this intrusion of a "smut store" into Redford. By the end of October, hundreds of letters had arrived at the offices of Mayor Roman Gribbs and the city council president, Mel Ravitz, not only from members of the Redford Presbyterian Church but also from neighborhood residents, parent-teacher groups, and homeowners' associations. Most of these letters

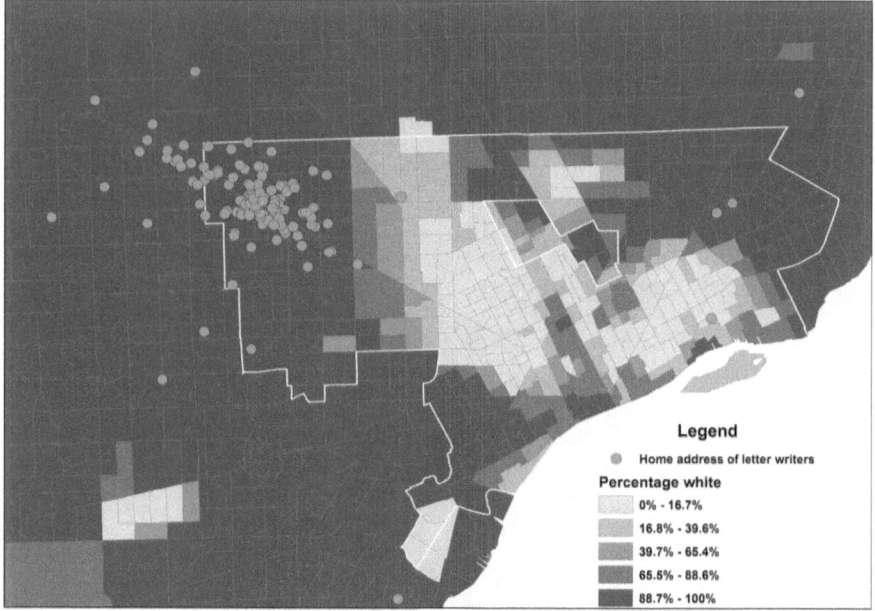

Figure 3.4. Origins of letters protesting the Adult World Bookstore with percentage of white residents in the Detroit metropolitan area, 1970 United States Census.

included a return address, making it possible to map where the writers resided, thereby giving us a sense of their demographics (see fig. 3.4). Not surprisingly, the vast majority of letters were sent from nearby households, with 80 percent coming from those living within two miles of the adult bookstore. Letters sent from other parts of the city, with a few exceptions, tended to come from areas in Detroit that were, like Redford, predominantly white. Meanwhile, roughly one in six of the letters originated from almost uniformly white suburban locales. Many of these suburbanite letter writers were former residents of the Redford area, while others did their shopping or went to church there. Taken together, then, it seems exceedingly likely that the vast majority of those writing protest letters were white.[8]

In total, these letters bore the signatures of roughly 280 individuals.[9] Of these, based on given names and gendered English honorifics, an estimated 194 letter writers were women and 67 were men, with the gender of the remaining 19 indeterminate. This gender imbalance is even starker when we omit those letters sent by a husband and wife together, which leaves 153 letters from women and 26 from men, or nearly six women for every man. This perhaps even understates the gender disparity given that many of the men who did send letters were acting in an official role as the head of a neighborhood organization or local business, meaning that just a handful were sent from individual male residents taking it upon themselves to write letters of protest. Though it might be tempting to see the marked prominence of women in Redford's protest campaign as a precursor to the feminist anti-porn movement, there is no indication that these women identified as feminists, and as we will see, their letters did not draw on anything resembling feminist rhetoric. Moreover, as Strub has argued, mainstream feminist positions on pornography during the early 1970s were very much in flux, with no consensus on the issue, while the feminist anti-porn movement would not fully coalesce until the latter half of the decade.[10]

Instead, this preponderance of women writing letters protesting the Adult World might be better contextualized within two separate but related histories. The first is the way women have long played a crucial role in spearheading anti-porn efforts at the grassroots level, as previously observed in chapter 1 with the work done by Catholic women in monitoring retailers for indecent literature. The second is to place the activism of Redford's letter writers within the broader context of the history of white women's prominent position in grassroots conservative politics and neighborhood resistance to racial integration. As Elizabeth Gillespie McRae argues, white women at the grassroots level "were central to massive resistance to racial equality." And while McRae focuses most of her attention on the South, white women similarly played a critical role in grassroots campaigns against efforts to redress racism and end segregation in the North. As Thomas Sugrue writes of the battles over neighborhood integration in Detroit: "Concerns about family, domesticity, and community all undergirded white women's role in neighborhood resistance in the postwar city.... [Women] had even more at stake than men in the preservation of a neighborhood. They viewed neighborhood transition as a profound threat to the sense of community they had constructed. And they feared the introduction of outsiders—in the case of Detroit, blacks—as a threat to the domestic unit." Though the perceived outsiders had changed, the prominence of white women remained the constant in neighborhood resistance to both racial integration and the opening of adult businesses. It should therefore come as no surprise that much of the rhetoric employed by those protesting the Adult World bookstore was steeped in and adapted from language used in fights over the racial integration of white neighborhoods.[11]

Though the letters sent to the mayor and city council protesting Adult World vary greatly in style and content, three main threads ran through most of them: the need to protect children, fears surrounding invasion by unwanted outsiders, and a belief that Adult World would hurt the local economy and lower property values. Pointing to the way such anti-porn discourse proliferated in the years that followed, Marilyn Adler Papayanis found similar arguments used in neighborhood fights about adult businesses in 1990s New York City. As she writes, "Citizens feared that the presence of such establishments would expose their children to obscene material (either as a result of graphic signage or lax policing), flood their streets with so-called undesirable elements from other areas, and, perhaps most importantly, lower property values." Rhetorical strategies that were fully calcified by the 1990s were, however, still in their infancy in the early 1970s, and the authors of Redford's protest letters were actively devising new forms of anti-porn discourse that would later become widespread. Moreover, as can be seen through an examination of Redford's anti-porn campaign, these discursive strategies were highly mutable and able to adapt to specific local contexts.[12]

THE THREAT TO CHILDREN

One of the most potent rhetorical devices used by anti-porn advocates has long been the invocation of the figure of the idealized and innocent child imperiled by the proliferation of pornography. The deployment of this discursive strategy was particularly prevalent in anti-porn politics in the United States, where, as Walter Kendrick writes, this notion "exercised a power unknown in Europe." Anthony Comstock, America's most famous and notorious antiobscenity crusader, largely built his career on the perceived endangerment of children in the face of indecent media, and he intended his 1883 book, *Traps for the Young*, as "a plea for the moral purity of children." As seen in chapter 1, Fredric Wertham framed much of his postwar crusade against comic books in similar terms, highlighted by his 1954 book, *Seduction of the Innocent*.[13]

Given the popularity of these campaigns and the aforementioned proximity of the Adult World bookstore to Redford High School, it is not surprising that many letter writers invoked the need to protect children from pornography. The first example of this strategy was a flyer, "How to Protest against the Adult World," distributed by the Redford Presbyterian Church in early October 1972. The flyer called on residents to write to key city officials—including the president of the city council, the mayor, and the police commissioner—and implore them to take action against the spread of pornography in the city. It also included a sample letter that distilled the church's preferred rhetoric for the fight against Adult World. Taking center stage was the argument that the bookstore would represent a threat to neighborhood children: "[Pornography] corrupts our youth and works against what we are trying to do in our families in teaching good sex and the disciplined mind and body. It stands over against what we are wanting to see taught in our schools yet our High School youth must pass this shop on the way to and from the Redford High School each day." In drawing on the perceived vulnerability of Redford's youth, the letter immediately set out the stakes of the issue for area residents.[14]

While some residents ignored the flyer's instructions to "state your own convictions in your own words" and simply signed their name to the sample letter, most instead drafted their own original letters. But even these letter writers tended to place the protection of children at the heart of their argument. For example, Mr. A. Schanenberger, writing on behalf of the Burt Area Citizens Committee, worried that children might venture into the store despite laws restricting their admission.[15] In a typo-filled letter, he argued that "while the present controls limit admittance to 18 years or older this adult bookstore is within 900 feet of Redrord [sic] High School and a posted age limit does not guarantee constraint by the owner when that level of curoisity [sic] and and [sic] money is readily available." Schanenberger also expressed the fear that entrance into the store itself might not even be necessary for the corruption of children: "Unconcern is again reflected in the present choice of building advertising. The flashing lights are contemporary enough but to blatently [sic] flash: 'Pleasure is what we sell.'" It was not just the products sold within the store that troubled him but the very presence and visibility of the store itself. In other words, Redford's youth might not even need to enter the bookstore to be corrupted by its influence; a peek at the storefront signage might be enough on its own.[16]

Similarly, a letter from Evelyn Ginn expressed particular concern over the exposure of children to pornography. "Naturally," she wrote, "we do not care to have curious youngsters reading this pornographic material. It nurtures an unhealthy attitude toward sex, most especially when a child's knowledge has not been fully developed." But Ginn went beyond just rehashing the well-worn trope of the innocent youth in danger from the perils of pornography, positing that the adults going into the store were developmentally stunted and had not truly achieved adulthood. She argued that "these are not really 'adult' bookstores. A mature adult with a normal sex life and a healthy attitude toward sexual love, does not seek this type of entertainment. Only a warped or undeveloped personality needs the kind of stimulus that comes from reading and seeing this type of material." Ginn here evoked a similar conception of the adult consumer of indecent media as the one offered up by those supporting Detroit's literary censorship operation, as discussed in chapter 1. As Alex Canty of the Detroit Recorder's Court Psychiatric Clinic said in 1953, "The regular reader of obscene literature is a person who receives some stimulation by it because he has not matured emotionally." For Ginn and Canty, questioning whether adults who consumed pornographic material really qualified as adults was concomitant with the presumed innocence of children, the implication being that these "undeveloped" adults had once been innocent children whose minds had been warped by pornography.[17]

ATTRACTING "UNDESIRABLE ELEMENTS"

The belief that only mentally stunted adults could become consumers of pornography also fueled the argument that adult businesses attracted "undesirable" individuals who posed a danger to residents. While this line of argument did not appear in the sample letter, it nevertheless was a recurring theme in many of the letters protesting Adult World. Some letter writers raised the specter of unwanted homosexual outsiders who were interested in children. As Ginn wrote, "Last summer my teenage son was approached by a man who used filthy sexual language and spoke of 'smoker' movies. I wonder if he had just been to see one. Or perhaps he had just read some pornographic material that stimulated him to the point that he had to go out and pick up a young boy." Here Ginn drew on the long-standing association of homosexuality with child molestation to again emphasize the threat Adult World posed to neighborhood children through the type of sexually deviant clientele drawn to the business and through the impact of indecent "'smoker' movies" on the adult mind.[18]

Redford's protesting residents also wrote of unwanted outsiders in ways that drew on contemporaneous debates surrounding race, in particular the way white suburbanites frequently complained of a "racial invasion" of their neighborhoods by Black city dwellers. As David Freund writes, white homeowners in the postwar Detroit suburb of Dearborn "insisted that blacks had destroyed residential neighborhoods in Detroit and now posed an immediate threat to suburban residents, who needed to prevent a 'Negro invasion.'" Similarly, letters objecting to Adult World often used derivatives of the term *invasion* to describe how the bookstore was drawing unwanted types into the area. "The Northwest Redford-Detroit area has been invaded by 'The Adult World,'" Ann M. Sullivan's letter complained, while Mrs. Wm. D. Murphy implored, "Please help Northwest Detroit clean out this dirty mess that has invaded us."[19]

But even as the Redford protesters drew on the racialized rhetoric of invasion, the fact that they lived within Detroit's borders and not in the suburbs meant that the presumed "invaders" they feared—the undesirable individuals supposedly threatening to tarnish the community—were not the poor Black city dwellers feared by white suburbanites but rather white suburbanites themselves. Myron Gelt, owner of Gigi Floral Fashions, located next door to Adult World, explicitly made this point in his letter of protest: "Most of the patrons of 'porno' shops are usually the white middleclass suburbanites who live in their suburban utopia." Mrs. Overly similarly complained to the mayor: "If our neighborhood does not patronize this establishment, it still does not prevent people out of the neighborhood from coming in, who would not have it in their own neighborhood." Given the relative dearth of adult businesses in the suburbs in comparison to the nearly fifty spread throughout Detroit at this time, the suburban origins of the individuals to whom she is referring are all too clear. The notion across these letters, then, was that hypocritical white suburbanites, while not allowing adult businesses in their own neighborhoods, would be the ones actually patronizing Adult World.[20]

The fact that the letter writers focused on outsiders also points to the way all involved seemed to assume that no residents of the Redford area could possibly be among the customers of Adult World. Of course, these assumptions are unlikely to have matched reality. Still, given the proximity of Redford to the suburbs, as well as the fact that Grand River Avenue in this area was something of a shopping destination, it does stand to reason that Adult World had a substantial number of suburbanites among its clientele. The fact that many of these suburban dwellers resided in places that were, at least in the estimation of Redford's protesting letter writers, both economically prosperous and free from porn only exacerbated frustrations over the perceived invasion of unwanted suburban outsiders into Redford.

PROPERTY VALUES AND WHITE FLIGHT

The final common theme of these letters was concern over falling property values and the economic vitality of Redford and Detroit. This issue, much like the fear that Adult World would attract undesirable individuals, did not appear in the sample letter put out by the Redford Presbyterian Church but was nevertheless frequently invoked by letter writers. These economic concerns were almost always couched within expressions of civic pride and were tied to a sense of loss and fear for the city's economic and social health. As Mrs. F. H. Wilcox wrote, "I was born in Detroit, so were my parents, and so were my children. I've been proud of being a 'Detroiter' <u>but</u> the new business which recently moved into my neighborhood is spoiling my pride in my city." Similarly, Evelyn Ginn wrote, "Please do anything you can to put all the 'adult' bookstores and movies out of business. We don't need them in our city. They are dangerous to the mental health of some, and an insult to all the people in Detroit who care about our city and the people in it. I care." Ginn was referring to the "I Care About Detroit" campaign, which had been initiated by downtown business interests following the violence and turmoil that hit the city in the summer of 1967. As part of the campaign, flyers and buttons with the "I Care About Detroit" slogan were distributed at special events held downtown, and Motown star Smokey Robinson recorded a song of the same name in support of the cause. The expression was meant to evoke pride in the city and a sense of ownership over Detroit's future, and its deployment in the fight over Adult World is evidence that the protesters viewed the spread of adult businesses as part of the broader threat to the future prospects of the city.[21]

These expressions of civic pride were often linked with allusions to the growing tendency of white Detroiters to flee the city for the suburbs. Mr. and Mrs. Houslander expressed this perspective when they asked, "Is this another way to drive people from Detroit? We have lived here all our lives, however, if this is the beginning of things to come, perhaps there will be more of an exodus." Such threats to join the white flight to the suburbs were often described in terms of political retribution for inaction on the part of city officials. As Mrs. James Gilligan put it, "As a taxpayer on two residences in Detroit, and a city income tax payer, I will withdraw from this city unless some action is taken on these places, and also cost my vote likewise!!!" No doubt the threat of leaving the city and the promised response come election time should adult businesses continue to proliferate were strategies designed to induce political action.[22]

Linked to concerns about white flight were fears that adult entertainment in Detroit would cause "legitimate" businesses to flee to the suburbs. Letter writers displayed their awareness of the city's already-visible economic decline by expressing the fear that the presence of adult theaters and bookstores in the city would only hasten the trend of businesses leaving for the suburbs or closing. Gelt, the aforementioned proprietor of Gigi Floral Fashions, succinctly expressed this view by writing, "When a porno shop moves in, five regular businesses leave the city as does your tax base." As a small-business owner himself, Gelt further claimed that he "would hate to be classified as one of those businesses fleeing to the suburbs; but with neighbors such as 'porno' shops, it leaves very little choice." Gelt was by no means alone in expressing the view that the economic health of the city depended on closing adult businesses. Echoing this sentiment, Marie Mitchell wrote: "If the Common Council is sincerely trying to get Detroit 'back on its feet,' this type of smut store should be closed." Though, in reality, the fall of Detroit's economy had been set in motion decades earlier by the forces of structural racism and economic inequality, undoubtedly the belief that adult businesses were a major cause of the economic decline of Detroit was widely held.[23]

Fears regarding the economic effect of adult businesses were particularly acute when it came to their perceived impact on residential neighborhoods. As Burt Area Citizens Committee president A. Schanenberger said of Adult World: "This use on Grand River within a shopping area may at first seem to be appropriate on a major thoroughfare, but its performance and outward effect on our residential community is what concerns us and makes it objectionable." The emphasis, then, was on the effect that adult businesses might have on residential neighborhoods, and there is an implied acceptance of adult entertainment if sequestered within business districts like the city's downtown. Another letter writer, Karen Fink, phrased this argument very directly, saying, "I wish to protest, mainly, the location of this store."[24]

These concerns led many Redford residents to call for laws preventing such establishments from opening in their neighborhoods. Irene Stein, for example, argued that "some laws should be passed forbidding these adult book + peep stores from operating in primarily residential areas." James Gilligan combined his complaint with the threat that he was planning on "moving to a community where the local governmental authorities has [sic] sufficient ingenuity to pass legislation whereby these stores will only operate with the approval of the local neighborhood." Notably, this view that residents should have the right to decide whether or not to allow adult businesses echoed the strategies that had become central to white racial politics of the era, which had increasingly come to rely upon a color-blind rhetoric that sought to distance its purveyors from charges of racism while still allowing them to argue against efforts to combat racial segregation and inequality. As Matthew Lassiter has argued, "Color-blind ideology shaped a collective politics of white, middle-class identity that defined 'freedom of choice' and 'neighborhood schools' as the core privileges of homeowner rights and consumer liberties." Though the particulars had changed, the rights-based rhetoric of white suburbanites was mirrored in the letters of anti-porn activists. As one letter protesting Adult World succinctly put it, "We, as residents, have rights too!"[25]

Writing on behalf of the North Rosedale Park Civic Association in Detroit, an organization that represented some 1,400 households, Charles Allegrina summarized many of the key issues: "We believe the use of freedom of the press as a rationale [for permitting adult businesses] amounts to a total disregard for the affect [sic] this type of amusement has on the surrounding neighborhoods. Various people have described it as the first signs of blight." Allegrina's use of the term *blight* holds particular significance due to its association with the racial conflicts that were central to the discourse on the urban crisis. *Blight* had long been the word used to describe condemned and economically impoverished neighborhoods, which meant that it had come to be linked to predominantly Black urban areas. As Freund writes of Detroit's suburbs, "By the 1950s, whites were preoccupied with distinguishing their suburban havens from what they viewed as its urban antithesis, as well as the minority population associated with it. Suburban whites talked constantly about the necessity of preventing 'urban blight' and keeping their communities clean." Neighborhoods linked with blight were potential targets of urban renewal, which often meant the total destruction of communities and the displacement of their residents. In Detroit, the postwar urban renewal program aimed to rehabilitate "blighted areas" of the city, which in practice meant leveling many of the city's most densely populated Black neighborhoods. Thus, the threat of Redford becoming associated with blight carried with it very real economic consequences for residents. Allegrina's word choice here was no mere coincidence, then, as it tied the fight over Adult World to a longer history of white backlash against an expanding Black urban center.[26]

It is also significant that Allegrina explicitly rejects defenses of adult businesses based on the ideal of the "freedom of the press" and the First Amendment, countering with an argument about the economic vitality of residential neighborhoods. In drawing on economic arguments to make their case, those protesting the Adult World bookstore were able to sidestep debates over morality and censorship, with many explicitly denying the relevance of those issues altogether. "This protest is not made in the interest of establishing moral standards for the people of this city," Ralph Williams insisted. "Each adult has the duty and right to set his own standards within the framework of the US Constitution. All open minded people will accept the fact that our own values are not necessarily best for everyone." This insistence that moral concerns were not the motivation for their protest allowed letter writers to avoid debates over censorship; they sometimes even explicitly denied that questions about the morality of pornography were at all germane to the issue at hand.[27]

This rhetorical move drew much of its inspiration from color-blind ideology, which, as Freund argues, had "enabled whites to defend segregation and even to dismiss civil rights protest while claiming to be nonracist." Similarly, then, grassroots anti-porn activists of the early 1970s crafted morality-neutral economic- and rights-based rhetorical strategies that could advocate in favor of censorship and the shuttering of adult businesses while simultaneously distancing themselves from the stereotype of the religion-driven, bluenosed, and prudish anti-porn crusader of old. Of course, this is not to say that morality was absent entirely from the arguments being made by these anti-porn activists, just as racism was never absent from color-blind rhetoric either. As Freund writes of color-blind discourse, "Of course it still represented a racist worldview and whites' actions systematically discriminated against certain racial groups. But the language and assumptions were very different and, critically, whites believed what they were saying." In much the same way, morality still undergirded the assumptions behind this new form of anti-porn discourse, and the goals of Redford's protesting residents remained largely the same as those of previous generations of anti-porn activists. Nevertheless, this morality-neutral anti-porn rhetoric marked a profound shift for anti-porn politics by making it better attuned to the social and political landscape of the post–sexual revolution era. And though Redford's protesting residents were by no means synonymous with the anti-porn movement as a whole, their campaign was indicative of broader anti-porn trends occurring at the grassroots level across the United States in the early 1970s.[28]

As discussed further in chapter 5, Redford's letter-writing campaign helped spur the city to enact new anti-porn laws. Present at the bill signing were Betty Hedeen, president of the Redford Community Council, and Virginia Fuller, representing the Redford Parents Club, both given personal invitations by the mayor. Each subsequently received a letter from Mayor Gribbs, complete with an autographed photo from the bill signing, with Gribbs expressing his gratitude for their help in "gaining passage of these vitally needed laws." The letter went on to say, "I look forward to having your support as we continue our efforts to eliminate the blight of indecency from Detroit." As indicated by these words, if the morality-based arguments of old never fully disappeared, living on in Gribbs's invocation of "indecency," this rhetoric had become inextricably linked with a new anti-porn discourse emphasizing issues of blight and urban decay.[29]

CONCLUSION: THE DEATH OF ADULT WORLD

On October 11, in the midst of the deluge of letters sent by Redford residents protesting Adult World, the Detroit City Council directed the heads of three city departments to look into the possibility of taking action to close the bookstore. Anti-porn laws on the books in the city at that time had limited ability to shutter existing adult businesses, though, and so the reply came back that the city had no way of closing Adult World. Even so, Redford's residents soon got their wish when Adult World quietly closed its doors in November. Though one woman wrote a letter thanking city council president Mel Ravitz for closing the bookstore, in reality it appears to have shut down of its own accord due to community pressure and feared legal action against the business.[30]

Adult World was not the last adult business Redford would have to deal with, as in early 1973, the Pussycat Theater opened its doors in northwest Detroit just over a mile from where Adult World had been. The community again organized in response, if not perhaps with quite the same level of passion as they had against Adult World. The same arguments were again used in opposing the Pussycat, with the *Detroit Free Press* writing, "The Redford Park Community Association believes that the Pussycat Theater, which opened about a month ago at Telegraph and Grove, has hurt property values and will eventually have a bad effect on neighborhood businesses." That group's leader further argued that the Pussycat, despite being in operation for just one month, had already made an impact on the community in that potential home buyers were being "deterred by the proximity of the theater." Still, the protests of the community failed to close the Pussycat, and the theater continued to operate for years to come.[31]

The notion that adult businesses directly cause neighborhood decay and the decline of housing prices is questionable, but what is surely true, though, is that the anti-porn protesters examined in this chapter firmly believed this to be the case. And, regardless of the underlying validity of this belief, it could have profound real-world effects. In the years ahead, Redford changed in all the ways one might expect, with white residents moving out to the suburbs in droves and the area looking increasingly like the rest of the city by declining economically while becoming more racially diverse. Given the complex structural forces at work driving these changes, it seems fair to assume that no neighborhood letter-writing campaign against an adult business was likely to alter Redford's fate. Still, the furor over Adult World did fuel a belief among the residents of Redford that the neighborhood was in trouble. This belief, in turn, led many residents to more seriously consider moving out to the suburbs, accelerating the flight of people and businesses from the area. The residents who galvanized their community to protest against Adult World were fervently trying to save their neighborhood; in reality, they may well have only hastened its decline.

The campaign by Redford's residents against the Adult World bookstore—alongside similar campaigns waged in countless neighborhoods both in Detroit and across the country—helped fundamentally alter the political strategies used by those advocating in favor of censorship. Concerns about homeowners' rights and the economic impact of adult businesses would, in turn, come to reshape the legal strategies used to censor pornography and adult entertainment.

As discussed in chapter 5, the deluge of letters sent by Redford residents to city officials came while the mayor and city council were debating new laws designed to curb the spread of adult businesses in the city. Meanwhile, the city had also been engaged in a years-long debate over how to regulate the growing number of establishments catering to exotic dance in Detroit. Many residents opposed to topless bars and the like sought to use similar arguments as those used by Redford's residents by emphasizing the negative economic impact such businesses supposedly had on neighborhoods. And yet, as the following chapter explores, these economic arguments had the potential to be turned on their head; in the early 1970s, the owners of topless bars and the dancers who worked in them fought back against proposed new regulations by making their own case about the importance of the thriving exotic dance industry to the city's ailing economy.

NOTES

1. James O. Banks to Roman S. Gribbs, October 12, 1972, box 333, folder 6, Roman Gribbs Papers, Burton Historical Collection, Detroit Public Library.

2. Whitney Strub, *Perversion for Profit: The Politics of Pornography and the Rise of the New Right* (New York: Columbia University Press, 2011), 146.

3. See Carolyn Bronstein, *Battling Pornography: The American Feminist Anti-Pornography Movement, 1976–1986* (Cambridge: Cambridge University Press, 2011); Carolyn Bronstein and Whitney Strub, eds., *Porno Chic and the Sex Wars: American Sexual Representation in the 1970s* (Amherst: University of Massachusetts Press, 2016); Strub, *Perversion for Profit*, 146–78.

4. Gayle S. Rubin, "Thinking Sex: Notes for a Radical Theory of the Politics of Sexuality," in *Deviations: A Gayle Rubin Reader* (Durham, NC: Duke University Press, 2011), 138; Robert O. Self, *All in the Family: The Realignment of American Democracy since the 1960s* (New York: Hill and Wang, 2012), 7. Other notable work emphasizing the intersections among the histories of race, sex, and cities includes Clayton Howard, "Building a 'Family-Friendly' Metropolis: Sexuality, the State, and Postwar Housing Policy," *Journal of Urban History* 39, no. 5 (September 2013): 933–55; Tim Retzloff, "City, Suburb, and the Changing Bounds of Lesbian and Gay Life and Politics in Metropolitan Detroit, 1945–1985" (PhD diss., Yale University, 2014); Josh Sides, *Erotic City: Sexual Revolutions and the Making of Modern San Francisco* (Oxford: Oxford University Press, 2009).

5. See Thomas J. Sugrue, *The Origins of the Urban Crisis: Race and Inequality in Postwar Detroit* (Princeton, NJ: Princeton University Press, 1996).

6. Frank B. Woodford and Arthur M. Woodford, *All Our Yesterdays: A Brief History of Detroit* (Detroit: Wayne State University Press, 1969), 277. All census

data come from the National Historical Geographic Information System. See Steven Manson, Jonathan Schroeder, David Van Riper, and Steven Ruggles, IPUMS National Historical Geographic Information System: Version 12.0 (database, University of Minnesota, 2017), http://doi.org/10.18128/D050.V12.0.

7. Joe T. Darden et al., *Detroit: Race and Uneven Development* (Philadelphia: Temple University Press, 1987), 127, 221–22; John Hartigan Jr., *Racial Situations: Class Predicaments of Whiteness in Detroit* (Princeton, NJ: Princeton University Press, 1999), 69; David M. P. Freund, *Colored Property: State Policy and White Racial Politics in Suburban America* (Chicago: University of Chicago Press, 2010), 33.

8. Banks to Gribbs, October 12, 1972, Roman Gribbs Papers.

9. Those who sent multiple letters to either Ravitz or Gribbs or who sent letters to both Ravitz and Gribbs were only counted once.

10. Strub, *Perversion for Profit*, 213–16. For more on the history of the feminist anti-porn movement, see Bronstein, *Battling Pornography*.

11. Elizabeth Gillespie McRae, *Mothers of Massive Resistance: White Women and the Politics of White Supremacy* (New York: Oxford University Press, 2018), 4; Sugrue, *The Origins of the Urban Crisis*, 251. For more on the role played by white women in grassroots opposition to racial integration, see Michelle M. Nickerson, *Mothers of Conservatism: Women and the Postwar Right* (Princeton, NJ.: Princeton University Press, 2014); Lisa McGirr, *Suburban Warriors: The Origins of the New American Right* (Princeton, NJ: Princeton University Press, 2002); Matthew F. Delmont, *Why Busing Failed: Race, Media, and the National Resistance to School Desegregation* (Oakland: University of California Press, 2016), 142–67.

12. Marilyn Adler Papayanis, "Sex and the Revanchist City: Zoning Out Pornography in New York," *Environment and Planning D: Society and Space* 18, no. 3 (2000): 343.

13. Walter Kendrick, *The Secret Museum: Pornography in Modern Culture* (Berkeley: University of California Press, 1987), 141; Anthony Comstock, *Traps for the Young* (New York: Funk & Wagnalls, 1883), 1; Fredric Wertham, *Seduction of the Innocent: The Influence of Comic Books on Today's Youth* (New York: Rinehart, 1954).

14. Mrs. Naomi Morgan and John R. Morgan to Mel Ravitz, October 17, 1972, box 42, folder 1, Mel Ravitz Papers, Walter P. Reuther Library, Wayne State University. It is worth noting that the letter's mention of "teaching good sex" is by no means an indication of support for sex education. As Janice M. Irvine argues in her book *Talk about Sex*, the issue of sex education, not unlike pornography, was a critical lynchpin for the rise of the New Right. This sample letter's linking of the issues of pornography and sex education therefore not only connected two major debates over sexual speech but also sought to draw on the grassroots fervor that had helped propel debates over sex education into the forefront of American

politics and turned opposition to unfettered sexual speech into a matter of conservative doctrine. Janice M. Irvine, *Talk about Sex: The Battles over Sex Education in the United States* (Berkeley: University of California Press, 2004), 2.

15. I have tried to use names as given by the letter writers themselves, meaning the name they signed at the end of their letters, regardless of whether their full name was given elsewhere, such as on a letterhead or as part of a return address on the envelope.

16. Mr. A. Schanenberger to Roman S. Gribbs, October 26, 1972, box 333, folder 6, Roman Gribbs Papers, Burton Historical Collection, Detroit Public Library.

17. Evelyn Ginn to Roman S. Gribbs, October 18, 1972, box 333, folder 6, Roman Gribbs Papers, Burton Historical Collection, Detroit Public Library; Charles Manos, "5 More Face 'Smut' Charges," *Detroit Free Press*, February 16, 1953, 3.

18. Ginn to Gribbs, October 18, 1972, Roman Gribbs Papers.

19. Freund, *Colored Property*, 334; Ann M. Sullivan to Mel Ravitz, October 17, 1972, box 42, folder 1, Mel Ravitz Papers, Walter P. Reuther Library, Wayne State University; Mrs. Wm. D. Murphy to Roman S. Gribbs, September 26, 1972, box 333, folder 6, Roman Gribbs Papers, Burton Historical Collection, Detroit Public Library. For more examples of white suburbanites speaking on a "racial invasion" of their neighborhoods, see Darden et al., *Detroit: Race and Uneven Development*, 130–31; Freund, *Colored Property*, 286, 395; Kevin M. Kruse, *White Flight: Atlanta and the Making of Modern Conservatism* (Princeton, NJ: Princeton University Press, 2007), 66; Sugrue, *The Origins of the Urban Crisis*, 231, 249.

20. Myron Gelt to John Nichols, Mel Ravitz, and Roman S. Gribbs, October 11, 1972, box 333, folder 6, Roman Gribbs Papers, Burton Historical Collection, Detroit Public Library; Mrs. Harold Overly to Roman S. Gribbs, October 10, 1972, box 333, folder 6, Roman Gribbs Papers, Burton Historical Collection, Detroit Public Library.

21. Mrs. F. H. Wilcox to Mel Ravitz, October 8, 1972, box 42, folder 1, Mel Ravitz Papers, Walter P. Reuther Library, Wayne State University (emphasis in original); Ginn to Gribbs, October 18, 1972, Roman Gribbs Papers; Diane J. Edgecomb, "News Bulletin," July 1, 1968, box 426, folder 7, Jerome P. Cavanagh Collection, Walter P. Reuther Library, Wayne State University; Julie Morris, "5,000 Show They Care about City," *Detroit Free Press*, August 11, 1969, 3.

22. Mr. and Mrs. Houslander to David Eberhard, September 25, 1972, box 333, folder 6, Roman Gribbs Papers, Burton Historical Collection, Detroit Public Library; Mrs. James Gilligan to Mel Ravitz, September 28, 1972, box 42, folder 1, Mel Ravitz Papers, Walter P. Reuther Library, Wayne State University.

23. Gelt to Nichols, Ravitz, and Gribbs, October 11, 1972, Roman Gribbs Papers; Marie Mitchell to Mel Ravitz, October 13, 1972, box 42, folder 1, Mel Ravitz Papers, Walter P. Reuther Library, Wayne State University.

24. Schanenberger to Gribbs, October 26, 1972, Roman Gribbs Papers; Karen L. Fink to Mel Ravitz, October 18, 1972, box 42, folder 1, Mel Ravitz Papers, Walter P. Reuther Library, Wayne State University.

25. Irene Stein to Mel Ravitz, October 15, 1972, box 42, folder 1, Mel Ravitz Papers, Walter P. Reuther Library, Wayne State University; James Gilligan to Mel Ravitz, September 15, 1972, box 41, folder 7, Mel Ravitz Papers, Walter P. Reuther Library, Wayne State University; Matthew D. Lassiter, "The Suburban Origins of 'Color-Blind' Conservatism: Middle-Class Consciousness in the Charlotte Busing Crisis," *Journal of Urban History* 30, no. 4 (May 2004): 550; Mr. and Mrs. Michael Mayer to Mel Ravitz, October 11, 1972, box 42, folder 1, Mel Ravitz Papers, Walter P. Reuther Library, Wayne State University.

26. Charles D. Allegrina to Mel Ravitz, October 21, 1972, box 42, folder 1, Mel Ravitz Papers, Walter P. Reuther Library, Wayne State University; Freund, *Colored Property*, 358; Sugrue, *The Origins of the Urban Crisis*, 48–49.

27. Ralph E. Williams to Roman S. Gribbs, September 23, 1972, box 333, folder 6, Roman Gribbs Papers, Burton Historical Collection, Detroit Public Library.

28. Freund, *Colored Property*, 13, 17.

29. Roman S. Gribbs to Mrs. Betty Hedeen, November 1, 1972, box 333, folder 7, Roman Gribbs Papers, Burton Historical Collection, Detroit Public Library; Roman S. Gribbs to Mrs. Virginia Fuller, November 1, 1972, box 333, folder 7, Roman Gribbs Papers, Burton Historical Collection, Detroit Public Library.

30. George C. Edwards to Creighton C Lederer, William E. Clexton, and Philip Tannian, October 11, 1972, box 333, folder 7, Roman Gribbs Papers, Burton Historical Collection, Detroit Public Library; Philip Tannian to Common Council, November 9, 1972, box 333, folder 7, Roman Gribbs Papers, Burton Historical Collection, Detroit Public Library; Mrs. Stanley Taylor to Mel Ravitz, November 13, 1972, box 41, folder 7, Mel Ravitz Papers, Walter P. Reuther Library, Wayne State University.

31. Louis Heldman, "Ban Helps Smut Peddlers Thrive," *Detroit Free Press*, February 12, 1973, 3, 8.

FOUR

TOPLESS DETROIT

Regulating Industry and Exotic Dance

AS DISCUSSED IN THE PRECEDING chapter, one of the key lines of argument used by anti-porn advocates during the early 1970s was the notion that adult businesses are toxic to the overall business environment of a neighborhood. Thus, the notion went, both area residents and "legitimate" nonsexual businesses would flee from neighborhoods rife with adult businesses, thereby hurting the local economy. And yet, adult entertainment was one of the only thriving industries in Detroit during this time, creating hundreds, perhaps thousands, of new jobs in a city whose unemployment rate was rapidly escalating. Adult entertainment in Detroit also generated millions of dollars in revenue each year, thereby contributing badly needed money to the city's depleted tax coffers. The notion that adult businesses might actually be a part of a healthy economy rather than a hindrance to one was largely alien to public discourse of the era, save for one notable exception. Even as the early 1970s saw numerous adult theaters and bookstores targeted by protest campaigns and shut down by the city due to their supposed negative impact on Detroit's economy, owners of topless bars successfully marshaled their own economic arguments to make the case that to shutter them would kill a thriving industry that was materially aiding Detroit's ailing economy.

This chapter explores the history of exotic dance in Detroit, focusing in particular on fights over topless dancing in the early 1970s. Anti-porn advocates fought against the spread of topless entertainment in both the judicial and legislative arenas with the aim of shutting down this burgeoning form of adult entertainment. And yet, even as anti-porn activists had so successfully mined economic arguments in their fight against other forms of adult entertainment in Detroit, owners of topless bars managed to appropriate this rhetoric for their own use by tying the fate of Detroit's shaky economy to that of topless bars. Bar owners emphasized the gross revenue of the topless entertainment industry in Detroit, the tax revenue collected by the city and the state, and the sheer number of individuals employed by the industry. In emphasizing these economic figures, owners of topless bars managed to largely succeed in their fight against efforts to shutter their businesses. If anti-porn activists never fully accepted topless bars as part of the landscape of Detroit, they nevertheless eventually came to see them as a less pressing matter than other forms of adult entertainment.

Though it was rarely ever made explicit, debates over the fate of topless dance in Detroit largely revolved around the regulation of female bodies. Anti-porn advocates viewed male lust over the female form as natural and self-evident, whereas female incitement of male lust was dangerous and in need of regulation. Meanwhile, in their efforts to stamp out topless dancing, city officials spoke of morals and the need to guard against prostitution but paid little more than lip service to the interests of the dancers themselves. Exotic dancers were viewed as victims in need of protection by the state, yet ironically, the illicit nature of the industry, itself a result of the work of anti-porn forces, had created real problems for dancers, with working conditions and employment practices that were at times exploitative in nature. In this chapter, I therefore highlight the voices of exotic dancers as they spoke of both the labor problems they faced in the industry as well as the way efforts by the city to further regulate the industry exacerbated these same problems as well as created new ones. In looking at these labor issues alongside the rhetoric used by the industry, this chapter examines the debates over women's bodies and the economics of topless dancing that so often underlay fights over indecent media in Detroit.[1]

GO-GO AND PASTIES

Throughout the first half of the twentieth century, the Detroit Police Department, led by the Censor Bureau, sought to clamp down on exotic dancing in the city. At times, as discussed in chapter 2, this involved targeted raids on "smoker" parties that included as part of their entertainment offerings either striptease shows or stag films. At other times, though, this meant going after any bars, nightclubs, or burlesque theaters that featured performances by dancers in various states of undress. The officers of the Censor Bureau frequently dropped in unannounced to such establishments to make sure performers were wearing a minimum level of clothing, typically defined as a "nontransparent brassiere and trunks." Female dancers found to be wearing attire deemed too revealing would usually be arrested and charged with indecent exposure, and bar owners or managers were also often charged. On rare occasions, male bodies came under police regulation as well. In 1937, the police announced that they would be going after performances of "male revues" at bars and nightclubs.[2] Even worse in the police's eyes were "female impersonators," whose violation of gender norms made them a prime target for the Detroit Police Department at that time. When one nightclub proprietor asked what he should do about the "female impersonator" still under contract, the police superintendent replied that the performer should "complete the engagement in male attire."[3]

The close of the 1950s saw an uptick in the preponderance and prominence of exotic dancing in Detroit. A 1959 *Detroit Free Press* article spoke on the growing visibility of exotic dancing in the city. As the article began:

> Bright lights and show girls have come back to Detroit.
>
> The reasons could make a social study in dusty textbook language—but what they spell out is Girls! Girls! Girls!
>
> History may link the new girlie era with "the fluctuating economy of an industrial city," or work out ponderous theories on "urban depletion in [the] face of suburban expansion."
>
> But meantime—tonight—Detroiters and conventioneers will sit happily beating out the rhythm of bumps and grinds in any of the 24 night spots that now feature Girls! Girls! Girls!

The way the article draws a connection between "the new girlie era," on the one hand, and suburbanization and urban decay, on the other, illustrates how the history of commercial sex and adult entertainment has long been understood as intertwined with urban history. In this case, this meant arguing that the growth of exotic dance in Detroit might well be the natural by-product of the demographic shift from the city to the suburbs. The article expanded on this point later on, stating, "Many of the bar owners now employing strippers dislike the whole project. But since the population swing to the suburbs, their business has been dying, especially in the loop area. They are using the girls to bring in enough business just to survive." Whether bar owners, in reality, "disliked" the trend toward more explicitness may be debatable, but no doubt exotic dancing indeed acted as a means of survival for bar owners who were increasingly seeing their customers move out to the suburbs.[4]

The article went on to connect the availability of adult entertainment to major downtown redevelopment projects of the era. Critical here was the Cobo Center, a massive convention center then under construction that, it was hoped, would fuel a renewal of the downtown area. But, as the article stated, "Veteran policemen and entertainment world figures point out that no conventions will be coming into Detroit to use the 53 million-dollar convention building if Detroit takes in its sidewalks after dark." In other words, the article predicted that no conventions would come to Detroit if the city killed its nightlife scene by shutting down exotic dancing. This linking of the convention trade with the lure of adult entertainment would define the discourse surrounding exotic dancing in the city for decades to come. As the article stated, "Inspector Melville Bullach, of the Censor Bureau, admitted that one of the reasons for downtown gaity [sic] is the 70,000 conventioneers visiting from now through September." In other words, conventions and exotic dancing sustained one another, neither able to flourish in Detroit without the other.[5]

Finally, this same 1959 *Free Press* article also placed the rise of exotic dancing within the broader context of a potential loosening of morals in the Motor City: "But this mushrooming use of 'Exotic Dancers' is new in staid old Detroit. An indication that the big city may be coming out of its 18-year-old period of Victorian purity." As discussed in chapter 1, two years earlier, the ruling in *Butler v. Michigan* had put a dent in Detroit literary censorship, and the late 1950s were, at least on the surface, perceived to be a period of loosening moral standards in the city. Within this context of curbs on media censorship, the Censor Bureau, in the words of the *Free Press*, had "relaxed a couple of Detroit's frigid entertainment rules" when it came to exotic dancing.[6]

Still, though the Censor Bureau may have eased the rules for exotic dancing to a small degree, they continued to maintain very real control over such entertainment. In July of 1959, Bullach and the Censor Bureau led a seminar for exotic dancers in the city, giving instructions as to what was and was not permissible (see figs. 4.1 and 4.2). Some of these restrictions included "bumps and grinds must be limited to two in succession," "no snuggling up to microphones, curtains, or pieces of furniture," and "flat-footed bumping and grinding is out." The *Detroit Times* noted that "Bullach bore down hard on two points." The first related to elements that he feared might encourage prostitution, with Bullach warning dancers that he would "not tolerate table-hopping and drink-hustling by strippers. They can sit with friends between acts—if they put on clothes." The feared slippage between exotic dance and prostitution drove the regulatory mechanisms used by the Censor Bureau, in this case through keeping dancers away from customers between their performances. The other key point Bullach zeroed in on was what the *Times* called the issue of "oversized ladies in undersized garments and panties." As Bullach so eloquently put it, "I don't want any of you big girls trying to squeeze into a size eleven or 32-A." A Detroit police officer giving women instructions on what clothes were suitable

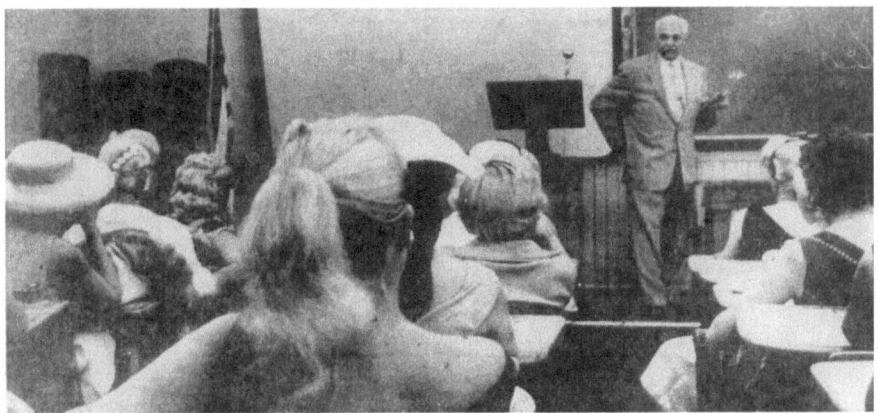

Figures 4.1 and 4.2. Inspector Melville Bullach of the Censor Bureau instructs exotic dancers on police regulations for proper clothing and technique. *Detroit Free Press*, July 10, 1959.

for their particular bodies is indicative of the way regulating exotic dancing always entails regulating women's bodies, whether made explicit, as was the case here, or more often not.[7]

Bullach's instructions for how to dance with decency were seemingly adhered to for the most part, as throughout much of the 1960s, there was little in the way of controversy regarding exotic dancing in Detroit. At the national level, however, this period saw major developments in exotic dancing that would soon affect Detroit. In 1964, Carol Doda famously inaugurated topless dancing in San Francisco, setting off a trend that would spread to cities throughout the country before long. Meanwhile, go-go dancing grew enormously in popularity during the mid-1960s. In its most "clean" form, go-go was simply a type of rhythm dancing; in practice, though, go-go was inextricably tied with adult entertainment and exotic dance. As the *Free Press* put it in 1966, "Much has been written about go-go and the phenomenon has been called a curiosity, a fad, decadent, one more piece of evidence to prove that the younger generation is going to hell and dragging the older one with it.... But most have not said, squarely, what any studious observer of go-go must conclude: That go-go has a lot to do with sex." Critically, too, whereas a clear dividing line between performer and audience was often upheld in burlesque houses featuring striptease performances, go-go most often occurred at bars, where the separation between dancer and customer was often blurry or even practically nonexistent.[8]

Beginning in 1965 and accelerating in the following years, go-go dancing as erotic spectacle spread rapidly to bars and restaurants across Detroit. By the end of 1966, estimates pegged the number of Detroit businesses offering go-go dancing at somewhere between twenty-five and sixty, or roughly one out of every five bars in the city. As the *Detroit News* wrote in 1966, "For better or worse, go-go has become an important and increasingly popular part of the Detroit entertainment scene." Businesses adopted go-go to lure in customers, with one bar owner reporting a 30 percent increase in business after adding go-go dancing as entertainment. Go-go dancing's popularity was such that it soon appeared beyond the boundaries of Detroit, with bars in numerous suburbs offering go-go dancing as well. In late 1967, the *Detroit Daily Dispatch* published an article expressing wonder at the fact that the go-go phenomenon had grown so popular that it had made it out to more rural parts of Michigan, including to one bar located outside Alpena, a city of just over thirteen thousand people located in the northern part of the state. As the *Daily Dispatch* wrote, "And now the ordinary folks of the country can have the same enchanting show as the ordinary folks of the city.... From San Francisco to Detroit, on up to Alpena, the go-go beat goes on." It was not the last time that commentators would state their astonishment at the presence of adult entertainment outside of major cities; in reality, however, topless bars frequently were found in suburban locales.[9]

Though bars sometimes advertised in local newspapers that they featured topless dancing, during performances, female go-go dancers in Detroit always wore pasties covering their nipples and a sheer blouse or shawl on top of that. This was to keep in line with guidelines laid down by the Detroit Police Department about what was acceptable for exotic dancing in the city. Deputy police superintendent John Nichols had signed an order mandating this minimum

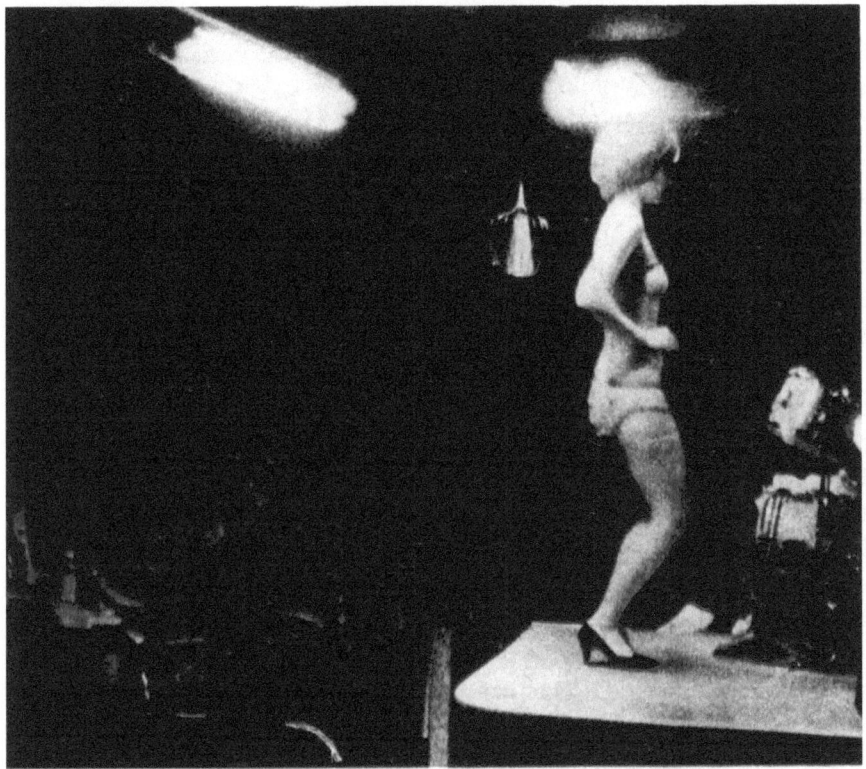

Figure 4.3. Exotic dancing in a bar on Michigan Avenue in 1969. *Detroit Free Press Magazine*, August 24, 1969.

of attire for dancers and also barring any "movement of the body which is designed to arouse the prurient interests of the customers." Exactly what type of dancing tended to "arouse the prurient interests" was left hazy, and such vague regulations pointed to the way exotic dancing, perhaps even more so than other forms of adult entertainment, always had its legal status dependent on the whims of police officers and judges. One constant among industry opponents, however, was the fear that dancers would sell their bodies more directly to customers, leading the city to put in place regulations regarding what dancers could wear when conversing with patrons between their sets. Meanwhile, female bartenders and waitresses had more stringent restrictions on what they could wear, with a "non-sheer blouse" a requirement, meaning no topless or semi-topless.[10]

All this meant that, as the *Detroit News* wrote in early 1967, Detroit did not have "'topless' in the fashion of the West Coast," with semi-topless instead the standard in the city. As Bob Young, manager of the Detroit bar the Sax Club, explained at that time, "They won't let us go to topless in Michigan. This [semi-topless] is the same effect, but it's legal." However, Young went on to suggest that even more risqué erotic dancing was on the horizon in Detroit, saying, "This is just a hint of what's to come. I can't say yet, but we'll go as far as we can within the limits of law. The public wants topless; they've read about it, they want to see it—and we're giving it to them, as much as the law allows, anyway."[11]

Fully topless dancing in a public venue, rather than a private stag show, finally arrived in Detroit in May of 1969, when Tyra Lea LaRue removed her pasties during a performance at the Sip 'n' Chat Bar on the city's west side. LaRue went topless with the approval of the bar owner, Theodore Manolakas, who called the police in advance of the performance, hoping to challenge the ban on topless in Detroit. The police ticketed LaRue on the charge of indecent exposure, and two months later, she and Manolakas appeared in court to contest the ticket. The local newspapers covered the case in detail, though much of their coverage seemed to focus on Tyra Lea LaRue herself, in particular on her body. Both the major newspapers included a large photo of LaRue, each carefully shot so that her full body was on display. The *Free Press* called her "something of a cross between Carol Channing and Mae West," going on to list her height, weight, and body measurements before stating, in a lofty bit of journalism at its finest, that "she has big brown eyes, a wide smile, and is sexy without being lewd."[12]

Ultimately, in July of 1969, traffic court referee John G. Carney fined LaRue $300 for indecent exposure while Manolakas was fined $200 for allowing an act of indecent exposure at his establishment. In handing down the fines, Carney explicitly noted that the Supreme Court had set the precedent that community standards ought to be used for judging what is or is not indecent, with Carney stating, "I don't think the majority of people approve of girls going topless in bars." LaRue and Manolakas vowed that they would appeal the fine, with the latter explaining, "This is a test case. She has a right to dance topless under the First Amendment of the Constitution, which guarantees freedom of speech."[13]

LaRue and Manolakas requested a jury trial to appeal the fines and challenge Detroit's indecent exposure ordinance. Their attorney argued that "the person in the bare flesh is not obscene," with the case hinging on a jury of ten women and two men determining whether topless dancing violated "contemporary community standards" with regards to indecent exposure. Newspaper

Figure 4.4. Tyra Lea LaRue outside court.
Detroit Free Press, September 17, 1969.

accounts again focused on LaRue's body, with both the *Free Press* and *News* making sure to give her measurements and detail the clothes she wore to the trial and *Free Press* writer John Oppedahl opening his article by stating, "A slightly chubby, demurely clad topless dancer began a full-dress attack Tuesday on the city's anti-bare-bosom law."[14]

The jury ruled in favor of the city in September of 1969, with LaRue and Manolakas found guilty. LaRue was sentenced to a thirty-day prison term or a $300 fine while Manolakas was given ninety days or a $500 fine, though the sentences were stayed while another appeal was mounted. After the trial, jury foreman Francis Semelsberger explained of the reasoning behind their ruling, "We figured it was time somebody stood up to be counted on just how far is far enough.... We figured, 'we will take a stand on morals if no one else will.'" Such language spoke to an implied "silent majority" of citizens fed up with this new sexually permissive moral landscape. Still, the reality was that even this ruling did little to stop the spread of topless in Detroit, with the attorney for the city in the case saying that he thought there would be no more topless arrests "since Detroit police have more essential places to put their efforts."[15] This comment spoke to the way, as discussed in chapter 2, in the years immediately following the civil unrest of the summer of 1967, the Detroit police placed somewhat less of a priority on the regulation of sex media and adult entertainment. The night of the trial, the *Detroit News* visited three topless establishments in the city, finding that two of them, including Manolakas's Sip 'n' Chat Bar, featured fully topless dancers sans pasties.[16]

"THE STRIP"

LaRue and Manolakas appealed the decision, though it would take two years for the case to be heard. In the meantime, topless dancing flourished in the Detroit metropolitan area. While topless bars could be found throughout the region, a number of them congregated along a stretch of Michigan Avenue moving out from west Detroit, through Dearborn, and into Inkster, with the area coming to be known informally as "the strip." Michigan Avenue in Dearborn was perhaps the main hub of topless bars in the region, as by the end of the decade, most of the bars on that strip had turned to topless entertainment. The spread of topless dancing quickly altered popular conceptions of Dearborn, with the *Free Press* writing in 1969: "Until recently nothing much more than a main street shopping area for Dearbornites, the place has suddenly sprouted glitter and turned the reclusive, historic town into nothing less than a frantic nightly frolic of imported bare thighs, big name acts and wide-open double-clutching sounds." The same article speculated as to why Dearborn had seen this flourishing of topless bars, saying, "Orville Hubbard's town grabbed it because if there ever was a city waiting for something to come along and give it an identity, it's Dearborn." Some might object to this characterization of Dearborn as lacking an identity by noting that it was, in fact, world renowned throughout much of the twentieth century for being a bastion of white racism, with this history stretching from the racism and antisemitism of Henry Ford to beloved mayor Orville Hubbard, who led the fight against integration during the postwar era. On this front, at least, the rise of topless entertainment in Dearborn did not change much, with the same *Free Press* article reporting, "In Orville Hubbard's town, as the bar owners will tell you, Negro entertainment is not encouraged."[17]

If the rise of exotic dance in Dearborn did little to challenge Dearborn's racial order, it did serve to push back on the popular conception of suburbs as sexless and sedate. The seeming irony that, rather than the big city of Detroit, the suburb of Dearborn was at the center of adult entertainment in the region was not lost on contemporaneous commentators, with one *Free Press* article stating, "The real action is now where only months or so ago, no wise man would have expected it to go—the safe and sensible suburbs." In truth, the view of the suburbs as being safe, sensible, and sexless was largely a fiction. Adult entertainment had long been a mainstay in the suburbs of Detroit, even at times, as with the case of topless dancing in Dearborn, surpassing the big city in both the number of adult venues and the level of sexual explicitness on offer in those venues. As the same article said of this contrast between city and suburb, Dearborn's topless bars "mak[e] up a sort of Las Vegas side street and escape hatch for fun-hungry migrants from Detroit's nightlife ghost town." Contrary to popular imagination, then, while the major city of Detroit was at times known for its dreary, sexless nightlife, the suburb of Dearborn, by contrast, promised unfettered sexual entertainment.[18]

THE GREAT COVER-UP

The case against Tyra Lea LaRue and Theodore Manolakas wound its way through the courts, eventually appearing before Wayne County Circuit Court judge Joseph G. Rashid. In any number of ways, Rashid was exactly the wrong person for LaRue and Manolakas's chances. As one lawyer put it at the time, "If there was going to be a judge against sin, it would be Joe Rashid."[19] For one, Rashid was a prominent member of the Catholic community in Detroit, having formerly been president of the Detroit Council of Catholic Laymen, on the board of directors of the Detroit Guild of Catholic Lawyers, and a member of the executive board of the National Council of Catholic Men, all in addition to being a regular at St. Alphonsus Church in Dearborn.[20]

More centrally, Rashid was no stranger to the fight against pornography. In the mid-1950s, Rashid had been a Wayne County assistant prosecutor and, in the words of the *Detroit News*, "specialized in the prosecution of such [obscenity] cases." This meant that Rashid collaborated closely with the Detroit Police Department's Censor Bureau and groups like the Committee for Better Literature for Youth, whom he met with in 1956. In 1962, after becoming a judge, Rashid publicly warned parents of the dangers of obscene literature, calling on the "intelligent public" to lobby merchants to keep such reading material off store shelves.[21] In one editorial he penned that year, Rashid made clear what he thought of constitutional objections to censorship campaigns, writing, "While many people contend that suppression of obscenity violates our constitutional concepts of free speech and free press, community efforts directed to the elimination of such obscenity is no wise censorship, nor is it in any way a violation of the Constitution." He went on to compare the need to suppress obscene literature for children and the "mentally disturbed or sick adult" as being akin to the need to "suppress gambling paraphernalia, narcotics and guns."[22] In his public statements, Rashid also issued a grave warning as to the potential consequences of failing to act against pornography, couching his statement in terms that made clear the ways his religion was inextricably linked with his belief in the need for censorship. As he said, "Unless this is done we can look for a gradual weakening of the moral fibers of the community so that such things as the sanctity of marriage is destroyed and the fathers and mothers of the next generation throw basic morality and the Ten Commandments out the window."[23]

Rashid's anti-porn views were widely known, to the extent that, in late 1963, when a case involving an arrest over obscene literature was set to come up before him, the attorney representing defendant William Doerfler filed a motion to disqualify Rashid from hearing the case based on the judge's previous procensorship statements as well as his prominent membership in a number of Catholic groups that were allied with the NODL. Rashid denied the accusation that he could not be impartial in the case, telling the *Detroit News*, "I have absolutely no prejudice or bias as related to the subject matter. While I have spoken on the subject, I have at no time publicly said that any given publication does not comply with Michigan statutes." Rashid therefore dismissed the lawyer's motion, a decision that was upheld on appeal. Rashid subsequently ruled against Doerfler, affirming his obscenity conviction.[24]

In light of all this, it came as no surprise when, in June of 1971, Judge Rashid ruled against LaRue and Manolakas in their appeal of their indecency convictions. What was notable, though, was the breadth of his ruling, with Rashid condemning not only the defendants on trial but also seemingly all topless dancing—and indeed all adult entertainment. Crucially, he went beyond just ruling that topless dancing was indecent by also declaring that pasties and other forms of semi-topless dancing were illicit as well. As he said after handing down his decision, "In my opinion, pasties do not comply with the test of decency. What the hell, a pasty, a piece of adhesive tape, a Band-Aid? It's not adequate." He went on to declare that "the female mammary gland should be covered by the generally accepted standard of modesty." As was typical for anti-porn advocates, exactly what would constitute an acceptable standard for covering breasts was left unsaid by Rashid.[25]

Following this ruling, the initial comments by city officials seemed to indicate that the decision would not affect the state of topless entertainment in Detroit. Police inspector Russell Gallaway, who headed the Vice Squad, said that the police had stopped enforcing the pasties requirement at least a year prior to this ruling, believing that the city's indecent exposure law was unenforceable. As he said, "Most of the go-go girls don't use pasties and we don't believe we are empowered to do anything about it." William Doran, an attorney for the city assigned to matters related to the Detroit Police Department, at first suggested that topless bars would not be shut down as a result of Rashid's ruling, saying, "We are not attempting to enforce a topless ban or the use of pasties because the U.S. Supreme Court has ruled that the nude body is not in and of itself obscene."[26]

Just days later, though, the police and prosecutors reversed course, and a ban on topless dancing was put in place in Detroit. Police lieutenant Joseph Areeda, who had once headed the Obscenity Detail, announced the move, declaring that all female dancers in the city must "henceforth wear a brassiere of some sort" during performances and that "Rashid's ruling will be enforced to the letter." This meant that, in addition to topless itself being banned, the previous compromise use of pasties by dancers was no longer adequate either. Lieutenant Areeda promised that "any dancers without brassiere-type tops from now on will be cited," with potential penalties including a one-hundred-dollar fine or ninety-day jail sentence. The decision went into immediate effect, with the fifty-nine bars in Detroit offering up topless dancing at that time warned that violations would be prosecuted, though some bar owners vowed to appeal the ruling. Just days later, two dancers at the Rumpus Lounge on the city's east side were ticketed for indecent exposure after they went topless, while the bar's manager was ticketed for allowing "improper dancing" at the bar. Following the tickets, in subsequent performances at the bar that night, the dancers performed while wearing bras.[27]

Meanwhile, in the days following his ruling, Rashid became something of a minor celebrity in Detroit, and he boasted that he "had received fan mail which stacked three inches high."[28] Favorable local newspaper profiles of Rashid allowed him to respond to his critics and flesh out the rationale behind his stance against exposed flesh. Echoing the proclamations made countless times by the censorial minded, Rashid declared, "I don't consider myself a moralist. I don't look upon myself as a prude or a puritan." Rather, his ruling was, in his mind, a response to the "so-called new morality which dictates that all social restraints on sexual freedom must go." Though acknowledging that his ruling would have its detractors, he nevertheless stated his conviction that his beliefs were shared by most people, though in his view, "the voices they raise in objection aren't being heard."[29]

This invocation of a supposed silent majority of citizens opposed to pornography was a recurring rhetorical strategy used by anti-porn advocates during this period. The era's most influential anti-porn group, Citizens for Decent Literature, repeatedly drew on this notion, with one 1970 article in their newsletter stating, "How loudly does the 'silent majority' have to shout before 'somebody' listens? Far from remaining silent on the vital subject of smut control, the people *are* speaking out—and demanding action." In deploying this rhetorical strategy, anti-porn advocates appropriated a discursive formation that was newly ascendant in white racial politics of the era. Notions of a silent majority opposed to the supposed overreach of the civil rights movement had fueled grassroots conservative politics and helped elect Richard Nixon to the presidency. The deployment of this rhetoric by anti-porn advocates speaks not only to the overlap between the groups involved in the concurrent fights against both indecent media and racial integration but also to the way the discourse used in white racial politics came to infuse other arenas of American politics. Moreover, in invoking the idea of a silent majority opposed to pornography, activists could inflate notions of a consensus among "right-minded" citizens as to the need to censor pornographic material. Thus, Rashid could portray himself as merely being a lone voice empowered to speak for this silent moral majority.[30]

In reality, the exact opposite was more accurate. Just a few days after his ruling, a *Detroit Free Press* poll of its readers found 68.3 percent opposed to Rashid's ruling, with just 31.7 percent in support. Though the poll may have been unscientific (and one imagines that a similar poll by the more conservative-leaning

Detroit News would have given at least somewhat different results), it nevertheless speaks to the fact that Judge Rashid and his supporters in many ways bore more resemblance to a very vocal minority than they did a silent majority. The real silent majority were the citizens who either supported adult entertainment or were simply indifferent to it and unmoved by efforts to curtail its availability. This fits with a repeated trend in fights over pornography, as touched on in chapter 1. As Walter Kendrick writes, "Those who feel that no harm is being done are unlikely to form pressure groups in order to advance that view. Contentment and indifference are silent, while fear and outrage bellow; and in the pornography debate, hysteria on the part of a few has traditionally been given free rein by the obliviousness of the many." With many liberals uneasy about being too vocal in their defense of adult entertainment, the stage was set for those like Rashid to dominate the conversation by invoking the idea that they were simply speaking for the silent majority of people who agreed with their views. This, in turn, allowed Rashid to present himself as courageously giving voice to most of the city's citizens when there was little to indicate that most Detroiters agreed with him.[31]

In the days following Rashid's ruling and the subsequent effort by the city to ban topless dancing, the debate over the issue played out in local newspapers. Those in favor of the ban tended to celebrate the way it would uphold morals, while those opposed found the move to be a form of censorship that would hurt local businesses. At times, this debate was even waged between husband and wife. On the first night of the topless ban, John Kratsas, proprietor of the Sip 'n' Chat Bar, lamented, "My business is off 45 percent tonight. That judge is limiting business in Detroit bars." His wife, on the other hand, took a more favorable view of the ruling. As she said, "It's the greatest thing that could happen as far as I'm concerned as a woman. I think it will help business because now men can bring their wives." For Violet Kratsas, then, the rolling back of topless would make these bars an acceptable place for women to attend (at least women accompanied by their husbands).[32]

The notion of women going to see exotic dancing was treated as a mark of legitimacy on both sides of this debate. Along these lines, Ron Clark, owner of the topless bar Gold Diggers, boasted, "I get couples in here. They wouldn't come if there was anything raw or dirty or sickening about topless." The shared view, then, was that female customers would in some way legitimize bars featuring exotic dancing, firmly establishing them as decent and respectable establishments. This mirrored a trend in the world of adult cinema, wherein the late 1960s and early 1970s had seen producers and distributors actively court the "coveted couple or date market," which, it was thought, would lend respectability to adult film. Of course, such perspectives failed to account for the multiplicity of reasons—beyond merely accompanying their husbands—women might decide to attend a topless bar, including the potential pleasure they may have gotten from the experience.[33]

One line of argument often used by opponents of topless was a supposed concern for the dancers. For example, Robert L. Kincheloe, executive director of the Detroit Council of Churches, stated, "I personally am opposed to women being treated strictly as sex objects, things." As he went on to explain, "The topless scene certainly treated women as objects.... I am not opposed to nudity or sex. But I am opposed to women being treated as less than complete people." This opposition to topless was born out of Kincheloe's broader concern over what he called "the playboy philosophy which treats half of humanity as if they are not people." Of course, left out of this equation was the notion that a woman being paid to dance topless might still, in fact, be a complete person with her humanity intact. As Gayle Rubin writes, "While antiporn activists often claim to want to protect women in (and from) the sex industry, much of their analysis is based on condescension and contempt toward sex workers."[34]

In the debate over topless bars, the group that was quite often ignored entirely were those most directly affected by Rashid's ruling: the dancers themselves. The fifty-nine topless bars in Detroit employed hundreds of dancers who, according to Mike Sherwin, an agent for exotic dancers in the city, faced nearly 50 percent salary cuts as a result of the city's decision to crack down on topless, with dancers who normally made five or six dollars an hour set to see their wages cut to as little as three dollars an hour. As Sherwin said, "Several of the girls are leaving town. They're in the business for the money, and there's not as much money in dancing covered." For many dancers, the concern over what would happen to them due to the topless ban was acute. One agent for a number of dancers said, "Lots of girls will be going on welfare."[35]

Similar arguments were made by the sixteen exotic dancers who showed up outside the City-County Building on June 10, 1971, to protest the city's ban on topless. The demonstration was organized by Mrs. Gerry Hernandez, who told the *Detroit News*, "This is a financial rap to Detroit. There are more than 200 girls who work straight shifts at the city's 59 topless places who will be out of work. Instead of taxes we pay, we'll be forced on welfare and ADC [Aid to Dependent Children]. Most of us are married or divorced and have children to support. The city is denying us jobs." One protesting woman carried a sign in one hand that said, "The most beautiful legs on welfare," while in her other hand she pushed a baby carriage. News coverage of the rally was largely condescending in tone, with the *Detroit News* detailing the types of clothing worn

Figure 4.5. An exotic dancer performs in Detroit after Judge Rashid's ruling. *Detroit Free Press*, June 10, 1971.

by the protesting women and speculating that two of the women may not have been wearing bras. The *Free Press*, meanwhile, ran photos of women at the rally on page one but did not actually include an article covering the protest or quote any of the protesting dancers, instead only giving a brief caption to the photos that quoted an unnamed police officer present at the scene who joked, "I'm here to make sure they walk two abreast." Despite the sexist news coverage, the protest still drew attention to the harsh reality felt by these dancers in the wake of Detroit's ban on topless—a rather typical result of efforts to curb adult entertainment, with calls to protect female sex workers from their alleged exploitation as sexual objects frequently leading to worse pay and working conditions for these same workers.[36]

The drop in pay for dancers following the topless ban was the predictable outcome of a steep drop in patronage at topless bars in Detroit. One *Detroit News* reporter described how Rashid's decision had "brought a wake-like silence to many of Detroit's 59 go-go bars," with estimates of the decline in business ranging from 45 percent all the way up to 75 or 80 percent. Stories abounded of bar owners forced to lay off cooks, dancers, and door bouncers, and many bar owners pondered switching to live music or other entertainment formats to survive. As Johnny Nicholas, owner of the Blue Note Lounge, said, "Every place in the country has got it (topless) and they're just setting the city back. They talk about helping Detroit, but this is making it a dead town."[37]

While Detroit was becoming a "dead town" in the face of enforced bra wearing for exotic dancers, topless bars in neighboring Dearborn were flourishing. There Rashid's ruling went unenforced, and so "customers almost to the man had fled across the border to the more liberated climate of Dearborn." Reports of packed bars with lines out the door only further demonstrated the oddity of this neighboring suburb becoming a hub of adult entertainment while the city remained, both literally and figuratively, buttoned up. Commenting on the trend, Detroit bar owner John Kratsas said, "If Dearborn wasn't right across the street, maybe it wouldn't be so bad. But they charge the same for a drink there." Likewise, Hernandez, organizer of the protest by exotic dancers outside the City County Building, said, "I'm sure Mayor (Orville) Hubbard in Dearborn is sitting back and smiling at all the Detroit go-go patrons who now have to take their money to the suburbs."[38]

Meanwhile, a similar situation was occurring in the suburb of Warren, just north of Detroit, where bars offering topless dancing saw an increase in patronage following the city's decision. This was again the result of Detroiters heading out to the suburbs for adult entertainment, with one Warren dancer saying, "The only difference now is that our crowd is made up of a lot more Detroit people." Still, there was concern that too much attention to the flourishing topless industry in the suburbs would result in them, too, being targeted with a ban on topless. The *Detroit News* noted that the manager of one Warren bar pleaded with their reporter, saying, "Hey, don't say a thing about this place. We don't want to make waves. You start talking about our crowd and we're going to have to cover up, too." The same manager expressed fear that his revenue would drop by 75 percent if topless was banned in Warren, with the bar's dancers then looking at a 50 percent pay cut to their weekly salary of two hundred dollars.[39]

The flight of topless customers and their paying dollars to suburban bars fueled concerns that Detroit's already ailing economy would be materially hurt by the city's ban on topless. As the *Detroit News* reported, the main message of the protest outside the City County Building was "more revenue for Detroit, keep topless." In particular, fears abounded that barring topless would hurt Detroit's chances of attracting major conventions to the city. Just weeks prior to Judge Rashid's ruling, it had been reported that the American Bowling Congress's championship tournament in Detroit had brought in more than forty thousand visitors to the city, with those visitors pumping some $5 million into Detroit's economy with their spending. Of that spending, a not-insignificant portion of it went to the city's adult entertainment venues, with the manager of one downtown topless bar reporting of the impact of the bowling tournament patronage, "These guys spend money like it's going out of style." In mid-June, *Free Press* columnist Bob Talbert reported that Detroit had lost out on one major convention due to the national news coverage surrounding Rashid's decision and two other contemporaneous newsworthy local court rulings, one of which involved an Oakland County judge banning the Kurt Vonnegut book *Slaughterhouse-Five*. As Talbert wrote, the negative press surrounding these rulings "may have already cost Detroit a major, multi-million convention which would perk up the city's economy in 1974." Talbert reported that the head of a national manufacturing firm in New York told the firm's Detroit representative, "Forget those plans about our convention in Detroit in '74. If that's the way Detroit thinks, who needs it." The association of Detroit with censorship and puritanism, then, had seemingly already damaged the city's national reputation alongside its economic prospects.[40]

TOPLESS STRIKES BACK

In the weeks and months following Judge Rashid's June 1971 decision, Detroit bar owners and their attorneys developed rhetorical strategies designed to win over public sentiment on the issue of topless. Sometimes this meant emphasizing topless as a form of speech that was worthy of the same protections as other artistic forms. Connected to this was the argument, long used by defenders of adult entertainment, that there is a blurry line between pornography and art, with one attorney for the bar owners stating, "The next time the African Ballet comes to Detroit I can see no reason why these women won't be arrested. They dance bare-breasted without even pasties." Likewise, one article posed the question, "Is topless dancing on bar stages different than the nude dancing with exotic props allowed in a Detroit burlesque house? Is it different than the topless dancing of visiting African troupes barebreasted, or the brief but total nudity of [the musical] *Hair* at the Vest Pocket Theater in Detroit?" Though the line between topless dancing at a bar versus in an African ballet or burlesque house may have been blurry, the real distinction was perhaps best summed up by burlesque producer Mike Todd, who stated, "At $4.40 a ticket, it's art; for a buck, it's striptease." For this reason, the rhetorical defense of the topless industry based on arguments about the blurry line between different forms of topless or exotic dancing exposed a crucial aspect of nearly all censorship efforts, which is that they are almost never just about the narrowly defined object being censored. In other words, it was the cheap price and the venue of a bar that made the dancing indecent, not just the dance itself.[41]

Even as owners of topless bars argued that there was little to distinguish dancing at their establishments from more artistic and culturally accepted forms of dance, they also sought to distance themselves from a lower (in every sense of the word) form of exotic dance: bottomless. As one bar owner said, "What they should be doing is fighting against bottomless, keeping that out of Detroit. I'd spend the last penny I've got to keep bottomless dancing out." At this point bottomless was more theory than practice in the region, and there is little to suggest that bottomless dancing had actually occurred in any of the city's bars. Still, the rhetorical strategy of distinguishing topless as respectable in contrast to the indecency of bottomless went hand in hand with efforts to tie it to higher, more culturally accepted art forms.[42]

Another rhetorical device used by owners of topless bars was to emphasize the economic effects of the topless ban. This went beyond just stories regarding the economic woes of bar owners seeing their revenues drop precipitously. Rather, in their public comments, bar owners stressed the loss of jobs and reduced pay for employees, with one bar owner warning that in the wake of Rashid's ruling, "Lots of girls will be going on welfare." Beyond the effect on workers, bar owners also emphasized the size and economic importance of the topless dancing industry in Detroit, with the *Free Press* noting, "Some observers call [topless] the biggest entertainment business in Detroit." Meanwhile, a bartender at the Town Talk bar stated, "I think the city is nuts, killing a million dollar a year industry and handing it over to Dearborn and any other city that wants it." In the years to come, supporters of topless would increasingly deploy this line of argument, with the (likely overstated) claims as to the size of the industry growing exponentially over time.[43]

Meanwhile, owners of topless bars also organized to fight back in the courts against the city's ban on topless. Thirty-two bar owners chipped in one hundred dollars each to hire attorney Casey Ambrose, who sought to coordinate the attack on the topless ban. They received a victory just weeks after Judge Rashid's ruling when circuit court judge Thomas Roumell issued a temporary restraining order barring the city from enforcing its ban on topless, believing that Judge Rashid's ruling might only apply to the Tyra Lea LaRue case, rather than all topless dancing. The *Detroit News* subsequently reported, "Lifting of the topless go-go ban apparently cheered Detroit officials, who said they feared the ban would hurt the city's convention business." Though few city officials wanted to go on the record in support of topless, many understood the broader economic implications of the topless ban. As Tom Delisle, an aide to Detroit mayor Roman Gribbs, said at the time, "Can you imagine a group of conventioneers coming to town, having a couple of drinks and then heading out for a hot time at the public library?"[44]

Days later, though, the case was remanded back to Judge Rashid, who quickly affirmed his earlier decision, putting the ban on topless back in place. Within weeks, the owners of topless bars filed a new lawsuit attacking the constitutionality of the ordinance being used by the city to prohibit topless dancing. The ordinance in question, passed in 1954, read: "No person shall make any indecent exposure of his or her person in the streets, lanes, alleys, markets, or public places of the city." The attorney representing Detroit's bar owners, Ivan Barris, argued that the ordinance was "unconstitutionally vague and uncertain" and thus violated the Fourteenth Amendment. In particular, Barris contended that "exposure of female mammary glands does not constitute indecent exposure."[45]

Moreover, Barris made the argument that the ordinance had never been intended to apply to bars. As he said, "We feel the legislative intent of this ordinance is aimed not at so-called topless go-go dancing, but rather is aimed at sexual deviates who might expose themselves in public places," similarly saying elsewhere that the ordinance was meant to apply only to "sexual deviates and perverts who exposed themselves in public places." By invoking the notion of "sexual deviates and perverts," Barris sought to distance topless bars from the imagined specter of the homosexual or pedophile terrorizing public places through his indecent behavior. More centrally for legal purposes, Barris argued that the "public places" referred to in the city ordinance did not apply to bars. As he said, "A liquor bar is not a public place—not public in the sense of a park or a street. Only certain individuals go into a bar and they have to be over 21."[46]

In the end, this argument won the day. After bar owners won a temporary stay against the enforcement of Judge Rashid's ruling in July of 1971, their case finally went up before the Michigan Court of Appeals a year later. The court ruled against the city, overturning the convictions of LaRue and Manolakas. As its justification, the court did not address any free speech questions and did not rule on whether topless dancing fell under the heading of "indecent exposure." Instead, the court based their ruling on the notion that a bar does not count as "a 'public place' within the meaning of the ordinance." Thus, the notion of topless bars as "private" places, or at least not "public" in the sense defined by the indecent exposure ordinance, meant that they were exempt from prosecution under that particular law. Topless had won the day. Predictably, the victory would prove short lived.[47]

OF FINGERPRINTS, BOTTOMLESS, AND EXOTIC DANCE

As discussed in detail in chapter 5, over the course of 1972, the Detroit City Council focused its attention on the drafting of legislation designed to curb the spread of adult businesses, including adult movie theaters and bookstores alongside nude modeling studios and massage parlors. By contrast, topless bars were seen as more of a back-burner issue. In light of the new form of hard-core pornography available on movie theater screens in Detroit, exotic dancing, even in topless form, was evidently seen as relatively tame and old hat by comparison. And so, whereas thousands of letters streamed into the offices of city officials regarding adult movie theaters and bookstores, anti-porn activists were comparatively muted when it came to topless bars. No council members, even the most anti-porn-leaning among them, made topless dancing a major issue in 1972, and neither did Mayor Gribbs, who that year had made enacting new and effective anti-porn legislation a top priority of his administration.

All that, however, is not to say that city officials were entirely inactive when it came to the issue of topless bars. In the fall of 1972, the mayor's office unveiled a slate of new anti-porn ordinances, which soon after were passed by the city council and signed into law. This included new legislation requiring 51 percent of nearby residents to give their approval to any new adult business. Newspaper coverage highlighted the effect this would have on adult bookstores and movie theaters, which had been the primary focus of the mayor's office in drafting the legislation. Also regulated under this particular ordinance, though, was the newly formed category of "class D cabarets," defined as "a Cabaret which features topless dancers, go-go dancers, exotic dancers, strippers, mail [sic] or female impersonators, or similar entertainers." Still, this ordinance only applied to businesses trying to open after the new law had been passed, meaning the (by then) roughly ninety existing topless bars in the city were unaffected.[48]

Other, less heralded provisions of the law more directly affected existing topless bars. Namely, the ordinance sought to more closely regulate topless dancers themselves through two major legal changes. The first required that all dancers receive a "group 'D' entertainer's identification card from the Detroit Police Department." This new identification requirement meant that all dancers had to go to a police station to be fingerprinted, questioned, and undergo a criminal background check, with "a record or conviction for an offense involving gambling, narcotics, prostitution, pandering or any other offense involving moral turpitude" leading to the police's refusal to grant the identification card. The second major change was in dictating the roles of dancers before and after their acts by barring any dancer from "perform[ing] a secondary service such as selling cigarettes, photographing patrons, waiting tables, bartending or hat checking."[49]

These provisions in the new law were specifically a reaction to the fear that dancers might also act as prostitutes. Animating this fear was the specter of "B-girls," the nickname given to female bar employees who interacted with male customers to entice them into buying expensive drinks, with such behavior, it was thought, potentially leading to prostitution. The specific provision against dancers acting as bartenders or waitresses had been a point of contention back in 1959, when Censor Bureau chief Melville Bullach instructed exotic dancers in the city "that he would not tolerate table-hopping and drink-hustling by strippers." Some thirteen years later, Bullach's informal policy was passed into law, with fears of prostitution again driving this regulatory approach. As Lieutenant Leo Martin, head of the Detroit Police Department's Liquor License section, said at the time of the new ordinance's enactment, "We're not saying all these girls are prostitutes. We're not down on go-go girls, don't get us wrong. But we don't want B-girls dancing in Detroit." Still, even as the ordinance was supposedly designed to halt prostitution among exotic dancers, more than a few viewed the new provisions as merely the newest way to harass and attack those working in adult entertainment. Numerous dancers and bar owners argued that the real aim of the law was "to kill go-go" and "close down all go-go bars."[50]

The aspects of the law regulating the work of exotic dancers would prove controversial. The restraint on dancers working as bartenders or waitresses between sets particularly hurt given that the industry had long relied on interaction between dancers and customers to stimulate business and generate tips for the dancers. Dancer Kay Meloche claimed the new ordinance would have a counterintuitive effect, saying, "We all have our regular customers who come just to see us dance. But now they're not coming back. We can't talk to them or dance for them. This is going to drive some girls into prostitution, I'm convinced." Others connected the economic hit felt by dancers to the economic hit the city would feel if trends continued. Larry Zoline, manager of Gold Diggers, tied the industry to the lucrative convention trade for the city, noting that the recent Society of Automotive Engineers had been a flop for his bar, saying, "The guys came in and wanted to enjoy themselves and they couldn't. They asked

Figure 4.6. A dancer employed at the Waterland Lounge after getting fingerprinted at police headquarters. *Detroit Free Press*, November 29, 1972.

'Why can't the girls talk to us.' They left. This is going to hurt the city. They're not going to come here for conventions." Numerous newspaper articles in the months following the law cataloged the drop in business at topless bars. At least one dancer noted that Dearborn topless bars were prospering in the face of the misfortune of Detroit's topless industry, saying, "In Dearborn, just a few blocks away, it's wide open. They sit with customers, they go bottomless."[51]

The fingerprinting and identification card requirement particularly drew the ire of dancers, with dancer Diane Norris saying of the experience, "My daughter (aged 7) overheard me saying I had to come down and be fingerprinted and she said: 'What's the matter, Mommy, did you steal something?' I hope she doesn't talk about it at show and tell." Likewise, another dancer said, "I don't like coming down here and being fingerprinted. I haven't even committed a crime. It takes away your dignity." In reality, the inconvenience and loss of dignity that came from having to go to the police station to get fingerprinted were not ancillary by-products of the law but its direct purpose. The deliberate inconvenience of this requirement provided another hurdle for dancers to deal with and further stigmatized their work. It was also another way police could exert their power over workers in the adult entertainment industry. In addition to questioning dancers, the *Free Press* noted that the program was "providing police officers with some pleasant afternoon diversion," quoting one unnamed police officer as saying, "Hey, catch that stunning blond over there!"[52]

Even so, at least one dancer embraced the law as a way of cleaning up the industry. As Annette Ellis said, "At first I didn't like it, but now, I think it's good. This benefits us all by screening the hookers and addicts out of the business. I don't want to work with them."[53] Not unlike distinguishing topless from the indecency of bottomless, by denigrating a select few "bad apples" among exotic dancers, Ellis and many others in the industry sought to lend themselves a degree of respectability. Ironically, this same logic was used by belly dancers in Detroit to fight the new ordinance and distance themselves from topless dancing. Crucially, the new law required belly dancers to register with the city the same as topless dancers. Not long after the ordinance was passed, belly dancers began to lodge complaints at being "classified with strippers, go-go dancers and impersonators." In their view, whereas belly dancing was centuries old and required skill, go-go dancing had barely been around a decade and was seemingly for the talentless. Such distinctions were seen as real and substantial among members of the city council. As one article said, "Councilmen David Eberhard, a Lutheran minister, said his only objections were to lewd dancing. And belly dancing, he added, does not fall in that category. Belly dancing is a cultural activity which is proper and even popular at some ethnic festivals, he said."[54] Another article said of one belly dancing venue in particular, "Council members all said they had no intention [of] putting a 'high class' place like The Cedars out of business."[55]

The issue came down to the particular language used in the ordinance—specifically its mention of "exotic" dancing. As Councilman Anthony Wierzbicki explained, "We hadn't intended to get into this particular field (belly dancing). Exotic is kind of a vague term. When we said exotic, I don't think we meant foreign types of dancing. I think it was intended to cover strippers and go-go dancers." Confusion over what exactly the council members had voted for was surprisingly prevalent. Councilman Nicholas Hood admitted that he had no knowledge of any of the regulations against topless dancing when he voted for the larger package of anti-obscenity ordinances. As he said, "The regulation against the girls was in the fine print. We didn't realize that they were being regulated too. We were after the Adult Bookstores, peep-movies and massage parlors." Beyond indicating the fact that he apparently had not fully read the bill he voted for, Hood's statement is indicative of the relatively low priority topless bars tended to be given by city officials, with other forms of adult businesses seen as more threatening to the social order. In large part because of this, in early 1973, there were signs that many on the city council were open to fully repealing the new provisions regulating exotic dance in the city.[56]

Even as debate raged over these new regulations on exotic dancing, a new form of indecent dance emerged in earnest: bottomless. In early 1973, in the suburb of Inkster at the western end of the Michigan Avenue "strip" of topless bars, there appeared the region's first confirmed sightings of bottomless dancing. As the *Free Press* explained in an April 25 article, bottomless in Inkster had become a regular attraction "except when a suspicious-looking stranger walks through the door." When a bar owner felt confident no police officers were in attendance, G-strings were removed and fully nude dancing reigned. As the same article reported, "Parking lots are routinely jammed at Inkster's three bottomless bars on Michigan Ave., and on a recent Friday night, there were long waiting lines at the door. Topless bar owners on Detroit's Michigan Ave. glumly say their business is off up to 50 percent." The same day the *Free Press* published its story on bottomless in Inkster, Mayor Gribbs sent a letter to the city attorney's office stating, "In view of recent publicity concerning the influx of bottomless dancing in Wayne County and its potential introduction into the city, I am directing you to immediately review the City Ordinances and make the necessary amendments for my submission to Common Council prohibiting such dancing in the city of Detroit." On April 27, just two days after the *Free Press* first reported on bottomless in Inkster, Gribbs sent the city council a series of ordinances designed to prevent the spread of bottomless into Detroit. Even as Gribbs was seeking to strengthen the city's laws against exotic dancing, though, the city council was thinking about loosening them. The same day that Gribbs sent them his anti-bottomless ordinances, the city council also took up a proposal to revoke the requirement that exotic dancers be fingerprinted and licensed, with a majority of council members tentatively indicating support for the repeal. This set up a clash between the mayor and the city council over what to do about exotic dance in Detroit.[57]

In a press release upon the unveiling of his new anti-bottomless proposals, Gribbs stated, "We don't need it [bottomless dancing] in Detroit and we don't want it. I believe that the people of our City have made it very clear that this offends the public morality. I personally think it is degrading to women and insulting to basic human dignity." Gribbs's statement was indicative of the type of rhetoric he and fellow anti–topless dancing advocates often deployed against exotic dancing. In emphasizing morality and the protection of women, Gribbs attacked the industry by emphasizing the continuities with other decency-based anti-obscenity campaigns. And, when it came to the issue of bottomless, Gribbs met little resistance to his proposals. Even Carl Ranno, attorney for the bar owners, indicated to the city council that "bar owners would agree to a ban on bottomless dancing, providing the language of the proposed ordinance was made more exact." If there were many issues of contention between the various parties involved in the fight over exotic dancing in Detroit proper, seemingly the one point of agreement was that bottomless dancing was a line that dare not be crossed.[58]

Before long, though, it was revealed that Gribbs's proposals went beyond just banning bottomless dancing. On the chopping block as well were simulated performances of sex acts and, as it turned out, all topless dancing. The surprise announcement was delivered by Philip Tannian, one of Gribbs's top aides, in mid-May of 1973, when he disclosed that the administration was moving not only against bottomless but against topless as well. The mayor's office proposed to respond to the 1972 ruling by the Michigan Court of Appeals by adding bars and cabarets to the list of places where indecent exposure was banned under existing city law. The industry immediately recognized the implications of the plan, with attorney Carl Ranno saying, "This is not just a matter of writing tickets. This becomes a matter of putting an industry right out of the city."[59]

Unsurprisingly, in the face of all this, the topless industry in Detroit mounted a multipronged campaign to fight back against its proposed extinction. Perhaps the most visible part of these efforts was a letter-writing campaign directed at Gribbs. Though details of how this campaign was waged remain murky, it appears that flyers were handed out, likely at bars themselves, with individuals asked to sign their name and mail the flyer to Gribbs at city hall. Roughly two thousand of these can be found in the archived papers of Gribbs—exponentially more than ever wrote to the city in support of any other form of adult entertainment, though that number likely inflates the actual number of individual letter writers. Given that letter writers were not asked to give their address, it is nearly impossible to verify that each person signed their own name and that they only signed a name to one flyer. We can, for instance, fairly assume that the person who signed one flyer as "Mayor Roman Gribbs" was not, in fact, Mayor Roman Gribbs. Still, even if the exact total number of letters is inflated, the campaign does speak to the widespread support the industry had in Detroit. This fact was also indicated by *Free Press* polls on this issue, with one poll in May of 1973 finding that 61.7 percent of readers agreed with the notion that topless dancing is not obscene and does not harm citizens. Amazingly enough, a *Free Press* poll from a month prior had even found that a majority of readers, 57 percent, believed the much-maligned bottomless dancing should also be permitted in the city.[60]

The flyer itself also speaks to a newly developed rhetorical strategy used by the industry. Namely, while Gribbs was speaking of the immorality of topless, the industry was hitting back by focusing on the economics of topless. The flyer provides six facts about the industry, mostly focusing on the economic size of topless go-go in Detroit. It reads:

> Fact: Gross sales are in excess of 12 million per year.
> Fact: Staff employees earn between 3 and 4 million per year.
> Fact: Entertainers earn an estimated 1.7 million per year.
> Fact: Topless go-go has been in the city for 7 years can the city of Detroit justify new laws to ban it now.
> Fact: U of M survey finds that each dollar spent is respent in the economy 17 times resultin[g] in a potential 200+million added to the Detroit economy.
> Fact: 4% state sales tax is divided up the following way, 2% goes directly to education, ½ of the balance of 2% goes into the city of Detroit treasury........ who benefits???????????

Though the figures regarding the size of the industry are likely exaggerated—the numbers often varied widely when industry advocates gave interviews to the press—their deployment is indicative of the broader strategy used by the topless industry. Rather than battling the city on questions of morality and decency, supporters of topless mounted an argument about the economic impact of the industry on the city, in this case by giving statistics on the net earnings of the industry, the number of employees and their pay, and the industry's contributions to the city's tax revenue.[61]

These arguments were at the heart of the complaints leveled at the city by Sonny Clark, manager of the National Burlesk, Detroit's last remaining burlesque theater, in 1973. The city's newly proposed indecent exposure ordinance was set to affect the National Burlesk just the same as topless bars, and in comments to the *Detroit News*, Clark spoke out against the proposal: "It's all pretty ridiculous. This town's already dead. What are they trying to do, bury it?" He went on to explain that, in his view, "banning bottomless or topless dancing would be the final blow to the city's dwindling night life," and he unfavorably compared Detroit's live entertainment options to those offered in New York City and San Francisco. Echoing the economic arguments being pushed by bar owners, Clark went on to say, "As it is, it's a wonder we get any conventioneers. We get maybe 60 or 70 people a night. They just don't want to come downtown anymore."[62]

This type of economic argument could be particularly effective in the Detroit of the early 1970s, where the flight of businesses from the city to the suburbs had not gone unnoticed. Losing the patronage of topless bars to the suburbs was a particularly acute fear given that Detroit's more permissive neighbors had often prospered from the city's relative prudishness. More than one supporter of topless made the connection between what the Gribbs administration was proposing now and the temporary ban on topless following Judge Rashid's ruling. As one article said, "Carl Ranno, an attorney for the bars, predicted financial disaster in event of a ban, saying income dropped drastically during the last ban in June, 1971." Meanwhile, dancer Nora McKiddie similarly recalled the impact of Rashid's ruling, saying, "All the business just went to Dearborn. It was a bleak period for Detroit bars. Is the city trying to drive an industry right out of Detroit and into the suburbs once again?"[63]

These arguments were made forcefully by industry advocates at public hearings held by the city council in May of 1973. There, attorney Carl Ranno told the city council that a ban on topless "would jeopardize a $6 million investment in the bars, $3 million in wages to bar workers and $13 million in liquor sales." He further emphasized that the move would hurt the city's convention business. Meanwhile, dancer Roberta Chilson also spoke before the city council, forcefully arguing against those opposed to topless dancing in saying, "I do not believe my work is in any way obscene. I do not think the human body is obscene, but I know some people may find it so, even to the extent of finding obscenity in the sight of a mother nursing her baby. This sort of attitude is not morality—it is sickness." Beyond tying the issue to a broader societal disgust and urge to regulate women's bodies, Chilson went on to argue specifically about the impact a ban on topless would have on dancers like her. As she said, "I ask the city not to take our livelihoods away. Our performances are not obscene, and we will not, by dancing, harm any of this city's citizens. . . . I dance topless to support my child and my mother. I think of how obscene it would be not to be able to feed my child."[64]

The effectiveness of the industry's economic arguments meant that supporters of the topless ban were forced to respond. Mayor Gribbs's aide Philip

Tannian specifically expressed his doubt "that customers in Detroit would flee to more liberal minded communities, such as Inkster." He also responded to the economic arguments in favor of topless in saying, "We did not make the (anti-topless) decision on the basis of economics but on the basis of human dignity." This statement tried to shift the conversation away from the economic impact a topless ban would have on the city to more traditional morality-based grounds for regulating adult entertainment. However, this attempted pivot met with limited success in the public arena. Indeed, the triumph of the exotic dance industry in setting the terms of the debate is indicated by the words of Councilman Hood, who, when pressed on whether he wanted to see topless dancing banned, stated, "Oh, I don't know about that. I don't want to be in favor of restraint of trade."[65]

ORGANIZED GO-GO LABOR

The efficacy of these economic arguments ultimately led organized labor to take an interest in the fight over topless dancing in Detroit. In particular, Myra Wolfgang, secretary-treasurer of the Hotel and Restaurant Employees Union Local 705, became involved in debates over the fate of exotic dancing in the city in 1973. Wolfgang was at the tail end of an incredibly successful career as a labor organizer, with the *Detroit News* having once called her "the most effective leader for the working poor in Michigan." In the world of go-go dancing, while others saw either immorality or big business, Wolfgang saw exploitative labor practices that needed rectifying.[66]

This was not the first time Wolfgang had been involved in a battle over adult entertainment in Detroit. Over the course of 1963 and 1964, she led a highly publicized fight against the newly opened Playboy Club. The club, the eighth in the chain of Hugh Hefner–endorsed entertainment and eatery venues, was in the practice of not paying its "bunnies" a salary, with waitresses instead relying entirely on tips for their pay. Wolfgang organized pickets outside the Playboy Club that lasted some seven and a half months, the longest in Local 705's history (see fig. 4.7).[67] As part of her campaign, Wolfgang made explicit arguments about what she saw as the immorality of the Playboy Club. When protesting against the Michigan Liquor Control Commission's decision to give a liquor license to the restaurant, she commented that the commission "should not be used by those who would bring Sodom and Gomorrah to Detroit," further calling the club "licensed immorality."[68] Nevertheless, these concerns about morality were always linked with the club's labor practices, with Wolfgang saying, "I'm not opposed to sex. I'm sure it's here to stay. But I do think every waitress should receive a wage, not just tips alone." Eventually, the pickets succeeded,

Figure 4.7. A member of the Hotel and Restaurant Workers Union Local 705 protests the Playboy Club in Detroit. *Detroit Free Press*, October 30, 1963.

and on August 13, 1964, the "union shop" card went up in the Playboy Club, and wages were guaranteed to workers.[69]

Nearly a decade later, the battle over the fate of go-go and topless in Detroit similarly drew Wolfgang's attention, though the rhetoric she now deployed was decidedly different from the moralizing language she had used in the fight over the Playboy Club. Wolfgang focused on the plight of dancers, hoping to unionize them or, at the very least, improve labor practices among topless bars. This meant that she had something of an uneasy relationship with the city's efforts to regulate exotic dancing. She did agree with the mayor and city council on one point—the ordinance prohibiting dancers from acting as waitresses or in other support jobs. When a judge upheld that part of the ordinance, Wolfgang approved of the decision, saying, "A waitress is a waitress and an entertainer is an entertainer." As one article said of her reaction, "Mrs. Wolfgang said she was not concerned about the moral aspects of the ruling. She approves it because the dancers were taking work away from union waitresses." Whereas morality-based rhetoric had been an explicit part of her campaign against the Playboy Club, here she focused exclusively on labor issues.[70]

In May of 1973, when the city council convened to discuss a variety of issues surrounding exotic dancing in Detroit, Wolfgang was there to lend her support in the interests of dancers. Again, she sought to distance her views from issues of morality, saying, "I am not taking a moral stance on the question. The question of morality to me is the immorality of the exploitation of human beings." In regard to the controversial fingerprinting and identification card requirement, Wolfgang was strongly against the measure, arguing that the male customers should be fingerprinted rather than the dancers. As she said, "They (men) are the ones soliciting, and the dancers, I assure you, would be glad to have their unwelcome advances curbed." This was in keeping with her perspective on exotic dance, wherein she sought primarily to defend the rights of female workers—in this case to not be forced to be fingerprinted and register with the police.[71]

While appearing before the city council, Wolfgang also fought against a Detroit law that required all dancers to gain employment via a booking agency rather than directly with the bars themselves. In her view this "denied dancers the right to get their own jobs, and also denies them rights and benefits obtained by other employees such as workmen's compensation." On May 29, Mayor Gribbs met with Wolfgang on the matter, after which he expressed to aides that "he would now like to have language drafted he can submit to Council making the booking agent section in regard to bar entertainers merely permissive rather than an absolute requirement." It is not entirely clear what came of this in the end, as these booking agencies would continue to dominate the industry in Detroit in subsequent years.[72]

Ultimately, efforts to unionize dancers in Detroit died down, as did organized labor's interest in Detroit's topless battle. Still, Wolfgang's involvement in the matter highlighted important issues regarding exotic dance in the city. The battle over the fate of topless in Detroit quite often pitted the mayor, the city council, and the police against bar owners, with the actual dancers quite often forgotten in the proceedings. Though reconstructing the exact working conditions for exotic dancers at the time may be impossible, anecdotal evidence points to real problems for dancers in the industry. Stories abound of dancers being threatened with termination if they did not go topless or bottomless or facing repeated harassment from customers without any intervention from bar owners. There were also bar owners or booking agents who took exorbitant cuts from the money supposedly being made by the dancers themselves. Opponents of the industry often used these stories as backing for new laws designed to regulate and even stamp out exotic dancing in Detroit. In reality, problems with labor practices were greatly exacerbated by these anti-obscenity crusaders. As Gayle Rubin writes, "The underlying criminality of sex-oriented businesses ... renders sex workers more vulnerable to exploitation and bad working conditions. If sex commerce were legal, sex workers would be more able to organize and agitate for higher pay, better conditions, greater control, and less stigma." Though it would be a mistake to place topless dancing neatly in the same category as prostitution, society's reoccurring demonization of all forms of sexual commerce outside the bounds of marriage meant that dancers in Detroit were vulnerable to the same types of anti-vice and anti-obscenity crusades long weathered by other types of sex workers. If Wolfgang's championing of exotic dancers was short lived, it nevertheless was a moment of possibility that saw the rights of sex workers defended rather than sex workers being made mere passive objects subject to the whims of bar owners and the regulatory decisions of city officials, the police, and judges.[73]

TOPLESS GO-GO GOES ON AND ON

In May of 1973, the city council voted on three ordinances related to exotic dance, with the results something of a mixed bag for both supporters and detractors. Unsurprisingly, a ban on bottomless dancing passed easily. More controversially, the council voted to repeal the requirement for exotic dancers to get an identification card from the police. On June 4, Gribbs sent a letter to the council informing them of his decision to veto their repeal and keep in place the fingerprint and identification card requirement. He did so at the behest of the police department, which had sent a memo detailing how infractions at cabarets in the city had been sharply down since the law's enactment. Ultimately the council proved unable to overturn Gribbs's veto.[74]

Most significantly, the city council voted to amend the indecent exposure ordinance to apply to bars and cabarets and not just "public places" in the city. Crucially, though, the city council left it up to the courts to decide whether topless dancing in bars constituted indecent exposure. In other words, bars and nightclubs were now legally rendered places in which indecent exposure could occur, but the courts would have to decide whether topless dancing actually constituted indecent exposure. In this way, the city council avoided having to directly ban topless dancing themselves by instead punting the decision to judges while simultaneously appeasing anti-porn advocates wanting to see the city council to take action.[75]

Indicating how the economic arguments deployed by the owners of topless bars had come to dominate the debate, in reporting on the council's actions, the *Free Press* wrote, "In passing a new indecent exposure ordinance last week, the Common Council may have destroyed one of Detroit's few multimillion dollar entertainment industries—topless go-go dancing." In the face of continuing pressure from those criticizing the city council and the mayor for the economic effect of their war against topless, Gribbs issued a statement that read, "It is very questionable whether bars in Detroit will lose any appreciable amounts of money by complying with the law. Nevertheless, the question of profit and loss by itself cannot be a deciding factor in the law-making process. It is up to the mayor and the Common Council to pass such ordinances as will benefit the public health, safety, and welfare. This is what has been done." Even as Gribbs tried to shift the conversation back toward morality, the fact that he felt it necessary to respond to the point regarding the size of the industry speaks to the way this economic argument had gained real traction locally.[76]

Following the ordinance's passing, all indications were that the days of topless dancing in Detroit were numbered. However, just one day before the ordinance was set to go into effect, a major flaw in the mayor and city council's approach came to light. Namely, as part of the zoning ordinance targeting adult entertainment passed back in October of 1972, the city had included "topless dancers" as part of the definition for class D cabarets that were regulated under the law, a fact that made it dicey for the city to now legally ban such activity. As Maureen P. Reilly, an attorney for the city, put it, "We can't charge someone for doing what we've given them a license to do." The irony, then, was that an ordinance that had been intended to halt the spread of adult entertainment in the city was now preventing the out-and-out extinction of topless bars. And so, topless in Detroit was given a last-minute reprieve, leaving the mayor's office, the driving force behind the law, looking foolish and clumsy.[77]

Gribbs immediately proposed an amendment to the previous year's ordinance to remove the reference to "topless dancers" from the definition of class D cabarets. However, the city council had evidently seen enough and so tabled the matter. The *Detroit News* noted that the council was "disturbed at the flood of hearings and discussions it has had to schedule on a whole series of cabaret ordinances," while the *Free Press* wrote, "Councilmen appear to be weary of the long hassle over topless, bottomless and belly dancing. And they are miffed by some of Mayor Gribbs's actions in the matter." Council president Mel Ravitz, in denying Gribbs's request for further action to clarify the ordinance licensing class D cabarets, stated, "I just can't consider this (topless) issue as one of the high-priority matters. I think we have done what is right and reasonable to ban bottomless. I think we should leave it at that." And so, despite the wishes of the mayor, the city council largely put aside the issue of topless, moving on to some of the city's more pressing concerns.[78]

TOPLESS SUBURBS

As noted previously, the suburbs were often more permissive than Detroit proper when it came to exotic dancing. The suburb of Inkster is illustrative in this regard, as it had inaugurated the bottomless era in the region in early 1973 when dancers went fully nude at three bars located along Michigan Avenue in Inkster. After newspaper reports revealed the bottomless practices of these bars, police arrested fourteen dancers in May of that year, charging them with indecent exposure. Outside the trial location, half a dozen women protested against bottomless dancing, with one protester saying, "The moral fiber of our city is being undermined, and we certainly don't need that." Reflecting the fear that bottomless would come to define Inkster, one sign read, "Inkster is not sin city."[79]

Yet bottomless continued, as did arrests. In July of 1974, four women were arrested for indecent exposure after dancing bottomless at the Nite Lite Lounge, one of the three Inkster bars that had initially inaugurated bottomless. In fact, from 1973 to 1975, reportedly over 150 arrests were made at two Inkster bars alone. The wave of arrests did not amount to much, though, especially since they gummed up the works of the judicial system, with one judge lambasting the Inkster police for the mass arrests. Still, the police harassment and arrests continued. In 1976, two police officers were suspended after they claimed they had acted on orders to harass the Nite Lite Lounge out of business, a claim that was denied by Inkster's chief of police, who said the officers' statement showed "a flagrant lack of loyalty."[80]

A constant throughout these proceedings was a recognition of the political problem nude dancing posed for Inkster. On the one hand, the outcry from anti-porn advocates over the preponderance of exotic dancing in Inkster made inaction a risky political decision for elected officials. On the other hand, outlawing exotic dancing came with its own set of problems, even putting aside the legal questions surrounding the constitutionality of banning topless and bottomless. In particular, the political calculus was complicated by the fact that John Hamilton, the owner of two topless bars and a restaurant in Inkster, was estimated to be either the first- or second-largest employer in town.[81] City officials had to strike a balance between adequately responding to citizens' complaints against exotic dancing while not actually driving out a major employer in the local economy. Still, no politician wanted to be too closely associated with adult entertainment. When one exotic dancer said to the press that Inkster mayor Edward Bivens Jr. had been in the topless bar she worked at, Bivens was forced to clarify that he had merely "been in and out for a few minutes during a civic dinner."[82]

A similar story played out in Highland Park, the suburb situated within the city boundaries of Detroit. There, a controversy erupted after it was reported in 1975 that Highland Park mayor Robert Blackwell went to the Tender Trap, a topless bar, nearly every day for lunch and was, in fact, on a first-name basis with the dancers. Unlike Mayor Bivens of Inkster, though, Blackwell did not shy away from the association and indeed was often linked with adult entertainment in the city. In addition to frequenting the Tender Trap, Blackwell had also attended the grand opening of a nude modeling studio, the Blue Orchid, where he reportedly "personally painted one of the nude employees." Another time, Blackwell took a group of reporters to see the adult film *The Devil in Miss Jones* (1973) at Highland Park's Krim Theater. In fact, at least in part due to Blackwell's liberal stance, Highland Park was, by the mid-1970s, something of a haven for adult businesses, with the area often referred to in the press as "Smut City" and "Sin City."[83]

In 1975, Mayor Blackwell came up for reelection, and the race centered on his perceived permissive attitude toward, and even embrace of, adult entertainment. The *Free Press* endorsed the challenger, Jesse Miller, saying that under Blackwell Highland Park had "degenerated into an open haven for prostitution and pornography." Miller ran on the platform of cleaning up the city, a message that ultimately won the day when he narrowly defeated Blackwell in the election. The day after being voted out of office, Blackwell was back at the Tender Trap giving an interview to the *Free Press*. His successor, meanwhile, was quickly caught up in scandal when it turned out that one of the new mayor's largest campaign contributors was the operator of a bottomless dancing bar and that, once in office, he had asked the police to "take it easy" on the bar owner. In 1979, Blackwell ran for mayor again, only this time he was quick to distance himself from adult entertainment. When asked about his history of patronage at the Tender Trap, Blackwell claimed he no longer frequented it or similar locales, saying, "Under no circumstances would I be involved in having lunch at those places anymore because it would give the cloud that I'm giving support, when actually I'm not." Asked directly if he would "get rid" of places like that, Blackwell replied, "Oh, yes, oh, yes, oh, yes." Blackwell later won back his mayoral seat, going on to serve another two terms.[84]

CONCLUSION

The rest of the 1970s saw more battles over exotic dancing in Detroit, though they never reached the fever pitch of the early part of the decade. Rather, an uneasy truce was seemingly reached whereby topless dancing was permitted while bottomless was not. When bottomless was inevitably introduced into Detroit proper in 1974, city officials' reaction against it was swift. After a judge ordered seventeen bars to scale back their acts, which were said to feature bottomless and simulated sex acts, Rick McNeil, manager of the Royal Coach Lounge, responded by saying, "This town wants to be a convention town, but it closes down the only fun around." Responding to such claims, city council president Carl Levin said, "We don't need the bottomless business in Detroit, as difficult as our economic conditions are." This statement again reflected the oddity of a city that was desperately trying to attract businesses simultaneously moving to shut down a prosperous industry. No matter how much money topless bars raked in or how much tax revenue they contributed to city coffers, their association with commercial sex would always make them suspect. Therefore, the potential increased revenue from bottomless was not enough to prevent city officials from barring it in Detroit.[85]

A constant throughout this era was that customers followed new "innovations" in exotic dancing. That meant that when the era of topless was inaugurated, those bars still sticking with bras and pasties found their customer base fleeing. When topless was briefly banned in Detroit in 1971, customers simply went to topless bars in Dearborn. When Inkster inaugurated bottomless, bars there started filling up, to the detriment of topless bars in Detroit. In his dissertation on the history of gay life in Detroit, Tim Retzloff explores the "queer sexual commute" whereby individuals traveled by automobile across Detroit and its suburbs in search of gay sexual encounters. The movement of customers between topless bars offering varying levels of sexual explicitness indicates another type of sexual commute, one in which seekers of adult entertainment traveled across the city and beyond its borders in search of the latest salacious offerings.[86]

One of the inevitable results of Detroit's war on exotic dancing was the way it drove customers to neighboring suburbs. If the suburbs were at times uneasy about this turn of events, they nevertheless reaped the economic benefits of housing a thriving business that Detroit had rejected. This "race to the bottom" among bars also meant that whichever city or suburb was most willing to tolerate commercial sex would reap the very real economic benefits. That nevertheless few locales were willing to permit exotic dance in its most permissive forms therefore speaks to the political toxicity of adult entertainment.

This reluctance of elected officials to embrace the economic potential of exotic dance also points to the way adult entertainment, for better or worse, could come to be seen as defining a city. This explains the protesters in Inkster saying their suburb would not become "Sin City" and the widespread labeling of Highland Park as "Sin City" and "Smut City." Meanwhile, those on the other side of the debate took to calling Detroit a "ghost town" and a "dead town" on those occasions when the city did manage to actually shut down topless dancing. Adult entertainment was thereby more than just one industry among many in these places. Rather, it had the potential to define places as a whole.

This is significant given the way urban historians have long sought to understand how cities and suburbs define themselves as distinct from one another. In his book *Colored Property*, David Freund writes, "Suburban residents fighting to protect the homogeneity of their new neighborhoods often lived in places indistinguishable, at least physically and architecturally, from the Detroit neighborhoods that many had recently left behind." So how then did suburbanites distinguish their neighborhoods from their urban neighbors? For Freund, the answer comes down to "suburban political culture." While this is undoubtedly true, the history of exotic dance in the Detroit metropolitan region suggests that a proliferation of commercial sex in an area could also come to define a place, creating widely held beliefs as to the distinction between city and suburb.[87]

Crucially, though, the landscape of exotic dance often challenged the popular conception of urban centers as dens of adult entertainment while the suburbs were free from such commercial sex. In reality, the suburbs of

Detroit were often offering more explicit adult entertainment options than the city itself. The reasons for this are varied, but which suburbs were the ones that saw commercial sex thrive helps elucidate this issue. Namely, not all suburbs had a thriving adult entertainment industry. Whereas working-class Inkster, Dearborn, and Highland Park all, at various times, saw topless bars flourish in their midst, the more middle- and upper-class suburbs of Oakland County and Grosse Pointe were nearly free from such businesses. Given the mobility of customers, it would be a mistake to think this indicates that working-class individuals made up the customer base for topless bars. Customers very often lived in different neighborhoods, or even different cities, than the adult entertainment establishments they were attending, preferring the anonymity offered by more distant adult businesses to the convenience of nearby ones.

For those suburbs where topless bars did flourish, it was something of a double-edged sword. On the one hand, adult businesses could provide much-needed jobs and tax revenue in a suburb in desperate need of both. On the other hand, too much adult entertainment and a place could become known for it, becoming, like Highland Park, "Smut City." Of course, this was only a problem to the extent that people thought it was a problem, and Mayor Blackwell in Highland Park evidently only considered it an issue after voters turned against him. And, given the struggling economy in Highland Park, the city may well have been better off as "Smut City" than the alternative. As Laurence Wolf, owner of the Krim Theater, said, "Blackwell knows if those theaters weren't adult theaters, they'd be boarded-up theaters."[88]

NOTES

1. Here I am influenced by scholarship on the history of sex work that centers the voices of those in the industry. See Heather Berg, *Porn Work: Sex, Labor, and Late Capitalism* (Chapel Hill: University of North Carolina Press, 2021); Melinda Chateauvert, *Sex Workers Unite: A History of the Movement from Stonewall to SlutWalk* (Boston: Beacon, 2014); Melissa Gira Grant, *Playing the Whore: The Work of Sex Work* (London: Verso, 2014); Andrea Friedman, *Prurient Interests: Gender, Democracy, and Obscenity in New York City, 1909–1945* (New York: Columbia University Press, 2000).

2. "Potter Does a Quick Encore on His Strip-Tease Number," *Detroit Free Press*, May 3, 1937, 7; "Jail Strip Dancer at Night Club," *Detroit News*, May 1, 1937, 2.

3. "Public Blamed for Strip Acts," *Detroit Free Press*, May 6, 1937, 2.

4. Ralph Nelson, "It's Girlie Era, but Police Watch for Error," *Detroit Free Press*, June 8, 1959, 1, 10.

5. Nelson, 1.

6. Nelson, 1, 10.

7. Louis Cook, "This Is the Limit, Police Censor Tells City Strippers," *Detroit Free Press*, July 10, 1959, 4; Bernard F. Mullins, "Strippers Thrown a Curve," *Detroit Times*, July 10, 1959, 3.

8. Kurt Luedtke, "Glimpsing Two Girls a Go-Go: A Search for the Reasons Why," *Detroit Free Press Magazine*, January 9, 1966, 17–18. On Doda, see Josh Sides, *Erotic City: Sexual Revolutions and the Making of Modern San Francisco* (Oxford: Oxford University Press, 2009), 45–48.

9. Arnold S. Hirsch, "Go-Go: A Nightmare of Sex and Sounds," *Detroit News*, November 10, 1966, 15; Robert Selwa, "Go-Go Fever Spreads into Outstate Michigan," *Detroit Daily Dispatch*, December 28, 1967, 4.

10. Mark Beltaire, "Dreams Cashed In," *Detroit Free Press*, October 10, 1967, 12-D; Hirsch, "Go-Go," 15.

11. Hirsch, "Go-Go," 15; Doc Greene, "A Look at Topless Go-Go Girls, Detroit Style," *Detroit News*, January 20, 1967, 20-D.

12. Bob Carr, "Little Richard Is Rocking Again," *Detroit News*, May 16, 1969, 10-D; Susan Holmes, "Topless Dancer Befuddles Court," *Detroit Free Press*, July 24, 1969, 3.

13. John Gill, "Fine Shakes Up Topless Dancer," *Detroit News*, July 24, 1969, 4-B; Holmes, "Topless Dancer Befuddles Court," 3.

14. Beverly Eckman, "Jury Courted by Topless Act," *Detroit News*, September 17, 1969, 6-C; John Oppedahl, "Bared Bosom Goes on Trial," *Detroit Free Press*, September 17, 1969, 3.

15. Beverly Eckman, "The Moral Issue in 2-Inch Pasties," *Detroit News*, September 18, 1969, 17; "Topless Dancer Sentenced," *Detroit Free Press*, November 11, 1969, 12.

16. Eckman, "Jury Courted by Topless Act," 6-C.

17. Robert Kraus, "Way Out on Michigan Avenue; Join Us Where the Gawkers Go," *Detroit Free Press Magazine*, August 24, 1969, 22–23, 29. For more on the history of white racism in Dearborn, see David M. P. Freund, *Colored Property: State Policy and White Racial Politics in Suburban America* (Chicago: University of Chicago Press, 2010), 284–327.

18. Kraus, "Way Out on Michigan Avenue," 23.

19. Edward Shanahan, "'No Prude,' Rashid Declares," *Detroit Free Press*, June 5, 1971, 3.

20. Hiley H. Ward, "Clergy, Girls, Debate Topless Dancing," *Detroit Free Press*, February 12, 1972, 5-B; "Magazine Plea Denied by Judge," *Detroit Free Press*, January 9, 1964, 10-B.

21. Robert D. Kirk, "Curb Obscene Literature, Rashid Warns Parents," *Detroit News*, April 1, 1962, 2-B; "Meeting in Prosecutor's Office of the Citizens

Committee for Better Youth Literature," September 19, 1956, box 12, folder 11, Metropolitan Detroit Council of Churches Records, Walter P. Reuther Library, Wayne State University; Evelyn S. Stewart, "Police Censorship of Books Is Under Fire," *Detroit Free Press*, October 25, 1956, 22.

22. Joseph A. Rashid, "A Community Problem: Effects," *Citizen-Inquirer*, March 26, 1962, 1, 3.

23. Kirk, "Curb Obscene Literature," 2-B.

24. Motion to Disqualify Judge and Affidavit in Support Thereof, *Samuel H. Olsen v William Doerfler and Royal News Company*, Circuit Court for the County of Wayne, no. 12328, December 31, 1963, box 65, folder 1, Ernest Goodman Papers, Walter P. Reuther Library, Wayne State University; Robert D. Kirk, "Rashid Won't Step Down in Smut Case," *Detroit News*, January 9, 1964, 10-B; "Magazine Plea Denied by Judge," 10-B; Order Denying Motion to Disqualify Judge Rashid, *Samuel H. Olsen v William Doerfler and Royal News Company*, Circuit Court for the County of Wayne, no. 12328, March 17, 1964, box 65, folder 1, Ernest Goodman Papers, Walter P. Reuther Library, Wayne State University; Opinion of the Court, *Samuel H. Olsen v William Doerfler and Royal News Company*, Circuit Court for the County of Wayne, no. 12328, December 1, 1964, box 65, folder 1, Ernest Goodman Papers, Walter P. Reuther Library, Wayne State University.

25. Jim Neubacher, "Go-Go Gal Put Under Wraps," *Detroit Free Press*, June 3, 1971, 3.

26. "Judge's Decision Won't Put Pasties on Go-Go Dancers," *Detroit News*, June 3, 1971, 2-B.

27. Susan Holmes, "Cover Up, Police Tell Go-Go Gals," *Detroit Free Press*, June 8, 1971, 2; Arthur W. O'Shea, "Stop Topless Dancing, Detroit Bars Ordered," *Detroit News*, June 8, 1971, 3; "Police Enforce Ban, Arrest 2 Dancers," *Detroit News*, June 10, 1971, 25.

28. Judy Diebolt, "Bar Owners Lose Round in Topless Fight," *Detroit Free Press*, June 15, 1971, 3.

29. Shanahan, "'No Prude,' Rashid Declares," 3, 14.

30. "Majority Shouts—Who's Listening?," *National Decency Reporter* 7, no. 3–4 (April 1970): 12. For more on the use of the "silent majority" in white racial politics, see Matthew D. Lassiter, *The Silent Majority: Suburban Politics in the Sunbelt South* (Princeton, NJ: Princeton University Press, 2007).

31. "Sound Off," *Detroit Free Press*, June 10, 1971, 1; Walter Kendrick, *The Secret Museum: Pornography in Modern Culture* (Berkeley: University of California Press, 1987), 226.

32. James Graham, "Go-Go Trips on Topless Ban," *Detroit News*, June 9, 1971, 1.

33. George Cantor, "Dancers Cover Up and Lunch Is a Bore," *Detroit Free Press*, June 10, 1971, 4; Eric Schaefer, "Pandering to the 'Goon Trade': Framing

the Sexploitation Audience through Advertising," in *Sleaze Artists: Cinema at the Margins of Taste, Style, and Politics*, ed. Jeffrey Sconce (Durham, NC: Duke University Press, 2007), 35.

34. "Church Leaders Differ on Banning Topless Dancers," *Detroit News*, June 9, 1971, 17; Gayle S. Rubin, *Deviations: A Gayle Rubin Reader* (Durham, NC: Duke University Press, 2011), 268.

35. Graham, "Go-Go Trips on Topless Ban," 17; Cantor, "Dancers Cover Up and Lunch Is a Bore," 4.

36. Stephen Cain and Michael F. Wendland, "Well-Clad Pickets Protest Topless Ban," *Detroit News*, June 11, 1971, 2; "Protesting Topless Ban," *Detroit Free Press*, June 11, 1971, 1.

37. Graham, "Go-Go Trips on Topless Ban," 1, 17; Judy Diebolt, "Topless Dancers' Reprieve Extended," *Detroit Free Press*, July 7, 1971, 14.

38. Cantor, "Dancers Cover Up and Lunch Is a Bore," 3–4; Cain and Wendland, "Well-Clad Pickets Protest Topless Ban," 2.

39. Cain and Wendland, "Well-Clad Pickets Protest Topless Ban," 2.

40. Cain and Wendland, 2; Mike O'Hara, "ABC Brings City $5 Million," *Detroit News*, May 19, 1971, sec. D, 1, 4; Bob Talbert, "Strange Judicial Rulings Give Our Town a Bad Image in Nation," *Detroit Free Press*, June 15, 1971, 11.

41. Judy Diebolt, "Topless Ban Lifted during Appeal," *Detroit Free Press*, June 26, 1971, 3, 12; Ward, "Clergy, Girls, Debate Topless Dancing," 5-B; John Weisman, "A Star Stripper Relives the Golden Days of Burlesk," *Detroit Free Press*, January 25, 1973, 14-B.

42. Cantor, "Dancers Cover Up and Lunch Is a Bore," 4.

43. Ward, "Clergy, Girls, Debate Topless Dancing," 5-B; Cantor, "Dancers Cover Up and Lunch Is a Bore," 3–4.

44. James Graham and Mike Maza, "Roumell Lifts Topless Ban; Rashid Angry," *Detroit News*, June 12, 1971, 1–2.

45. Eckman, "Jury Courted by Topless Act," 6-C.

46. Michael Brogan, "Suit Fights Topless Ban," *Detroit News*, June 21, 1971, 11; "Another Bar in Bra Fight," *Detroit Free Press*, June 22, 1971, 12.

47. Gary Schuster, "Convictions Upset in Topless Case," *Detroit News*, July 5, 1972, 8-C; Judge Charles Levin, Jads, Inc. v. City of Detroit, 200 N.W.2d 715 (Mich. Ct. App. Div. 1 1972).

48. Don Lenhausen, "City Tightens Anti-Smut Laws," *Detroit Free Press*, October 25, 1972, 3; Ordinance to Amend Chapter 5, Article 4 of the Code of the City of Detroit, 1972, box 333, folder 7, Roman Gribbs Papers, Burton Historical Collection, Detroit Public Library; Julie Morris, "Go-Go Girls Grouchy about Police Census," *Detroit Free Press*, November 29, 1972, 4.

49. Ordinance to Amend Chapter 5, Article 4 of the Code of the City of Detroit, Roman Gribbs Papers.

50. Cook, "This Is the Limit, Police Censor Tells City Strippers," 4; Morris, "Go-Go Girls Grouchy about Police Census," 4; Jim Neubacher, "Topless Go-Goers Restrained, Bar Business Is Gone-Gone," *Detroit Free Press*, January 22, 1973, 3.

51. Neubacher, "Topless Go-Goers Restrained, Bar Business Is Gone-Gone," 3.

52. Morris, "Go-Go Girls Grouchy about Police Census," 4.

53. Neubacher, "Topless Go-Goers Restrained, Bar Business Is Gone-Gone," 4.

54. Don Lenhausen, "Belly Dancers Protest," *Detroit Free Press*, February 15, 1973, 12.

55. Stephen Cain, "Council Rallies to Aid of City's Belly Dancers," *Detroit News*, April 13, 1973, B-1-D.

56. Lenhausen, "Belly Dancers Protest," 12; Chuck Thurston, "Detroit's Go-Go Dancers Get Squeezed Where It Hurts," *Detroit Free Press*, January 24, 1973, 8.

57. Maryanne Conheim, "Bar Dancers Go Bottomless—But Only Off and On," *Detroit Free Press*, April 25, 1973, 1; Roman S. Gribbs to Michael Glusac, April 25, 1973, box 457, folder 4, Roman Gribbs Papers, Burton Historical Collection, Detroit Public Library; Roman S. Gribbs to Common Council, April 27, 1973, box 457, folder 4, Roman Gribbs Papers, Burton Historical Collection, Detroit Public Library; Don Lenhausen and Peter Benjaminson, "Go-Go Crackdown Is Sought by Gribbs," *Detroit Free Press*, April 28, 1973, 3.

58. "Statement of Mayor Roman S. Gribbs," April 27, 1973, box 457, folder 4, Roman Gribbs Papers, Burton Historical Collection, Detroit Public Library; Stephen Cain, "Bottomless Vote Nears," *Detroit News*, May 24, 1973, B-1.

59. Don Lenhausen, "Topless Dancing Faces Ban," *Detroit Free Press*, May 16, 1973, 3, 11.

60. "Sound Off," *Detroit Free Press*, May 26, 1973, 1; "Sound Off," *Detroit Free Press*, April 27, 1973, 1. The flyers protesting the closing of topless bars can be found in box 458, folders 2–4, and box 459, folders 1–2, Roman Gribbs Papers, Burton Historical Collection, Detroit Public Library.

61. "Support Topless Go-Go," 1973, box 459, folder 2, Roman Gribbs Papers, Burton Historical Collection, Detroit Public Library.

62. James Graham, "Bottomless Ban to Hit Burlesque," *Detroit News*, May 21, 1973, 12.

63. Don Lenhausen, "Topless Dancer Blasts Proposed Ban," *Detroit Free Press*, May 24, 1973, 3; Bob Talbert, "I, Too, Think It's Shame about Sham," *Detroit Free Press*, May 22, 1973, 17.

64. Cain, "Bottomless Vote Nears," B-1; Lenhausen, "Topless Dancer Blasts Proposed Ban," 3.

65. Lenhausen, "Topless Dancing Faces Ban," 3, 11.

66. Jean Maddern Pitrone, *MYRA: The Life and Times of Myra Wolfgang, Trade-Union Leader* (Fort Wyandotte, MI: Calibre Books, 1980), 165.

67. Pitrone, 120, 122–24, 127–28.

68. Carter Van Lopik, "The Bunny Business Beckons," *Detroit Free Press*, October 29, 1963, 3.

69. Gene Roberts, "Myra Wolfgang, Thumb in the Playboy's Soup," *Detroit Free Press*, February 16, 1964, 2-C.

70. Ralph Orr, "Wolfgang: Dancer Can't Wait Table," *Detroit Free Press*, January 23, 1973, 8.

71. Stephen Cain, "Bottomless Ban May Cover Topless Bars, Too," *Detroit News*, May 16, 1973; Lenhausen, "Topless Dancing Faces Ban," 11.

72. Lenhausen, "Topless Dancing Faces Ban," 11; P. G. Tannian to Michael Glusac, June 1, 1973, box 457, folder 4, Roman Gribbs Papers, Burton Historical Collection, Detroit Public Library.

73. Lee Winfrey, "An Ex-Drummer Is King of Detroit's Go-Go World," *Detroit Free Press*, April 21, 1969, 3, 8; Cain, "Bottomless Vote Nears"; David Ashenfelter, "Bottomless Dancer Trades Music for Lawn Mower," *Detroit News*, May 11, 1973, B-1-W; Rubin, *Deviations*, 160.

74. Stephen Cain, "Council Helps Gribbs in Fight against Topless Dancers," *Detroit News*, May 30, 1973, 5-B; Don Lenhausen, "Council Bans Indecency; Topless Go-Go Could Go," *Detroit Free Press*, May 30, 1973; Roman S. Gribbs to Common Council, June 4, 1973, box 457, folder 4, Roman Gribbs Papers, Burton Historical Collection, Detroit Public Library.

75. Cain, "Council Helps Gribbs in Fight against Topless Dancers," 5-B; Lenhausen, "Council Bans Indecency."

76. John Miller, "As Go-Go's Go, So Go Bars?," *Detroit Free Press*, June 4, 1973, 3, 12.

77. Tim McNulty, "Topless Go-Go Goes On and On," *Detroit Free Press*, June 8, 1973, 3.

78. Stephen Cain, "Bottomless Dancing Banned in Detroit," *Detroit News*, June 13, 1973; Don Lenhausen, "Council Skips Ban on Topless," *Detroit Free Press*, June 20, 1973, 6.

79. Louis Heldman, "Go-Go Dancers Bared All but Toes, Policeman Says," *Detroit Free Press*, May 17, 1973, 5-B.

80. "Police Grab 4 Dancers in Topless Raid," *Detroit Free Press*, July 28, 1974, 6; Ron Ishoy, "Everytime the Girls Take It All Off John Hamilton Gets a Little Richer," *Detroit Free Press Magazine*, November 23, 1975, 10; Leonard Yourist, "Nude Performers Given a Break," *Detroit News*, June 26, 1975, 1-B-W; Sara Rimer, "Irate Judge Strips Bottomless Dance Cases off Docket," *Detroit Free Press*, June 26, 1975, 12; "Ticketed: Loyal to His Lady," *Detroit Free Press*, March 17, 1976, 3.

81. Ishoy, "Everytime the Girls Take It All Off," 15.
82. Heldman, "Go-Go Dancers Bared All but Toes," 5-B.
83. Jo Thomas and Peter Benjaminson, "Smut City: Sex Strip Flourishes in Highland Park," *Detroit Free Press*, January 20, 1975, 1–2; James Kenyon, "Highland Pk. Attacks Smut," *Detroit News*, June 26, 1973, 3-B.
84. "Highland Park Needs Change," *Detroit Free Press*, November 1, 1975, 8; Peter Benjaminson, "Blackwell at Topless Lunch: Showy Mayor Turns Bitter," *Detroit Free Press*, November 6, 1975, 14-D; Jo Thomas, "HP Cleanup Attempt Stirs Political Dust," *Detroit Free Press*, June 13, 1976, 10; Tim Kiska, "Clean Up Highland Park?," *Detroit Free Press*, January 28, 1979, 1.
85. Thomas C. Fox, "Judge Curbs 17 Go-Go Spots," *Detroit Free Press*, December 4, 1974, 3; Tom Hennessy, "Bare Bottom Cold Shouldered," *Detroit Free Press*, February 21, 1975, 3.
86. Tim Retzloff, "City, Suburb, and the Changing Bounds of Lesbian and Gay Life and Politics in Metropolitan Detroit, 1945–1985" (PhD diss., Yale University, 2014), 129–39.
87. Freund, *Colored Property*, 29.
88. Thomas and Benjaminson, "Smut City," 2.

FIVE

EROGENOUS ZONING

The Creation and Dispersal of the "Detroit Model"

BY THE LATE 1960S, MOVIE theaters in Detroit were increasingly struggling due to demographic and economic changes in the city as a whole. In light of this, and much to the horror of the censorial minded, many theaters chose to turn to sexually explicit cinema to stay afloat. Even worse than this, in the view of anti-porn advocates, was the fact that the films they were showing grew more and more explicit over time. In 1967, the *Detroit Free Press* declared, "Detroiters can now see films in public theaters that 10 years ago they might have been arrested for having in their private possession." A year later, *Detroit News* film critic Ken Barnard published an article titled "Sex in Movies—How Far Will They Go?" Interviewed for the article was Ross Caccavale, owner of a series of art-house theaters in the Detroit metropolitan area, who correctly predicted, "With the public permissiveness of the last 10 years, we're only a few years away from commercial exhibition of hard-core pornography." By October of 1970, the *Detroit News* found itself declaring, "These are the sordid '70's. Now you can see total nudity, front and rear, and almost every form of sexual perversion right there on the silver screen—in living color. . . . And some theaters—like the Stone Burlesk—just run stag film footage spliced together—no plot, not even a pretense of a socially-redeeming quality."[1]

This trend toward greater sexual explicitness was hardly confined to the movies. Adult bookstores also proliferated rapidly during this era. In September of 1970, one Detroit city council member estimated that the number of adult bookstores in the city had increased from three to eighteen that year alone. Meanwhile, as explored in chapter 4, the exotic dancing trade began to grow more explicit, with topless bars rapidly increasing in number around the start of the 1970s. The theatrical world in Detroit also embraced the trend, with the

"Apparently, sergeant, you just haven't been keeping up with the Supreme Court . . ."

Figure 5.1. Comic in *National Decency Reporter*, March–April 1969.

onstage nudity in the play *Hair* leading to a firestorm of controversy in the city in 1970. Likewise, Detroit's art scene also reflected the move toward greater sexual explicitness, with the January 1970 exhibition at a Detroit art gallery of fourteen drawings by John Lennon depicting his love life with Yoko Ono drawing much controversy in the city and even the attention of the Detroit Police Department.[2]

Detroit was hardly alone in seeing works labeled pornographic receive previously unheard-of levels of prominence and popularity. As the 1970s began, pornography assumed a prominent place in the urban landscape across the country as never before. Every major city in the United States seemed to suddenly find itself overrun with adult businesses, with a newfound sexual explicitness testing the limits of propriety. Meanwhile, these cities were, much like Detroit, struggling with how best to regulate pornography in this new era. Nearly every system of censoring movies before release at the state or local level had been ruled unconstitutional by the 1970s, as had been the case in Detroit in 1969. Many cities attempted to use obscenity law to prosecute individual films or filmmakers, only to find themselves stymied by liberal court decisions. Given the curtailment of the traditional legal means of regulating sexually explicit cinema and adult entertainment, cities were left seemingly helpless in the face of the rapid growth of adult entertainment.

It was within this context that, in the early 1970s, Detroit's city council and, in time, its mayor would be forced to come up with a new method for regulating pornography. Rather than using obscenity law, the city adopted the use of zoning law to regulate the location of adult businesses. The city's new anti-porn laws were quickly challenged in the courts, eventually making it all the way to the United States Supreme Court. After the high court affirmed the constitutionality of Detroit's zoning-based approach to anti-porn regulation, what came to be known as the Detroit Model was quickly copied by countless cities across the country, going on to reshape the preferred means for halting the growth of pornography.

Despite its immense influence, Detroit's zoning law has received little scholarly attention to date outside of legal histories, where the focus is exclusively on the Supreme Court case it generated rather than the origins of the law itself in Detroit. This chapter fills this gap by exploring the development of Detroit's anti-porn zoning ordinance, the debate over the law, and its influence on the country as a whole. I place this history centrally within the context of an early 1970s Detroit struggling with how to respond to urban decay and downward economic trends. I also seek to understand how the law was shaped by political actors who came at the issue of pornography from a variety of different perspectives that shaped their respective approaches to the question of how best to regulate pornography. In the end, I make the case for seeing the Detroit Model as an extension of efforts by the city to combat the urban crisis, with Detroit's innovative approach to regulating pornography, as well as the rhetoric and logic underlying it, in time coming to reshape anti-porn politics throughout much of the United States.

THE POLITICAL CONTEXTS OF DETROIT

Before delving into the city council's debates over pornography in the early 1970s, it is necessary to briefly examine the political context in Detroit at the time. For much of the 1960s, Detroit's political scene was centered around Jerome Cavanagh. In 1961, Cavanagh ran for mayor despite the fact that he was a thirty-three-year-old political neophyte who had never held or even ran for elected office and had little name recognition citywide. In a shocking turn, though, Cavanagh was carried into the mayor's post with the overwhelming support of roughly 85 percent of Detroit's African Americans voters, whom he had appealed to through a campaign that centered the state of race relations in the city and particularly the issue of excessive policing. With Cavanagh as mayor, during the first half of the 1960s, Detroit nurtured an image as a "model city" for race relations. This reputation helped make Cavanagh a rising political star nationally, with many predicting that his position as Detroit's mayor would be a springboard to higher office.[3]

The image of Detroit as a "model city" was shattered by the violence that shook the city in 1967. The alternately named riots or rebellion of that summer laid bare the simmering racial tensions in the city and the routine and systemic discrimination faced by African Americans. It also pointed to the failings of white liberals, with Cavanagh's rhetoric emphasizing racial harmony and his piecemeal policy initiatives designed to placate African American unrest far from sufficient to deal with the problem at hand. Though many still saw him as the favorite to win reelection in 1969, undoubtedly the shine had been taken off Cavanagh's political stardom, and in June of that year, Cavanagh announced that he would not seek a third term as mayor.

Cavanagh's decision left the race for mayor of Detroit wide open. One of the top candidates in the primary was the moderate liberal Richard Austin, the Wayne County auditor who was seeking to become the city's first Black mayor. Running on the far opposite side of the political spectrum was Mary Beck, the firebrand conservative city councilwoman who had garnered the support of many whites in the city with her racially charged rhetoric. Meanwhile, despite being the favored choice among many, in July of 1969, white liberal councilman Mel Ravitz announced that he would not run for mayor and would instead seek reelection to the city council. With Ravitz refusing to enter the race, the search was on for a white, liberal-leaning candidate to face off against Austin. Before long, Roman S. Gribbs stepped up to the plate.

Gribbs was a Detroiter through and through; born to Polish immigrants in the city, he had lived in Detroit his whole life outside of a stint in the army and had attended the University of Detroit as both an undergraduate and for law school. He became an assistant prosecutor for Wayne County in 1957, and he held the position into the mid-1960s before twice running for the position of recorder's court judge, losing both times. In June of 1968, Gribbs got his big break when he was appointed to the post of sheriff of Wayne County. In the months ahead, he received commendations in the press for appointing an African American man to be his second-in-command and chief deputy. He proceeded to win reelection that same year, setting him up for a four-year term as sheriff. After Ravitz refused to run, though, attention turned to Gribbs as a possible mayoral candidate, and a week later, he announced his candidacy.[4]

For scholars looking at the history of Detroit, Gribbs is often painted as a law-and-order figure who played to the racist fears of whites in the city during his mayoral bid.[5] And undoubtedly Gribbs at times engaged in this type of politics in the run-up to the 1969 election, particularly with some of the rhetoric surrounding his campaign's focus on crime in the city. And yet, this view of Gribbs leaves out the important ways he consciously distanced himself from race-baiting conservatives by carving out a moderate liberal position when it came to issues of race. Upon announcing his bid for mayor, Gribbs explicitly refused to be tagged as a "law and order" candidate, admitting that "many times citizens have legitimate complaints about police actions." His selection of an African American for the second position in his sheriff's office was repeatedly mentioned in press coverage of his campaign and again positioned him as a moderate liberal on race. Still, his role as sheriff meant he also had a reputation as someone who would tackle crime, perhaps the central issue of the election. Gribbs positioned himself as a candidate who could appeal to whites across the political spectrum, with conservatives seeing a sheriff who would deal with the issue of crime while liberals saw nominally progressive racial politics.[6]

In September, Austin and Gribbs finished as the top two candidates in the primary, advancing them to a runoff election. Though Austin received the most support with 38 percent of the vote, with Gribbs trailing at 31 percent, it was Beck's 21 percent that spelled trouble for Austin. Almost immediately after the primary, it was reported that many of Beck's supporters would shift their support to Gribbs come November. As one Beck supporter said, "I'm for Gribbs now. . . . In the first place, he is white, and besides Austin wants a police review board, and for that alone I wouldn't vote for him." Such sentiments were rife among whites in the city, who feared a Black takeover of the political structures of Detroit.[7]

Beyond the undeniable truth that many white Detroiters simply were unwilling to vote for an African American as mayor, the main challenge for Austin's campaign was that, in the words of the *Free Press*, "Gribbs nimbly combines moderate views with his image as a police officer." This allowed Gribbs to have his proverbial cake and eat it too, presenting a unifying and moderate vision of Detroit that could appeal to both racist white voters opposed to Austin as well as white voters concerned about crime in the city but nevertheless unwilling to support the explicit racism of more stringent law-and-order candidates. There was a decided irony to the fact that the mayoral race between Gribbs and Austin bitterly divided the city given that, when it came to their actual policy positions, the two candidates were nearly identical. Both were liberal-leaning moderates concerned about crime, and the two agreed on far more issues than they disagreed on. Nevertheless, the election exposed deep fractures in the city when it came to race. In the end, Gribbs defeated Austin by the narrowest of margins, 258,010 votes to 251,816. In his victory speech, Gribbs told Detroit, "I pledge to you my unrelenting efforts, and I assure you I will be mayor of all the people. We will have unity."[8]

Even as Gribbs's victory seemingly signaled the city's preference for the continuation of white liberal political leadership, the election also brought indications of the new political order that was coming to Detroit. Most obviously this was seen through Gribbs's narrow margin of victory; though Austin's loss was a major disappointment for his supporters, the closeness of the election showed clearly that a new era of Black political leadership in Detroit was near. Just as significantly, the city's readiness for political change was indicated in the makeup of the newly elected city council.[9] For the 1969 election, three of the nine members of the city council had chosen not to seek reelection, making for the biggest turnover in the council in a decade. The newcomers were Carl Levin, Ernest Browne Jr., and David Eberhard. Levin was known for his liberal politics and would eventually go on to serve six terms as a United States senator. Browne was also a liberal, and his election made him the third African American serving on the city council, then a record high for the city.[10]

Finally, David Eberhard was thirty-five years old when he was elected, having previously seen his star rise in the city as the pastor of Riverside Lutheran Church on the east side of Detroit. There, Eberhard had run a number of inner-city social services programs while building a reputation as a "liberal maverick in his denomination." During the 1960s, Eberhard became actively involved in city politics, frequently hosting key city officials, including Mayor Cavanagh, at his church. He was progressive when it came to racial issues, having actively sought to diversify his own church, which went from nearly all white to 40 percent Black during his tenure. He first ran for city council in a special election in 1968, and when it appeared that he might be matched up against Robert Tindal, a leader in the local chapter of the National Association for the Advancement of Colored People (NAACP), Eberhard said plainly that "it should be him over me. We need more black candidates." After narrowly losing that race to a white conservative candidate, Eberhard ran again a year later, easily winning a council seat while running on a liberal platform, though, as we shall see, he soon became the most stridently anti-porn voice on the city council.[11]

The three newcomers were all young and identified in the press as liberals, making a total of six liberals on the council (Ravitz, Levin, Browne, Eberhard, Robert Tindal, and Nicholas Hood), with two other incumbent city council members straddling the line between liberal and conservative (William Rogell and Philip J. Van Antwerp) and just one outright conservative (Anthony Wierzbicki). This was set to be the most liberal Detroit City Council in some time and one of the most racially diverse, though the departure of the aforementioned Councilwoman Beck notably left the council without any women.

The most prominent figure on the new city council was undoubtedly Mel Ravitz. Ravitz had been a sociology professor at Wayne State University when he first ran for city council in 1961, and after his surprising victory, he became an outspoken progressive voice on the council and a champion of working-class and African American interests in the city. His reputation as perhaps the city's most liberal-minded white politician helped his political standing rise over the course of the Cavanagh administration, with higher office seemingly an inevitability. After declining to run for mayor in 1969 despite rampant speculation about his possible candidacy, Ravitz received almost fifty thousand more votes than any other candidate for the city council, thus making him city council president and setting him up for a future run for mayor of the city, potentially against the newly elected mayor, Roman Gribbs.

1970: THE CITY COUNCIL DEBATES ANTI-PORN LEGAL APPROACHES

In May of 1970, the city council began discussing the issue of pornography and the city's efforts at halting its spread. This was prompted by both the rapidly increasing number of adult businesses in the city as well as the arrival of the musical *Hair*, which featured a brief nude scene. At a city council meeting, a number of council members, led by David Eberhard, pressed city attorney William P. Doran on how Detroit might control pornography. Doran responded in a circumspect manner, noting that "legally, control is almost impossible because one man's pornography may be another man's art." Without legal recourse to shut down *Hair*, the city council instead put to a vote a resolution calling for Detroit citizens to boycott the premiere of the play. The measure failed four to five, with Eberhard voting for the measure while Ravitz opposed it.[12]

In the weeks ahead, the city council continued to grapple with the issue. Eberhard led the attack against pornography, warning ominously of the rising tide of adult entertainment in the city. He charged that the number of adult bookstores had increased tenfold in the last year alone and warned of the increasingly racy content sold within such establishments.[13] As the *Detroit News* wrote of one city council meeting, "Eberhard spoke of a proliferation of 'dirty book' houses, some having 'novelette counters' offering erotic devices and back-room curtained rooms 'like voting booths' where persons can view obscene films in privacy." Driven by concern over these developments, Eberhard proposed a new obscenity ordinance for the city that he hoped would shut down adult businesses in Detroit.[14]

The challenge, of course, was in determining what exactly could be considered obscene, a question that had vexed the courts for decades by that point. The lack of clarity was such that even the city's pornography dealers wanted a clear ruling, with one adult bookstore owner saying, "It's hard to determine what's obscene. What's obscene to one person isn't to another. I wish they would set the guidelines, then we'd have something to go by." The city council therefore asked the Department of Corporation Counsel, which acted as the attorney's office for the city, to prepare a legally viable definition of obscenity. Their response was a near word-for-word recitation of what was then the United States Supreme Court's three-pronged test of obscenity based on the rulings in *Roth v. United States* (1957) and *Memoirs v. Massachusetts* (1966). Meanwhile, that same month, the legal coordinator of the Detroit Police Department prepared two proposals for new obscenity ordinances, each designed to toughen the penalties for obscenity and increase police discretion in such cases.[15] Still, it was clear to all that, given recent court rulings, none of these approaches would allow the city to easily begin shutting down adult businesses. Anthony Wierzbicki, the most reliably conservative member of the city council, responded that he thought the Supreme Court rulings should simply be ignored, saying, "We ought to be able to set up our own definition of obscenity and say, 'This is obscene.'" Unsurprisingly, the Detroit Corporation Counsel responded that simply ignoring Supreme Court precedents was not a legally feasible approach.[16]

Given the stalemate on obscenity, the city council began to ponder alternate methods for regulating adult businesses. Some council members suggested more stringently enforcing fire-safety regulations against adult movie theaters, particularly so-called mini adult theaters, which tended to seat fewer than a hundred. This strategy was something of a return to the early days of cinema, when the rapid growth in the number of nickelodeon theaters in Detroit starting in 1906 elicited major concerns over the safety of patrons in these small storefront theaters. As Lieutenant Joseph Areeda, head of the Detroit Police Department's Obscenity Detail, told the city council in 1970, "I can see the day when these small movie houses are all over the city. All they have to do is rent an old storefront, set up 40 chairs and show 16-millimeter films." Outside of the reference to the 16mm format, this statement would have seemed perfectly suited to debates over regulating movie theaters during the nickelodeon era of cinema.[17]

Another legal approach suggested by the city council was to place a special tax on adult businesses. As Eberhard said of this idea, "We're going into this now through the back door. If we can't run them out with the law, we could tax them out, perhaps." Eberhard's comments made clear that this proposal was less about the tax itself than the way the tax might, in a roundabout manner, drive adult entertainment venues out of business. This presented a legal quandary, though, in that if this tax forced out adult businesses, it would no doubt be seen as a violation of the First Amendment. The city council therefore directed the Department of Corporation Counsel to look into the legality of the idea. The *Detroit Free Press* found the notion novel enough to poll its readers on the proposal, with just over half opposing the idea of taxing pornography.[18]

The last major idea posited in the council for how to regulate pornography came from city council president Mel Ravitz, who suggested that the city's Anti-Skid Row Ordinance be extended to apply to adult businesses. This section of the city's zoning code had been adopted by the city council in 1962 and had at its center a provision that prohibited certain types of businesses— including pawnshops, second-hand stores, bars, lodging houses, shoe shine parlors, and pool rooms—from locating within one thousand feet of each other. The ordinance was aimed at combating the formation of "skid row" areas in Detroit, with the types of businesses in question seen as causing neighborhood decay and blight, therefore justifying their dispersal across the city. The bill was backed at the time by numerous neighborhood and homeowner' groups who saw these types of businesses as a major cause of the decline of some of the city's residential areas, with the newly elected Ravitz lobbying in favor of it. As it spread out rather than banned businesses seen as having a negative economic impact on neighborhoods, the ordinance was able to survive a legal challenge from local pawnbrokers in 1962.[19]

In fact, Ravitz had previously proposed expanding the "regulated uses" zoning ordinance to control sex-oriented businesses. In early 1965, in the wake of a wave of protests prompted by the opening of a new burlesque theater in midtown Detroit, Ravitz proposed that burlesque theaters be added to the list of regulated businesses under the skid row ordinance. Though this did not end up becoming law at that time, in the midst of the city council's debate in 1970 over how to regulate pornography, Ravitz revived the idea, suggesting that adult movie theaters and bookstores be included among the types of business dispersed under the city's existing skid row zoning ordinance. As Ravitz said of the idea, "We won't be able to eliminate them, but at least we can control their numbers and location." In contrast to Eberhard, then, who sought a means to eradicate pornography from the city entirely, Ravitz proposed a more measured approach that would prevent adult businesses from proliferating in any one area while still allowing them to function where there were no nearby "regulated use" businesses. Just as critically, whereas Eberhard emphasized moral concerns in proposing the use of obscenity law, Ravitz instead focused on economic concerns, meaning the secondary effects adult businesses allegedly had on neighborhoods, by utilizing zoning law. The differing priorities and approaches of Eberhard and Ravitz would come to dominate the debate in the city council over pornography.[20]

Eberhard's leadership on this issue and his hard-line stance against pornography were seen as something of a surprise at the time given his reputation as a liberal. Still, there had been some indications that he might take such a position. In 1963, as the pastor of Riverside Lutheran Church, Eberhard set up what he called a Christian Key Club for youth in the community and used the occasion to go out of his way to criticize the then newly opened Playboy Club in Detroit. As he said of his church's club, "There won't be any bunnies. . . . Bunnies are a symbol of a playboy attitude which is irresponsible. We want to show that church youth are responsible." Still, pornography and censorship had seemingly never come up when Eberhard ran for city council, leaving many confused and disappointed by his anti-porn stance. As the radical weekly paper *Fifth Estate* wrote in June of 1970, "All the liberals were campaigning hard to get good guy Rev. David Eberhard elected to the city council last year. Now that they were successful, he has repaid them by introducing a new ordinance dealing with obscenity and defamation of the flag and religion." Weeks later, *Fifth Estate* labeled Eberhard a "liberal-turned-censor."[21]

Meanwhile, Ravitz's views on the issue of pornography and censorship could hardly have been more different. Whereas Eberhard had proudly voted for the proposed boycott of *Hair*, Ravitz, after voting against it, divulged that he had already bought tickets to the play and planned to attend with his wife. Just eight days later, during the play's opening week in Detroit, Ravitz not only attended *Hair* but also reportedly "danced coatless" onstage after being invited up, along with other members of the audience, during the finale rendition of "Let the Sun Shine In." The sight elicited some laughs, with the *Free Press* publishing a cartoon rendition of Ravitz onstage with scantily clad women and hippies (see fig. 5.2). It also became a minor source of controversy, with fellow council members William Rogell and Anthony Wierzbicki—both of whom had voted in favor of the proposed boycott of the play—expressing their concern over the propriety of Ravitz's onstage appearance. Ravitz was reportedly reluctant to respond to the criticism at first but later said, "I enjoyed the show and I didn't find it obscene. I think it's a show you have to judge in its totality. In that respect

Figure 5.2. Comic depicting city councilman Mel Ravitz dancing onstage at *Hair*. *Detroit Free Press*, June 19, 1970.

it was a vital, affirmative performance. I was asked if I would join the cast on stage and I did. I participated and enjoyed it thoroughly."[22]

This was largely in keeping with Ravitz's liberal leaning when it came to issues of pornography and censorship. He tended to avoid taking a firm stance and particularly had little interest in the moral grandstanding that so often was attached to anti-porn activity. When he did dip his toes in anti-porn political waters, it was always with economic rather than moral concerns in mind, as was the case with his recommendation that the city's "regulated uses" zoning provision be applied to adult businesses. His thinking on the issue was no doubt influenced by his training as a sociologist, and both as an academic and subsequently as a politician, he had advocated for the inclusion of the voices of neighborhood residents in the debate over urban renewal. His proposal to disperse adult businesses can thus be seen as in line with his broader concern over neighborhood decay in the city rather than as a moralizing anti-porn stance.

There is also evidence for this in some of the responses sent by Ravitz's office to the many letters from constituents regarding pornography in the city—letters that arrived in growing numbers over the course of the early 1970s as pornography became widespread and the city council reckoned with how to respond. Most of these letters were in support of the enactment of new anti-porn laws, and to these Ravitz's office dutifully responded with variations on a form letter that stressed that the city council was trying to act against pornography but was hemmed in by court decisions and that Ravitz had proposed the use of zoning to regulate adult businesses. The rare constituents who wrote Ravitz criticizing the city's war on pornography received a very different and likely more forthright response. In December of 1970, one Detroit resident wrote Ravitz to express his view that, even as he was personally opposed to pornography, laws to prohibit its spread were just as self-defeating as Prohibition had once been. As the letter said, "You Can Not Legislate Morality. When you do, You drive the immorality underground.... If I thought for one second a new law would stop all the Pornography, I would be the first in line to back such a Law—But these types of laws have not worked in the past and I can not see how they could work now." To this, Ravitz gave a personalized response, saying, "I think that you are quite right, it is not going to be possible to legislate these stores and other purveyors of pornography out of existence. Indeed if people would simply cease visiting these establishments perhaps that would be the most effective means of making clear that they are unwanted."[23]

Ravitz stated his views on censorship perhaps most clearly in a response to a letter sent by Thomas Donohue in March of 1971. In his letter, Donohue criticized Wayne County prosecuting attorney William L. Cahalan's handling of the grand jury investigation into the police shooting of one Charles Calloway, with Donohue faulting Cahalan for failing to make a strong case while he was simultaneously vigorously pursuing legal action against the operators of adult businesses in Detroit. To this, Ravitz replied:

> Although I do not know the details of the Calloway case, I do share the general point of view expressed in your letter, namely, that our law enforcement agencies should concentrate on fundamental problems rather than to deal with rather questionable "morality" issues such as book stores and "skin flicks."
>
> My own general point of view is that we need to have a basic revision of our State Criminal Code removing from that Code many items that are items of personal morality. I think that this would free the Police Departments and the Prosecuting Attorney offices around the state to do a more effective job on those areas of more significant community concern.

This view was in keeping with the position of many liberals at that time who saw pornography as a matter of personal morality and a victimless crime that police departments should not bother trying to regulate. In fact, Ravitz's letter here in many ways mirrored the controversial majority opinion of the Presidential Commission on Obscenity and Pornography, which, in the fall of 1970, had issued a report (soon to be rejected by the United States Senate and President Nixon) that called for the repeal of all laws governing the circulation of pornography among consenting adults.[24]

There is great deal of irony in the fact that the anti-porn zoning law Detroit eventually came to adopt—which would then fundamentally reshape the legal means used to regulate pornography across the country—was masterminded not by an anti-porn crusader but rather by a politician who seemingly had no strong feelings regarding the morality of pornography and indeed thought the governmental focus on the issue was a misguided waste of time. As these letters make clear, Ravitz's views aligned far more closely with those who wanted to see pornography decriminalized than those, like Eberhard, who wanted to see pornography banned outright. Ultimately, then, it would be economic arguments—as well as, perhaps, pragmatic political considerations—that would help turn Ravitz into one of country's most influential architects of anti-porn legislation.

Still, Ravitz's zoning-based approach to regulating pornography had failed to pick up much momentum by the end of the summer of 1970, and the year was marked by much talk and little action by the city council on the issue. The problem on the legal front was the vagueness and uncertainty surrounding obscenity law, as Eberhard and the other anti-porn advocates on the city council struggled to deal with the reality that they could not simply ban pornography. A legally viable approach was needed, but at least at the time, there was no agreement on what exactly that might look like.

To try to untangle the legal mess, the city council requested two reports from city government agencies. The first was from the police department and concerned why the city's existing censorship ordinances were not being enforced. Police commissioner John Nichols replied by noting that the city ordinance dealing with movie censorship had been struck down a year earlier in the *Vixen* case while the municipal ordinance dealing with obscenity was not being enforced due to the belief that it too was unconstitutional, with the police instead relying on the state's obscenity law.[25]

The other report was from the city council's Support Service and focused on assessing the viability of the various methods of regulating pornography that had been proposed in the council. When it came to obscenity, based on recent

Supreme Court rulings that held that an individual had a right to privately own obscene material, the memorandum took as a given that the only constitutional method of controlling adult material through obscenity would be to regulate it based on "the protection of minors or unwilling persons." The report therefore concluded that a ban on adult businesses distributing or exhibiting obscene material to consenting adults was unlikely to stand up in court. The memorandum also took up the idea of levying a special tax on adult businesses. On this matter, the report was unequivocal, saying that such a proposal "is clearly constitutionally forbidden" since it would "be seen as a discriminatory regulation of the attempt to exercise a constitutionally protected right." Though the city could choose to tax all movie theaters and all bookstores, it could not discriminate by taxing only the adult ones.[26]

When it came to Ravitz's idea of using zoning to regulate adult businesses, two problems were cited in the report. The first was an inherent limitation of Ravitz's proposal, which is that such a plan would not have an impact on adult businesses already in operation, as it would only affect new businesses planning to open. The second issue was whether the proposal could withstand a legal challenge. As the report read: "It is unlikely that, constitutionally, the location of adult bookstores could be regulated by zoning laws, the same way liquor stores and bars are regulated. The problem is one of equal protection of laws. As in the question of taxing, the City could zone all bookstores and all movie theatres ... but not only those that deal with sexual subjects" (emphasis in original). The report thus identified what would later prove to be the central legal question surrounding the use of zoning to regulate adult businesses, which is whether the First Amendment protections granted to theaters and bookstores meant they could not be regulated by zoning in the same manner as liquor stores or bars. On this point, the support service made clear that Ravitz's proposal was thought to be unconstitutional. The memorandum instead suggested that the city adopt the obscenity guidelines laid down by the Supreme Court in *Redrup v. New York* (1967), with the proposed policy for Detroit being that "it is the duty of the government to protect its citizens from unwanted intrusions into their private lives, not to regulate their personal and private morals which do not interfere with the lives and morals of others." Still, such a proposal would have done little to shutter most adult businesses in the city and could hardly satisfy the demands of hard-line anti-porn advocates like Eberhard. Ultimately, then, the support service memorandum threw cold water on the various plans suggested in the city council while providing no comprehensive solution.[27]

In December of 1970, the city council held an open meeting on the issue, with the vast majority of the attending public who spoke at the meeting supporting new anti-porn regulations. Eberhard suggested that the city simply padlock "smut" bookstores and theaters and make the owners prove their material was not obscene, a move that undoubtedly would have been overturned by the courts. To this and other radical responses, Assistant Corporation Counsel William P. Doran urged caution, saying, "The concerns of these people who want us to take action certainly are legitimate and deeply and firmly held. But what they assume should be done and what can be done constitutionally are two entirely different things." In truth, Doran said, he had "no hope at all" that adult businesses in the city could be closed legally. The city council, then, was seemingly left without options, and so they decided to put the question of how to stop the spread of pornography on the back burner for the time being, moving on to other matters of concern.[28]

Beyond the lack of consensus on how to regulate pornography legally, a broader issue for Eberhard and his fellow anti-porn advocates was that the anti-porn rhetoric they tended to rely on increasingly appeared out of step with the times. Many proponents of new anti-porn legislation for the city continued to use the traditional moralizing and religious-based anti-porn discourse of old, but in the wake of the sexual revolution, no one wanted to be labeled a prude, particularly as public sentiment had congealed around a general aversion to media censorship. Advocates did themselves no favors either when they tried to tie the anti-porn fight to other morality-based issues, as happened when Mrs. Jacob Wenzel, secretary of the Metropolitan Detroit Council of Better Literature, said at a June 30, 1970, public meeting of the city council on the issue of pornography: "They should outlaw these things critical of organized religion and our nation. A reverent attitude is more appropriate in thinking of our government." This statement led the *Detroit Free Press* to publish an editorial responding to Wenzel's comments and more broadly to the city council's war against pornography. The paper harshly criticized the whole enterprise, saying, "It seems improbable in this city, with its diversity of religion and politics, that we should now be called upon to defend freedom of speech and religion at their most elemental level. Yet that is precisely the point to which Councilman Eberhard's crusade against the smut peddlers has brought the council." The editorial, while granting that Wenzel and Eberhard had good intentions, nevertheless evinced the type of opposition to censorship that was broadly symptomatic of liberal views on the issue at the time, with the piece going on to say, "We cannot have censorship without getting ourselves in trouble on the issue of whether we can be free to question our government and to exercise our independence. This is what has kept the Supreme Court hung up on trying to find a workable definition. This is why our society has to put up with some borderline stuff that has only the minutest kind of redeeming social value." Ultimately, then, what anti-porn advocates were lacking in 1970 was not just a legally viable approach to regulating adult media but also discursive strategies that might allow the movement to create separation between itself and the bluenosed moralizing censorship campaigns of old.[29]

By the start of the 1970s, though, a new form of anti-porn rhetoric had already begun to emerge and would ultimately coalesce into the type of anti-porn discourse seen in Redford in chapter 3. An example of this came in the July 1970 protests of Moulin Rouge and Candid Magazines, two adult bookstores in the Jefferson-Chalmers area of eastern Detroit. Every day for nearly three weeks, neighborhood residents picketed outside Candid Magazines from its ten o'clock opening time to its eight o'clock closing. The protest was organized by the Ad Hoc Committee for a Quality Community, a group formed in response to these two adult bookstores as well as the broader presence of adult businesses in residential areas. The very name of the group indicated that its opposition to pornography was, at least publicly, based on a grassroots neighborhood politics rather than traditional moralistic anti-porn politics. This distinction was reiterated in public comments by the leaders of the group, including the statement of Rev. Ronald Schmidt, who said of the Candid Magazines bookstore, "This is the death of our neighborhood." The group's official statement made clear that they hoped to distance themselves from the traditional rhetoric of anti-porn advocates by saying, "It is the express desire of our group to work toward the creation and maintenance of a quality community. It is not our desire to deprive anyone of their constitutional rights to read whatever literature they wish or to endanger an art form with censorship, nor are we against human sexuality as expressed in a truly loving relationship." The group acknowledged up front, then, the free speech arguments that had been winning the day and instead made clear that they sought to base their opposition to adult businesses on the grounds of the "maintenance of a quality community." By actively trying to distinguish themselves from their moralizing anti-porn predecessors, the Ad Hoc Committee for a Quality Community hoped to chart a new way forward for anti-porn politics that could respond to this new era in which censorship efforts were increasingly regarded with skepticism.[30]

One of the leaders of the Ad Hoc Committee for a Quality Community, Rev. Charles D. Robertson, further explicated the group's approach to anti-porn politics in the letter he sent to Mel Ravitz about the Candid Magazines bookstore. Robertson couched his statement by first discussing his hesitance to join the group due to his own liberal politics and aversion to being associated with more conservative anti-porn advocates, writing: "I had to do a great deal of 'soul searching' before joining with the Pastor of Faith Lutheran Church to form The Ad Hoc Committee for a Quality Community . . . because, I think there are more pressing issues facing the world and society like getting out of Indo-China and cleaning up our environment, etc. and also, as a clergyman . . . I did not want to join with broom riding Mary Beck types in some kind of a right wing witch hunt." In prefacing the letter this way—and, in particular, by invoking the specter of conservative Detroit politician Mary Beck—Robertson actively worked to distance himself and the Ad Hoc Committee from the rhetoric and tactics used by anti-porn advocates in previous decades. Instead, the group sought to shape a new form of anti-porn politics—one not opposed to liberalism but rather based in it through a defense of ordinary homeowners in residential neighborhoods whom they identified as the victims of the unchecked proliferation of pornography. Consequently, the focus for the reverend was less on banning such material entirely than it was on regulating its place in the urban landscape by keeping pornography out of residential areas. Such a position held real strategic value as a stance that might attract liberals who were uneasy about censorship and the rhetoric of older anti-porn campaigns but nevertheless were concerned about the potential impact of adult businesses on residential areas. As Ravitz responded to the reverend's letter, "I appreciate the difficulty of your position and I share it with you. I, too, would like to avoid association with any kind of witch hunters but I can likewise appreciate the necessity to keep undesirable literature out of our community."[31]

OBSCENITY ARRESTS AND POLICE ENTRAPMENT

It is worth taking a detour to discuss some of the ways the Detroit Police Department, alongside the Wayne County Prosecutor's Office, took matters into their own hands in the midst of this stalemate within the city council over how to deal with the issue of pornography. Though they no longer had the ability to censor movies before their release, throughout the early 1970s, police and prosecutors sought to clamp down on pornography through arrests using obscenity law. This was sometimes done in direct response to citizen complaints. And so, the picketing and protests of the Ad Hoc Committee for a Quality Community against the Moulin Rouge and Candid Magazines adult bookstores motivated the police to act. On July 17, 1970, the police raided the Moulin Rouge bookstore, arresting the owner and salesman on obscenity charges. The aforementioned Rev. Schmidt and Rev. Roberts, cochairs of the Ad Hoc Committee, both celebrated the news but vowed they would continue to picket outside Candid Magazines until further action was taken. Four days later, Lieutenant Areeda of the Obscenity Detail went into Candid and watched a two-minute stag film in one of the shop's peep show machines. Deeming the film obscene, the police returned later that day to confiscate three peep show machines, with Areeda saying he would next try to obtain a warrant for the arrest of the store's owner.[32]

These raids turned out to be a mere precursor to, less than three weeks later, what the *Free Press* deemed the "biggest anti-pornography strike ever conducted in Detroit." In one day, the police raided six adult bookstores, charging store owners with sale and possession of obscene material while confiscating a reported $50,000 worth of pornography, including hard-core adult films and peep show machines. It was a deliberate show of force, sending the message that the Detroit Police Department was here to clean up the city and rid it of adult entertainment. In reality, though, the results of the police's initiative were less definitive than anti-porn advocates might have hoped. Two weeks after the arrests, attorney Stephen M. Taylor, acting on behalf of five of the raided adult bookstores, filed a lawsuit against the police and the prosecutor's office, asking for $100,000 in damages and an order barring the enforcement of Michigan's obscenity law until a three-judge federal panel could rule on its constitutionality. A year later, the *Detroit News* reported that the obscenity cases against the bookstore owners had yet to go to trial and that numerous peep show machines were still in operation in the city.[33]

On August 20, 1970, less than two weeks after the biggest anti-porn raid in Detroit history, the *Detroit News* published an article that quoted Lieutenant Areeda as saying, "You can't hardly get a conviction on any form of obscenity anymore." Nevertheless, police and prosecutors were undeterred, and they continued to go after adult businesses in Detroit with decidedly mixed results. In September of 1970, Wayne County prosecutor William Cahalan filed suit to stop the showing of the adult film *He and She* at the Trans-Lux Krim Theater in Highland Park and the United Artists Theater in downtown Detroit. Rather than filing criminal charges against the exhibitors of the film, Cahalan instead tried the novel tactic of filing a civil suit seeking to declare the film obscene and legally bar it from exhibition in the state. The appeal of this approach was that, by putting the film on trial rather than the exhibitor, a civil suit could more hastily get a hearing on whether a movie was obscene compared to criminal charges, which often got bogged down with preliminary hearings and motions. This tactic was quickly stymied, though, with circuit judge Edward Bell declaring the 1963 state obscenity law used by Cahalan in this case unconstitutional due to it violating the Supreme Court's 1969 ruling in *Stanley v. Georgia*.[34]

In spite of Judge Bell's ruling, Cahalan continued to use civil suits while an appeal pended, with an assistant prosecutor saying, "We still think the law is operable." Even so, civil suits had their own limitations, as they were aimed at getting a speedy judgment on whether a film was obscene or not, rather than working to punish an exhibitor for showing a film deemed obscene. The problem was that adult films frequently played at theaters for only a short time before continuing on their run, meaning a civil suit often resulted in no real ramifications for the exhibitor. And so, by the time a Wayne County Circuit Court jury rendered their decision in December of 1970 that the adult film *101 Acts of Love* was obscene, the Summit Theater in downtown Detroit had already moved on to showing other adult films in the four weeks since the case was filed. Attorneys for the theater did not even bother to mount a defense since they were no longer showing the film and there would be no consequences to them for the film to be declared obscene in Michigan. The result of the case, then, was that a film no longer playing in Detroit was barred from Detroit while the film's exhibitor and distributor received no punishment of any kind. The same process played out months later when the Summit Theater showed the film *Animal Lovers*, prompting the Wayne County Prosecutor's Office to file a civil suit, which resulted in the film being declared obscene weeks after it had stopped showing.[35]

Whether utilizing criminal charges or a civil suit to determine obscenity, the problem for the Wayne County Prosecutor's Office was the fact that local courts were overrun with cases at this time, with lengthy court dockets making it hard to get before a judge in a timely manner. This was in large part the result of the Detroit Police Department racking up arrests on all manner of crimes in which there was no victim or injured party, which led some to wonder if the police needed to adjust their priorities. As the headline of a March 1972 *Detroit Free Press* article asked, "Do We Chase the Wrong 'Criminals'?" The paper's decision to place the word *criminals* in scare quotes was a deliberate one, as this article was the first in a five-part series dealing with the issue of victimless crimes, including not only pornography but also prostitution, drunkenness, and gambling. As the *Free Press* wrote, "In Detroit alone, hundreds of police spent thousands of man-hours last year arresting 497 vagrants, more than 3,000 prostitutes, almost 5,000 drug violators and more than 7,000 drunks, of whom 5,500 were taken to court and tried." The article went on to note that roughly half of all defendants in the city in 1971 had been charged with victimless crimes, with this having an "astronomical" cost to the taxpayers footing the bill while clogging up the court system.[36]

Even the police at times seemed hard pressed to explain why they placed such priority on victimless crimes, including pornography. Though the Detroit

Police Department had, for over a half century, practiced systematic forms of censorship out of the expressed belief that indecent media warped the minds of its consumers and led them down a path to criminality, some police officers began to use a decidedly different rhetoric. As the *Detroit News* wrote in August of 1971, "Detroit police make no attempt to claim that pornographic books seem to hurt anyone. When asked what effect the material has, [Obscenity Detail Patrolman Ralph] Guerrini suggested a call to the vice bureau." After a call to a vice officer, the *News* reported, "Inspector Russell Galloway says in eight years in vice control he's never found a sex maniac or anyone involved in prostitution or homosexual behavior whose acts related in any direct way to pornographic material." Obviously this was quite the departure from less than two decades earlier when Censor Bureau head Herbert Case had said, "There has never been a sex murder in the history of the Detroit Police Department in which obscene literature hasn't played a part."[37]

Though he denied a causal connection with pornography, Inspector Galloway's statement nevertheless points to the way the discourse surrounding the supposed link between pornography and sexual deviance often brought with it conflations of sexual criminality and homosexuality. Just as with the Redford letter writers who invoked the specter of predatory gay men lured to the neighborhood by the Adult World Bookstore, anti-porn advocates often suggested that pornography would lead to sexual deviance, including homosexuality as well as pedophilia, linking the two in the imaginary. To regulate pornography, then, always meant to regulate sexuality, with the war on pornography often seen as the tip of the spear in the war against the growing tide of homosexuality in society.

Meanwhile, a wholly different form of media regulation by the Detroit Police Department concerned not the content of films shown in theaters but rather the conduct and identity of audience members. In particular, the police, led primarily by the Vice Squad, had for decades monitored the auditoriums, balconies, and bathrooms of movie theaters for any suspected erotic activity. In practice, this amounted to the routine entrapment of gay men, with police officers flirting with men whom they suspected of being gay and then arresting them if they reciprocated. Timothy Retzloff, in his work on the history of gay and lesbian life in Detroit and the surrounding suburbs, found in court records from 1945 to 1965 "an average of fifty cases per year prosecuted as crimes of record for 'gross indecency between males' and 'accosting and soliciting for immoral purposes.'" While the Vice Squad focused most of their attention on public parks and restrooms known to be queer spaces during that time period, a number of movie theaters were heavily policed as well, including the Times Square, Regent, and Colonial.[38]

By the early 1970s, the Detroit Police Department had stepped up efforts at regulating the activities of gay men in public spaces. According to the *Gay Liberator*, the monthly newspaper put out by the Gay Liberation Front of Detroit, in 1972 the Detroit police arrested 1,065 men on accosting and soliciting charges, a 42 percent increase on the previous year. Though police records did not break down what percentage of men charged with accosting and soliciting were arrested based on suspected homosexual behavior as opposed to, for instance, soliciting a female sex worker, a Detroit police officer estimated that the number was roughly half in 1970. These arrests were the result of concerted efforts by the Detroit Police Department's eighty-man Vice Squad and four twenty-man "morality units" stationed in precincts. In the early 1970s, vice officers particularly targeted adult movie theaters as prime sites for entrapment. One anonymous individual wrote a letter to the editor of the African American newspaper *Michigan Chronicle* to express his frustration with the practice, saying, "Not all people who happen to visit an adult movie house or show are thinking about approaching another person. Many visit out of curiosity, only to find themselves approached by police. Without returning any conversation, a citizen can find himself jailed for accosting and soliciting when he has never said a word to an officer." Undercover police officers were a steady presence at adult movie theaters throughout the early 1970s, leading the *Gay Liberator* to repeatedly warn its readers about specific adult theaters where arrests had been reported, including the Projection Room, Colonial, Nortown, and Gem Art.[39]

Unsurprisingly, police particularly targeted any theaters showing gay-themed movies as prime sites for the entrapment of gay men. In 1972, the *Gay Liberator* published an article with a guide to cruising in bathrooms in the Detroit area, singling out the downtown Plaza Theatre while noting, "The Plaza Theatre used to be good when it was the old Telenews but now only if a gay movie is showing—but these type movies also bring the vice cops. Be careful." The way undercover vice cops sought to entrap and arrest men attending gay movies was widely known, to the point that one theater decided to warn its customers of the practice. As the radical newspaper *Fifth Estate* wrote in 1972, "Aware that the showing of the gay film, *Song of the Loon*, would attract the Detroit vice squad to prey upon show patrons, the management of the Roxy Theatre followed the suggestion of the Detroit Gay Switchboard and posted a sign in the men's room reading 'Beware of Entrapment.'" The first theater in the region to show gay pornography full-time, the Wood-Six Theater in 1973, was spared this type of constant police presence only through the fact that it was located in Highland Park, outside the Detroit Police Department's jurisdiction.[40]

Local gay rights activists sought to fight back against police entrapment through several avenues. The *Gay Liberator* repeatedly called on anyone arrested for accosting and soliciting to demand a jury trial, gumming up an already overburdened court system to, as they put it, "raise the price they [police and prosecutors] have to pay." Some gay male victims of police entrapment even sought to directly challenge the constitutionality of the accosting and soliciting ordinance itself in the courts. Meanwhile, gay rights activists also lobbied city officials to change anti-gay laws. In the fall of 1971, the organization Detroit Gay Activists sent a letter calling for the repeal of the accosting and soliciting ordinance to Mayor Gribbs, Commissioner Nichols, and city council president Mel Ravitz. Of these, Ravitz was the only one who responded to the group, setting up a meeting with local gay activists in which he expressed sympathy for their position while making no firm promises about a repeal of the accosting and soliciting law.[41]

All in all, even as the early 1970s saw the Detroit Police Department continue to try to regulate the morals of Detroit through obscenity arrests and the entrapment of gay men in movie theaters, they increasingly ran into challenges in the legal arena. Gay men accused of accosting and soliciting were increasingly unwilling to simply plead guilty and take whatever penalty was meted out to them by a judge. Similarly, the owners of adult businesses were also frequently fighting back against obscenity charges or moving through films so quickly that a determination that a film was obscene was ultimately irrelevant. However, the comparison diverges outside the legal arena. Gay rights activists had managed some inroads with a select few elected officials sympathetic to their cause and in 1973 achieved their greatest success yet when they managed to get a new city charter passed that protected all Detroit residents from discrimination based on sexual orientation, a first for major cities in the United States. The proprietors of adult movie theaters and bookstores, on the other hand, would never find any type of warm welcome from city officials, who were largely united in opposition to their businesses and what they represented. Indeed, the central question within the city council was how to regulate adult businesses, not whether to, a dilemma that continued to confound in 1971 even as pressure mounted on the city council to act.

1971: CONTINUED CITY COUNCIL INACTION

Over the course of 1971, adult entertainment in Detroit continued its unabated growth. Though statistics on the size of the industry in the city varied, one estimate put the number of adult bookstores at that time at twenty-two and the number of adult movie theaters at sixteen, while the *Detroit News* reported that the city's adult businesses grossed between $5 million and $10 million a year. Moreover, the type of adult material offered by these businesses had changed, with hard-core films and magazines replacing their soft-core predecessors. The *News* further noted, "Book stores also offer blatant sex items, sold as 'novelties.' These are rubber and plastic goods, replicas of sex organs and battery operated 'vibrators.'" Beyond the more explicit offerings of adult movie theaters and bookstores, pornography sent through the mail also became a newfound topic of alarm in the city in 1971. Meanwhile, that same year saw Judge Rashid's decision that temporarily outlawed topless dancing in the city, as discussed in chapter 4.[42]

New forms of adult entertainment also emerged. In May of 1971, the *Detroit Free Press* reported on a business in which, for five dollars, one could privately photograph a nude model for a half hour, with the rule evidently being that no touching was allowed. It quickly drew the attention of the authorities, with the paper reporting, "The police have been around—32 in the first four days of business, the proprietor claims—but could find nothing illegal. Business appears to be booming." More nude modeling studios soon followed. In the fall, one studio along Michigan Avenue drew the ire of some residents after it placed flyers under the windshields of parked cars in the area.[43]

Despite the growing prominence of adult entertainment in Detroit alongside the backlash it provoked, the challenges facing the city council in trying to come to an agreement on a legally sound way to regulate pornography had not measurably changed in the new year. In September of 1971, the city council met once again to discuss various ways they might halt the spread of adult entertainment in the city. At the meeting, several different methods for potentially regulating pornography were raised, including Ravitz's zoning approach and Eberhard's recurring suggestion that "they should padlock the places and make the dealers prove their stuff is not pornographic." A new idea up for consideration was to require all bookstores and theaters to get a license to operate each year under the purview of the Department of Buildings and Safety Engineering, thereby bringing them under closer control of the city. Finally, there was again a renewed push to craft a new obscenity ordinance for the city, this time at the behest of Thomas Gallagher, a member of the city's Department of Corporation Counsel. Gallagher's optimism about the potential utility of obscenity law diverged from the views expressed by Corporation Counsel William P. Doran a year prior. As Gallagher said at the meeting, "I think it can be done.... We're not quite as handcuffed as we thought in the first place." In Gallagher's view, the key was to focus on the category of obscenity rather than pornography because the former was easier to define than the latter. The city council then asked Gallagher to study further the various methods of regulating pornography discussed at the meeting and give his recommendation for a new anti-porn ordinance. Gallagher's confidence that he could come up with a viable ordinance was indicated when, in a response to a question about how long it would take to prepare a new obscenity ordinance, he boasted to journalists, "I can write it right now. Give me a piece of paper."[44]

Less than a week later, Gallagher sent the city council his response. In his letter, he argued against the approach of licensing adult businesses given that to do so would require that all movie theaters and bookstores be licensed, and in his view, "legitimate" businesses "should not be subjected to a regulatory law because of the misconduct of a relative few." The other problem with licensing, in Gallagher's view, was that to give licenses to adult bookstores would implicitly seem to condone them, even if it provided additional avenues of regulation. As he wrote of adult bookstores, "I don't think your honorable body should make any appearance of permissiveness so far as they are concerned." Such a line undoubtedly points to the strident anti-porn perspective Gallagher brought to this topic, and so it is perhaps no surprise that Gallagher preferred a return to an obscenity-based approach to regulating pornography. Gallagher sent the city council a proposed ordinance to update Detroit's obscenity code, though at least for the moment, the city council chose not to act on the measure.[45]

It was within this context that local gay and lesbian organizations—including ONE in Detroit, Detroit Gay Activists, and Daughters of Bilitis—sent a letter to Ravitz at the outset of 1972 setting out their opposition to the city council's efforts to enact further regulations against pornography. Given the differing politics of the various groups signing it, ranging from radical leftist to moderate liberal, the letter attempted to strike a position that would be acceptable to all its members. As it said, "The undersigned organizations are united in urging defeat of the proposed Detroit Ordnance [sic] to ban the sale of 'pornography' in the city. Our position is not an indorsement of material which many citizens, including a good number of our own members, find offensive. Rather we consider it regressive for a government body to legislate people's taste and morality when all such experiments in the past have utterly failed at tremendous cost in man-hours and money devoted to enforcement." The letter then took a vague, moderate-liberal position defending free speech while not mounting an argument in favor of pornography's worth or making clear the important role sex media had long played in gay and lesbian social circles. Nevertheless, it was one of the few examples of local organizations willing to take a stand against efforts to enact further regulations on adult entertainment.[46]

Altogether, at the outset of 1972, things looked much the same as they had a year prior in the city council. Council members continued to be stifled by the question of what would constitute a legally viable method of regulating pornography, even as the pornography trade in the city flourished. Soon, though, the anti-porn fight in Detroit was energized by the entrance of a new player on the scene—Mayor Gribbs.

1972: THE MAYOR AND CITY COUNCIL BEGIN TO TAKE ACTION

In early 1972, the debate over pornography in Detroit began to heat up. In January, Councilman Eberhard announced plans to sponsor two ordinances, both drawn up by Gallagher, aimed at closing many of the city's adult businesses.[47] The first of these ordinances, targeting adult bookstores, cleared a procedural vote in the city council later that month, with the only dissenting votes being Carl Levin, Philip Van Antwerp, and Mel Ravitz, who argued that the ordinance was likely to be ruled unconstitutional given the difficulties of separating out "adult" books and bookstores from "normal" ones. As Levin said, the ordinance "will cover almost every modern novel whether it's pornographic or not." Even Gallagher, author of the ordinance, admitted the thorniness of the issue, saying that it is "almost impossible to pick up a current novel which doesn't refer to human sexual activities." He indicated he would look to revise the ordinance in the days ahead while the council continued to debate its next action.[48]

On January 26, the city council held a two-hour public hearing. Of the roughly twenty-five members of the public who spoke at the meeting, all but two were in favor of the new ordinances. The opposing voices were Adrienne James of the ACLU, who argued against the proposals on constitutional grounds, and Paul Lowinger, a psychiatrist and professor at Wayne State University who contended that there was no evidence to support the supposed link between crime and pornography. Lowinger further argued that anti-pornography laws were "frequently used" to "persecute creative people." This drew the ire of many in attendance, including Councilman Van Antwerp, who told Lowinger, "I think you're nuts."[49]

The council members expressed differing opinions at the meeting, though most were broadly in favor of the proposed new obscenity ordinances. The two biggest naysayers were Ravitz and Levin, with the latter saying the proposed bookstore amendment "is not worth the paper it is written on." Instead, he argued that boycotts and picketing should be the methods used to "get rid of" adult businesses. Ravitz similarly expressed his misgivings about the constitutionality of the proposals, even as, in a gesture to the politics of the issue, he also made sure to publicly express that he was "as concerned about the problem [of pornography] as anybody."[50]

In the days following the public meeting, Creighton C. Lederer, the head of the Detroit Department of Buildings and Safety Engineering, submitted to both Levin and Ravitz the results of his study on different potential methods of regulating adult businesses. Lederer advocated for Ravitz's plan of using zoning law to control the spread of adult businesses, saying that they could be brought under the "regulated uses" section of the city's zoning code, which required that such establishments could not be within one thousand feet of each other. Lederer's memo spelled out the few exceptions to this rule in the city's existing zoning code, including one if "the proposed use will not enlarge or encourage the development of a 'skid row' area" and another if the business "will not be contrary to any program of neighborhood conservation nor will it interfere with any program of Urban Renewal." Such exceptions made clear that this section of the city's zoning code was primarily about the supposed negative economic impact that certain businesses had on surrounding neighborhoods. Unsurprisingly, then, for liberals like Levin and Ravitz, zoning presented an enticing alternative method for regulating pornography, one that could avoid the overt stifling of free speech through obscenity-based censorship while still mollifying the many citizens who wanted to see the city council take concrete action against pornography.[51]

Still, hard-liners on the city council continued to seek more radical measures to combat the spread of adult entertainment. By February of 1972, the city council was getting ready to vote on new obscenity ordinances proposed by Eberhard, including one making it a crime to operate a business where the "principal activity is the sale of books, magazines or other printed or recorded matter describing or portraying sexual activities or human nudity." Even as the city council was preparing to vote, some continued to call into question the legality of Eberhard's proposals. Among those questioning whether these ordinances would hold up in court was none other than the man who wrote them, Thomas Gallagher, who wrote the city council on February 10 to "reiterate that the bookstore ordinance should not be considered or passed by your honorable body.... After consultation with members of your honorable body and with members of the corporation counsel's staff, I am convinced that this amendment is constitutionally defective." Despite Gallagher's warning, Eberhard proceeded to call for a vote anyway, with the council deadlocking four to four on whether to adopt the ordinance aimed at adult bookstores as well as a separate one targeting nude photo studios, only agreeing to pass some smaller minor revisions to the existing obscenity ordinances. Two weeks later, though, Eberhard put the same ordinances up for a vote again, this time managing to get them passed while Councilman Van Antwerp, previously one of the nay votes, was away on vacation.[52]

After the council passed the ordinances, Levin repeated his objections, saying, "It will cover almost every modern novel, whether it's pornographic or not. I don't think we accomplished anything by passing it, and we're just kidding people into thinking we have." He again suggested that picketing adult bookstores might be a better course of action for residents while also arguing that a sounder regulatory measure would be to adopt the zoning-based approach favored by him and Ravitz. The city council at that time voted by a six-to-one margin to introduce a proposal bringing nude modeling studios under the "regulated uses" section of the city's zoning law and to hold a public hearing on the matter. The only nay vote on the proposal came from Wierzbicki, the most conservative council member, who no doubt found the proposal insufficient for his goal of shutting down adult businesses entirely. Meanwhile, with the passage of the anti–adult bookstore ordinance, Eberhard could finally claim some form of victory, having successfully passed a law that would, in theory, significantly alter the landscape of adult entertainment in Detroit. That was based on two conditions, though, one of them being the question of whether the ordinance was constitutional, with Eberhard issuing a challenge to the owners of adult businesses: "Let them take us to court." The other condition was more immediate and no less vexing: namely, would Mayor Gribbs even sign the bill?[53]

Up until this point, Gribbs had remained steadfastly silent on the question of what to do about the spread of pornography and adult entertainment in Detroit. Behind the scenes, though, he had already begun to make moves that would set the stage for him to come out strongly against adult media. In late 1971, Gribbs quietly established the Mayor's Task Force on Licensing Procedures, though he would tell neither the city council nor the public at large about the agency until March of 1972. A press release put out by the mayor's office at that time explained the mission of the task force by saying: "The Mayor's Task Force on Licensing Procedures was organized last year to investigate the growing number of citizen complaints and police problems with X-rated movie houses and adult bookstores. According to Phillip G. Tannian, assistant to the Mayor and the task force chairman, the task force has been given the responsibility of strengthening the ordinance pertaining to such establishments and developing, where necessary the means to deal with such problems swiftly and effectively." The task force was made up of representatives from five departments, including the City of Detroit's Department of Corporation Counsel, Health Department, Fire Marshal Division, Police Department, and Department of Buildings and Safety Engineering. One indication that the mayor was placing a high priority on the issue of pornography was that he chose Phillip Tannian to head the new task force. Tannian had been a key member of the mayor's campaign team in the 1969 election and was widely considered to be one of Gribbs's most influential aides and a growing political player in Detroit.[54]

On March 6, less than a week after the city council passed Eberhard's obscenity ordinance aimed at adult bookstores, Mayor Gribbs signed the bill into law. That same day the mayor also announced that he had decided to revoke the license for the peep show machines housed at Adult City, an adult bookstore operating on Eight Mile in northeast Detroit. The move was the result of the work of both the Mayor's Task Force on Licensing Procedures, which recommended the action, and the Detroit Police Department, which had an ongoing investigation into the business. As part of this investigation, on September 28, 1971, Patrolman Paul Smith entered the Adult City bookstore, first noting the "adult books & magazines" sold in the front of the store before moving to the back rooms, where small private viewing stations were set up wherein, for the price of a quarter, a patron could watch "80 to 90 seconds" of 8mm hard-core pornography. A search warrant was then issued, with the owner of the store arraigned a day later. Nearly six months after that, though, the case was still pending, leading both Commissioner Nichols and the Task Force on Licensing Procedures, in consultation with the Department of Corporation Counsel, to recommend that the mayor revoke the license used by Adult City for its peep show machines.[55]

The decision to revoke the Adult City bookstore's license and sign the city council's new obscenity ordinance into law on the same day was a calculated move by the mayor to signal his entrance into the debate over pornography in Detroit. As Mayor Gribbs said when announcing Adult City's license revocation, "This is only the first of many such actions to be taken whenever and wherever necessary to halt the proliferation of pornography in Detroit." There was a sense that, after so much debate on the issue in the city council, Gribbs was a latecomer to the anti-porn party, merely hopping on to the cause once it had become politically expedient to do so. This was implicit in how the *Detroit News* covered the mayor's announcement regarding the Adult City bookstore, with the paper writing, "With the action, Gribbs joins a crusade against pornography begun two months ago by the City Council." Meanwhile, the *Free Press* wrote that the attorney for Adult City "believes Gribbs took the action because of recent publicity about Common Council's action in passing a new city law aimed at adult bookstores." Still, if Gribbs had perhaps shown up late, he had undoubtedly appeared in full force, making clear that going after the adult entertainment industry in Detroit would henceforth be a major priority for his administration.[56]

As luck would have it, Gribbs was immediately given an opportunity to draw attention to his administration's anti-porn work when, on March 19, less than two weeks after he publicly entered the anti-porn fray, the *Detroit News* announced it would no longer run any ads for X-rated movies. The move set off a firestorm of controversy, with Jack Valenti, head of the Motion Picture Association of America, visiting the paper to express his displeasure with the move while director Stanley Kubrick, whose film *A Clockwork Orange* (1971) was affected by the ban on X-rated ads, wrote a scathing letter to the editor of the *News*. In the midst of this, the mayor's office quickly drafted a letter from Gribbs to the *News* in which he commended the paper's decision, saying it would be "applauded by all concerned citizens." He also used the letter to draw attention to the anti-porn work being done by his administration and specifically the Mayor's Task Force on Licensing Procedure, further saying, "I am earnestly and vigorously seeking to stem the tide of printed and visual smut." Between Eberhard's ordinance becoming law, Gribbs's actions, and the move by the *Detroit News* to bar ads for X-rated movies, the anti-porn movement in Detroit was undoubtedly picking up steam in March of 1972.[57]

Still, Mayor Gribbs, along with Eberhard and his fellow anti-porn advocates in the city council, faced almost immediate setbacks. The mayor's move against Adult City was the first to run into difficulties. On March 16, Judge John Feikens ordered the city not to interfere with the peep show machines housed in the Adult City bookstore until he could come to a final ruling on the constitutionality of the obscenity restrictions in Detroit's licensing ordinance. In the end this would prove irrelevant, though, as the city's Department of Buildings and Safety Engineering had, in the meanwhile, proceeded to grant Adult City a license renewal, seemingly unaware that the mayor had ordered those same licenses revoked two weeks prior. The *News* reported that "city officials were more than a little embarrassed at the 'clerical error,'" with the commissioner of the department, Creighton Lederer, admitting, "We goofed."[58]

Other mistakes soon followed. On March 22, Gribbs announced that he would refuse to approve the operating license for the Riviera Theater because its owner, Arthur Weisberg, had allegedly previously pled guilty to charges of conspiring to exhibit pornography. Within a week, Gribbs was forced to go back on this announcement after lawyers for Weisberg pointed out that it was not Weisberg but rather RGW Enterprises Inc., a corporation Weisberg then belonged to, that had pled guilty to the charges, while the charges against Weisberg had been dismissed. Once again, then, the move to use existing licensing laws to go after an adult business in Detroit had backfired for the mayor, leaving his administration's first entries into anti-porn politics looking haphazard and ill conceived.[59]

Still, the mayor's office pushed on, continuing to emphasize the use of licensing law as its preferred mechanism for controlling pornography in Detroit. In late March, the mayor, with the aid of his dedicated task force, unveiled a tentative proposal for new licensing procedures for all bookstores, cabarets, dance halls, and bars, among other types of businesses. The plan made two major substantive changes to city law, the first being that bookstores would now be required to get licensed to operate, which had not been the case up until this point (it was for this reason that the mayor went after the peep show machines in Adult City, rather than the nonexistent license for the bookstore itself). The second major change was that both new and existing adult businesses would have to receive approval from a majority of nearby neighborhood residents to be able to operate. The notion was to put power back in the hands of citizens, who would now get to decide which adult businesses could and could not operate in their communities.[60]

Ravitz and Levin immediately came out against the plan. Ravitz particularly lambasted the fact that the licensing procedures would apply to all bookstores, regardless of the type of literature they sold. Crafting the proposal in this way allowed the mayor to sidestep questions of how to legally distinguish between regular bookstores and their adult counterparts, but it also meant burdensome new regulations for nonadult bookstores in the city. While expressing his opposition to the plan, Ravitz also made sure to reiterate his disapproval of pornography, saying, "I'm as much opposed to pornography as anyone else but I just don't know that you can do anything legally at all about bookstores." Levin, meanwhile, attacked the aspect of the plan requiring that businesses get consent from their neighbors, saying, "You can't require that someone receive the permission of his neighbors to talk or write. It's clearly unconstitutional."[61]

Ravitz's and Levin's vocal opposition to the proposal also spoke to the growing tensions between the city council and Mayor Gribbs at this time. After a honeymoon period following Gribbs first taking office in early 1970, the relationship between Mayor Gribbs and the city council soon began to fray considerably. By March of 1972, the main source of rancor was over the implementation of some commercial-strip redevelopment proposals that the city council had previously passed but that had been held up by the mayor's office. The city council grew increasingly frustrated with the mayor as a result, showing their disapproval by refusing the formality of approving one report from the mayor and even threatening to hold up the payroll of the city's legal staff unless Gribbs approved the projects. On March 29, the *Detroit News* said of the fight, "The 'honeymoon' may not quite be over, but Detroit's city councilmen are having their first major spat with Mayor Gribbs." Underlying this growing tension was the fact that the next city elections were set to be held in 1973, and a number of city council members were eyeing a possible run for mayor. It was within this context that Ravitz and Levin spoke out against the mayor's proposed anti-porn ordinances, with Levin calling the proposals "a curious transference of power to the mayor's office."[62]

―⚋―

The rash of anti-porn activity in Detroit in March of 1972 encapsulated the variety of different approaches under consideration for how to regulate adult entertainment. Mayor Gribbs was pushing the use of licensing law by both relying on existing ordinances and proposing new ones. This approach had the benefit of granting greater regulatory control to the city government as well as to neighborhood residents under the proposed new plan. The downsides were the potential legal complications of giving residents this type of power as well as the challenge of how, or whether, to distinguish adult bookstores from regular ones. Councilman Eberhard, on the other hand, was driving forward with various obscenity-based plans that would allow the city to immediately shutter many if not most adult businesses. All this, though, was dependent on whether Eberhard's obscenity ordinances could survive the inevitable legal challenges, which seemed unlikely to most observers. Finally, Councilman Ravitz's proposal was to add adult businesses to the city's already established skid row zoning ordinance so as to disperse adult businesses. The plan would be unable to close existing adult businesses, only prevent new ones from opening, which, along with Ravitz's track record of voting nay on Eberhard's proposed obscenity ordinances, led many to view it as too lenient of a strategy. In the months ahead, these three approaches continued to compete with one another to see which would take hold as the city's main method for regulating pornography.

Eberhard's obscenity-based approach was quickly put to the test. Just weeks after his new obscenity ordinance targeting adult bookstores was signed into law by the mayor in early March, it was challenged in the courts by Royal News Co., an Ohio-based distributor of adult material. Representing them was famed civil rights attorney Ernest Goodman, who had also served as lead counsel on some of Royal News's previous legal tussles with the city of Detroit. The suit contended that the city's new obscenity ordinance targeted at adult bookstores violated the First and Fourteenth Amendments, was overly vague, and denied equal protection under law in its singling out of only adult-oriented bookstores for further regulation.[63]

Three months later, in June of 1972, Judge Philip Pratt ruled against the city, calling the new ordinance "constitutionally defective" and "obviously overbroad and vague." The judge particularly singled out the way constitutionally protected speech would be harmed by this ordinance, saying, "This unqualified language would erase from human knowledge such disparate founts as photographs of carvings in some pyramids and textbooks on zoology and animal husbandry." The ruling was hardly a surprise given the serious reservations nearly all parties had about the ordinance's constitutionality prior to the vote approving it in the city council. After the ruling was announced, Assistant Corporation Counsel Thomas Gallagher said of the judge's decision, "Even though I drafted the ordinance and defended it as fully as possible in federal court, I must admit that I tried to talk the Council out of adopting it this spring and I'm not surprised that Judge Pratt ruled against it." Evidently reality had set in since the time that, less than a year prior, Gallagher had confidently bragged to the press that he could write a new constitutionally sound obscenity ordinance on the spot.[64]

Needless to say, Councilman Eberhard was less than pleased with the judge's ruling. He called the decision "a typical example of what the courts are doing; we're having government by the courts, not by referenda or by elected officials." A day later, and expressly in response to the judge's decision, Eberhard unexpectedly announced that he would be running for mayor in the next year's election, making him one of the first major candidates to enter the race. His announcement was a clear indication not only of his political aspirations but, just as importantly, of the way he viewed pornography as central to his politics, with the judge's decision seemingly spurring him to announce his candidacy with the election still over a year away. Still, in the short term, and in light of the judge's ruling, Eberhard indicated a willingness to take another look at the other proposed methods of regulating pornography, saying, "We'll just have to take another tack. We'll try dealing with the problem from the angle of licensing and zoning if we can't do it the other way."[65]

Meanwhile, the Gribbs administration continued to push forward with the use of licensing to regulate adult entertainment. Undeterred by his bungling of the licensing revocations of the Adult City bookstore and the Riviera Theater, Gribbs continued to use existing licensing law to harass and crack down on adult businesses. On March 30, the Department of Buildings and Safety

Engineering, under the leadership of Creighton Lederer, began to require further "administrative review" for all permit applications in which the building housed any type of business that might be adult oriented, including movie theaters, bookstores, and modeling studios. This allowed the city to deny a building permit to American Mini Theatres, which had planned to open an adult theater in northwest Detroit. American Mini Theatres then sued the city, resulting in circuit court judge Joseph A. Moynihan, on May 17, ordering that Lederer and the Department of Buildings and Safety Engineering issue the permit for the theater.[66]

One day earlier, though, the city council passed an ordinance granting a ninety-day suspension on the issuance of licenses and permits for all new bookstores, modeling studios, and movie theaters. The bill passed five to three, with Ravitz, Levin, and Van Antwerp again making up the dissenting votes. Critics accused the ordinance of being unconstitutional while also noting that it applied to all new movie theaters and not just adult ones. This latter issue quickly led to an embarrassment when, just a few days later, a group hoping to bring children's movies and cartoons to the old Kramer Theater on the city's west side was denied a license due to the moratorium.[67]

With this ninety-day suspension in place, the city upped its use of licensing to curtail the spread of adult businesses. The mayor soon denied a license to John Clark, who was hoping to get a permit to operate the Adult Fare Theatre, a move that then sparked a legal fight. In late May, Clark combined his complaint with that of American Mini Theatres and a few other owners of adult businesses and together filed suit against the city over what they saw as the city's unlawful use of licensing restrictions to harass adult businesses. While the case was pending, American Mini Theatres wrote the mayor to inform him that, with renovations now complete, its new adult movie theater, the Playboy, would be opening its doors on August 2, 1972, without the still-pending license. On the day of its opening, a city building inspector came to the theater and cited its owners for a defective furnace and having no certificate of occupancy. The theater's attorney fired back that the city had "continually placed stumbling blocks" in the way of the Playboy's opening. Within a week, the furnace was fixed, and the Playboy reopened despite still lacking an operating permit from the city. Perhaps emboldened by the move, weeks later John Clark announced that he too would open his Adult Fare Theatre without a license.[68]

While these efforts to prevent new adult businesses from opening via licensing law achieved some limited success, they were also met with significant resistance, pointing to the limitations of this piecemeal approach when it came to dealing with the broader problem. Moreover, it seemingly had done little to quell the growth of the adult entertainment industry in Detroit. Estimates in mid-1972 put the number of adult bookstores and movie theaters in the city anywhere from fifty to around seventy-five, many of them having opened that very year. Meanwhile, the number of topless bars in the city continued to grow, particularly following the July 1972 Michigan Court of Appeals ruling overturning the 1969 conviction of Tyra Lea LaRue for indecent exposure. Undoubtedly, then, as summer came to a close, and despite the obscenity ordinances passed by the city council and the denial of licenses by the mayor's office, pornography and adult entertainment were continuing to flourish in Detroit. Just at that moment, though, the mayor and his chosen task force were getting ready to take action.[69]

THE BIRTH OF THE DETROIT MODEL

On October 2, 1972, Mayor Gribbs sent the city council the final version of the proposals recommended by his Task Force on Licensing Procedures. The press release sent out by the mayor demonstrated the way new currents in anti-porn politics had affected the formation of the proposed ordinances. The statement began by saying, "Our purpose is not in acting as a censor, but acting in response to the needs and requests of the citizens of Detroit." Immediately denying that the ordinances in any way amounted to censorship—which seemingly had become a four-letter word by this point—the mayor instead emphasized the grassroots neighborhood-based support for the plan, saying, "Our neighborhoods need protection from businesses our citizens feel are undesirable." Marshaling this grassroots support, the mayor called on citizens to attend the public hearings for the ordinances on October 17 before the city planning commission and on October 20 before the city council.[70]

In using language that emphasized grassroots opposition to adult businesses, the mayor was drawing on the anti-porn activism taking place in residential neighborhoods across the city at that very moment. Beyond the campaign of Redford against the Adult World Bookstore, as discussed in chapter 3, a similar effort had begun against the Frisco Theatre at Woodward and Eight Mile in northern Detroit. There, homeowners protested outside the adult movie theater for weeks using rhetoric largely similar to that used in Redford, including one resident saying that the Frisco had "invaded" the neighborhood. Evoking the white racial politics of the era, that same resident also said of the protesters, "We're all family people—normal silent majority people." Meanwhile, countless letters demanding action were simultaneously streaming into the offices of the mayor and city council.[71]

The groundswell of grassroots support for new anti-porn legislation was further evidenced by the two public hearings held on the issue that month. At the first of these, held on October 17 before the city planning commission, Gribbs himself appeared, telling those present, "The constitution of our country guarantees freedom of speech, but it does not guarantee that such freedom be allowed to hinder the rights of others and that it have the effect of severely crippling the morale and vitality of our neighborhoods." Much like the grassroots protesters who were then flooding his office with letters, Gribbs sought to elide questions of free speech by instead emphasizing the rights of residents and homeowners along with the impact of adult businesses on neighborhoods. All but two of the roughly seventy-five speakers attending the public hearing favored the adoption of the new ordinances, with many of these supporters hailing from community groups and homeowners' associations. Meanwhile, the two lone naysayers were against the proposals only because they thought they did not go far enough in getting rid of pornography in the city, with anti-porn activist Delores Huber saying the city should close all adult businesses rather than them "being planned into the structure of the city of Detroit."[72]

The second public hearing on the matter was held October 20 before the city council. This meeting attracted around 180 people, nearly all of whom again supported the new proposals. A boost to these attendance numbers came from the chartered bus of 48 people that originated from the Sixteenth Precinct Police Station, which was located in northwest Detroit just a few blocks from the Adult World Bookstore and across the street from Redford High School. A *Detroit Free Press* reporter rode with them to the meeting, with the reporter downplaying the notion that these anti-porn activists were driven by religion and moralizing by saying that there was more "small talk than sermonizing" on the bus ride and that the riders were "far from a bluestocking brigade."[73]

Among those bus riders was Beverly Drylie, who had written letters to both Ravitz and Gribbs protesting the Adult World. Talking to the *Free Press*, Drylie stressed that her disapproval of adult entertainment was based solely on its entrance into residential areas, saying, "I wouldn't object to having such places in a business-type district. I know there's a certain demand for it." She also emphasized her concerns surrounding the flight of people from the city, saying, "People are using this as one more argument to say the city's done for.... I'd hate to go to the suburbs. I love the city. It has all kinds of people, and that's what I like." Similarly, Myron Gelt, who had also written letters protesting the Adult World bookstore as the owner of a floral shop located just next door, drew cheers from those assembled at the meeting when he told the city council, "If you're not gonna do something about it, stop calling meetings, because we've got more important things to do—like looking for homes in the suburbs."[74]

The lone dissenting voice at the hearing was Sheridan Holzman of the ACLU, who spoke directly to the proposed use of zoning: "An adult bookstore is not the same as a bar, a pawnshop or the like. It is protected by the sanctity of the First Amendment to the Constitution." Holzman also argued that the ordinance might jeopardize the showing of "prize-winning movies of obvious merit, like *The Graduate, Ryan's Daughter* and *Clockwork Orange.*" This strategy of emphasizing the harm that censorship would do to prestigious art-house cinema, while ignoring the censoring of less high-minded material, nevertheless fell on deaf ears here, with Councilman Van Antwerp drawing laughter and applause when he replied to Holzman, "Who gave them prizes? Some bunch of New York City screwballs?"[75]

On October 24, the set of anti-porn ordinances recommended by the Mayor's Task Force on Licensing Procedures became the first anti-porn proposal passed by this city council unanimously. The two city officials who were most closely associated with the ordinance publicly were Ravitz and Gribbs, and each used rhetoric drawn from contemporaneous grassroots anti-porn campaigns. Upon helping pass the ordinance, Ravitz expressed confidence that it would hold up better than previous bills struck down in the courts, saying, "I think this time the ordinances will pass (a court test) because we're taking the view that these establishments have a blighting effect on neighborhoods by downgrading and depreciating property values." Press coverage surrounding the ordinance similarly emphasized the rights of homeowners and the economic impact of adult businesses rather than questions or morality or free speech. A *Detroit News* editorial on the new law said, "Basically, the ordinances do not pass moral judgment on adult book stores, nude modeling studios and the like." For this reason, the editorial predicted the law would have an easier time in the courts than "past laws dealing with moral definitions." Such language indicated the success of the ordinance's architects in crafting a law that could, at least rhetorically, elide these debates over morality.[76]

THE IMPACT AND INFLUENCE OF THE DETROIT MODEL

The ordinances passed by the city council and signed into law by the mayor were a mixture of zoning- and licensing-based solutions to the rise of adult entertainment in the city. The measure that was seen as the most noteworthy at the time was a version of the provision the Mayor's Task Force on Licensing

Procedures had recommended earlier that year requiring new adult bookstores, adult theaters, and topless bars hoping to open in the city to first receive approval from at least 51 percent of residents and business owners within five hundred feet. This granted greater control to neighborhoods that could now exercise veto power over adult businesses trying to open in their communities. As Gribbs emphasized in his public statements, the ordinances were aimed at "truly giving power back to the people. We are giving the citizens the ability to oversee their neighborhoods and to decide what kinds of businesses they find desirable."[77]

Garnering far less attention were some other measures tucked into the bill, including the fingerprinting and identification requirements placed on exotic dancers, as discussed in chapter 4. Most centrally, the bill also adopted Ravitz's suggestion of placing adult businesses under the "regulated uses" clause of zoning, which had not been part of the plan first suggested by the Mayor's Task Force on Licensing Procedures back in March. This required "regulated uses" establishments—including not only previous regulated businesses like bars and pawnshops but also now adult businesses—to not be within one thousand feet of each other. Despite eventually proving to be the most influential component of the ordinances, at the time this was perhaps the least heralded part of the law, not even garnering a single mention in any of the news articles covering the passage of the ordinances or in the mayor's statements.[78]

The ordinance had its limitations, the most notable being that it offered few opportunities for the city to close existing adult businesses, instead focusing on preventing news ones from opening. Eberhard bemoaned this, saying, "This is an essential weakness of these laws, so really we're only giving a partial answer to the problem."[79] In mid-November, Assistant Corporation Counsel Maureen P. Reilly, who would soon become one of the law's principal defenders in court, wrote a letter to the city council to tell them that the offices of the Corporation Counsel were currently drafting legislation to crack down on existing adult businesses. Meanwhile, the police were also taking action on the matter by trying to build cases against already-operating adult businesses. What this meant in practice, contended those in the industry, was simply that the police took to routinely harassing adult establishments to try and drive them out of business.[80] The notion that the police's investigation of adult businesses just amounted to harassment was confirmed by one Highland Park police officer, who said of their efforts to crack down on nude modeling studios, "Quite frankly, we harass the hell out of them."[81]

In February of 1973, the *Detroit Free Press* surveyed the landscape of pornography in Detroit in a two-part series by staff writer Louis Heldman. The articles provided a forum for the advocates and foes of the new anti-porn ordinances to square off in debate. In the second of the two articles, Rick Lawson, who had helped shape the city's anti-porn platform through his role as safety engineering supervisor for the Department of Buildings and Safety Engineering, emphasized that the ordinances were born out of the notion that adult businesses have a "blighting influence on nearby businesses and residential neighborhoods." He further claimed that homeowners' groups had threatened the city with lawsuits due to their contention that adult businesses had lowered property values in their neighborhoods.[82]

Stephen Taylor, attorney for many of the area's adult businesses, refuted Lawson's claims in the article, saying, "I think that rationale is ridiculous. There's been absolutely no evidence introduced by anyone that an adult-type bookstore or theater has any effect on the property values or business in the surrounding area." He went on to tell the *Free Press*, "I find it interesting to note that what people are saying now in regard to property values and adult-type bookstores and theaters is very similar to what they were saying when blacks began moving into an area, and just as untrue. They used the excuse to hide basic racism in the first case and they're using the excuse again to hide their basic, unfounded prejudice." Taylor's argument here illustrates the one at the heart of this book, which is that the rhetoric used against pornography during this era drew heavily on contemporaneous white racial politics. In fact, to my knowledge, his statement stands as the sole occasion that someone in Detroit during this era pointed out the similarities between the rhetoric used in battles over both racial integration and pornography. Seemingly no one else wanted to make this connection at the time or engage with the implications of Taylor's argument, as his charge went unanswered in the article.[83]

This *Free Press* series also examined the state of the adult entertainment industry in Detroit, with Heldman reporting that "the pornography trade has never been healthier in Detroit." In part this was because of an unintended consequence of the city's three-month-old anti-porn ordinances. As Heldman explained, "The new ordinances actually benefit bookstores and theaters that opened before November because there are no new sources of competition." In other words, by preventing new adult businesses from opening, those already in operation stood to benefit. Heldman also noted that another crucial factor in the flourishing of pornography in the city was the way *Deep Throat* had helped spur the growth of adult entertainment in the months following its summer 1972 opening in Detroit, with the film having "given the whole adult picture business a shot in the arm." In particular, *Deep Throat* was credited with bringing in new types of audiences, with Stuart Gorelick, operator of three adult theaters in Detroit, saying, "We're getting a tremendous amount of white collar workers coming in to see it—a Birmingham-Grosse Pointe type of crowd. This picture has opened the door to a certain respectability (for people) going to an X-rated theater." At that time, *Deep Throat* was setting records for an adult film in the United States, becoming one of the highest-grossing movies of the year while inaugurating the "porno chic" era. The film's success was often attributed to its ability to attract young couples, with their patronage seen as an emblem of newfound respectability for the adult film industry. Reflecting the way race and the relationship between city and suburb tended to dominate discussion in Detroit, Gorelick's statement, rather than focusing on couples and the presence of (accompanied) women at *Deep Throat*, instead emphasized the patronage of middle-class suburban whites as a marker of the respectability achieved by the film.[84]

In April of 1973, the Detroit Police Department's Obscenity Detail submitted a memorandum to Assistant Corporation Counsel Maureen Reilly listing every adult movie theater, adult bookstore, and nude photo studio in the city. This memo, which eventually found its way into court documents, provides an ideal snapshot for mapping the landscape of pornography in Detroit in early 1973. At that time, the police estimated that there were thirty-five adult bookstores, twenty-five adult movie theaters, and seven nude modeling studios in Detroit. Notably, though, the memo did not list topless bars, despite the fact that they were among those businesses regulated by the new zoning law. This no doubt was reflective of the fact that topless bars were often seen as operating in a separate category from adult theaters and bookstores in the mind of the public, if not necessarily in the legal realm.[85]

Looking at the map of adult businesses in Detroit at this time, it is clear that pornographic outlets congregated in three key areas of the city (see fig. 5.3). Unsurprisingly, downtown was a hub for pornographic outlets, boasting a total of eight adult businesses in early 1973, many of them older movie theaters that had recently converted to showing adult material. North from there, the Woodward corridor, particularly in Highland Park, also saw a flourishing of adult entertainment, with the area sometimes known as "porno row." Most of the adult businesses in Highland Park congregated either around its center, where Davison Freeway intersects with Woodward, or else at the northern end of Highland Park at the cross section of Woodward and McNichols. Each of these locations provided easy automobile access to both the suburbs and other parts of the city. Finally, a number of adult businesses also congregated along the Detroit side of West Eight Mile, the northern edge of the city. In particular, one area near the intersection of Eight Mile and Schaefer was a hub for

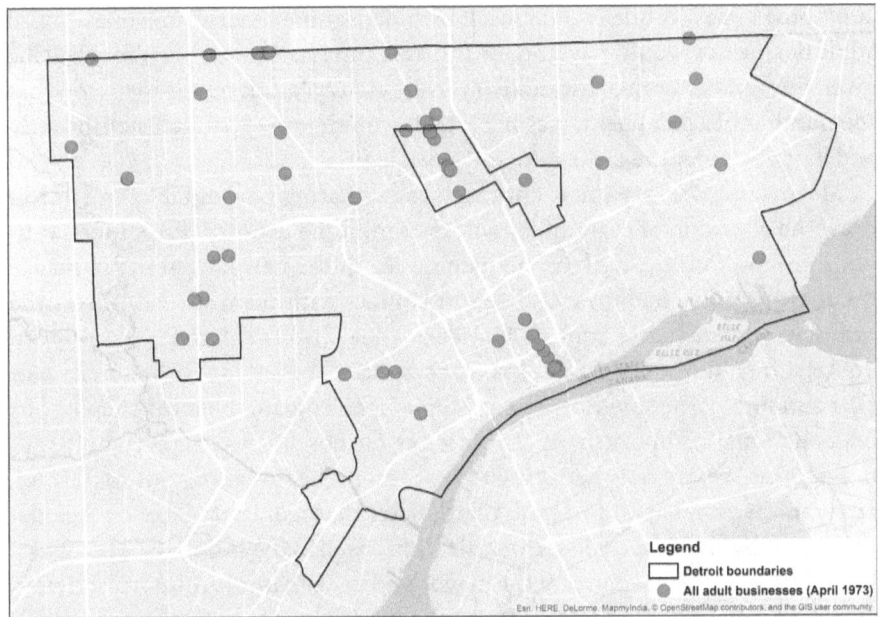

Figure 5.3. Map of adult businesses in Detroit in April of 1973.

adult entertainment, boasting six adult businesses and eventually coming to be known as the city's "sex strip." Once again, the location of these businesses provided easy access to customers traveling from other locales, particularly those coming from the suburbs north of the city. There were also adult businesses dotting residential neighborhoods across the city, many of which had opened over the course of 1972 in the months preceding the zoning law's adoption. On the whole, this map of the landscape of adult entertainment in Detroit lends credence to the notion that adult businesses were drawing a substantial portion of their customer base from the suburbs.

All in all, months after the city's much-heralded anti-porn ordinances had taken effect, there was little indication that the industry in Detroit was suffering. Of course, the nature of the ordinance was such that, as discussed prior, in certain ways existing adult businesses stood to gain from the new law. In April, it was estimated that just two of the city's adult bookstores had closed since the law's passing—a particularly low number given that adult businesses often only survived for a few months at a time. The real effect of the law was felt in the way the industry was unable to continue to expand through the opening of new adult businesses. While it is impossible to determine exactly how many more adult businesses would have opened in this time had it not been for the law, given the rapid growth of the industry in previous years, it stands to reason that the number of adult businesses in Detroit would have expanded significantly had it not been for the city's new anti-porn legislation.[86]

Meanwhile, the city's new approach to regulating pornography in Detroit drew the attention of certain key actors around the country. Prominent anti-porn groups, for one, took immediate notice of the new law, in part because the mayor's office had, in fact, been in contact with them for months as the ordinances were being crafted. Just days after Gribbs entered the anti-porn political fray in March of 1972, his office replied to a letter that had been sent over a month earlier by Morality in Media of Michigan, the local chapter of a major national anti-porn group. In his letter, Gribbs detailed the actions his administration would now be taking to try to stem the spreading tide of pornography in the city. He sent a similar letter later that month to Citizens Against Pornography and Smut, a local organization based in the suburb of Allen Park. These letters served to connect the mayor's office with local anti-porn activists, currying their favor by demonstrating the work being done by the city on this issue.[87]

The Gribbs administration's contact with anti-porn activists was not limited to local groups. Two months before the mayor's anti-porn proposals came up for a vote in the city council, the mayor sent drafts of the ordinances to Morality in Media of Western New York at the group's request. In the letter to them, the mayor also noted that the legislation had been sent to the legal staff at Citizens for Decent Literature, the most prominent anti-porn group at the national level during the era, further stating that "we expect to hear from them shortly with their recommendations and evaluation." This was not the only way the city leaned on Citizens for Decent Literature; in November, an internal memo revealed that the Detroit Police Department was doing an anti-porn training program "in collaboration with the Cleveland Office of the Citizens for Decent Literature, which will be extremely helpful in preparing evidence for our civil nuisance actions."[88]

Meanwhile, as the city was reaching out to and getting help from anti-porn groups, it was also interfacing with other cities similarly struggling with how to regulate pornography. Around the time that they were being passed and signed into law, copies of the licensing and zoning ordinances were sent out to numerous cities requesting them, including Michigan cities like Warren and River Rouge but also Perry, Georgia, and even Portland, Oregon, after a city official there saw a news story on the ordinances on a national television network. No doubt numerous other cities also studied Detroit's new anti-porn law at this time while leaving no archival paper trail.[89]

THE LEGAL CHALLENGES

Still, any rush to copy Detroit's new anti-porn legislation would depend first on its constitutionality being affirmed by the courts. Over the course of 1973, numerous legal challenges were filed against the law. The first of these was from American Mini Theatres and Pussy Cat Theatres of Michigan, which had hoped to open a new adult movie theater in northwest Detroit before the ordinance went into effect. The two firms acquired the necessary building permit in May of 1972 to convert a gas station into a movie theater and in the months ahead went about making the necessary alterations. Come October, the renovations were not yet done, but with the city getting set to adopt new anti-porn ordinances, the theater's owners applied to the Department of Buildings and Safety Engineering for a license to operate the theater. They were denied at that time after the Detroit Health Department refused to give its approval with the renovations still unfinished. By the time that all city departments had signed off on the theater in late December, the new anti-porn ordinance was in effect, requiring the theater to get approval from at least 51 percent of residents within a five-hundred-foot radius. The Pussy Cat Theater opened soon after without the necessary signatures, quickly resulting in a court fight.[90]

The case landed in circuit court, with the plaintiffs arguing that they had a "vested interest" in their theater prior to the law's enactment and thus should be exempt from the new law's requirements. On May 16, 1973, Judge Thomas Roumell ruled in favor of the city. His decision was purposefully limited in scope, finding only that the theater did not have a vested interest prior to the law given that they had not yet acquired all the necessary permits. As to the law itself, the judge wrote, "The reasonableness or propriety of the new ordinance ... is not in issue." Despite the narrowness of the decision, it was nevertheless seen as an important first victory for the city and its mayor. Gribbs had his aides write a letter on his behalf thanking Rick Lawson, a member of the Department of Buildings and Safety Engineering, and Maureen Reilly, who had argued the case as an attorney in the city's Corporation Counsel.[91]

Reilly was given little time to rest on her laurels, though, as one week after Judge Roumell's decision, she had to appear before Judge Lawrence Silverman of the Detroit Recorder's Court to give oral arguments on another case against the ordinance. This one was brought by the owners of the Nortown Theater in northeast Detroit, which had been ticketed by the city after it began showing adult movies in March of 1973 without first gaining the approval of 51 percent of nearby residents. This lawsuit focused squarely on the constitutionality of the law itself, with the theater's attorney, Stephen Taylor, arguing that the ordinance violated the First Amendment's guarantee of freedom of speech and the Fourteenth Amendment's equal protection clause. Judge Silverman rejected this argument, siding in favor of the city on all counts. As he wrote: "A 'skid row' condition in any one area can be caused by a numerical existence of several 'adult' establishments or uses.... To protect property values of surrounding businesses and residences and to maintain the public's confidence in the stability of neighborhoods is a sufficiently important, compelling, and substantial interest of government to justify regulations of First Amendment freedoms." This line of reasoning drew directly on the rhetoric used by those who had crafted the law and the attorneys now defending it regarding the economic impact of adult businesses on surrounding areas and the need to guard against neighborhood decay. Unsurprisingly, the ruling was celebrated by Gribbs, who publicly said, "I am delighted by this decision because the ordinances have proved most effective in controlling the spread of so-called adult theaters in Detroit."[92]

The Nortown and its attorney pressed on, though, indicating that they would separately go to trial in August over the specific ticket issued by the city against the theater. Meanwhile, Taylor and the Nortown Theater also took their fight to federal court, and just a week after Judge Silverman's ruling, they were appearing before United States District Court judge Lawrence Gubow. As Taylor said, "The Federal Court has a duty to proceed. We intend to stay open, and we will take our appeals all the way (to the Supreme Court) if necessary." As it turned out, it would indeed prove necessary.[93]

In the short term, though, the number of cases leveled against the city's anti-porn ordinances multiplied. At that time, a separate case brought by the adult-oriented Variety Book Store was also on the docket before Judge Gubow. Meanwhile, the owners of the Pussy Cat Theater continued their legal battle with the city even after Judge Roumell's ruling, and in mid-June, their challenge to the ordinance was set to appear before United States District Court judge Cornelia Kennedy. Finally, adult businesses in Southfield and East Detroit were also busy fighting ordinances patterned after Detroit's that had been passed in those two suburbs, with the case pending at that time before United States District Court judge Robert E. DeMascio. All this legal action had also drawn the attention of the ACLU, which was lending aid in some of the cases against the city.[94]

In the midst of this mass of legal maneuverings against the city's ordinance, the United States Supreme Court intervened with a ruling that seemed, at first blush, to instantly reshape battles over pornography across the country. On June 21, 1973, the court issued a decision in the case of *Miller v. California* that significantly broadened the scope of obscenity law. Replacing the old standard that obscene material must be "utterly without redeeming social value" was a new test asking "whether the work, taken as a whole, lacks serious literary, artistic, political, or scientific value." This effectively meant that adult media could no longer justify its legality based on a mere morsel of social value. Just as significantly, the decision replaced the previous test of obscenity, which relied on national standards, for a test based on "contemporary community standards," leaving the door open for localities to set their own, more stringent definitions of obscenity.[95]

The decision was immediately seen as a landmark that would set off a nationwide crackdown on hard-core pornography, with Charles Keating, head of Citizens for Decent Literature, writing that the decision was a "green light to combat smut." Among anti-porn forces in Detroit, the belief was that the court's ruling had ushered in a new era, with the city once again able to use obscenity to target adult businesses. Upon hearing the news of the decision, Maureen Reilly, the city's lead attorney on these matters, reportedly "literally screamed with delight," later saying, "I feel like somebody gave me a present." Meanwhile, Wayne County prosecutor William Cahalan quickly said his office would reopen its obscenity division, and Oakland County prosecutor L. Brooks Pattern called the court's decision "a breath of fresh air."[96]

Not surprisingly, owners of adult businesses were disappointed by the court's decision and anxious over the anticipated wave of prosecutions in the city. Following the ruling, brothers Burton and Stuart Gorelick—the men behind American Mini Theatres—decided to immediately close their three adult theaters in the city, the Pussy Cat, Penthouse, and Lido. The Follies also closed after the decision was announced before tentatively reopening its doors a few days later. Joseph Busik, owner of the Six Mile Theatre, said, "I'm dropping X-rated movies. I'm going to show PG's and R's. I stayed in it as long as it was legal. When it's no longer legal, I'm getting out of it." One local attorney, Bruce Randall, offered the pessimistic view when he said of the adult theaters and bookstores he represented, "There's a good possibility that they will not be able to exist any longer in the sense we know them now." Still, attorney Stephen Taylor urged patience and caution, saying, "No one knows what the law is in Michigan today.... We don't know what the courts are going to do, what the Legislature is going to do or what the police are going to do."[97]

Less than a week after the court's decision was announced, it became clear what the Detroit Police Department was intending to do when they began visiting every one of the city's twenty-nine adult bookstores and fourteen adult movie theaters, issuing warnings that would lay the groundwork for arrests. These visits also allowed the police to accumulate evidence against theaters through efforts by plainclothes officers to entrap and arrest gay men. As the *Gay Liberator* wrote at that time, "In preparing a case against the theaters, plainclothes vice cops are being sent in to observe the film, audience, and tearoom [slang for bathroom] action. We know that entrapments are taking place at the Colonial and Gem Theaters downtown. Probably elsewhere too."[98]

At this point, it appeared that the city finally had the ability to shutter existing adult businesses. Attention thus momentarily turned away from the battles over the city's licensing and zoning anti-porn ordinances, which were, after all, only half measures that could not close existing adult businesses. Obscenity law had seemingly made a grand comeback, with pornography in Detroit and across the country on the ropes as a result.

However, though it was initially imagined that *Miller v. California* would be a knockout blow for pornography, the actual results wound up being far less decisive. Owners of adult businesses in Detroit, unwilling to wait around to be arrested, sought and were granted a temporary restraining order preventing the city from raiding businesses or making arrests. Meanwhile, the question that soon took center stage was whether the state's existing obscenity ordinances were still valid in light of the Supreme Court's ruling. Maureen Reilly advised the police to hold off on arrests while the question was unresolved and suggested that the law should be rewritten. After Wayne County prosecutor William Cahalan proceeded anyway by filing charges against ten theaters, a three-judge recorder's court panel ruled that the existing state law had to be rewritten, giving adult businesses a stay of execution. As this legal wrangling was proceeding, adult entertainment in Detroit began to return to normal. The theaters that had closed immediately after the ruling soon reopened, and before long pornography was as available as ever throughout the city.[99] As attorney Stephen Taylor said in September, "At this point, the air is clearing somewhat. They (owners) now have the general idea the ruling is not as restrictive as they originally thought."[100]

This was largely the case across the country, with *Miller v. California* not resulting in the type of outright banning of pornography that anti-porn advocates had initially hoped for. The reality instead was that obscenity law continued to be a legal tangle throughout the United States in the years to come. The Supreme Court even scaled back the breadth of the *Miller* ruling a year later in overturning the conviction of a Georgia man who had been found guilty of distributing obscene material for screening the film *Carnal Knowledge* (1971).

In 1977, a *New York University Law Review* article summed up legal opinion in saying that the court's decision in *Miller v. California* in fact had "little effect on the day-to-day regulation of obscene materials."[101]

This made the court battles over Detroit's anti-porn licensing and zoning ordinances all the more important. In October of 1973, the city won another skirmish in the battle over its anti-porn laws when Judge Lawrence Silverman ordered the maximum possible sentence—a $500 fine and ninety days in jail— against the owner of the Nortown Theatre for operating an adult movie house without a city license. His opinion made clear that he would not be a friend to adult businesses in this or any other case, with the judge warning that the "panderers and purveyors of hard-core pornography" would be punished to the fullest extent of the law in his court. He further wrote, "Those who reap financial benefits should be punished for not only contributing to the destruction of a favorable environment in which to rear children, but for corrupting the community itself to the detriment of its citizens." The actual punishment was put on hold while the theater appealed the decision, but even so, Judge Silverman's ruling was taken as a major victory for the city. As building department official Rick Lawson said, "We will run out of problems with the so-called adult stores and theaters if we can get this kind of sentencing from all the judges." Still, attorney Maureen Reilly, who argued the case on behalf of the city, cautioned that the constitutionality of the ordinance itself would remain something of an open question until a higher court ruled on the matter.[102]

In March of 1974, the city finally received a ruling on the constitutionality of its anti-porn licensing and zoning ordinances from the United States District Court of Michigan, though it proved something of a mixed bag. The bad news for the city was that the provision requiring that all adult businesses gain the signatures of at least 51 percent of nearby residents to open was struck down. On this point, Judge Cornelia G. Kennedy and Judge Lawrence Gubow gave as their reasoning that "no arguments are advanced by Defendants as to how the prohibition of the regulated uses within 500 feet of a single dwelling or rooming unit furthers the legitimate interest the City has in preserving a residential area or neighborhood." This "imperceptible benefit" was weighed against the "severe impact imposed" by that provision of the ordinance, which, in the plaintiffs' view, had made it nearly impossible for new adult businesses to open in the city.[103]

However, the ruling nevertheless gave the city a major victory with the district court's decision that the provision mandating that no new adult business could be located within one thousand feet of an existing adult business was constitutional. Here, the court found that the city did have a "compelling State interest" for this regulatory approach given the importance of the "preservation of neighborhoods, upon which adult establishments have been found to have a destructive impact." On this point, the court cited none other than Mel Ravitz, who had submitted two documents to the court on the matter: one an April 1973 affidavit from Ravitz regarding the anti-porn ordinance and the other a letter from him to the Corporation Counsel from October of 1962.[104]

The latter document laid out the reasoning behind the city's 1962 Anti-Skid Row Ordinance, which was the progenitor of the 1972 zoning ordinance by acting to disperse bars, pawnshops, and other businesses that were seen as having an adverse effect on neighborhoods. In his 1962 letter—originally written to aid in legal challenges to the city's Anti-Skid Row Ordinance—Ravitz stressed that many people held the view that the concentration of the businesses regulated under the ordinance was bad for neighborhoods. Ravitz made a key distinction on this point, though, by drawing on his background as a sociologist (he had gotten his PhD in sociology from the University of Michigan in 1955, soon after getting a faculty position at Wayne State University):

> Here a basic sociological axiom is relevant: if people believe something is true, even if it is not originally, they will tend to act as if it were true, and in so doing help produce the condition that was originally only believed. If residents of any neighborhood believe that the concentration of the proscribed uses damage the neighborhood, they will act as if it were true and will seek to move away and allow in people with different standards; they will allow their property to decline; they will not engage in the full range of conservation attitudes and activities so necessary to the maintenance of a healthful residential neighborhood....
> A residential neighborhood is a very fragile thing. It can be ruined very easily. And ruin comes usually not by dramatic physical events, such as sheer age or the sudden invasion of barbarians to an area. Ruin comes to a neighborhood because its residents somehow begin to have their confidence in their area shaken. It matters not what the cause of this shaken confidence, whether it be a legitimate or phony cause.

This stands as perhaps the single best encapsulation of Ravitz's views on the anti-porn zoning law he engineered, even as he was not talking about that law in particular but rather its predecessor, the skid row ordinance. In Ravitz's opinion, whether bars and pawnshops (in the 1962 ordinance) or adult businesses (in the 1972 one) actually directly caused neighborhood decay was irrelevant to the issue; rather, the mere idea that such businesses caused blight would be enough for that feared scenario to become reality. Residents' beliefs that undesirable businesses would cause neighborhood decline created a self-fulfilling prophecy, then, as individuals would subsequently begin to act as if their neighborhood was indeed on a path toward decay and blight. Regardless of the veracity of the underlying notion about the direct impact of these businesses, if enough people believed it to be true, residents would take actions—such as putting their homes up for sale en masse—that would drive down property values. In Ravitz's reasoning, then, the notion that adult businesses caused the economic decline of neighborhoods held just as much truth value as a sufficient number of residents collectively believing that painting one's house orange or placing garden gnomes on one's lawn caused neighborhood decay.[105]

Notably, in the affidavit Ravitz gave in April of 1973 specifically on the anti-porn ordinance, he repeated almost verbatim this argument from his 1962 letter. The decision of the city to submit the 1962 letter from Ravitz on the anti-skid row ordinance and a nearly identical 1973 affidavit on the anti-porn ordinance was a calculated move to draw connections between the two. That the anti-porn zoning provision in question built upon an older law that had nothing to do with pornography seemed to lend credence, in the eyes of the district court, to the city's argument that the ordinance was concerned only with the economics of neighborhood decay rather than morality. This no doubt helped shape the court's decision, wherein they ruled that the provision requiring the approval of 51 percent of residents within five hundred feet was unconstitutional—a provision spearheaded by Gribbs and emblematic of his preferred emphasis on licensing law—while the Ravitz-backed one-thousand-foot zoning-based dispersal provision was affirmed as constitutional. For the latter, the judges gave as their justification that "the affidavit of Dr. Mel Ravitz clearly established that the prohibition of more than one regulated use within 1000 feet is necessary to promote the interest" of the city regarding the "preservation of neighborhoods."[106]

Press coverage of the district court's ruling focused on the city's loss when it came to the five-hundred-foot provision rather than its victory on the one-thousand-foot part of the ordinance, with the *Detroit News* headline blaring, "Court Eases Curb on 'Adult' Stores," while the *Free Press* declared, "Court Relaxes Sex Shop Curbs." This was perhaps unsurprising; after all, up until that point, almost all news coverage of the 1972 anti-porn ordinance had focused on the licensing provision granting residents the power to nix the opening of adult businesses in their neighborhoods, with little attention paid, by contrast, to the provision regarding the use of zoning to disperse adult businesses. The five-hundred-foot provision was no doubt an easier sell to the general public, who could readily understand that it promised greater power for residents to control the entrance of adult businesses into their neighborhoods. By contrast, the one-thousand-foot provision was opaque and bureaucratic, with residents never getting to witness the unseen work of city officials using maps and charts to determine whether an adult business could open in their community.[107]

Still, there were those who recognized that the city's legal victory on the one-thousand-foot dispersal section of the ordinance might prove, in the words of Carl Levin, "more significant" in the long run than its loss on the five-hundred-foot provision. In his public comments following the decision, Levin, by this time the city council president, focused on the importance of the victory on the zoning provision, perhaps unsurprisingly so given that he had been Ravitz's closest ally in the 1972 battles over pornography in the city council. No doubt in large part because of Levin's statements, two days after the *Detroit News* first ran its story on the judge's decision with the headline "Court Eases Curb on 'Adult' Stores," it published an article that, while nearly identical in content, featured a new headline reading, "Ruling May Aid Detroit's Control of Porno Shops."[108]

City attorney Maureen Reilly also spoke positively of the ruling in her public comments, calling the decision "a victory for the city, as far as I'm concerned." As she noted when appearing before the city council soon after, "The decision basically upheld our contention that the city could zone deleterious businesses." Moreover, she pointed out that the court ruling indicated that "First Amendment rights could be incidentally regulated." These were crucial legal points, and while the overturning of a major part of the ordinance was a blow, the decision had given the city's attorneys much to build on. She therefore urged the city not to appeal the ruling.[109]

The adult businesses behind the case did decide to appeal, though, and the case wound up before the Sixth Circuit Court of Appeals. On June 16, 1975, in a two-to-one decision, the court ruled against the city, overturning the city's anti-porn zoning ordinance as unconstitutional. The court did buy the city's argument that the presence of adult businesses in residential areas led to the decay of neighborhoods, meaning that in the court's view, Detroit did have a "compelling public interest" to regulate the location of adult businesses. However, the majority opinion found that the city failed to clear the higher bar of "showing that the method which it chose to deal with the problem at hand was necessary and that its effect on protected rights was only incidental." This greater burden of proof was necessary due to the way the ordinance classified certain types of movie theaters and bookstores as requiring further regulation based on the "content of the constitutionally protected materials which they purvey to the public." Therefore, the majority of the court found that the city's ordinances were in violation of the equal protection clause of the Fourteenth Amendment and declared them invalid.[110]

Even as it ruled against the city, the majority opinion also expressed sympathy for Detroit's position. As Judge Lively wrote for the majority, "This court is keenly aware of the serious problems created in the major cities of the country by the deterioration of established neighborhoods. We are particularly sensitive to the problems of Detroit, the largest city within this Circuit." There was seemingly no question among the judges as to the validity of the notion that adult businesses cause neighborhood decay, and the majority did not engage with the charge that the city's anti-porn zoning ordinances were merely a way of bypassing obscenity law while still enacting censorship. Indeed, even as the majority opinion struck down the ordinances themselves as unconstitutional, it pointedly suggested that the city might come up with alternative solutions to the problem that could prove valid, saying, "In holding that the two ordinances under review are unconstitutional we do not suggest that the City of Detroit is powerless to deal with its urban problems."[111]

The dissenting opinion, delivered by Judge Anthony Celebrezze, the former mayor of Cleveland, drew on similar rhetoric in declaring his view that "the Detroit ordinance before us is a legitimate exercise of the City's police power. The plight of our cities requires that public officials have tools adequate to prevent their decline and collapse as centers of life and work." Judge Celebrezze repeatedly quoted from Ravitz's affidavits to back the idea that the ordinances were only concerned with economic effects, not content control. He rejected free speech arguments, contending that the First Amendment "was not intended to be the death-knell of cities" and that "preserving neighborhoods is not a subterfuge for censorship." As he concluded, "It seems to me that if we are to prevent our cities from becoming uninhabitable jungles, we must, within constitutional safeguards, restore to our cities the right of self-government."[112]

The city quickly appealed the ruling, and in October of 1975, the United States Supreme Court agreed to review the case. The news was immediately recognized as a potentially momentous event in anti-porn politics. On November 28, 1975, the *New York Times* published an article titled "Foes of Pornography Winning a Few Skirmishes, but Not the Major Battles." The article found that obscenity prosecutions across the country were being stymied by the courts even after the *Miller* decision. Given this, the *Times* reported that several cities were awaiting the Supreme Court's decision on the Detroit case to see if they should adopt their own anti-porn zoning ordinances. Beyond those cities looking to possibly emulate Detroit's specific law, though, this was also the first time the Supreme Court would rule on the use of zoning to regulate adult entertainment altogether. This meant that the case was seen as potentially opening up a host of new zoning-based solutions to the problem of pornography. As the news magazine *Time* wrote in the months leading up to the court's decision, "Though Detroit's policy is to disperse rather than cluster its porn shops, the court's decision, due in June, will presumably settle a community's right to use zoning against porn."[113]

In March of 1976, Maureen Reilly and her fellow lawyers for the city squared off against Nortown Theatre attorney Stephen Taylor and American Mini Theatres attorney John H. Weston before the United States Supreme Court. Afterward, the legal team for the city expressed confidence that the court would rule in their favor, noting that the justices had mostly grilled the opposing attorneys. Three months later, the court handed down its ruling in the *Young v. American Mini Theatres* case: in a narrow five-to-four decision, Detroit's anti-porn zoning ordinance was declared constitutional.[114]

Though the case was large and unwieldy, touching on a number of legal points, the questions surrounding the ordinance's impact on the First Amendment were of primary importance to the Supreme Court. Justice John Paul Stevens, who had joined the court only a year prior, wrote the majority opinion, in which he said regarding the question of the law's impact on speech, "There is surely a less vital interest in the uninhibited exhibition of material that is on the borderline between pornography and artistic expression than in the free dissemination of ideas of social and political significance." When it came to pornography that was not legally obscene, then, even though such speech held First Amendment rights, "society's interest in protecting this type of expression is of a wholly different, and lesser, magnitude than the interest in untrammeled political debate." As Justice Stevens reasoned, "Whether political oratory or philosophical discussion moves us to applaud or to despise what is said, every schoolchild can understand why our duty to defend the right to speak remains the same. But few of us would march our sons and daughters off to war to preserve the citizen's right to see 'Specified Sexual Activities' exhibited in the theaters of our choice." Whereas the court had upheld content-based restrictions when it came to protecting minors or nonconsenting adults, this marked the first time that, in the words of legal scholar Richard F. Hixson, the Supreme Court had upheld "the *general* regulation of otherwise protected speech on the basis of content." This decision, then, was a landmark in introducing what would come to be known as the "sliding-scale approach to First Amendment jurisprudence."[115]

Justice Lewis F. Powell, while siding with the majority, nevertheless wrote a concurring opinion that disagreed with Justice Stevens on this notion that sexually explicit nonobscene speech should be granted lesser constitutional protections. Instead, he found that the ordinance was more an example of an "innovative land-use regulation" that would not have a major impact on the availability of pornography in the city. As he wrote, "There is no indication that the application of the Anti-Skid Row Ordinance to adult theaters has the effect of suppressing production of or, to any significant degree, restricting access to adult movies." In truth, there was considerable evidence that the city's anti-porn zoning law had curtailed the spread of adult businesses in the city and with it the availability of sex media, but Powell nevertheless used this reasoning to side with the majority opinion in finding the city's ordinances constitutional based on their mere "incidental and minimal" impact on free speech.[116]

Justice Potter Stewart—who had once famously written that when it came to defining hard-core pornography, "I know it when I see it"—wrote a blistering dissent in which he called the majority opinion a "drastic departure from established principles of First Amendment law," further saying that the decision "rides roughshod over cardinal principles of First Amendment law." While granting that Detroit's ordinances were "well-intentioned efforts" by the city to "'clean up' its streets and prevent the proliferation of 'skid rows,'" Justice Stewart stressed that "it is in those instances where protected speech grates most unpleasantly against the sensibilities that judicial vigilance must be at its height." His opinion went on to detail what he saw as the very real impact that Detroit's zoning law, and in turn the court's decision, would have in limiting free speech.[117]

In 1957, the Supreme Court struck down the obscenity law used by the city of Detroit to censor literature. The court's decision was because the stated goal of keeping indecent media out of the hands of children was not sufficient to justify a law effectively barring even consenting adults from purchasing such material. Even if the aim of the law was justifiable, its application was too broad, with the obscenity ordinance casting too wide a net. Nineteen years later, the city was back before the highest court in the land, once again defending its censorial practices. The key innovation of the city's new zoning-based anti-porn regulatory approach proved to be the way it could mask the fact that it was still a form of censorship, with seemingly morality-neutral arguments about the economics of neighborhood decay instead taking center stage. It mattered little that this new approach ultimately sought the same goals of curtailing the spread of pornography as did earlier obscenity-based efforts, as the validity of its underlying assumption, that adult businesses cause neighborhood decay, came to be accepted as fact. This, in turn, allowed for the majority of the Supreme Court to view Detroit's anti-porn zoning law as neither stifling free speech in its purpose or its effect, or if it did, then only to a minor and altogether insignificant degree. It was for this reason that Justice Powell could write, "Detroit has silenced no message, has invoked no censorship, and has imposed no limitation upon those who wish to view [adult movies]." Detroit, then, had finally figured out how to suppress sexually oriented speech without the baggage that came with explicit censorship.[118]

CONCLUSION: THE SPREAD OF THE DETROIT MODEL

It is difficult to estimate the direct impact of the Supreme Court's decision on the landscape of pornography in Detroit itself, as the ruling merely had the isolated effect of reinstating the zoning provision that the Circuit Court of Appeals had invalidated a year prior. As for measuring the overall impact of the original law in Detroit, given that the ordinance was designed to prevent new adult businesses from opening, we are forced to try to compare the actual landscape of pornography in Detroit after the ordinance's enactment to a road not traveled wherein adult businesses had been able to open freely. Certainly, though, in public statements following the Supreme Court's ruling, city officials boasted of the impact of the law on the city, with Maureen Reilly saying, "When we passed the zoning ordinance in 1972, there were 18 theaters, 21 adult bookstores and 70 go-go bars here. Since the ordinance passed, we have had only two new adult theaters open." If it may be unknowable exactly how many adult theaters would have opened during this period without the city's anti-porn zoning ordinance, it seems safe to assume that the number would have been significantly higher than two. In 1977, Carl Rubin, attorney for a number of Detroit's adult businesses, conceded, "The ordinance has had its desired effect by substantially stopping new adult businesses from coming into the city. The sex business isn't what it used to be."[119] Regardless of the ordinance's overall effect in Detroit, though, the Supreme Court's 1976 decision mainly allowed Detroit to continue what it had been doing for much of the past three and a half years.[120]

The Supreme Court's decision had a far more decisive impact on the rest of the United States than it did Detroit itself, and press coverage of the ruling tended to emphasize the effect it would have on other cities. In the *Atlanta Constitution* and *Los Angeles Times*, articles covering the court's ruling just one day after it was announced mentioned that officials in both those cities were considering adopting ordinances similar to Detroit's. Meanwhile, the *New York Times* editorial board quickly interpreted the ruling as meaning that New York

City "no longer has to sit by and watch the heart of Manhattan turn into a sexual slum." Six months after the court's decision, Maureen Reilly reported that she had received calls from nearly one hundred cities asking for copies of Detroit's ordinance. By the end of the year, countless city officials across the country had introduced or adopted Detroit-style anti-porn zoning ordinances, including in Dallas, New York City, Des Moines, Kansas City, Portland, Indianapolis, Fairfax County, Pittsburgh, and San Jose. Over the course of 1977, similar laws would be taken up in San Antonio, Philadelphia, Chicago, and dozens of other cities.[121] Many more would follow suit by the decade's end, including nearly all of the country's largest metropolises.[122]

City officials across the country tended to adopt the rhetoric that Detroit officials had used both when the city first passed its anti-porn zoning law and subsequently when defending it in court. One aide to a Los Angeles city councilwoman drew on morality-neutral discourse and the argument that adult businesses cause urban decay when she said of her city's proposed Detroit-style anti-porn zoning ordinance, "It's not really a moral question. The ordinance aims at breaking up the economic concentration that debilitates the area. You can't get a guy to open a delicatessen next to a massage parlor." Speaking of blighted areas in Hollywood, the same aide continued, "We see the Detroit ordinance as a way to break that up and allow an area to come back economically."[123] A city councilman in Kansas City similarly said, "Zoning is the most powerful tool in the city arsenal to control pornography, the only way we can, as a city, regulate activity that leads to deterioration of neighborhoods." At other times, the economic-based morality-neutral arguments used by city officials gave way to the reality that zoning adult businesses amounted to censorship by another name. As Alan Magazine, county supervisor of Fairfax County in Virginia, said after Fairfax adopted a Detroit-style anti-porn zoning ordinance, "In practical terms we have made it impossible for them [pornography businesses] to locate here, even though we were unable constitutionally to ban them completely."[124] However, more often city officials drew on the idea that Detroit's zoning approach did not amount to censorship at all, with Jane Stern, spokesman for Fairfax County, saying, "Zoning seems to be the most legal, legitimate method of control. It's the best tool, without getting into censorship."[125]

The Supreme Court's decision thus led to both the discursive and legislative anti-porn strategies used in Detroit being exported to the rest of the United States. Before long, Detroit's approach to regulating pornography—using zoning law to disperse adult businesses—had come to be known as the Detroit Model. This approach stood in contrast to the other major model for urban regulation of pornography, which was on display in Boston. Rather than trying to disperse adult businesses, Boston went in the opposite direction by attempting to quarantine them in an area that had come to be popularly known as the Combat Zone. The city officially made the Combat Zone the exclusive home to adult entertainment in Boston in 1974, with the move immediately receiving a tremendous amount of national attention.[126]

Some news coverage of the Combat Zone noted the irony that out of all cities, it was Boston, with its famous history of banning indecent media, that was setting up an area in which pornography might be allowed to flourish. As one *Los Angeles Times* article said, "The city that once made 'banned in Boston' a household phrase is zoning a district that will be the exclusive domain of porno shops, sex films and girlie shows." By contrast, there was no such similar discussion centered on Detroit's history of book banning when discussing the Detroit Model. The success of Herbert Case in keeping the Detroit Police Department's literary censorship operation secret was such that, in September of 1973, even the *Detroit Free Press* could somehow write that "Detroit has never been a hotbed of rabid book-banners."[127]

Because the Supreme Court's ruling in *Young v. American Mini Theatres* had marked the first time that the high court had weighed in on a zoning-based solution to regulating pornography, it also spurred interest from a number of cities regarding the possibility of using zoning law to mimic Boston's Combat Zone. Most chose not to do so, though, with the *New York Times* in November of 1976 writing, "Officials in a few cities, including Las Vegas and Oklahoma City, have proposed creation of special 'adult business districts' patterned after Boston's so-called 'combat zone.' ... But community resistance to the idea and reports of widespread prostitution, organized crime activities and muggings by prostitutes and others in the Boston district have so far kept it from spreading elsewhere."[128] A member of the New York City Planning Commission in late 1976 summed up popular opinion in saying, "The Boston experiment has not been successful. It has led to breeding additional crime."[129] This view resulted in the lack of imitation of Boston's approach, and in 1984, ten years after Boston first formally set up the Combat Zone, city officials there admitted that it remained the only city in the United States to try concentrating its adult businesses in one area.[130] William Toner, who in 1977 published a report on different methods of regulating adult businesses, explained the reason for the lack of enthusiasm for copying Boston's anti-porn model when he said, "Nobody wants to be known as the councilman who helped set up Pornography City."[131]

By contrast, the popular view of the Detroit Model was that, if it could not eliminate pornography entirely from the urban landscape, it could at least significantly curtail its growth. Press coverage of the Supreme Court decision and the ruling's subsequent impact often included stories that highlighted Detroit's success in preventing new adult businesses from opening, with these accounts in turn driving other cities to copy Detroit's approach. The Detroit Model was never a cure-all, as by its nature it could only prevent new adult businesses from opening rather than close existing ones. Because of this, it could never accomplish what hard-line anti-porn advocates had always wanted, which was the virtual elimination of all pornography from society. An article in the *National Decency Reporter*, the anti-porn journal published by Citizens for Decency Through Law (previously known as Citizens for Decent Literature), encapsulated the view of strident anti-porn voices on what it called the "Detroit Plan" in saying, "If you live in a city or state where obscenity nuisance abatement laws are weak or lacking or where criminal prosecutions are not vigorously pursued or are a losing battle because of liberal courts or prosecutors, then the zoning approach may be at least an alternative. Zoning will not eliminate pornography, but it can be effective in keeping porno theaters and stores out of the neighborhoods and away from churches and schools. . . . Though not a total or acceptable victory, some relief is probably better than none." In truth, the Detroit Model was never going to fully please the Eberhards and Citizens for Decency Through Laws of the world, and it was not designed to do so. But for city officials writing laws across the country, the Detroit Model presented an alluring package: the promise of effective anti-porn legislation that would actually hold up in court. The combination of the two was something no other approach to regulating pornography during this era could offer, thus driving countless cities to follow Detroit's lead in adopting zoning laws to disperse adult businesses.[132]

The convergence of urban politics with anti-porn politics would not last indefinitely. By the end of the decade, the prominence of the morality-neutral anti-porn rhetoric deployed by Redford's protesting residents began to decline as the feminist anti-porn movement began to gain in stature. The centrality of anti-porn discourse focusing on property values and neighborhood decay was thus gradually replaced by rhetoric emphasizing pornography's alleged exploitation of women and contribution to the epidemic of violence against women. It would be a mistake, though, to say that the type of anti-porn politics I have cataloged in this book wholly disappeared with the rise of the feminist anti-porn movement. Language similar to that used by Redford's letter writers continued to be deployed in urban battles over pornography for decades to come, as was the case in the battle over pornography in New York City during the 1990s. Just as importantly, though, feminist anti-porn activists often drew inspiration from the tactics and rhetoric of urban anti-porn politics of the early 1970s.[133]

The anti-porn machinations of San Francisco in the late 1970s are a useful case study in this regard. As historian Josh Sides writes of this period, "[San Francisco Mayor] Dianne Feinstein was taken with the Detroit ordinance and began conducting research on the implementation of a similar ordinance in San Francisco, even before the Supreme Court upheld its constitutionality." Immediately following the court's ruling, Feinstein pushed through a four-month moratorium on the issuance of permits for adult businesses. By January 1977, she was ready to reveal her proposed ordinance, which was, in Sides's words, "virtually identical to that in Detroit." Despite facing some strong opposition from, among others, owners of adult businesses, gay community leader Harvey Milk, the San Francisco chapter of the ACLU, and African American mothers of the Bayview Hunters Point Neighborhood Association (who feared that the ordinance would drive adult businesses into their neighborhood), the city ultimately enacted a version of Detroit's ordinance in September of 1978.[134]

As Sides writes, crucial to the construction and passing of this anti-porn zoning law in San Francisco was the "ideological and logistical support from Bay Area feminists and particularly those affiliated with Women Against Violence in Pornography and Media (WAVPM)." WAVPM had only recently been founded to fight against the depiction of violence against women in both mainstream cinema and pornography, though it tended to focus most of its attention on the latter category. The group's director and national coordinator at that time was Laura Lederer, and she regularly met and communicated with Feinstein regarding the mayor's efforts to enact a Detroit-style anti-porn zoning ordinance. In fact, as Sides explains, Lederer played an important and unique role in helping Feinstein pass San Francisco's version of the Detroit Model. As Sides writes, "Lederer traveled to Detroit, conducting interviews with city officials and collecting data on the effectiveness of the ordinance, which she then passed on to Feinstein."[135]

No doubt Lederer found it easy enough to gain access to Detroit city officials for this research given that she was a Detroit native whose father was none other than Creighton Lederer, who had been head of Detroit's Department of Buildings and Safety Engineering under Mayor Gribbs. The elder Lederer had played a crucial role in Mayor Gribbs's campaign against pornography, working to drive adult theaters and bookstores out of business through his department's strategic deployment of licensing law. Behind the scenes, he had also helped steer the city toward Ravitz's zoning-based anti-porn approach, writing a memo recommending its usage in early 1972. Meanwhile, as to the younger Lederer, after helping San Francisco adopt a version of the ordinance her father had helped enact in Detroit, she went on to edit the 1980 book *Take Back the Night: Women on Pornography*, which historian Carolyn Bronstein later called "the single most influential and widely read collection of feminist anti-pornography writings," thus cementing her status as one of the most important voices in the early feminist anti-porn movement.[136]

The case of Laura Lederer and the role she played in San Francisco's adoption of a Detroit-style anti-porn zoning law points to the continuities between the early 1970s morality-neutral urban anti-porn politics discussed here and the era of feminist anti-porn politics that followed. These connections were also born out in other campaigns waged by feminist anti-porn leaders of the time, as with the decision by the group Women Against Pornography to ally with the 42nd Street Redevelopment Corporation and various real estate and business interests in their effort to rid Times Square of adult entertainment. The connections between these two eras of anti-porn politics have been underexamined by scholars looking at the feminist anti-porn movement, who have tended to focus on the way the movement developed out of particular strands of feminism and the debate between anti-porn feminists and opposing anti-censorship feminists. This work has given little attention, though, to the way the feminist anti-porn movement also drew on existing strands of the broader anti-porn movement, including specifically the rhetorical strategies and regulatory approach pioneered in Detroit. Bringing in this broader historical perspective enables an understanding that the feminist anti-porn movement did not simply emerge wholly out of feminism with no real connections to the history of the anti-porn movement; rather, there were very real continuities with established anti-porn political strategies.[137]

Moreover, the feminist anti-porn movement, and the debates surrounding it, have tended to dominate much of the scholarly discourse around pornography even up to today. This has been the case despite the reality that the feminist anti-porn movement had little lasting impact on the actual regulation of pornography, a phenomenon that is perhaps best illustrated through the example of the Antipornography Civil Rights Ordinance. In the early to mid-1980s, Andrea Dworkin and Catharine MacKinnon, perhaps the two most prominent anti-porn feminists of that era, crafted a law defining pornography as a civil rights harm against women, thus allowing women to sue the producers, distributors, and exhibitors of adult material in civil court. The duo first sought to get the ordinance enacted in Minneapolis in 1983 but were twice stymied by the mayor vetoing the bills due to fears that the inevitable resulting legal case against the ordinance would prove highly costly for the city. Indianapolis adopted a slightly altered version of the law a year later, which was a major milestone for the feminist anti-porn movement. However, the law was quickly challenged in the courts and ruled unconstitutional by the Seventh Circuit Court of Appeals. The Supreme Court subsequently refused to hear the appeal, thus letting the lower court's ruling stand. Undeterred, Dworkin and MacKinnon managed to get Bellingham, Washington (the state's eighth-largest city), to approve the ordinance as a ballot initiative. That law was quickly challenged in the courts and again ruled unconstitutional.[138]

All in all, the ordinance was enacted into law only in two midsize cities, was struck down in court both times, resulted in exactly zero prosecutions, and seemingly had no tangible impact on the spread of pornography. Even so, the ordinance has generated a bounty of scholarly attention, whereas Detroit's anti-porn zoning ordinance has yet to be studied in detail outside of legal histories and law journals. This is despite the fact that Detroit's anti-porn zoning ordinance was copied by nearly every major city across the United States—and many minor ones to boot. Indeed, it stands as likely the single most influential municipal anti-porn ordinance of the twentieth century.

NOTES

1. James H. Dygert, "The Standards—And the Times That Hold Sway over Movies," *Detroit Free Press*, August 13, 1967, sec. B, 1; Ken Barnard, "Sex in Movies—How Far Will They Go?," *Detroit News*, November 17, 1968, sec. E, 1; James A. Treloar, "Skin Flicks in Livid Color (Green)," *Detroit News*, October 19, 1970, 3–4.

2. Michael Brogan, "Smut Houses: Growing Problem in Detroit," *Detroit News*, September 21, 1970, 10; "'Hair' Here to Stay Despite Police Frowns," *Detroit Free Press*, June 18, 1970, sec. B, 4; Mike Maza, "Detroit to Get First Peek at Banned Lennon Prints," *Detroit Free Press*, January 20, 1970.

3. Joseph Turrini, "Phooie on Louie: African American Detroit and the Election of Jerry Cavanagh," *Michigan History Magazine*, December 1999, 11–17.

4. Judd Arnett, "High Cost of Justice," *Detroit Free Press*, June 28, 1964, sec. B, 3; "Runs for Judge," *Detroit Free Press*, April 30, 1966, 3; "Sheriff's Top Aide a Negro," *Detroit American*, June 5, 1968, 1; "Voting Tables," *Detroit Free Press*, November 7, 1968, sec. B, 12; Ladd Neuman, "Ravitz Rejects Mayor's Race," *Detroit Free Press*, July 19, 1969, 3; David Cooper, "Sheriff Gribbs Enters Race for Mayor; To Seek Unity," *Detroit Free Press*, July 26, 1969, 3.

5. See, for example, Heather Ann Thompson, *Whose Detroit?: Politics, Labor, and Race in a Modern American City* (Ithaca, NY: Cornell University Press, 2004), 80.

6. Cooper, "Sheriff Gribbs Enters Race for Mayor," 4.

7. Michael Maidenberg, "Beck Supporters Moving to Gribbs, Survey Shows," *Detroit Free Press*, September 11, 1969, 3.

8. Maidenberg, 4; Clark Hoyt, "Gribbs Wins Mayor Race," *Detroit Free Press*, November 5, 1969, 1.

9. Detroit's legislative body was, until July 1, 1974, called the common council, at which point its name was changed to the city council. For the sake of simplicity, I refer to it as the city council throughout this book.

10. Ladd Neuman, "Council to Get a Face-Lifting," *Detroit Free Press*, September 7, 1969, 3; Ladd Neuman, "Ravitz and Hood Win Top 2 Council Seats," *Detroit Free Press*, November 5, 1969, 1, 12.

11. Hiley Ward, "Militants Score for Council," *Detroit Free Press*, August 10, 1968, sec. B, 11; Hiley H. Ward, "'Direct Power:' Key to Pastor's Success," *Detroit Free Press*, January 7, 1967, 12.

12. Ladd Neuman, "Hands Off 'Hair,' City Told," *Detroit Free Press*, May 15, 1970, 3; Clark Hallas, "It's 'Hair'—By a Whisker," *Detroit News*, June 10, 1970, sec. B, 4.

13. "Definition of Obscenity Sought by Legal Expert," *Detroit News*, June 17, 1970, sec. C, 5.

14. Clark Hallas, "Council's War on Obscenity Is Sidetracked," *Detroit News*, July 1, 1970, sec. B, 7.

15. Louis Heldman, "What's Obscene? City Guide Asked," *Detroit Free Press*, June 30, 1970, sec. C, 10; "Definition of Obscenity Sought by Legal Expert," 5; William P. Doran to Common Council, June 25, 1970, box 25, folder 19, Mel Ravitz Papers, Walter P. Reuther Library, Wayne State University; John O'Leary, "Approach No. I—Obscenity," June 8, 1970, box 25, folder 19, Mel Ravitz Papers, Walter P. Reuther Library, Wayne State University; John O'Leary, "Approach No. II—Attack on Obscenity," June 8, 1970, box 25, folder 19, Mel Ravitz Papers, Walter P. Reuther Library, Wayne State University; Hallas, "Council's War on Obscenity Is Sidetracked," 7.

16. Ron Landsman, "Council Moves to Curb Smut Peddling in City," *Detroit Free Press*, July 1, 1970, 3.

17. Hallas, "Council's War on Obscenity Is Sidetracked," 7.

18. Landsman, "Council Moves to Curb Smut Peddling in City," 3; "Sound Off," *Detroit Free Press*, July 3, 1970.

19. "Anti-Skid Row Law Gets 7–2 Council OK," *Detroit Free Press*, February 21, 1962, 3; "Pawnbrokers Lose Bid for New City Locations," *Detroit Free Press*, October 26, 1962, 3.

20. "Burlesque, Skid Row Law Eyed," *Detroit News*, January 5, 1965, sec. D, 6; Hallas, "Council's War on Obscenity Is Sidetracked," 7.

21. Hiley H. Ward, "Church Features New Key Club," *Detroit Free Press*, February 15, 1963, 3; "Deee-Troit Seen," *Fifth Estate*, June 25, 1970, 4; "Deee-Troit Seen," *Fifth Estate*, July 9, 1970, 4.

22. Hallas, "It's 'Hair'—By a Whisker," 4; Louis Heldman, "Ravitz Fails to Impress Critics by Dancing in 'Hair,'" *Detroit Free Press*, June 19, 1970, 3.

23. Dennis McGuire to Mel Ravitz, December 6, 1970, box 25, folder 19, Mel Ravitz Papers, Walter P. Reuther Library, Wayne State University; Mel Ravitz to Dennis McGuire, December 22, 1970, box 25, folder 19, Mel Ravitz Papers, Walter P. Reuther Library, Wayne State University.

24. Thomas Donohue to Mel Ravitz and William L. Cahalan, March 9, 1971, box 32, folder 13, Mel Ravitz Papers, Walter P. Reuther Library, Wayne State University; Mel Ravitz to Thomas Donohue, March 23, 1971, box 32, folder 13, Mel Ravitz Papers, Walter P. Reuther Library, Wayne State University.

25. John Nichols to Common Council, December 21, 1970, box 25, folder 19, Mel Ravitz Papers, Walter P. Reuther Library, Wayne State University.

26. Common Council Support Service, "Memorandum of Law and Recommendations Regarding Proposed Ban of Adult Bookstores and Movie Theatres," December 7, 1970, 4, box 25, folder 19, Mel Ravitz Papers, Walter P. Reuther Library, Wayne State University.

27. Common Council Support Service, 4.

28. "Eberhard Wants Smut Shops Padlocked," *Detroit News*, December 10, 1970, 26; David L. Good, "Lawyer Doubts Smut Can Be Stopped," *Detroit News*, December 9, 1970, 12-C.

29. Landsman, "Council Moves to Curb Smut Peddling in City," 3; "No Room for Censorship in a Democratic Society," *Detroit Free Press*, July 2, 1970, 6.

30. Jody Ross, "Neighbors Picketing Racy Magazine Store," *Detroit Free Press*, July 18, 1970, 3; Rev. Charles D. Robertson to Mel Ravitz, July 13, 1970, box 25, folder 19, Mel Ravitz Papers, Walter P. Reuther Library, Wayne State University.

31. Robertson to Ravitz, July 13, 1970, Mel Ravitz Papers; Mel Ravitz to Rev. Charles D. Robertson, August 3, 1970, box 25, folder 19, Mel Ravitz Papers, Walter P. Reuther Library, Wayne State University.

32. "Police Charge 2 with Smut Sale," *Detroit Free Press*, July 19, 1970, 13; "Police Hit Peep Show in Raid," *Detroit Free Press*, July 22, 1970, 3.

33. "5 Dealers, 100 Films Seized in Biggest City Smut Raid," *Detroit Free Press*, August 8, 1970, 3; "Smut Raids Hit 6 Bookstores," *Detroit News*, August 8, 1970, 6; Ron Landsman, "Suit Challenges Michigan Obscenity, Seizure Laws," *Detroit Free Press*, August 22, 1970, 5; Allen Phillips, "Porno-Detroit: A Thriving Market," *Detroit News*, August 22, 1971, 9-B.

34. Tom Pawlick, "Underground Sex Ads: They're 'Healthy,' Says a Sociologist; They're 'Degenerate,' Says a Minister," *Detroit News*, August 20, 1970, sec. The Other Section, 10; "Police, Prosecutor Team Up in Drive on Adult Movies," *Detroit News*, September 26, 1970, 7; "Obscenity Statute Ruled Out by Judge," *Detroit News*, October 6, 1970, 4; "Judge Halts New Drive against Explicit-Sex Films," *Detroit Free Press*, October 7, 1970, 2.

35. "Suit Seeks to Halt Film," *Detroit News*, November 21, 1970, 2; Michael Brogan, "Jury Finds *101 Acts* Obscene," *Detroit News*, December 16, 1970, 20-C; "Judge Bars 'Animal' Film as Obscene," *Detroit News*, March 23, 1971, 17.

36. Jack Knight, "Do We Chase the Wrong 'Criminals'?," *Detroit Free Press*, March 26, 1972, 1–2.

37. Phillips, "Porno-Detroit," 9-B; *Investigation of Literature Allegedly Containing Objectionable Material: Hearings before House Select Committee on Current Pornographic Materials on H.R. 596 and 597* (1952), 140.

38. Tim Retzloff, "City, Suburb, and the Changing Bounds of Lesbian and Gay Life and Politics in Metropolitan Detroit, 1945–1985" (PhD diss., Yale University, 2014), 40, 101–2.

39. "The Vice Report," *Gay Liberator*, August 1973, 7; Barbara Stanton, "The Homosexuals of Detroit," *Detroit Free Press Magazine*, November 22, 1970, 35; "'Fake' Arrests X Rated," *Michigan Chronicle*, June 16, 1973, 9; "Cruise with Care," *Gay Liberator*, November 1971, 5; "Bits & Pieces," *Gay Liberator*, September 1974, 4.

40. Jon Queen, "Tiptoe through the Tearooms," *Gay Liberator*, November 1972, 5; "Deee-Troit Seen," *Fifth Estate*, May 20, 1972, 4.

41. "Jury Frees Gay!," *Gay Liberator*, November 1971, 1; Franz Martin, "Gays vs. Vice," *Fifth Estate*, October 14, 1971, 6; John Morales, "The Powers That May," *Gay Liberator*, November 1971, 1.

42. David L. Good, "Council May Move against Smut Peddlers," *Detroit News*, September 23, 1971, sec. B, 9; Phillips, "Porno-Detroit," 9-B; Jane Briggs, "You Can Stop Smut Mail," *Detroit Free Press*, February 3, 1971, sec. C, 5.

43. "Capitalism at Its Sexiest," *Detroit Free Press*, May 23, 1971, sec. B, 1; "Citizen of Detroit" to Mel Ravitz, October 6, 1971, box 32, folder 13, Mel Ravitz Papers, Walter P. Reuther Library, Wayne State University.

44. Good, "Council May Move against Smut Peddlers," 9.

45. Thomas H. Gallagher to Common Council, September 28, 1971, box 32, folder 13, Mel Ravitz Papers, Walter P. Reuther Library, Wayne State University.

46. ONE in Detroit et al. to Mel Ravitz, January 1972, box 41, folder 7, Mel Ravitz Papers, Walter P. Reuther Library, Wayne State University.

47. David L. Good, "Slowdown of Smut Flow Sought," *Detroit News*, January 5, 1972, sec. B: Metro-Detroit, 1.

48. David L. Good, "Levin Says Obscenity Ordinance Misses Target," *Detroit News*, January 19, 1972, sec. B: Metro-Detroit, 1.

49. Julie Morris, "Council Hears Blunt Plea for Curbs on Pornography," *Detroit Free Press*, January 27, 1972, 3.

50. David L. Good, "Obscenity Ordinance Faces Council Changes," *Detroit News*, January 27, 1972, sec. C, 4.

51. Creighton Lederer to Carl Levin, January 28, 1972, box 41, folder 6, Mel Ravitz Papers, Walter P. Reuther Library, Wayne State University.

52. Thomas H. Gallagher to Common Council, February 10, 1972, box 41, folder 6, Mel Ravitz Papers, Walter P. Reuther Library, Wayne State University; David L. Good, "Council Pulls Punches in Fight against Smut," *Detroit News*, February 16, 1972; "Council Rejects New Smut Curb," *Detroit Free Press*, February 16, 1972, 3; David L. Good, "Smut Stores Challenged to Fight New Ordinance," *Detroit News*, March 1, 1972, 6.

53. Good, "Smut Stores Challenged to Fight New Ordinance," 6; Julie Morris, "Council Bans Porno Stores," *Detroit Free Press*, March 1, 1972, 3.

54. "Mayor's Office Press Release," March 6, 1972, box 333, folder 7, Roman Gribbs Papers, Burton Historical Collection, Detroit Public Library; "Gribbs Appoints HP Council Chief as Legal Adviser," *Detroit Free Press*, February 11, 1970, sec. B, 1; John Oppedahl, "Gribbs' Moves Hint of Race for Re-Election," *Detroit Free Press*, August 27, 1972, sec. F, 13.

55. "Mayor's Office Press Release," March 6, 1972, Roman Gribbs Papers; John F. Nichols to Roman S. Gribbs, February 11, 1972, box 333, folder 7, Roman Gribbs Papers, Burton Historical Collection, Detroit Public Library.

56. "Mayor's Office Press Release," March 6, 1972, Roman Gribbs Papers; "Adult Bookstore Fights Revocation of License," *Detroit News*, March 7, 1972, sec. B, 2; "Peep Gallery Ordered Shut," *Detroit Free Press*, March 7, 1972, sec. B, 1.

57. Roman S. Gribbs to *Detroit News*, March 27, 1972, box 333, folder 6, Roman Gribbs Papers, Burton Historical Collection, Detroit Public Library.

58. "Peep Show Ban Delay Ordered," *Detroit News*, March 17, 1972, sec. B, 19; David L. Good, "'Peep' Permit OK'd; Gribbs Tried to Kill It," *Detroit News*, March 23, 1972, sec. C, 1.

59. Roman S. Gribbs to J.G.A. Enterprises, Inc., March 22, 1972, box 333, folder 6, Roman Gribbs Papers, Burton Historical Collection, Detroit Public Library; "Gribbs Refuses License to West Side Theater," *Detroit News*, March 24, 1972, sec. C, 8; "Theater License Ban an Error, Says City," *Detroit News*, March 30, 1972, sec. B, 2.

60. John Woolley, "License Plan Aims at Smut in Stores," *Detroit Free Press*, March 22, 1972, 11; David L. Good, "City Anti-Smut Plan Assailed," *Detroit News*, March 22, 1972, sec. B: Metro-Detroit, 1.

61. Good, "City Anti-Smut Plan Assailed," 1.

62. David L. Good, "Gribbs Delay on Commercial Strip Angers Council," *Detroit News*, March 29, 1972, sec. B: Metro-Detroit, 1; Good, "City Anti-Smut Plan Assailed," 1.

63. "Court Suit Fights City's Law on Smut," *Detroit News*, March 13, 1972, 11; "Smut Law Contested in Court," *Detroit Free Press*, March 14, 1972, 3; David L. Good, "Smut Business Booms, but Dealers Feel Heat," *Detroit News*, March 24, 1972, sec. C, 8.

64. Douglas Glazier and Jeffrey Hadden, "Obscenity Ruling Appeal Unlikely," *Detroit News*, June 21, 1972, sec. C, 16; Jonathan Miller, "Court Rejects City Ordinance against Smut," *Detroit Free Press*, June 21, 1972, 3.

65. Miller, "Court Rejects City Ordinance against Smut," 3; "Eberhard Says He'll Run for Mayor," *Detroit Free Press*, June 22, 1972, 10.

66. "Complaint," Lido Cinema Corporation v. Roman Gribbs, No. 38356 (E.D. Mich. S. Div. 1972), 11–13, exhibits F and I, box 41, folder 6, Mel Ravitz Papers, Walter P. Reuther Library, Wayne State University.

67. Julie Morris, "90-Day Ban Set on Smut Permits," *Detroit Free Press*, May 17, 1972, sec. C, 12; David L. Good, "New 'Adult' Licenses Halted," *Detroit News*, May 17, 1972, 7; "Kiddie Shows Blocked," *Detroit Free Press*, May 20, 1972, 3.

68. "Complaint," Lido Cinema Corporation v. Roman Gribbs, 11–12; Roman S. Gribbs to John Clark, June 10, 1972, box 333, folder 6, Roman Gribbs Papers, Burton Historical Collection, Detroit Public Library; Stuart Gorelick to Roman S. Gribbs, July 31, 1972, box 333, folder 6, Roman Gribbs Papers, Burton Historical Collection, Detroit Public Library; "Harassment Charged by 'X' Theater," *Detroit News*, August 4, 1972, 4; "X-Rated Theater Back in Business," *Detroit News*, August 9, 1972, sec. B, 12; Stephen M. Taylor to Roman S. Gribbs, August 17, 1972, box 333, folder 6, Roman Gribbs Papers, Burton Historical Collection, Detroit Public Library.

69. "Smut Shop Controls Urged," *Detroit News*, June 23, 1972, sec. B, 21; Tom Ricke, "Porno Shops Profit from Hang-Ups," *Detroit Free Press*, August 21, 1972, 12.

70. "Mayor's Office Press Release," October 2, 1972, box 333, folder 6, Roman Gribbs Papers, Burton Historical Collection, Detroit Public Library.

71. David L. Good, "Residents Give Up Fight against Adult Theater," *Detroit News*, October 10, 1972, 3.

72. Julie Morris, "All at City Hearing Want Anti-Smut Law," *Detroit Free Press*, October 18, 1972, sec. C, 10; Ronald L. Russell, "Planning Unit OK's Gribbs' Anti-Smut Rule," *Detroit News*, October 18, 1972, sec. B, 1.

73. Maryanne Conheim, "Council Hears Foes of Pornography," *Detroit Free Press*, October 21, 1972, 3.

74. Conheim, 3.

75. Conheim, 3; Ronald L. Russell, "Detroit Council to Vote Tuesday on Smut Curbs," *Detroit News*, October 21, 1972, 14.

76. Gloria Snead, "Council OK's Smut Store Rules," *Detroit News*, October 25, 1972, sec. B, 1; "A Try at Pornography Control," *Detroit News*, November 11, 1972, 4.

77. "Statement—Mayor Roman S. Gribbs, Morality and Media," October 26, 1972, box 333, folder 6, Roman Gribbs Papers, Burton Historical Collection, Detroit Public Library.

78. Don Lenhausen, "City Tightens Anti-Smut Laws," *Detroit Free Press*, October 25, 1972, 3, 8; Snead, "Council OK's Smut Store Rules," 1;

"Statement—Mayor Roman S. Gribbs, Morality and Media," Roman Gribbs Papers.

79. Snead, "Council OK's Smut Store Rules," 1.

80. Maureen P. Reilly to Common Council, November 17, 1972, box 41, folder 7, Mel Ravitz Papers, Walter P. Reuther Library, Wayne State University; Louis Heldman, "Pornography Trade Thrives in Detroit," *Detroit Free Press*, February 11, 1973, 6.

81. Michael Wendland and James Graham, "5 Detroit Area Art Studios Offer Sex for Sale," *Detroit News*, December 10, 1972, 20.

82. Louis Heldman, "Ban Helps Smut Peddlers Thrive," *Detroit Free Press*, February 12, 1973, 3.

83. Heldman, 8.

84. Heldman, 3; Heldman, "Pornography Trade Thrives in Detroit," 3, 6.

85. "Appendix," Young v. American Mini Theatres, 427 U.S. 50 (1976), exhibit 2.

86. Don Lenhausen, "Irate Citizens Storm Council Protesting Porno Movies," *Detroit Free Press*, April 3, 1973, sec. D, 8.

87. Roman S. Gribbs to S. H. Murphy, March 9, 1972, box 333, folder 6, Roman Gribbs Papers, Burton Historical Collection, Detroit Public Library; Roman S. Gribbs to Mrs. John E. McNeal II, March 23, 1972, box 333, folder 6, Roman Gribbs Papers, Burton Historical Collection, Detroit Public Library.

88. Roman S. Gribbs to Morality in Media of Western New York, August 8, 1972, box 333, folder 7, Roman Gribbs Papers, Burton Historical Collection, Detroit Public Library; Reilly to Common Council, November 17, 1972, Mel Ravitz Papers.

89. David Eberhard to George L. Dimas, September 28, 1972, box 1, folder 3, David Eberhard Papers, Burton Historical Collection, Detroit Public Library; David Eberhard to George L. Dimas, October 4, 1972, box 1, folder 3, David Eberhard Papers, Burton Historical Collection, Detroit Public Library; David Eberhard to George L. Dimas, November 13, 1972, box 1, folder 3, David Eberhard Papers, Burton Historical Collection, Detroit Public Library; David Eberhard to John McEwan, November 13, 1972, box 1, folder 3, David Eberhard Papers, Burton Historical Collection, Detroit Public Library; Clyde Cox to David Eberhard, December 7, 1972, box 1, folder 3, David Eberhard Papers, Burton Historical Collection, Detroit Public Library; "Untitled List of Incoming Phone Calls," October 30, 1972, box 333, folder 6, Roman Gribbs Papers, Burton Historical Collection, Detroit Public Library; Francis J. Ivancie to Roman S. Gribbs, November 30, 1972, box 333, folder 6, Roman Gribbs Papers, Burton Historical Collection, Detroit Public Library.

90. American Mini Theatres vs. Detroit, No. 72 225–448 AW (Circuit Court for the County of Wayne May 16, 1973); "Detroit," *Boxoffice*, February 5, 1973, sec. ME, 2.

91. *American Mini Theatres* at 8; Roman S. Gribbs to Maureen P. Reilly, May 30, 1973, box 457, folder 4, Roman Gribbs Papers, Burton Historical Collection, Detroit Public Library; Roman S. Gribbs to Richard E. Lawson, May 30, 1973, box 457, folder 4, Roman Gribbs Papers, Burton Historical Collection, Detroit Public Library.

92. Stephen Cain, "U.S. Courts to Test Detroit's Smut Ban," *Detroit Free Press*, June 16, 1973, 5; Louis Heldman, "City Wins 1st Smut Battle," *Detroit Free Press*, June 12, 1973, sec. B, 5.

93. Cain, "U.S. Courts to Test Detroit's Smut Ban," 5.

94. Cain, 5.

95. Miller v. California, 413 U.S. 15 (1973).

96. Charles Keating, "Green Light to Combat Smut," *Reader's Digest*, January 1974, 147–50; "Smut Ruling Worries Detroit Adult Theaters," *Detroit News*, June 22, 1973, 15; Louis Heldman, "Sex Movies, Smut Shops Put On Spot," *Detroit Free Press*, June 22, 1973, 3; "3 Porno Theaters Close Down in City," *Detroit Free Press*, June 23, 1973, 3.

97. "3 Porno Theaters Close Down in City," 3; Paul M. Branzburg, "Police Set for Smut Arrests," *Detroit Free Press*, June 27, 1973, 17; Heldman, "Sex Movies, Smut Shops Put On Spot," 3.

98. Branzburg, "Police Set for Smut Arrests," 3; "The Vice Report," 7.

99. "Judge Delays Action on Adult Movies," *Detroit Free Press*, June 30, 1973, 3; Paul M. Branzburg, "High Court Obscenity Ruling Puts Prosecution in Limbo," *Detroit Free Press*, July 1, 1973, 3, 7; "Good Ruling on Censors," *Detroit Free Press*, September 14, 1973, 8.

100. Betty DeRamus, "Pornography Curbs Are a Legal Jungle," *Detroit Free Press*, September 16, 1973, 12.

101. Whitney Strub, *Perversion for Profit: The Politics of Pornography and the Rise of the New Right* (New York: Columbia University Press, 2011), 171–72; Obscenity Law Project, "An Empirical Inquiry into the Effects of Miller v. California on the Control of Obscenity," *New York University Law Review* 52 (1977): 810.

102. Don Lenhausen, "Sex Films Bring Term of 90 Days," *Detroit Free Press*, October 17, 1973, 3, 12; Stephen Cain and Robert S. Wisler, "Officials Praise Sentences of Adult Movie Operators," *Detroit News*, October 17, 1973, sec. B: Metro-Detroit, 1.

103. Nortown Theatre, et al., v. Gribbs, No. 39796, 40168, 40198 (E.D. Mich. S. Div. 1974).

104. *Nortown Theatre.*

105. "Appendix," *Young*, exhibit 1.

106. "Appendix," *Young*, exhibit 1; *Nortown Theatre.*

107. "Court Eases Curb on 'Adult' Stores," *Detroit News*, March 23, 1974, 2; Louis Heldman, "Court Relaxes Sex Shop Curbs," *Detroit Free Press*, March 23, 1974, 3, 9.

108. "Court Eases Curb on 'Adult' Stores," 2; Michael Wowk, "Ruling May Aid Detroit's Control of Porno Shops," *Detroit News*, March 25, 1974, 4.

109. Beverly Eckman, "Council Will Bar New 'Adult' Outlets," *Detroit News*, March 30, 1974, 3; Dave Anderson, "City Council Explodes at Sex Shop Hearing," *Detroit Free Press*, March 30, 1974, 3.

110. American Mini Theatres v. Gribbs, No. 74–2129, 74–2303 (6th Cir. Ct. App. 1975).

111. *American Mini Theatres.*

112. *American Mini Theatres.*

113. Seth S. King, "Foes of Pornography Winning a Few Skirmishes, but Not the Major Battles," *New York Times*, November 28, 1975, 52; "The Porno Plague," *Time*, April 5, 1976, 63.

114. Dave Anderson, "High Court Case Is an Experience," *Detroit Free Press*, March 29, 1976, 3, 13.

115. Young v. American Mini Theatres, 427 U.S. 50 (1976); Richard F. Hixson, *Pornography and the Justices: The Supreme Court and the Intractable Obscenity Problem* (Carbondale: Southern Illinois University Press, 1996), 138, 141.

116. *Young*, 427 U.S. 50.

117. *Young*, 427 U.S. 50.

118. *Young*, 427 U.S. 50.

119. Robert Lindsey, "Drive by Cities on Pornography Spurred by Detroit Zoning Case," *New York Times*, November 28, 1976, 34; Francis Ward, "Detroit's Zoning Law Helps Clean Up Sex Shop District," *Los Angeles Times*, July 18, 1977, 14.

120. It is worth mentioning that even though every adult movie theater in Detroit would shut down in time—victims of competition from pornography available via home video and then the internet—the city's adult bookstores proved to have greater staying power. In part this was because many of them began to specialize in sex toys and then home video pornography beginning in the 1980s, but this staying power was also a result of the way adult businesses operating at the time of the zoning law's adoption were grandfathered in. This has led to an impressive eight total adult bookstores having managed to survive in Detroit from the early 1970s to the time of this writing.

121. Robert Lamb, "Relief, Caution Expressed Here on Porno Ruling," *Atlanta Constitution*, June 25, 1976, 11; "Court Upholds Curbs on 'Adult' Movie Theaters," *Los Angeles Times*, June 25, 1976, sec. B, 1; "Zoning 'Adult' Movies," *New York Times*, July 8, 1976, 30; Richard J. Cattani, "Cities Forced to Go It Alone in Pornography Struggle," *Christian Science Monitor*, December 14, 1976, 9; Philip Hager, "Zoning Laws New Weapon in Smut Fight," *Los Angeles Times*, September 4, 1976, 1, 15; Lindsey, "Drive by Cities on Pornography Spurred by Detroit Zoning Case," 1, 34; Phil Kerby, "Putting Pornography in Its Place," *Los Angeles Times*, December 2, 1976, sec. C, 1; Lenny Litman, "Peeps, Strips, Go-Go, Screen

Sex in Pittsburgh on Detroit Plan?," *Variety*, December 1, 1976, 66; "Kansas City Adopts Ord 'Zoning' on Lines of Boston, Detroit," *Variety*, December 15, 1976, 36; "Philly Council Passes Antipornography Bill," *Boxoffice*, May 16, 1977, sec. E, 6–7; "Chicago 'Zoning' versus Pomo Sites Is Taking Shape," *Variety*, July 13, 1977, 16; "San Antonio Latest to Keep Porn Away from Residences," *Variety*, September 28, 1977, 28.

122. Remarkably enough, the rush to adopt similar laws was not just limited to cities in the United States, with Toronto's executive alderman calling for the city to adopt similar anti-porn zoning laws, saying just days after a United States Supreme Court ruling that had no legal bearing on the city he represented, "It's been tried in Detroit and it works there." David Miller, "Zoning Clout Urged to Curb Porn," *Toronto Star*, June 29, 1976, sec. B, 2.

123. Hager, "Zoning Laws New Weapon in Smut Fight," 15.

124. Lindsey, "Drive by Cities on Pornography Spurred by Detroit Zoning Case," 1.

125. Hager, "Zoning Laws New Weapon in Smut Fight," 15.

126. See Eric Schaefer and Eithne Johnson, "Quarantined! A Case Study of Boston's Combat Zone," in *Hop on Pop: The Politics and Pleasures of Popular Culture*, ed. Henry Jenkins, Tara McPherson, and Jane Shattuc (Durham, NC: Duke University Press, 2002), 430–53.

127. "Sex-Oriented Business Gets Own Zoned Area in Boston," *Los Angeles Times*, June 7, 1974, 2; DeRamus, "Pornography Curbs Are a Legal Jungle," 12.

128. Lindsey, "Drive by Cities on Pornography Spurred by Detroit Zoning Case," 1, 34.

129. "Dispersal of Porno Is Sought," *Atlanta Constitution*, December 2, 1976, 20.

130. Jonathan Kaufman, "From Scollay Sq. Tattoo Parlors to Combat Zone Porno Film," *Boston Globe*, December 27, 1984, 25.

131. David Gumpert, "Problems in the Combat Zone," *Wall Street Journal*, June 30, 1977, 12.

132. Bruce Taylor, "Ask a CDL Attorney: Is 'Zoning' the Solution?," *National Decency Reporter* 15, no. 2 (April 1978): 8.

133. See Marilyn Adler Papayanis, "Sex and the Revanchist City: Zoning Out Pornography in New York," *Environment and Planning D: Society and Space* 18, no. 3 (2000): 341–53.

134. Josh Sides, "Excavating the Postwar Sex District in San Francisco," *Journal of Urban History* 32, no. 3 (2006): 369–74.

135. Sides, 369–71.

136. Carolyn Bronstein, *Battling Pornography: The American Feminist Anti-Pornography Movement, 1976–1986* (Cambridge: Cambridge University Press, 2011), 190.

137. For more on Women Against Pornography's campaign against adult entertainment in Times Square, see Bronstein, 200–37.

138. For more on the law, see Bronstein, 323–31; Donald Alexander Downs, *The New Politics of Pornography* (Chicago: University of Chicago Press, 1989); Lisa Duggan and Nan Hunter, *Sex Wars: Sexual Dissent and Political Culture* (New York: Routledge, 1995), 30–42, 64–67; Nadine Strossen, *Defending Pornography: Free Speech, Sex, and the Fight for Women's Rights* (New York: New York University Press, 2000), 59–82; Carole S. Vance, "More Danger, More Pleasure: A Decade after the Barnard Sexuality Conference," *New York Law School Law Review* 38, no. 1–4 (1993): 289–317.

EPILOGUE

The Election of Coleman Young and the Politics of Pornography and Race

PRACTICALLY ALL THE POLITICIANS INVOLVED in the debate over the adoption of Detroit's new anti-porn ordinances in 1972 had higher political aspirations. For figures like Roman Gribbs, Mel Ravitz, and David Eberhard, the groundswell of grassroots anti-porn protest in the city fueled each to take on pornography in their own way as a central issue that they hoped would help them reach their respective goals. In the end, though, the 1973 elections in the city demonstrated the electoral limits of the politics of pornography in the face of the politics of race.

Through the first two years of Mayor Gribbs's term, his administration had shown little interest in censorship or pornography, instead following in the same vein as his predecessor, Jerome Cavanagh, by keeping clear of a public stance that might align him with the censorial minded. In early 1972, though, with the city's next mayoral election a year and a half away, Gribbs made pornography a top priority for his administration, evidently because he saw it as an issue that could be leveraged for political gain. Throughout 1972, his team carefully responded to every anti-porn letter it received to extol the mayor's action against pornography. And, after the city council passed the anti-porn licensing and zoning ordinances in October of that year, his administration was quick to take credit for the legislation. After a WXYZ Radio editorial lauded the city council for its action, Gribbs's press secretary, Phill Jourdan, wrote to the station's editorial director:

> I received a copy of your October 25 editorial regarding the new obscenity ordinances. I agree that this new approach is laudable and I also agree that the Common Council deserves some credit for passing the ordinance.

However, I think you should be aware that the genesis of these proposals is Mayor Gribbs and his Task Force on Licensing Procedures. If the Mayor had not acted so firmly and if the Task Force had not put in so many hours of research and hard work, this revolutionary new approach would not have been made. I have included copies of our press release and the Mayor's letter to council.

I don't mean this to be critical . . . but credit is important in the business of government and I think that credit should go where it is due.

This letter points to both the rivalry between Gribbs and the city council as well as the importance the mayor's office placed on getting credit for these anti-porn ordinances. This issue of credit was particularly important in light of the fact that the whole city was starting to prepare for the next mayoral election, which by that time was just a year away.[1]

On November 15, 1972, two days before Gribbs's press secretary wrote his letter to WXYZ Radio, *Detroit Free Press* columnist Frank Angelo sized up the state of the mayoral race. As he wrote, there was an ongoing search for a "'unity' black candidate." Former circuit court judge Edward Bell had already declared his intention to run, while some of the other potential major Black candidates were likely contenders, including Councilman Ernest Browne, State Senator Coleman Young, and Michigan Secretary of State Richard Austin, who had narrowly lost to Gribbs in the 1969 election. As Angelo wrote, though, "There may be others, but this group pretty well cuts across the major currents and undercurrents that exist in the black community—and that's the rub. Because, chances are, not one of the men is likely to muster the kind of all-out support from blacks and so-called liberal whites that would be needed to beat Mayor Gribbs next November." Angelo was dubious about whether any of the potential African American candidates could become the consensus choice of the Black community in Detroit while still holding the requisite support of white liberals necessary to challenge Gribbs in the mayoral election.[2]

Thus, the expectation was that Ravitz would be the one to emerge as Gribbs's chief rival, with Angelo writing of Ravitz, "There's a feeling that he's the one man who can really bring together the black community and the white liberal community for a challenge to Gribbs, the establishment heavy." Ravitz had citywide name recognition, strong institutional support among unions, and was highly popular among both left-leaning whites and African Americans. Despite being seen as a potential front-runner in the 1969 mayoral race, he had passed up the opportunity to run then, and there was a widespread feeling that his time had now come. During his intervening years as city council president,

Ravitz had modulated his strident liberalism with a moderate pragmatism that, he hoped, would help elect him mayor. The prominent role he played in the debate over pornography can be seen as one extension of these efforts to set himself up for a mayoral run. Indeed, the fact that Ravitz took on the issue of pornography whatsoever despite his seeming apathy on the question of the morality of pornography and his decided aversion to censorship points to the way he saw anti-porn politics as another rung on the ladder that would lead him to the mayor's office. All this led many prognosticators in late 1972 to predict that the city was headed for a showdown between Gribbs and Ravitz in the following year's mayoral election.[3]

Still, Gribbs had yet to actually announce that he would be running for reelection, though there were signs that he was preparing to run again. Staff shake-ups by the mayor in August of 1972 were widely seen as an indication that Gribbs was gearing up for a reelection run. The letter from Gribbs's press secretary to WXYZ can also be seen as an indication of his intention to run again, with the letter acting as a way for the mayor to take credit for the anti-porn ordinances while undercutting Ravitz, his presumed chief rival. In Angelo's view, Gribbs was also actively working to boost his "good guy" liberal bona fides by touting progressive city initiatives like the police department's push for more African American officers, the idea being to cut off the opening to Gribbs's left politically.[4]

Just over a month after Angelo's column, though, Gribbs shocked the city's political establishment by declaring that he would not seek reelection. The mayor's aides learned of the decision only an hour before it was announced, and it apparently caught his staff entirely by surprise. Gribbs had been raising money for a reelection campaign just a week prior only to change course, declining to run so that he could spend more time with his family. Though his term as mayor had lacked the pizazz of his predecessor (and, as it turned out, his successor), he was still fairly popular in the city, and Gribbs, for one, claimed that he made his decision despite private polls that he said indicated he would win reelection easily.[5]

After Gribbs's announcement, the *Free Press* instantly declared Ravitz "the man to beat for mayor of Detroit in 1973." Even as Ravitz had yet to formally declare his candidacy for the position, his public remarks at that time made it evident that a mayoral run was in his future, with Ravitz saying, "Somebody has to be and is going to be the mayor. With 12 years of training I am as knowledgeable and perhaps more so than most other candidates I can think of." He went on to position himself as the unifying candidate, saying, "I believe this town can be put together again."[6]

Still, alternatives to Ravitz quickly began to emerge, with a number of white politicians soon mentioned as possibilities who might appeal to the moderate and conservative vote. Among these was police commissioner John Nichols, who was seen as a candidate able to appeal to the "law-and-order and homeowner support Gribbs enjoyed." Nichols at that point denied any interest in the post, though, saying, "I'm a policeman. That's all I know. I don't know anything about politics."[7] Meanwhile, there was also David Eberhard, who, as discussed in chapter 5, had previously announced his plan to run for mayor in June of 1972 after the obscenity law he had championed was overturned by a court decision. Eberhard reversed course later that year and declared that he would not run given the belief that Gribbs would seek reelection and win. However, after Gribbs pulled out of the race, Eberhard immediately expressed renewed interest, announcing his candidacy a week later.[8] Still, most prognosticators gave him little chance of winning the race, and many expected Eberhard to drop out before the primary to instead run again for city council. However, Eberhard spoke confidently of his chances, pledging in his campaign announcement that he would clean up "a dirty, filthy, junky city."[9] The *Free Press* wrote of the approach taken by Eberhard in his mayoral run that he "was elected to the council as a liberal, but has said he will make a conservative campaign for mayor."[10] In the months ahead, Eberhard tried to drum up support by focusing on the drive to halt the spread of pornography in the city, with the *Detroit News* writing that he was "basing much of his mayor campaign on the obscenity issue."[11]

When Ravitz officially announced his candidacy in February of 1973, he did so by positioning himself as a candidate who could unite Detroit, saying, "I don't want to be mayor of a divided city." He indicated that he saw himself as a middle-ground choice positioned between the supposed divisiveness of radical Black mayoral candidates and conservative-leaning white ones, able to build a broad coalition across racial and ethnic lines while attracting business and labor interests. If Ravitz was not quite seen as a shoo-in for mayor, he was undoubtedly the front-runner at this point—the candidate that everyone else was trying to catch.[12]

Still, Ravitz was playing a tricky game by positioning himself in the center of opposing forces, and his candidacy soon took a hit when the Michigan Supreme Court issued a ruling in May of 1973 that the state's constitution did not preclude Coleman Young from running for mayor despite him serving in the state legislature at that time. Young immediately kick-started his campaign by attacking the Detroit Police Department and its commissioner, John Nichols—who was expected to announce his mayoral candidacy shortly—by saying that Nichols was "following the old blackjack rule by terror." The *Free*

Press explained that Young's strategy "is intended to make the primary campaign into a battle between himself and Nichols, hoping to cut the political middle ground away from Common Council President Mel Ravitz." Indeed, Young positioned his candidacy as something of a critique of the legacy of white liberal leadership in an increasingly Black city. As he said, "Detroit today is a racially polarized city, and now is the time we need to have a black mayor." He also took aim directly at Ravitz. After a report detailed how Ravitz had received more votes for city council from the Black community in 1969 than three out of six Black candidates, Young said flatly, "I don't think the Black community will be tricked by Mel Ravitz again."[13]

In the end, this strategy worked for Young, thus dooming Ravitz's candidacy. With Nichols and Young in the race, to say nothing of a host of other white liberal-leaning candidates, Ravitz finished a distant third in the September primary. Ravitz's path through the middle became no path at all, as he failed to win either predominantly white or predominantly African American neighborhoods. Meanwhile, as the top two vote getters, Nichols and Young advanced to the general election. Unlike in the 1969 election, when the white and Black mayoral candidates had largely similar politics, Nichols and Young could agree on little and presented unambiguously different visions for the city. The liberal-leaning moderation embodied by Gribbs in the 1969 race had given way to the Nichols campaign's full-on embrace of racist-tinged law-and-order politics. Meanwhile, Young's brash style and full-throated embrace of Black politics was far removed from the mild-mannered moderate liberalism of Richard Austin's 1969 mayoral run. Ultimately, after a hotly contested campaign, Young eked out a narrow win to become Detroit's first African American mayor.[14]

The 1973 elections in Detroit demonstrated the limitations of anti-porn politics in the face of racial polarization. For all Gribbs's work against adult entertainment throughout 1972, it had not transformed him into the type of popular mayor who could scare off potential competitors angling for his job. Ravitz's pragmatic attempt to appropriate anti-porn politics as a means to boost his electoral chances in the end satisfied no one, and the white liberalism he represented was seemingly no longer satisfactory to either African Americans or moderate whites in the city. Finally, centering his campaign around the issue of pornography drew little popular or institutional support for Eberhard's mayoral run, and he quietly bowed out of the race in July to instead run again for city council.[15]

Meanwhile, the city council race also proved the limited political capital provided by anti-porn politics. Phillip Tannian, a top mayoral aide who had spearheaded Gribbs's campaign against pornography as head of the Mayor's

Figure E.1. Coleman Young pictured at Detroit's Playboy Club during the 1970s.

Task Force on Licensing Procedures, ran for city council that year but finished just twentieth in the primary, outside of the top eighteen who advanced to the general election. Katherine Gribbs, the wife of the mayor, also ran for city council and fared better than Tannian in the primary, finishing seventh overall. However, come November, she dropped to fourteenth, finishing far outside the top nine candidates who were elected to the council.[16]

Mayor Young, meanwhile, showed little interest in engaging in anti-porn politics. During his twenty years as the mayor of Detroit, Young rarely if ever spoke about the issue of pornography or signed any major pieces of anti-porn legislation into law. Young did, however, have his picture taken at Detroit's Playboy Club (see fig. E.1), beaming while standing next to two "bunnies"—an image one would be hard pressed to imagine his predecessor posing for. Given all this, there is more than a bit of irony to the fact that, because of the timing of when the Supreme Court heard the appeal, the legal case on Detroit's anti-porn zoning law came to have Young's name rather than Gribbs's affixed to it. In reality, Coleman Young had nothing to do with *Young v. American Mini Theatres* or the law that prompted the case.

Coleman Young ushered in an era of ascendance for Black politics in Detroit—one in which there was far less interest in the battles over pornography and censorship that had preoccupied his white predecessors. Indeed, his apathetic stance toward pornography points to an essential component to the history of the anti-porn movement in Detroit that I have catalogued in this book, which is the degree to which it was dominated at all levels by whiteness. The city's grassroots anti-porn protesters, from Catholic postwar opposition to indecent literature to those protesting the Adult World Bookstore in Redford, were predominantly, almost exclusively, white. Likewise, from Herbert Case to Roman Gribbs, all the key figures who spearheaded media censorship efforts by the city government were white. Moreover, as I have argued, all these anti-porn advocates stretching from the grassroots level up to the mayor's office drew on, in varying ways, white racial politics. In the end, though, the all-consuming whiteness of the anti-porn movement meant that it had little political utility for white politicians once the city was majority Black. White politicians like Gribbs, Ravitz, and Eberhard no doubt saw anti-porn politics as a unifying issue that could create solidarity among Blacks and whites who were—in their imagination, at least—equally opposed to pornography. In reality, anti-porn politics had always been a more compelling political issue to whites in the city, whereas African Americans frustrated with the state of racial relations in Detroit had little interest in the "unifying" power of anti-porn politics when far more pressing issues were impacting their daily lives. Throughout the time that Detroit was majority white in both its population and political leadership during the twentieth century, anti-porn politics held a central place in the city; not coincidentally, once the city became majority African American and its political leadership eventually came to reflect that, the era of preeminent anti-porn politics in Detroit came to an end.

All this is not to say that all African Americans in Detroit were entirely apathetic when it came to the issue of pornography, as there were occasional grassroots anti-porn efforts by Black residents of the city. In 1973, the group Angry Residents Mobilized (ARM) was organized by African American parents and homeowners to protest the stretch of adult businesses along Eight Mile Road in northern Detroit. ARM members drew on similar arguments to those of white Redford residents, emphasizing the threat to property values and the notion that those patronizing adult businesses in the neighborhood were suburban whites who would not allow such establishments in their own communities. They also argued that adult businesses were conglomerating, particularly in Black neighborhoods of the city. As Mrs. Jay Fowler said of pornography, "We are Black people. Everywhere we move, they bring this stuff in." Likewise, Frederick T. McClure, Michigan executive of the prominent civil rights organization Southern Christian Leadership Conference (SCLC), similarly said at that time, "Smut is something new for SCLC to fight, but it's a legitimate battle because the pornography problem didn't begin until blacks were allowed to buy homes here." Black anti-porn activists also often linked this notion to the charge that the city was deliberately allowing adult businesses to proliferate in Black neighborhoods rather than white ones. Robert Glenn, president of a homeowners group and spokesman for ARM, argued that point before a public meeting of the city council in May of 1974. As the *Free Press* said of the meeting, "Glenn explained that the city was able to keep the sex shops out of the all-white neighborhoods and that many suburbs were also able to keep the porno shops out, but Detroit couldn't." These arguments drew on assertions Black activists had been making for years about the prevalence of commercial sex in Black neighborhoods in Detroit. As one Black resident said in 1963 about the prevalence of prostitution in their neighborhood: "You would think the Negro community had been designated as the city's official 'red light' district." Such rhetoric highlighted the reality that city officials and the police had long been more responsive to white residents making an issue of commercial sex in their neighborhoods than they were to Black residents doing the same.[17]

All told, though, even as there certainly was Black activism against adult businesses rooted in concern about issues like property values and neighborhood deterioration, anti-porn sentiment never seemed to hold quite as much sway among African Americans in Detroit as it did with the white anti-porn activists catalogued throughout this book. In part this was because the African American community in the city was busy debating another form of "indecent" media that was, to some Black residents, far more dangerous than pornography. Over the course of the early to mid-1970s, the city's most prominent Black newspaper, the *Michigan Chronicle*, only published a few articles dealing with the issue of pornography in the city. Over that same time frame, it published dozens, perhaps hundreds, of news stories and opinion pieces on the flourishing of blaxploitation cinema in Detroit and across the country. Blaxploitation was a loosely defined genre of 1970s films that tended to be set in poor urban centers and focus on Black male action heroes. The genre was immensely popular in Detroit, particularly among younger African Americans, who celebrated blaxploitation for the stories it told of empowered Black men fighting against racist forces in society. For many other Black Detroiters, though, blaxploitation reified negative stereotypes of African Americans and glorified criminality and drug use, supposedly representing a new nadir in representations of Black people onscreen. In early 1974, the Detroit chapter of the NAACP began a drive against downtown theaters showing blaxploitation, with picketers holding signs like "Distorted Stories Corrupt Young Minds" and "Pollution in Detroit Theatres Inspires Crime." As these signs make clear, protests against blaxploitation in Detroit often linked the popularity of blaxploitation films with the problems of crime and drug use in the African American community in the city. After months of these protests, Joe Madison, executive secretary of the Detroit NAACP, claimed victory in getting downtown theaters to change the films they played, telling the press, "Now that people have worked to eliminate the images of pimps, prostitutes, and dope-dealers from the screens of downtown movie theaters, it's only a matter of time before they want them off the streets as well." This controversy was hardly unique to Detroit, with blaxploitation cinema lambasted by many Black newspapers and civil rights organizations across the country.[18]

Much of this debate catalyzed around the film *Super Fly* (1972). Whereas blaxploitation pictures like *Cotton Comes to Harlem* (1970) and *Shaft* (1971) focused on cops and private detectives, *Super Fly* was the story of a cocaine dealer trying to evade corrupt white police officers while selling thirty kilos meant to fund his exit from the drug trade. The film opened in Detroit in August 1972 at the Fox Theatre, where it posted the biggest opening day ever at the theater and then proceeded to do about twelve times the theater's average business in the first week of its release.[19] The film's success was fueled in part by its soundtrack by Curtis Mayfield, and just weeks after its debut, it was reported that the soundtrack album was "without question Detroit's number one seller."[20]

Beyond the success of the film itself and its soundtrack in Detroit, *Super Fly* also affected fashion in the city, with the flashy and flamboyant look of the main character setting off something of a fashion craze among young African American men. Long coats with fur and fedoras began appearing everywhere, with the *Free Press* reporting in February of 1973, "Walk down almost any street in Detroit and you'll see what men's clothiers have known since last September: Super Fly clothes are super hip." So-called Super Fly outfits were advertised in the pages of the city's newspapers, and stores had trouble keeping them on the shelves. A *Free Press* columnist even claimed that the Super Fly look was actually "started by Detroit pimps and was picked up quickly by the show business and sporting worlds." It reportedly got to the point that Detroit's undercover police officers took to wearing Super Fly outfits to blend into Black Detroit, a fact that also points to the way the fashion of the film was often linked with racist popular images of Black criminality.[21]

To some, *Super Fly* and the craze it set off in Detroit provided a breath of fresh air emphasizing Black liberation and independence; to others, the film glorified drugs and promoted negative stereotypes of African Americans. The debate was perhaps best encapsulated in the pages of the *Michigan Chronicle*. On the one hand was an August 1972 article by Bill Lane, in which he wrote of the film, "At last the screen has a story about the seamy side of Black life in the ghetto as manipulated by people who are white—and wearing the badge of law and order." On the other hand, three weeks later, the paper published an article by Steve Holsey in which he wrote, "A number of concerned Black people feel that it's time for Black-oriented movies to stop glorifying the criminal element of the Black community. *Superfly*, some say is the last straw."[22]

It was within this context of debate over blaxploitation in Detroit's African American community that Coleman Young gave his famous mayoral inauguration speech in early 1974. In it, Young said, "I issue an open warning now to all dope pushers, to all ripoff artists, to all muggers: It's time to leave Detroit. Hit Eight Mile Road. And I don't give a damn if they are black or white, if they wear Super Fly suits or blue uniforms with silver badges: Hit the road!" This quote has been repeated ad nauseum in the decades since, most often by white suburbanites who interpreted it as Young telling the city's criminals to move into the suburbs. Others have focused on Young's mention of those wearing "blue uniforms with silver badges" or his reference to "dope pushers." Drawing far less attention, though, was his invocation of "Super Fly suits," with its allusions to the battle over blaxploitation in the city.

Young's decrying of African Americans in their Super Fly suits put him firmly on the side of those opposed to blaxploitation in the city, with fashion choices inspired by blaxploitation seemingly a sign of criminality. Just as importantly, though, Young's comments are an indication of the way his politics engaged directly with long-standing debates over what media was considered "indecent" and thus out-of-bounds for respectable mainstream society. Although this indecency had once been defined by sexually explicit pornographic content, now it was the depiction of race and blackness that was at issue. Remaining constant, though, was the belief that the consumption of indecent media could have harmful negative effects on the individual and on society. Though the media targeted had changed, as had certain contours of the discourse, there were very real continuities among Herbert Case's belief that indecent literature would turn the young and impressionable into deviants and sex criminals, the view that adult businesses would cause neighborhoods to decay and be overrun by blight, and the notion posited by Young and others that blaxploitation was linked to Black urban criminality and drug use. Even as anti-porn politics waned in prominence during Young's tenure in Detroit, the inauguration speech of the city's first African American mayor points to the fact that the debate over what media was indecent, and what effects such indecent media might have, would remain central in this new era.

NOTES

1. Phill Jourdan to Lowell Newton, November 17, 1972, box 333, folder 7, Roman Gribbs Papers, Burton Historical Collection, Detroit Public Library.
2. Frank Angelo, "Mayoralty Race Shaping Up for '73," *Detroit Free Press*, November 15, 1972, 9.
3. Angelo, 9; Peter Benjaminson, "Ravitz Loses in Neighborhoods He Cultivated," *Detroit Free Press*, September 12, 1973, 10.
4. John Opendahl, "Gribbs' Moves Hint of Race for Re-Election," *Detroit Free Press*, August 27, 1972, sec. F, 13; Angelo, "Mayoralty Race Shaping Up for '73," 9.
5. Billy Bowles, "Gribbs Picks Family over a 2d Term," *Detroit Free Press*, December 29, 1972, 1, 11.
6. Ladd Neuman, "Mel Ravitz Front-Runner—As of Now," *Detroit Free Press*, December 29, 1972, 1.
7. Neuman, 6.
8. Jim Neubacher, "Eberhard Eying Mayor's Race Again," *Detroit Free Press*, December 30, 1972, 3.
9. Billy Bowles, "Eberhard Announces He'll Run for Mayor," *Detroit Free Press*, January 6, 1973, 3.
10. Remer Tyson, "Young's Entrance Sets Battle Lines in Mayoral Race," *Detroit Free Press*, May 14, 1973, 5.
11. Stephen Cain, "Council Rallies to Aid of City's Belly Dancers," *Detroit News*, April 13, 1973, B-1-D.
12. Billy Bowles, "Ravitz Enters Mayoral Race, Seeks Unity," *Detroit Free Press*, February 13, 1973, 3.
13. Remer Tyson, "Sen. Young Opens Race for Mayor," *Detroit Free Press*, May 11, 1973, 3, 12; Tyson, "Young's Entrance Sets Battle Lines in Mayoral Race," 3; "Ravitz Rapped by Young," *Michigan Chronicle*, September 1, 1973, 5.
14. Benjaminson, "Ravitz Loses in Neighborhoods He Cultivated," 10.
15. Peter Benjaminson, "Rogell, Eberhard Seek Council Re-Election," *Detroit Free Press*, July 21, 1973, 3.

16. "Results of Detroit Election," *Detroit Free Press*, September 13, 1973, 14; Julie Morris, "6 Stay on Council; 3 Newcomers Win," *Detroit Free Press*, November 7, 1973, 1.

17. Gary Baumgarten, "Black Parents up in ARMS against 'Sex Strip,'" *Michigan Chronicle*, June 30, 1973, 11; Dave Anderson, "City Council Explodes at Sex Shop Hearing," *Detroit Free Press*, March 30, 1974, 14; Douglas Glazier, "Neighbors Want a Jury Probe of 'Sex Strip,'" *Detroit News*, March 28, 1974, 20; Roy W. Stephen, "Prostitutes Run Wild on John R at Canfield," *Michigan Chronicle*, August 10, 1963, 1.

18. Nadine Brown, "New NAACP Secretary Vows More Picketing of Blaxploitation Films," *Michigan Chronicle*, February 23, 1974, 4; Fred Girard, "Downtown Flicks Getting Better," *Detroit Free Press*, July 18, 1974, 14.

19. "'Super Fly' 1,250 at Detroit Fox and 1,000 at Mercury in 1st Week," *Boxoffice*, September 25, 1972, sec. ME, 2.

20. Steve Holsey, "Reflections," *Michigan Chronicle*, September 16, 1972, sec. B, 7.

21. Susan Watson, "'Super Fly' Look: Film Sets Fashion," *Detroit Free Press*, February 20, 1973, 3; Bob Talbert, "Zany Stan Spreads into Social Scene," *Detroit Free Press*, August 24, 1974, 13; "Occupational Hazards for STRESS," *Detroit Free Press*, June 3, 1973, sec. B, 1.

22. Bill Lane, "'Super Fly' Is Super First Look at Dope Dealings," *Michigan Chronicle*, August 26, 1972, sec. B, 8; Holsey, "Reflections," 7.

BIBLIOGRAPHY

DETROIT AREA NEWSPAPERS

Detroit Free Press
Detroit News
Detroit Times
Fifth Estate
Gay Liberator
Michigan Catholic
Michigan Chronicle

TRADE PRESS

Billboard
Boxoffice
Exhibitors Herald
Film Daily
Hollywood Reporter
Motion Picture Daily
Motion Picture News
Moving Picture World
Variety

ARCHIVE COLLECTIONS

American Civil Liberties Union of Michigan/Metropolitan Detroit Branch Collection, Walter P. Reuther Library, Wayne State University.

David Eberhard Papers, Burton Historical Collection, Detroit Public Library.
Edward Mooney Papers, Archdiocese of Detroit Archives.
Ernest Goodman Collection, Walter P. Reuther Library, Wayne State University.
Jerome P. Cavanagh Collection, Walter P. Reuther Library, Wayne State University.
Mel Ravitz Papers, Walter P. Reuther Library, Wayne State University.
Metropolitan Detroit Council of Churches Records, Walter P. Reuther Library, Wayne State University.
Roman Gribbs Papers, Burton Historical Collection, Detroit Public Library.

BOOKS AND ARTICLES

Abel, Richard. *Motor City Movie Culture, 1916–1925.* Bloomington: Indiana University Press, 2020.

Bailey, Marlon M. *Butch Queens Up in Pumps: Gender, Performance, and Ballroom Culture in Detroit.* Ann Arbor: University of Michigan Press, 2013.

Bates, Stephen. "Father Hill and Fanny Hill: An Activist Group's Crusade to Remake Obscenity Law." *First Amendment Law Review* 8, no. 2 (March 2010): 217–82.

Beaty, Bart. *Fredric Wertham and the Critique of Mass Culture.* Jackson: University Press of Mississippi, 2005.

Berg, Heather. *Porn Work: Sex, Labor, and Late Capitalism.* Chapel Hill: University of North Carolina Press, 2021.

Black, Gregory D. *Hollywood Censored: Morality Codes, Catholics, and the Movies.* Cambridge: Cambridge University Press, 1996.

Brasell, R. Bruce. "'A Dangerous Experiment to Try': Film Censorship during the Twentieth Century in Mobile, Alabama." *Film History* 15, no. 1 (January 2003): 81–102.

Bronstein, Carolyn. *Battling Pornography: The American Feminist Anti-Pornography Movement, 1976–1986.* Cambridge: Cambridge University Press, 2011.

Bronstein, Carolyn, and Whitney Strub, eds. *Porno Chic and the Sex Wars: American Sexual Representation in the 1970s.* Amherst: University of Massachusetts Press, 2016.

Calvert, Clay. "Of Burning Houses and Roasting Pigs: Why Butler v. Michigan Remains a Key Free Speech Victory More Than a Half-Century Later." *Federal Communications Law Journal* 64, no. 2 (March 2012): 247–74.

Carmen, Ira H. *Movies, Censorship, and the Law.* Ann Arbor: University of Michigan Press, 1966.

———. "State and Local Motion Picture Censorship and Constitutional Liberties with Special Emphasis on the Communal Acceptance of Supreme Court Decision-Making." PhD diss., University of Michigan, 1964.

Chafets, Ze'ev. *Devil's Night: And Other True Tales of Detroit*. New York: Random House, 1990.
Chateauvert, Melinda. *Sex Workers Unite: A History of the Movement from Stonewall to SlutWalk*. Boston: Beacon, 2014.
Comstock, Anthony. *Traps for the Young*. New York: Funk & Wagnalls, 1883.
Conot, Robert. *American Odyssey: A History of a Great City*. Detroit: Wayne State University Press, 1986.
Czitrom, Daniel. "The Politics of Performance: From Theater Licensing to Movie Censorship in Turn-of-the-Century New York." *American Quarterly* 44, no. 4 (1992): 525–53.
Darden, Joe T., Richard Child Hill, June Thomas, and Richard Thomas. *Detroit: Race and Uneven Development*. Philadelphia: Temple University Press, 1987.
Darden, Joe T., and Richard W. Thomas. *Detroit: Race Riots, Racial Conflicts, and Efforts to Bridge the Racial Divide*. East Lansing: Michigan State University Press, 2013.
Davis, Kenneth C. *Two-Bit Culture: The Paperbacking of America*. Boston: Houghton Mifflin, 1984.
Delmont, Matthew F. *Why Busing Failed: Race, Media, and the National Resistance to School Desegregation*. Oakland: University of California Press, 2016.
Denning, Michael. *Mechanic Accents: Dime Novels and Working-Class Culture in America*. London: Verso, 1987.
Detroit Police Department. *Annual Reports*. Detroit: Detroit Police Department, 1942–65.
Doherty, Thomas. *Hollywood's Censor: Joseph I. Breen and the Production Code Administration*. New York: Columbia University Press, 2007.
———. *Pre-Code Hollywood: Sex, Immorality, and Insurrection in American Cinema; 1930–1934*. New York: Columbia University Press, 1999.
Downs, Donald Alexander. *The New Politics of Pornography*. Chicago: University of Chicago Press, 1989.
The Drive for Decency in Print: Report of the Bishops' Committee Sponsoring the National Organization for Decent Literature. Huntington, IN: Our Sunday Visitor, 1939.
Duggan, Lisa, and Nan Hunter. *Sex Wars: Sexual Dissent and Political Culture*. New York: Routledge, 1995.
Erickson, Mary P. "'In the Interest of the Moral Life of Our City': The Beginning of Motion Picture Censorship in Portland, Oregon." *Film History* 22, no. 2 (2010): 148–69.
Fine, Sidney. *Violence in the Model City: The Cavanagh Administration, Race Relations, and the Detroit Riot of 1967*. East Lansing: Michigan State University Press, 2007.

Freund, David M. P. *Colored Property: State Policy and White Racial Politics in Suburban America*. Chicago: University of Chicago Press, 2010.

Friedman, Andrea. *Prurient Interests: Gender, Democracy, and Obscenity in New York City, 1909–1945*. New York: Columbia University Press, 2000.

Garner, Donald W. "Fighting the Tobacco Wars on First Amendment Grounds." *Southwestern University Law Review* 27, no. 3 (1998): 379–400.

Geltzer, Jeremy. *Dirty Words and Filthy Pictures: Film and the First Amendment*. Austin: University of Texas Press, 2016.

Gilbert, James. *A Cycle of Outrage: America's Reaction to the Juvenile Delinquent in the 1950s*. New York: Oxford University Press, 1986.

Grant, Melissa Gira. *Playing the Whore: The Work of Sex Work*. London: Verso, 2014.

Grieveson, Lee. *Policing Cinema: Movies and Censorship in Early-Twentieth-Century America*. Berkeley: University of California Press, 2004.

Hajdu, David. *The Ten-Cent Plague: The Great Comic-Book Scare and How It Changed America*. New York: Picador, 2009.

Hartigan, John, Jr. *Racial Situations: Class Predicaments of Whiteness in Detroit*. Princeton, NJ: Princeton University Press, 1999.

Hixson, Richard F. *Pornography and the Justices: The Supreme Court and the Intractable Obscenity Problem*. Carbondale: Southern Illinois University Press, 1996.

Howard, Clayton. "Building a 'Family-Friendly' Metropolis: Sexuality, the State, and Postwar Housing Policy." *Journal of Urban History* 39, no. 5 (September 2013): 933–55.

Irvine, Janice M. *Talk about Sex: The Battles over Sex Education in the United States*. Berkeley: University of California Press, 2004.

Kendrick, Walter. *The Secret Museum: Pornography in Modern Culture*. Berkeley: University of California Press, 1987.

Kruse, Kevin M. *White Flight: Atlanta and the Making of Modern Conservatism*. Princeton, NJ: Princeton University Press, 2007.

Kruse, Kevin M., and Thomas J. Sugrue. "Introduction: The New Suburban History." In *The New Suburban History*, edited by Kevin M. Kruse and Thomas J. Sugrue, 1–10. Chicago: University of Chicago Press, 2006.

Kurashige, Scott. *The Fifty-Year Rebellion: How the U.S. Political Crisis Began in Detroit*. Oakland: University of California Press, 2017.

Lancaster, Roger N. "The New Pariahs: Sex, Crime, and Punishment in America." In *The War on Sex*, edited by David M. Halperin and Trevor Hoppe, 65–125. Durham, NC: Duke University Press, 2017.

Lassiter, Matthew D. "Pushers, Victims, and the Lost Innocence of White Suburbia California's War on Narcotics during the 1950s." *Journal of Urban History* 41, no. 5 (2015): 787–807.

———. *The Silent Majority: Suburban Politics in the Sunbelt South*. Princeton, NJ: Princeton University Press, 2007.

———. "The Suburban Origins of 'Color-Blind' Conservatism: Middle-Class Consciousness in the Charlotte Busing Crisis." *Journal of Urban History* 30, no. 4 (May 2004): 549–82.

Leff, Leonard J., and Jerold L. Simmons. *The Dame in the Kimono: Hollywood, Censorship, and the Production Code*. Lexington: University Press of Kentucky, 2001.

Lewis, Jon. "'American Morality Is Not to Be Trifled With': Content Regulation in Hollywood after 1968." In *Silencing Cinema: Film Censorship around the World*, edited by Daniel Biltereyst and Roel Vande Winkel, 33–47. New York: Palgrave Macmillan, 2013.

———. *Hollywood v. Hard Core: How the Struggle over Censorship Created the Modern Film Industry*. New York: New York University Press, 2000.

Lockhart, William B., and Robert C. McClure. "Censorship of Obscenity: The Developing Constitutional Standards." *Minnesota Law Review* 45, no. 5 (November 1960): 5–121.

———. "Literature, the Law of Obscenity, and the Constitution." *Minnesota Law Review* 38, no. 4 (March 1954): 294–395.

Luckett, Moya. *Cinema and Community: Progressivism, Exhibition, and Film Culture in Chicago, 1907–1917*. Detroit: Wayne State University Press, 2014.

Lvovsky, Anna. *Vice Patrol: Cops, Courts, and the Struggle over Urban Gay Life before Stonewall*. Chicago: University of Chicago Press, 2021.

McCarthy, Kathleen D. "Nickel Vice and Virtue: Movie Censorship in Chicago, 1907–1915." *Journal of Popular Film* 5, no. 1 (January 1976): 37–55.

McGehee, Margaret T. "Disturbing the Peace: Lost Boundaries, Pinky, and Censorship in Atlanta, Georgia, 1949–1952." *Cinema Journal* 46, no. 1 (2006): 23–51.

McGirr, Lisa. *Suburban Warriors: The Origins of the New American Right*. Princeton, NJ: Princeton University Press, 2002.

McRae, Elizabeth Gillespie. *Mothers of Massive Resistance: White Women and the Politics of White Supremacy*. New York: Oxford University Press, 2018.

Milliken, Christie. "Rate It X?: Hollywood Cinema and the End of the Production Code." In *Sex Scene: Media and the Sexual Revolution*, edited by Eric Schaefer, 25–52. Durham, NC: Duke University Press, 2014.

Muñoz, José Esteban. "Cruising the Toilet: LeRoi Jones/Amiri Baraka, Radical Black Traditions, and Queer Futurity." *GLQ: A Journal of Lesbian and Gay Studies* 13, no. 2–3 (June 2007): 353–67.

Nickerson, Michelle M. *Mothers of Conservatism: Women and the Postwar Right*. Princeton, NJ: Princeton University Press, 2014.

Nyberg, Amy Kiste. *Seal of Approval: The History of the Comics Code*. Jackson: University Press of Mississippi, 1998.

Obscenity Law Project. "An Empirical Inquiry into the Effects of Miller v. California on the Control of Obscenity." *New York University Law Review* 52 (1977): 810–939.

O'Connor, Thomas F. "The National Organization for Decent Literature: A Phase in American Catholic Censorship." *Library Quarterly* 65, no. 4 (1995): 386–414.

Ooten, Melissa. "Censorship in Black and White: *The Burning Cross* (1947), *Band of Angels* (1957) and the Politics of Film Censorship in the American South after World War II." *Historical Journal of Film, Radio and Television* 33, no. 1 (March 2013): 77–98.

Papayanis, Marilyn Adler. "Sex and the Revanchist City: Zoning Out Pornography in New York." *Environment and Planning D: Society and Space* 18, no. 3 (2000): 341–53.

Pitrone, Jean Maddern. *MYRA: The Life and Times of Myra Wolfgang, Trade-Union Leader*. Fort Wyandotte, MI: Calibre Books, 1980.

Pratt, Henry J. *Churches and Urban Government in Detroit and New York, 1895–1994*. Detroit: Wayne State University Press, 2004.

Rabinowitz, Paula. *American Pulp: How Paperbacks Brought Modernism to Main Street*. Princeton, NJ: Princeton University Press, 2014.

Randall, Richard S. *Censorship of the Movies: The Social and Political Control of a Mass Medium*. Madison: University of Wisconsin Press, 1968.

Reed, Rebecca. "Regulating the Regulators: Ideology and Practice in the Policing of Detroit, 1880–1918." PhD diss., University of Michigan, 1991.

Retzloff, Tim. "City, Suburb, and the Changing Bounds of Lesbian and Gay Life and Politics in Metropolitan Detroit, 1945–1985." PhD diss., Yale University, 2014.

Rorty, James. "The Harassed Pocket-Book Publishers." *Antioch Review* 15, no. 4 (December 1955): 411–27.

Rubin, Gayle S. *Deviations: A Gayle Rubin Reader*. Durham, NC: Duke University Press, 2011.

———. "Thinking Sex: Notes for a Radical Theory of the Politics of Sexuality." In *Deviations: A Gayle Rubin Reader*, 137–81. Durham, NC: Duke University Press, 2011.

Sandler, Kevin S. *The Naked Truth: Why Hollywood Doesn't Make X-Rated Movies*. New Brunswick, NJ: Rutgers University Press, 2007.

Schaefer, Eric. "Pandering to the 'Goon Trade': Framing the Sexploitation Audience through Advertising." In *Sleaze Artists: Cinema at the Margins of Taste, Style, and Politics*, edited by Jeffrey Sconce, 19–46. Durham, NC: Duke University Press, 2007.

Schaefer, Eric, and Eithne Johnson. "Quarantined! A Case Study of Boston's Combat Zone." In *Hop on Pop: The Politics and Pleasures of Popular Culture*, edited by Henry Jenkins, Tara McPherson, and Jane Shattuc, 430–53. Durham, NC: Duke University Press, 2002.

Self, Robert O. *All in the Family: The Realignment of American Democracy since the 1960s*. New York: Hill and Wang, 2012.

———. "Sex in the City: The Politics of Sexual Liberalism in Los Angeles, 1963–79." *Gender & History* 20, no. 2 (2008): 288–311.

Sides, Josh. *Erotic City: Sexual Revolutions and the Making of Modern San Francisco*. Oxford: Oxford University Press, 2009.

———. "Excavating the Postwar Sex District in San Francisco." *Journal of Urban History* 32, no. 3 (2006): 355–79.

Smoodin, Eric. "Going Hollywood Sooner or Later: Chinese Censorship and *The Bitter Tea of General Yen*." In *Looking Past the Screen: Case Studies in American Film History and Method*, edited by Jon Lewis and Eric Smoodin, 169–200. Durham, NC: Duke University Press, 2007.

Somerville, Don Smith. "A Study of Local Regulations and Group Actions on the Circulation of Newsstand Publications." MA thesis, University of Illinois, 1956.

Strossen, Nadine. *Defending Pornography: Free Speech, Sex, and the Fight for Women's Rights*. New York: New York University Press, 2000.

Strub, Whitney. "Black and White and Banned All Over: Race, Censorship and Obscenity in Postwar Memphis." *Journal of Social History* 40, no. 3 (2007): 685–715.

———. *Obscenity Rules: Roth v. United States and the Long Struggle over Sexual Expression*. Lawrence: University Press of Kansas, 2013.

———. *Perversion for Profit: The Politics of Pornography and the Rise of the New Right*. New York: Columbia University Press, 2011.

Sugrue, Thomas J. *The Origins of the Urban Crisis: Race and Inequality in Postwar Detroit*. Princeton, NJ: Princeton University Press, 1996.

———. *Sweet Land of Liberty: The Forgotten Struggle for Civil Rights in the North*. New York: Random House, 2008.

Tentler, Leslie Woodcock. *Seasons of Grace: A History of the Catholic Archdiocese of Detroit*. Detroit: Wayne State University Press, 1990.

Thomas, June Manning. *Redevelopment and Race: Planning a Finer City in Postwar Detroit*. Detroit: Wayne State University Press, 2013.

Thompson, Heather Ann. *Whose Detroit?: Politics, Labor, and Race in a Modern American City*. Ithaca, NY: Cornell University Press, 2004.

Tsika, Noah. *Screening the Police: Film and Law Enforcement in the United States*. New York: Oxford University Press, 2021.

Turrini, Joseph. "Phooie on Louie: African American Detroit and the Election of Jerry Cavanagh." *Michigan History Magazine*, December 1999.

Vance, Carole S. "More Danger, More Pleasure: A Decade after the Barnard Sexuality Conference." *New York Law School Law Review* 38, no. 1–4 (1993): 289–317.

Wertham, Fredric. *Seduction of the Innocent: The Influence of Comic Books on Today's Youth*. New York: Rinehart, 1954.

Wittern-Keller, Laura, and Raymond J. Haberski Jr. *The Miracle Case: Film Censorship and the Supreme Court*. Lawrence: University Press of Kansas, 2008.

Wolcott, David B. *Cops and Kids: Policing Juvenile Delinquency in Urban America, 1890–1940*. Columbus: Ohio State University Press, 2005.

Woodford, Frank B., and Arthur M. Woodford. *All Our Yesterdays: A Brief History of Detroit*. Detroit: Wayne State University Press, 1969.

Wyatt, Justin. "The Stigma of X: Adult Cinema and the Institution of the MPAA Ratings System." In *Controlling Hollywood: Censorship and Regulation in the Studio Era*, edited by Matthew Bernstein, 238–63. New Brunswick, NJ: Rutgers University Press, 1999.

Zurcher, Louis A., Jr., and R. George Kirkpatrick. *Citizens for Decency: Antipornography Crusades as Status Defense*. Austin: University of Texas Press, 1976.

INDEX

Note: Page numbers in *italics* indicate illustrative material

abortion, in censored materials, 56
accosting and soliciting law, 223
ACLU (American Civil Liberties Union), 62, 87, 100, 107, 244, 258
Adam and Eve (film), 87
Adams, Paul L., 104
Ad Hoc Committee for a Quality Community, 217–18
adult bookstores: and obscenity law, 104–5, 118, 218–19, 245–46; popularity and staying power of, 202, 203, 208, 223–24, 235, 240, 268n120; protests against, 217, 226–27, 228 (*see also* Redford anti-porn campaign); regulation of, 209, 224, 225, 226–31, 232–34, 245–53. *See also* adult films
Adult City, 229, 231
adult entertainment. *See* pornography and adult entertainment
adultery, in censored materials, 56
Adult Fare Theatre, 234
adult films: ads for, 136, 230; incarceration of distributors of, 90–93, 103, 118; mainstream respectability of, 136, 202, 239–40; peep show machines, 118, 219, 229, 230, 231; perceived audience of, 136, 221; raids on viewings of, 87–90, 97, 103, 158, 218–19. *See also* adult bookstores; adult movie theaters

adult movie theaters: and art-house theaters, 79, 82, 84, 86, 99, 100, 114–15; decline in, 254, 268n120; and obscenity law, 219–20, 245–46; police entrapment in, 222, 246; popularity of, 136, 192, 224, 240; protests against, 235; regulation of, 209, 224, 225, 234, 243–44, 245–53. *See also* adult films
Adult World: closure, 151–52; location, 140–41, *141*; opening, 135, 140. *See also* Redford anti-porn campaign
African Americans. *See* Black community
African ballet, 175
Alaska, censorship in, 65
alcohol. *See* drug use and addiction
Allegrina, Charles, 149–50
Allied Theatres of Michigan, 32
Ambrose, Casey, 176
American Book Publishers Council, 62
American Civil Liberties Union (ACLU), 62, 87, 100, 107, 244, 258
American Mini Theatres, 234, 243, 245, 252
American News Co., 47
Angelo, Frank, 272, 273
Angry Residents Mobilized (ARM), 277–78
Animal Lovers (film), 220
Antipornography Civil Rights Ordinance, 259–60
Areeda, Joseph, 117–18, 169, 209, 219

291

Aroused (film), 113
art galleries, 117, 203
art-house theaters, 79, 82, 84, 86, 99, 100, 114–15
Ashbaugh, R. H., 21
Atlanta, GA, 119
Atlanta Constitution (newspaper), 254
Attaway, William, *Blood on the Forge*, 56–57
Austin, Richard, 205, 206–7, 272, 275
Authors League of America, 62
Baker, Ralph, 33

Baker, Royal A., 22–25, 59–60, 63, 88
Bandit, The (film), 81
Banks, James O., 135, 141
banned materials. *See* literary censorship; movie censorship
Baraka, Amiri: *The Slave*, 103; *The Toilet*, 103
Barnard, Ken, 202
Barris, Ivan, 177
bars. *See* topless bars
bartending/waitressing, 163, 179, 186–88
Bates, Stephen, 64
Baxter, Anne, 56
Bayview Hunters Point Neighborhood Association, 258
Bazin, André, 38
beatnik cafés, 102
Beck, Anthony, 28
Beck, Mary, 205, 206, 208, 218
Bell, Edward, 219, 272
Bellingham, WA, 260
belly dancers, 181
Berg, Haskell, 90–91
Bergman, Ingmar, 130n62
B-girls, 179
Billboard (magazine), 23, 24
Billera, Jau, 102
Bivens, Edward, Jr., 192
Black community: anti-porn protests, 258, 277–78; demographics in Detroit, 4, 57, 138; Detroit Rebellion (1967), 124, 138, 205; and perceived threat of racial integration, 4–5, 139–40, 143, 146, 150, 239; police targeting of, 19, 80, 120, 124; political gains, 5, 9, 206–7, 272, 275, 277; representation in literature, 31–32, 56–57,

103; representation in movies, 78–79, 278–81
Blackwell, Robert, 192–93, 195
blaxploitation films, 278–81
Blue Note Lounge, 174
Blue Orchid, 192
Le Bonheur (film), 111, 112
book censorship. *See* literary censorship
booking agencies, 188–89
bookstores: compliance checks and canvassing of, 1, 35, 41, 42, 44–45; cooperation with censorship regulations, 30–31, 39–40, 47. *See also* adult bookstores; publishers and distributors
Boston, MA, 31, 255–56
bottomless dancers, 176, 180, 182–83, 184, 191, 193
Bourke, William J., 97
Boxoffice (magazine), 79, 81, 111
Breen, Joseph I., 26
Bronstein, Carolyn, 259
Brooks, Van Wyck, 30
Brown, Eugene, *Trespass*, 56
Brown, John, 77, 77
Browne, Ernest, Jr., 207, 272
Brute Force (film), 80–81, 118
Bullach, Melville E., 161; adult entertainment regulation, 103, 104, 105, 160–61, 179; on Censor Bureau qualifications, 121; on censorship, 105–6, 122; literary censorship campaign, 43, 59, 65; movie censorship campaign, 84, 96, 98–99
burlesque and cabaret shows: performer-audience separation, 162; regulation of, 37, 101–2, 158–59, 178, 190–91; *vs.* topless bars, 175–76. *See also* exotic dancers; topless bars
Burning Cross, The (film), 78–79
Burroughs, William S., *Junkie*, 56
Burstyn v. Wilson, 82, 83, 107
Burton, H. Ralph, 53
Busik, Joseph, 245
Butler, Alfred E., 61–62
Butler v. Michigan, 61–65, 94, 96, 106–7, 115, 160

cabaret. *See* burlesque and cabaret shows

Caccavale, Ross, 202
Cahalan, William L., 213, 219–20, 245, 246
California: censorship in, 45, 54; zoning law in, 255, 258
Calloway, Charles, 213
Calvert, Clay, 65
Cameron, Raymond, 29
Canada, zoning law in, 269n122
Candid Magazines, 217, 218–19
Canty, Alex, 58, 145–46
Carmen, Ira, 108–9, 111, 112, 113, 114, 115–16, 119, 120–21
Carnal Knowledge (film), 246
Carney, John G., 164
Case, Herbert W., 34; censorship system developed by, 38–40, 45–46; cooperation with print industry, 30–31, 35, 47, 49; cooperation with religious and community groups, 36–37, 42; influence outside of Detroit, 35; movie censorship practices, 83, 85, 91; on obscenity law, 83, 94; perceived audience of censored materials, 58, 59–60, 221; promotion to head censor, 32; secrecy of operations, 48–53, 54, 77
Casino (movie theater), 19
Catholic Action movement, 26
Catholic Legion of Decency, 24, 26, 49, 85
Catholics: literary censorship campaigns, 1, 26–30, 27, 35, 41–45, 168; movie censorship campaigns, 1, 24, 26, 49, 85; political power in Detroit, 25–26, 167–68
Cavanagh, Jerome, 106–7, 125, 204–5, 207, 271
CBLY (Detroit Committee for Better Literature for Youth), 41–44, 106, 168
Celebrezze, Anthony, 251
Censor Bureau, Detroit Police Department (later Obscenity Detail): comic book censorship operation, 32–35; complaint-based *vs.* proactive approach, 31, 35–37; compliance checks, 20, 34, 35, 41; comprehensive system for censorship, 20, 38–40, 47–48; cooperation with movie industry, 22, 23, 77, 87, 98–99, 110, 113; cooperation with print industry, 30–31, 35, 39–40, 43–44, 46–48, 49; cooperation with religious and community groups, 29, 30, 35, 41–45, 168; cooperation with stage theaters, 103; decline in operations, 65, 108, 117, 125; extralegal and subjective practices, 39, 40, 43–44, 78, 81, 82–83, 94, 98, 108, 110–19; incarceration of pornography distributors, 90–93, 103–5, 118; influence outside of Detroit, 34–35, 45–47, 77–78; inspection of adult bookstores and theaters, 118, 218–19, 245–46; inspection of beatnik establishments, 102; inspection of dancing venues, 101–2, 158–59; inspection of modeling studios, 238; inspection of stage plays, 85, 103, 117–18; lack of legal expertise, 120–21; and movie censorship ordinance, 20, 74, 78, 82, 98, 100–101, 107–8, 111–12, 115–16, 117; and obscenity law, 39, 62–64, 83, 93–97, 98, 103–5, 108, 109, 110–19; paperback book censorship operation, 36–37; perceived audience of censored materials, 57–61, 85, 114–15, 221; political and ideological leanings, 54–57, 78–82, 83–84, 85–86, 112–13; power wielded by, 119–20; public opposition to, growth of, 79, 105–7, 121–23; public opposition to, lack of, 53–54; raids on pornographic film viewings, 87–90, 97, 103, 158, 218–19; rebranding as Obscenity Detail, 109–10; resistance from movie industry, 81, 84, 85, 86–87, 99–100, 116–17; secrecy of operations, 48–53, 54, 76–77, 109; statistics on operations, 37, 38, 101–2; tolerant approach under Baker, 22–25, 59–60; women in, lack of, 21–22, 121
censorship: scholarship on, 6–7, 9–10; shift in rhetoric, 2–4, 135–37, 150–51. *See also* legislation; literary censorship; movie censorship
Chambers, Whitman, *The Come-On*, 56
Chicago, IL: censorship in, 64, 98, 107, 115, 119–20; NODL in, 42; zoning law in, 255
Child Birth (film), 86
Child Online Protection Act, 65
children and teenagers: juvenile delinquency, 21, 33–34, 57–58, 59–61, 79, 80; perceived threats to, 21–22, 29, 33–34, 57–58, 59–65, 114–15, 144–46

Chilson, Roberta, 185
Christianity. *See* Catholics; Protestants
cinema. *See* adult films; movie censorship
Citizens Against Pornography and Smut, 242
Citizens for Decent Literature, 41, 170, 242, 257
city council: Catholics on, 26; elections, 275–76; exotic dancing regulation, 178, 181–83, 185, 188, 189–91, 193; liberal transformation of, 207–8; movie censorship regulation, 20, 100; pornography regulation proposals and debates, 208–16, 224–28, 231, 232, 235–37 (*see also* licensing law; zoning law); and Redford anti-porn campaign, 141, 151; tension with Gribbs, 231–32, 272
city-suburb distinction, 5–6, 150, 194
civil rights, 259–60
Clark, John, 234
Clark, Ron, 171
Clark, Sonny, 184–85
Clockwork Orange, A (film), 230, 237
clubs. *See* burlesque and cabaret shows; topless bars
Cole, James, 110, 112
Colmes, Walter, 79
Colonial Theater, 246
color-blind rhetoric, 4–5, 149, 150–51
Combat Zone, Boston, 256
Come-On, The (film), 56
comic books, 32–35
Comics Code Authority, 35
Communications Decency Act (1996), 65
communism and fascism, 33, 50–51
Comstock, Anthony, 144
Concept East, 103
Congressional Select Committee on Current Pornographic Materials (1952), 46, 50, 53, 55
Conot, Robert, 19
convention business, 159–60, 175, 177, 179–80, 185
Cook, Louis, 99
Coronet Theater, 86
Cotter, Thomas M., 29
Cotton Comes to Harlem (film), 279
Couzens, Frank, 24

criminality: and blaxploitation, 279–81; in censored materials, 56, 57; and decriminalization, 213–14; and homosexuality, 146, 177, 221; juvenile delinquency, 21, 33–34, 57–58, 59–61, 79, 80; and pornography, 59, 220–21, 226

Dallas, TX, 255
Damaged Lives (film), 86
Darden, Joe T., 80, 139
Daughters of Bilitis, 225
Davis, Kenneth C., 36
Dearborn, MI, 166–67, 174, 180, 185, 195
decriminalization, 213–14
Deep Throat (film), 136, 239–40
deindustrialization, 138
Delisle, Tom, 177
DeMascio, Robert E., 244
Denning, Michael, 36
Department of Justice, 46
desegregation, 4, 139, 143
De Sica, Vittorio, 99
Des Moines, IA, 255
Detroit, MI: and city-suburb distinction, 5–6, 150; demographics, 19, 57, 138, *139*, *140*; economic decline, 2, 8, 124, 138, 148–49, 175; economic growth, 1, 19; political context, 204–8; scholarship on urban history of and media censorship in, 9–10
Detroit City Council. *See* city council
Detroit Committee for Better Literature for Youth (CBLY), 41–44, 106, 168
Detroit Council of Catholic Organizations, 29
Detroit Council of Churches, 28, 41, 43–44
Detroit Daily Dispatch (newspaper), 162
Detroit Department of Buildings and Safety Engineering, 224, 227, 229, 233–34, 239, 243
Detroit Department of Corporation Counsel, 209, 210, 224, 229, 238
Detroit Federation of Women's Clubs (DFWC), 21–22, 24, 41, 43
Detroit Fire Marshal Division, 229
Detroit Free Press (newspaper): adult entertainment coverage, 152, 159–60, 162, 164, *165*, 166–67, 170–71, 173, 175, 181,

182, 184, 190, 192, 211, 212, 224, 229–30, 236, 238–39, 249, 278; anti-porn rhetoric criticism, 216–17; crime coverage, 60, 220; friendly relationship with Censor Bureau, 50; literary censorship coverage, 46, 50–52, 57, 58, 65, 256; movie censorship coverage, 20, 21, 23, 24, 82, 91, 98, 99, 109, 110, 113, 115, 116, 122, 219; obscenity law coverage, 83, 94–95, 116; political campaign coverage, 206, 272, 273, 274–75; reader polls, 170–71, 184, 210; Super Fly fashion coverage, 279; theater inspection coverage, 103

Detroit Gay Activists, 223, 225

Detroit Gay Switchboard, 222

Detroit Health Department, 229, 243

Detroit Jewish Community Council, 41, 43

Detroit Line, 45–46

Detroit Model, 255, 256–57

Detroit News (newspaper): adult entertainment coverage, 162, 164, 166, 172–73, 184, 191, 202, 224, 229, 249, 250; commercial-strip redevelopment coverage, 232; friendly relationship with Censor Bureau, 50, 53; literary censorship coverage, 46, 102, 125, 168; movie censorship coverage, 78, 82, 84, 98, 107–8, 110, 111; obscenity law coverage, 40, 94, 96, 97, 111, 219; organized labor coverage, 186; political campaign coverage, 274; X-rated movie ads, 230; zoning law coverage, 237

Detroit News Co., 35

Detroit Parent-Teacher Association (PTA), 1, 35, 41

Detroit Police Department: anti-porn training program, 242; arrest and incarceration rates, 93, 120, 220, 221–22; collaboration with Wayne County Prosecutor's Office, 29, 40, 43–44, 96, 117–18, 213, 219–20; demographics, 19, 57, 121; disproportionate targeting practices, 19, 21, 120, 124; entrapment, 90, 92, 221–23, 246; Juvenile Crime Prevention Bureau, 33; and Mayor's Task Force on Licensing Procedures, 229; and negative portrayals of police, 21, 79–81; and rising crime rates, 125; and Super Fly undercover outfits, 279–80; Vice Bureau, 57, 108, 169, 221–22, 246; and victimless crimes, 220–21. *See also* Censor Bureau

Detroit Public Library, 28, 30–31

Detroit Rebellion (1967), 124, 138, 205

Detroit Times (newspaper), 160

Detroit Universal Film Exchange, 22

Devil in Miss Jones, The (film), 136, 192

Dezel, Albert, 79, 86

DFWC (Detroit Federation of Women's Clubs), 21–22, 24, 41, 43

dime novels, 36

discrimination, racial, 79

distributors (book). *See* publishers and distributors

distributors (film). *See* movie industry

distributors (pornography), incarceration of, 90–93, 103–5, 118

Doda, Carol, 161

Doerfler, William, 168

Donohue, Thomas, 213

Donovan, John A., 29

Doran, William P., 169, 208, 216, 224

Dos Passos, John, 55

Dowling, William, 29–30

drug use and addiction: and blaxploitation, 279–81; in censored materials, 56, 57, 79; and criminality, 60–61

Drylie, Beverly, 236

Duperrault, Doug, *Red Light Babe*, 56

Duvall, Evelyn Miller, *Facts of Life and Love for Teenagers*, 42–43, 44

Dworkin, Andrea, 259–60

Dyson, Taylor, *Bitter Love*, 55

Eberhard, David: background, 207; mayoral candidacy, 233, 274, 275; pornography regulation proposals and debates, 208–9, 210–11, 216, 227–28, 232, 238; topless bar regulation proposals, 181

economy: decline in Detroit, 2, 8, 124, 138, 148–49, 175; growth in Detroit, 1, 19; pornography's negative impact on, 147–50, 152, 237, 239, 244; pornography's positive impact on, 157, 159–60, 175, 176, 184–86, 190

Ellis, Annette, 181

Ellis, Havelock, *Psychology of Sex*, 56

Elysia (Valley of the Nude) (film), 24
entrapment, 90, 92, 221–23, 246
Esper, Clement, 41
Excelsior Pictures, 86, 87
Exhibitors Herald (magazine), 23
exotic dancers, 163, 173; and female audience, 171–72; perceived as victims needing protection, 172, 183; and prostitution, 160, 179; regulation of, 158–59, 160–61, *161*, 162–64, 169–70, 178–83, *180*, 185, 188, 189–90, 238; at stag parties, 88, 158; unionization, 188–89; wage concerns, 172, 176, 179, 188, 189. *See also* burlesque and cabaret shows; topless bars
"exotic" label, 181–82
exploitation films, 86, 100. *See also* blaxploitation films; sexploitation films

Facts of Love, The (film), 81
Fairfax County, VA, 255
Farrell, James T., 55
fascism and communism, 33, 50–51
Faulkner, Robert E., 93
FBI (Federal Bureau of Investigation), 46
FCC v. Pacifica Foundation, 64
Feikens, John, 230
Feinstein, Dianne, 258
female dancers. *See* exotic dancers
feminists, 93, 143, 257–60
Fifth Estate (newspaper), 211, 222
film. *See* adult films; movie censorship
Film Exchange Building, 76, 78, 110
fingerprinting, 179, *180*, 180–81, 182, 188, 190, 238
Fink, Karen, 149
fire safety codes, 19, 209, 234
First Amendment. *See* free speech
Florida, censorship in, 64
Follies Theatre, 245
Ford, Henry, 167
foreign films, 81–83, 85–86, 111, 112
Fourteenth Amendment, 62, 233, 244, 251
Fowler, Jay, 278
Fox Theatre, 81, 279
Franco, Francisco, 30
Frankfurter, Felix, 63
Freedman v. Maryland, 107–8, 110, 116, 117

free speech: in anti-censorship rhetoric, 25, 51, 100, 210, 237; in anti-porn rhetoric, 236, 251; legal rulings on, 64–65, 82, 97, 117, 136, 164, 168, 233, 244, 252–54; sliding-scale approach to, 252
Freund, David, 146, 150–51, 194
Frisco Theatre, 235
Fuller, Virginia, 151

Gaide, Howard, 102
Gallagher, Michael, 24
Gallagher, Thomas, 224–25, 226, 233
Galloway, Russell, 169, 221
Garden of Eden (film), 86–87
Gathings, E. C., 46
Gay Liberator (newspaper), 222, 223, 246
gay male sexuality, 55, 57, 221–23, 225
Gelt, Myron, 147, 148, 236–37
Gem Theater, 246
Georgia, censorship in, 119
Gerould, Christopher, *Sexual Practices of American Women*, 56
Gilbert, James, 45
Gillespie, John, 21–22
Gilligan, Mr. and Mrs., 148, 149
Ginn, Evelyn, 145, 146, 147–48
Girardin, Ray, 108, 109, 125
Girl Deputy, The (film), 23
Glenn, Robert, 278
go-go dancing, 162. *See also* exotic dancers
Gold Diggers, 171, 179
Goldstick, Nathaniel, 115
Goodman, Ernest, 100, 232–33
Gorelick, Burton, 245
Gorelick, Stuart, 239–40, 245
Graduate, The (film), 237
grassroots activism: adult bookstore protests, 217–18 (*see also* Redford anti-porn campaign); in Black community, 258, 277–78; influence of, overview, 11; literary censorship campaigns, 1, 26–30, 27, 35, 41–45, 168; movie censorship campaigns, 1, 24, 26, 49, 85
Grey, Harry, *The Hoods*, 56
Gribbs, Katherine, 276
Gribbs, Roman S.: background, 205; and credit for anti-porn ordinances, 271–72;

engagement with anti-porn activists, 242; engagement with gay activists, 223; and exotic dancing regulation, 178, 182–83, 185, 188, 189–91; licensing law, legal challenges to, 243, 244; licensing law task force, 228–31, 233–34, 235–38; mayoral campaigns, 205–7, 272, 273, 275; obscenity ordinance approval, 229–30; and Redford anti-porn campaign, 141, 151; tension with city council, 231–32, 272
Grieveson, Lee, 19
Griffin, John H., *The Devil Rides Outside*, 61–62
Grosse Pointe, MI, 195
Gubow, Lawrence, 244, 247
Guerrini, Ralph, 221
Gutch, Roy, 116

Haberski, Raymond J., Jr., 83, 98
Hair (musical), 117–18, 175, 203, 208, 211–12
Hajdu, David, 32
Hamilton, John, 192
Hand, Learned, 63–64
Hayden, Sterling, 56
He and She (film), 219
Hearn, Robert, 60
Hearn, Rose, 60
Hedeen, Betty, 151
Hefner, Hugh, 186
Heldman, Louis, 238–39
Hemingway, Ernest, 55; *To Have and Have Not*, 29–30
Hernandez, Mrs. Gerry, 172
Hickey, Paul J., 43
Highland Park, MI, 192–93, 195, 222, 240
Hill, Richard Child, 139
Himes, Chester B., *If He Hollers Let Him Go*, 56
Hixson, Richard F., 252
Holsey, Steve, 280
Holzman, Sheridan, 237
homeowners' rights, 2–3, 149, 152, 210, 236, 237, 239
homosexuality: activist groups, 223, 225; in censored materials, 55, 57, 111, 112; and police entrapment, 221–23, 246; and sexual deviancy, 146, 177, 221

Hood, Nicholas, 182, 186, 207
Hotel and Restaurant Employees Union Local 705, 186, 187
House Select Committee on Current Pornographic Materials (1952), 46, 50, 53, 55
Houslander, Mr. and Mrs., 148
Hubbard, Orville, 167
Huber, Delores, 236
Hughes, Theodore F., 95

identification card requirements, 178–79, 180–81, 188, 189–90, 238
Illinois: censorship in, 64, 98, 107, 115, 119–20; incarceration rates, 93; NODL in, 42; zoning law in, 255
immorality. *See* morality-based censorship
incarceration rates, 93
indecent exposure law, 164–66, 169–70, 176–78, 183–85, 189–90
Indiana, zoning law in, 255
Inkster, MI, 182, 186, 191–92, 195
integration, racial, 4–5, 139–40, 143, 146, 150, 239
Inter-Faith Rally Against Indecent Literature, 42
interracial romance, in censored materials, 30, 55, 56
Iowa, zoning law in, 255
Irvine, Janice M., 154–55n14

Jacobellis v. Ohio, 109
James, Adrienne, 226
Jews, literary censorship campaigns, 28, 41, 43
Joabar, Joseph, 122–23, 124
Jourdan, Phill, 271–72
Juvenile Crime Prevention Bureau, Detroit Police Department, 33
juvenile delinquency, 21, 33–34, 57–58, 59–61, 79, 80

Kaess, Fred W., 117
Kansas, censorship in, 85, 107, 119
Kansas City, MO, 255
Kantor, MacKinlay, 55
Keating, Charles H., 109, 245

Kendrick, Walter, 8, 49, 54, 58, 65–66, 144, 171
Kennedy, Cornelia G., 244, 247
Killer Inside Me (film), 56
Killing of Sister George, The (film), 111, 113, 125
Kincheloe, Robert L., 172
Kinsey, Alfred, 56
Kramer Theater, 234
Kratsas, John and Violet, 171
Krause, Paul E., 90, 91, 92, 102
Krim Theater, 192, 195
Kubrick, Stanley, 230
Ku Klux Klan, 26, 78

Lacey, James, 118
Lady Chatterley's Lover (film), 85–86
Lancaster, Burt, 80
Lancaster, Roger N., 93
Lane, Bill, 280
Lardner, John, 45, 46
LaRue, Tyra Lea, 164–66, 165, 167, 169, 177, 235
Lassiter, Matthew, 61, 149
Las Vegas, NV, 256
Latuko (documentary), 83–84
laws. *See* legislation
Lawson, Rick, 239, 243, 247
League of Jewish Women's Organizations, 28
Lederer, Creighton C., 227, 230, 234, 258–59
Lederer, Laura, 258, 259
Legion of Decency, 24, 26, 49, 85
legislation: on accosting and soliciting, 223; on building fire safety, 19, 209; on civil rights, 259–60; extralegal and subjective censorship practices, 39, 40, 43–44, 78, 81, 82–83, 94, 98, 108, 110–19; on indecent exposure, 164–66, 169–70, 176–78, 183–85, 189–90; and limitations of legal history of censorship, 10–11, 75; on movie censorship, 20, 78, 82, 98, 100–101, 107–8, 111–12, 115–16, 117, 214; on taxing adult businesses, 210, 215. *See also* licensing law; obscenity law; Supreme Court rulings; zoning law
Lennon, John, 117, 203
Leonard, Donald, 85
Leone, Sergio, 56
lesbian sexuality, 55, 57, 111, 113, 225

Levin, Carl, 207, 226–27, 228, 231, 232, 234, 250
Levine, Joseph, 99
Lewis, C. Day, *The Friendly Tree*, 28
Lewis, Freeman, 46, 49
Lewis, Jon, 64
libraries, 28, 30–31
License and Censor Bureau. *See* Censor Bureau
licensing law: city council proposal, 224, 225; constitutionality of, 244, 247, 249, 250–51; enforcement of, 243–44, 247; Gribb's task force on, 228–31, 233–34, 235–38; and movie censorship ordinance, 74, 83, 107–8, 111–12, 115–16, 117, 214; and obscenity law, 83, 103, 111–12, 116; residential approval provision, 178, 231, 238, 243, 244, 247, 249–50; and topless bars, 190–91. *See also* zoning law
Lido Theatre, 245
Like the Cat, They Came Back (film), 23
Lillies of the Field (film), 107
literary censorship: of beatnik poetry, 102; of comic books, 32–35; complaint-based *vs.* proactive approach, 31, 35–37; cooperation with print industry, 30–31, 35, 39–40, 43–44, 46–48, 49; decline of, 65–66; extralegal and subjective approach to, 39, 40, 43–44; lists of banned and objectionable publications, 29, 33–34, 39, 42–46, 50, 52, 54–57; and obscenity law, 39, 61–65, 106–7, 168, 227–28; of paperback books, 36–37; and perceived audience of censored books, 57–61, 221; racial motivations for, 31–32; religious and community campaigns for, 26–30, 27, 35, 41–45, 168; secrecy of operations, 48–53, 54; statistics, 37, 38
Literary Censorship Bureau, Detroit Police Department, 28–29, 30–31. *See also* Censor Bureau
Lively, Judge, 251
live performance. *See* burlesque and cabaret shows; exotic dancers; stage plays
Lockhart, William B., 71n68
Loftus, Richard, 40, 91
London, Ephraim S., 100
Loomis, Rae, *The Marina Street Girls*, 56

Lord, Daniel A., 26
Loren, Sophia, 99
Los Angeles, CA, 45, 54, 255
Los Angeles Times (newspaper), 254, 256
Lowinger, Paul, 226
Lucas, Curtis, 56
Ludington News Co., 35
Lupton, James, 108

M (film), 85
MacKinnon, Catharine, 259–60
MacLeish, Archibald, 30
Madison, Joe, 279
Magazine, Alan, 255
magazines: on ban lists, 43; and comic book censorship, 32–35, 37
Maguire, Arthur D., 29
Maher, John J., 24
mail-order pornography, 224
Maine, censorship in, 64
male dancers, 159
Mandel, George, *Flee the Angry Strangers*, 56
Manolakas, Theodore, 164, 166, 167, 169, 177
Marks, Edward, 103, 106, 110, 111, 114–15, 116–17, 121, 122
Martel, Frank X., 89
Martin, Leo, 179
Maryland, censorship in, 85, 95, 107, 119
Massachusetts: censorship in, 31; zoning law in, 255–56
mass market paperbacks, as genre, 36, 58
Matthews, Ernest L., Jr., *Out of Bounds*, 56
Mayfield, Curtis, 279
Mazey, Ernest, 87, 100
McClain, John, 97
McClure, Frederick T., 278
McClure, Robert C., 71n68
McCrea, Duncan C., 29
McKiddie, Nora, 185
McKinney, Doyle, 34
McNally, James N., 33, 35
McNeil, Rick, 193
McRae, Elizabeth Gillespie, 143
Meloche, Kay, 179
Memoirs v. Massachusetts, 209
Memphis, TN, 119
Meyer, Russ, 116–17
Michigan Catholic (newspaper), 28, 29

Michigan Chronicle (newspaper), 31, 32, 80, 222, 278, 280
Michigan Journalist (newspaper), 55, 63
Milk, Harvey, 258
Miller, Jesse, 192–93
Miller v. California, 245–47
mini adult theaters, 209. *See also* adult movie theaters
Minneapolis, MN, 259–60
Minneapolis Star (newspaper), 46, 47, 50, 52
Minnesota: anti-porn civil rights law in, 259–60; censorship in, 46, 95
Miracle Decision (*Burstyn v. Wilson*), 82, 107
Miriani, Louis, 106
Missouri, zoning law in, 255
Mitchell, Marie, 148
modeling studios, nude, 178, 192, 224, 226, 238, 240
Mom and Dad (film), 86
Mooney, Edward A., 29, 42
Moon Is Blue, The (film), 84–85, 115
morality-based censorship: movie censorship ordinance in Detroit, 20, 74, 78, 82–83, 98, 100–101, 109, 115–16; religious censorship campaigns, 26–30, 27, 35, 41–45, 168; rhetorical shift away from, 2–4, 135–37, 150–51, 213–14, 216–17. *See also* obscenity law
Morality in Media of Michigan, 242
Morgan, Nancy, *City of Women*, 55
Motion Picture Association of America, 117
Motion Picture News (magazine), 22
Moulin Rouge (bookstore), 217, 218
movie censorship: decline of, 107–9, 117; Detroit's ordinance, 20, 74, 78, 82, 83, 98, 100–101, 107–8, 111–12, 115–16, 117, 214; extralegal and subjective approach to, 78, 81, 82–83, 94, 98, 108, 110–16; and obscenity law, 83, 93–97, 98, 103–5, 108, 109, 110–19; and perceived audience of censored movies, 114–15, 136, 221; religious campaigns for, 1, 24, 26, 49, 85; scholarship on, 6–7; secrecy of operations, 76–77, 109; statistics, 37, 101; tolerant approach toward, 23–25, 59; types of movies cut and banned, 78–82, 83–86, 112–13, 116. *See also* adult films; adult movie theaters; movie industry; movie theaters

movie industry: cooperation with Censor Bureau, 22, 23, 77, 87, 98–99, 110, 113; Production Code, 6–7, 24, 26, 35, 64, 79, 84, 136; resistance to Censor Bureau, 81, 84, 85, 86–87, 99–100, 116–17
movie ratings system, 64, 117, 136
movie theaters: regulation of, 19, 20, 209, 234; sexually explicit cinema in, 202. *See also* adult movie theaters
Moving Picture World (magazine), 23
Moynihan, Joseph A., 234
Murphy, Frank, 26
Murphy, Mrs. Wm. D., 146
Murrow, Edward R., 54

NAACP, 207, 279
Naked Came the Stranger (film), 11
Naked Eye, The (documentary), 84
National Action Group, 4
National Burlesk, 184
National Council of Catholic Women, 42
National Decency Reporter (journal), 123, 203, 257
National Organization for Decent Literature (NODL), 26–30, 41, 42, 43, 168
Nevada, zoning law in, 256
newsstands, compliance checks and canvassing of, 34, 41, 43
Newsweek (magazine), 39, 45–46, 58, 80
New York: censorship in, 82, 83, 85–86, 107, 119; zoning law in, 255
New Yorker (magazine), 6
New York Times (newspaper), 251, 254–55, 256
Nicholas, Johnny, 174
Nichols, John, 162–63, 214, 223, 229, 274–75
nightclubs. *See* burlesque and cabaret shows; topless bars
Nite Lite Lounge, 191–92
Nixon, Richard, 170
NODL (National Organization for Decent Literature), 26–30, 41, 42, 43, 168
Norris, Alban J., 28
Norris, Diane, 180–81
Norris, Harold, 120
Nortown Theatre, 243–44, 247, 252
nudity: bottomless dancers, 176, 180, 182–83, 184, 191, 193; in censored materials, 83–84, 86–87, 99–100, 112–13, 116–17; indecent exposure law, 164–66, 169–70, 176–78, 183–85, 189–90; modeling studios, 178, 192, 224, 226, 238, 240. *See also* burlesque and cabaret shows; exotic dancers; topless bars

Oakland County, MI, 5–6, 195
Obscenity Detail, 109–18. *See also* Censor Bureau
obscenity law: and adult businesses, 103–5, 118, 218–20, 245–47; constitutionality of, 62–64, 94, 96–97, 168, 209, 215, 219, 233, 253; Detroit's ordinance, 209, 214, 224–25, 226–28, 229, 232–33; extralegal and subjective application of, 39, 40, 78, 83, 94, 98, 108, 110–19; Michigan's ordinance, 61, 94, 95, 96, 104–5, 115, 214, 246; and *scienter*, 104–5; variable obscenity doctrine, 64
O'Connor, Thomas, 27, 28
O'Hara, John, 55
Ohio: censorship in, 46, 85, 107; incarceration rates, 93
Oklahoma, zoning law in, 256
Once Upon a Time in America (film), 56
ONE, 225
101 Acts of Love (film), 220
One Summer of Happiness (film), 83
Ono, Yoko, 117, 203
Oppedahl, John, 166
ordinances. *See* legislation
Oregon, zoning law in, 255
organized labor, 186–89, *187*
Orwell, George, *Nineteen Eighty-Four*, 46
Outlaw, The (film), 49

Packer, Vin, *Spring Fire*, 55
Papayanis, Marilyn Adler, 10
paperback books, as genre, 36, 58
Parent-Teacher Association (PTA), 1, 35, 41
pasties, 162–63, 164, 166, 169
Patterson, L. Brooks, 4–6, 11, 245
Patterson, Paul, 91
peep show machines, 118, 219, 229, 230, 231
Pennsylvania: censorship in, 107; zoning law in, 255
Penthouse Theatre, 245

Peters, Fritz, *Finistère*, 55
Peters, Newton, 29
Phantom Peeper, The (film), 112–13, 132n97
Philadelphia, PA, 255
Philippe, Charles B., *Bubu of Montparnasse*, 56
Piggins, Edward, 65
Pittsburgh, PA, 255
Playboy (theater), 234
Playboy Club, 186–88, 211, 276
plays (stage theater), 85, 103, 117–18, 202–3
Plaza Theater, 88, 222
poetry, beatnik, 102
Poitier, Sidney, 107
police brutality, 19, 80–81, 120, 124
police department. *See* Censor Bureau; Detroit Police Department
policies. *See* legislation
poor population. *See* working class poor
pornography and adult entertainment: defined, 8; economic impact, negative, 147–50, 152, 237, 239, 244; economic impact, positive, 157, 159–60, 175, 176, 184–86, 190; perceived audience of, 57–61, 85, 114–15, 136, 145–46, 221; popularity and growth of industry, 202–3, 223–24, 240–41, 241; shift in public approval of, 84, 136, 170–71, 184. *See also* adult bookstores; adult films; adult movie theaters; exotic dancers; legislation; literary censorship; movie censorship; topless bars
porn studies, 7–8, 9
Portland, OR, 255
Potter, Lester, 88
Powell, Lewis F., 252–53, 254
Pratt, Henry J., 26
Pratt, Philip, 233
Preminger, Otto, 85
print industry. *See* bookstores; publishers and distributors
Production Code, 6–7, 24, 26, 35, 64, 79, 84, 136
property values, 152, 237, 239, 244, 249, 277
prostitution: in censored materials, 56, 57; and exotic dance, 160, 179

Protestants: adult bookstore protests, 135, 141; anti-censorship views, 122; literary censorship campaigns, 1, 28, 41, 42, 43–44
PTA (Parent-Teacher Association), 1, 35, 41
publicity, avoidance of, 31, 48–49, 52, 76, 107
public libraries, 28, 30–31
publishers and distributors, cooperation with censorship regulations, 35, 39, 43–44, 46–48, 49. *See also* bookstores
Publishers Weekly (journal), 46
Pussy Cat Theatre, 152, 243, 244, 245

Quaid, Robert S., 108
Quigley, Martin, 26

race: in censored materials, 31–32, 55, 56–57, 78–79, 103; demographics in Detroit, 19, 57, 138, 139, 142; and paperback book popularity, 36; white flight, 138, 148, 152, 236–37
racism: and blaxploitation films, 278–81; in censored materials, 78–79; and color-blind rhetoric, 4–5, 149, 150–51; in Dearborn, 167; and Detroit Rebellion (1967), 124, 138, 205; perceived threat of racial integration, 4–5, 139–40, 143, 146, 150, 239; and police targeting, 19, 21, 80, 120, 124; and silent majority rhetoric, 170; Southern exceptionalism myth of, 31–32, 79
Rahn, Sheldon, 43, 44
Randall, Bruce, 245
Randall, Richard S., 112–13
Ranno, Carl, 183, 185
rape, 130n62
Rashid, Joseph G., 43–44, 167–71, 176–77, 185, 224
Ravitz, Mel, 212; background, 208; and *Hair*, 208, 211–12, 212; mayoral candidacy, 205, 272–73, 274, 275; and Redford anti-porn campaign, 141, 151–52; views on censorship and obscenity law, 213–14, 218, 226–27; views on licensing law, 231, 234, 237; zoning law proposal, 210–11, 212–13, 214, 215, 227, 232, 237, 238, 248–49
Rebel, Adam, *Stable Boy*, 56
records, vinyl, 104

Redford anti-porn campaign: overview, 135–36, 141–44, *142*; color-blind rhetoric, 150–51; concern for attracting undesirables, 146–47; concern for children, 144–46; concern for economy, 147–50, 152; and neighborhood demographics, 138–40, *139*, *140*, *142*; outcome, 151–52
Redrup v. New York, 215
Red Squad, Detroit Police Department, 33
Reed, Rebecca, 19, 21
regulations. *See* legislation
Reilly, Maureen P., 190, 238, 240, 243, 245, 246, 247, 250, 252, 254, 255
Rekiel, Stanley, 90
religious groups. *See* Catholics; Jews; Protestants
Reno v. ACLU, 64–65
residential neighborhoods: homeowners' rights, 2–3, 149, 152, 210, 236, 237, 239; licensing provision on approving new adult businesses, 178, 231, 238, 243, 244, 247, 249–50; neighborhood decay rhetoric, 146–48, 149–50, 152, 159, 210, 239, 244, 248–49, 250, 251, 253; protests against adult businesses, 217, 235–36. *See also* Redford anti-porn campaign
Retzloff, Timothy, 194, 221
RGW Enterprises Inc., 231
Rhode Island, censorship in, 64
Ricca, John A., 62
Riviera Theater, 230
Robertson, Charles D., 217–18
Robinson, Smokey, 148
Rogell, William, 207, 211
Rogow, Meyer, 91–92, 94
La Ronde (film), 82, 83, 85
Rooney, Mickey, 79
Rosen, David, 92
Roth v. United States, 64, 97, 113–14, 209
Roumell, Thomas, 176–77, 243
Roxy Theatre, 222
Royal Coach Lounge, 193
Royal News Co., 232
Rubin, Carl, 254
Rubin, Gayle, 137, 172, 189
Rumpus Lounge, 169
Rusinack, John J., 39, 40, 41, 42, 43, 48, 49
Russell, Stanley, 92

Ryan, Harold M., 95, 96, 104–5
Ryan's Daughter (film), 237

Saginaw, MI, 45
Salinger, J. D., 55
San Antonio, TX, 255
San Francisco, CA, 258
San Jose, CA, 255
Sax Club, 164
Schanenberger, A., 145, 149
Schmidt, Ronald, 217, 218
Schroeder, Donald, 43, 103
SCLC (Southern Christian Leadership Conference), 278
secrecy, of censorship operations, 48–53, 54, 76–77, 109
See It Now (documentary series), 54
segregation, racial, 4, 139–40, 143, 149, 150
Self, Robert, 10, 137
Semelsberger, Francis, 166
sex and sexuality: in censored materials, 55–56, 67, 81–82, 83–84, 86, 111, 112–13; normative *vs.* commercial, 135. *See also* homosexuality; pornography and adult entertainment
sex education, 154–55n14
sex films. *See* adult films
sexploitation films, 112–13, 116–17
sexual assault, 130n62
sexual commute, 194
sexual revolution, 84, 136, 216
sex work. *See* prostitution
Shaft (film), 279
Shaw, Wilene, *The Fear and the Guilt*, 55
Sherwin, Mike, 172
Sides, Josh, 10, 258
silent majority rhetoric, 170
Silverman, Lawrence, 243–44, 247
Sip 'n' Chat Bar, 164, 166, 171
Six Mile Theatre, 245
skid row formation, 210–11, 227, 244, 248
Skillman, W. McKay, 62
Sky Above, the Mud Below, The (documentary), 99–100
Smith, John W., 26
Smith, Lillian, *Strange Fruit*, 30–32, 79
Smith, Paul, 229
Smith v. California, 104

smokers (stag parties), 88–90, 97, 103, 158
Smoodin, Eric, 6–7
Snyder, Charlie, 32, 77, 78, 79–81, 90
Somerville, Don, 53
Sonderegger, Leo, 50, 52, 71n68
Song of the Loon (film), 222
Southern Christian Leadership Conference (SCLC), 278
Southern exceptionalism myth of racism, 31–32, 79
Spanish Civil War, 30
stage plays, 85, 103, 117–18, 202–3
stag films, 88. *See also* adult films
stag parties, 88–90, 97, 103, 158
Stanley v. Georgia, 219
Stein, Irene, 149
Stern, Jane, 255
Stevens, John Paul, 65, 252
Stewart, Howard M., 82
Stewart, Potter, 253
Stone Burlesk, 202
Stoumen, Louis Clyde, 84
striptease shows. *See* burlesque and cabaret shows; exotic dancers; topless bars
Strohm, Adam, 28
Strub, Whitney, 8, 10, 51, 136, 143
Studio North Theater, 99
suburbs: *vs.* cities, 5–6, 150, 194; flight to, 148, 152, 159, 236–37; patronage of adult entertainment, 146–47, 167, 174, 180, 182, 191–92, 193–95, 240–41, 278
Sugrue, Thomas, 9, 31, 143
Sullivan, Ann M., 146
Summer Holiday (film), 79
Summit Theater, 220
Super Fly (film), 279–80
Supreme Court rulings: on free speech, 64–65, 82, 136, 252–54; on movie censorship, 82–83, 85–86, 98, 107–8, 121, 136; on nudity, 169; on obscenity law, 62–64, 96–97, 109, 113–14, 136, 209, 215, 219, 245–47, 254
Surf Theater, 86

Talbert, Bob, 175
Tannian, Philip G., 183, 185–86, 228–29, 275–76
Tarnapol, Arthur, 90
tax on adult businesses, 210, 215

tax revenue, 158, 184
Taylor, Stephen M., 219, 239, 244, 245, 246, 252
teenagers. *See* children and teenagers
Tender Trap, 192, 193
Tennessee, censorship in, 119
Tentler, Leslie, 26
Texas: censorship in, 62; zoning law in, 255
theater (stage plays), 85, 103, 117–18, 202–3. *See also* burlesque and cabaret shows
theaters. *See* adult movie theaters; movie theaters
This Naked Age (film), 86
Thomas, June, 139
Thomas, Richard W., 80, 139
Thompson, Jim: *The Alcoholics*, 56; *Killer Inside Me*, 56
Time (magazine), 33, 252
Times Film Corp. v. Chicago, 98
Timid May (film), 23
Tindal, Robert, 207
Todd, Mike, 176
Toner, William, 256
topless bars: patronage in suburbs *vs.* Detroit, 166–67, 174, 180, 185, 186, 193–94; politicians as patrons of, 192–93; popularity of, 161–62, 164, 202, 235; regulation of, 158–59, 160–61, 162–64, 169–70, 178–83, 188, 189–91, 238, 240; rhetorical and legal defense of, 175–77, 183–86, 190; and suburban flight, 159. *See also* burlesque and cabaret shows; exotic dancers
Toronto, Canada, 269n122
Torrès, Tereska, *Women's Barracks*, 55
Town Talk, 176
Toy, Harry S., 33, 35
Trans-Lux Krim Theater, 219
Two Women (film), 99, 130n62
Tyler, Harold, 50–52

Union Book Store, 31
unions, 186–89, *187*
United States v. Kennerley, 63–64
Universal Pictures, 81
urban crisis rhetoric: neighborhood decay, 146–48, 149–50, 152, 159, 210, 239, 244, 248–49, 250, 251, 253; white flight, 138, 148, 152, 236–37

urban renewal, 150, 159–60, 227
urban studies, 5, 9
Uskali, David A., 125

Valenti, Jack, 230
Van Antwerp, Philip J., 208, 226, 228, 234, 237
Van Etten, Winifred, *I Am the Fox*, 28
variable obscenity doctrine, 64
Variety (magazine), 23, 32, 84, 85, 87
Variety Book Store, 244
venereal disease, in censored materials, 86
Vest Pocket Theatre, 117, 175
Vice Bureau, Detroit Police Department, 57, 108, 169, 221–22, 246
victimless crimes, 220–21
vinyl records, 104
violence: in censored materials, 78–79; Detroit Rebellion (1967), 124, 138, 205; police brutality, 19, 80–81, 120, 124; sexual assault, 130n62
Virginia: censorship in, 64, 107, 119; zoning law in, 255
Virgin Spring, The (film), 130n62
Vixen (film), 116–17, 214
Vonnegut, Kurt, *Slaughterhouse-Five*, 175

Wahl, Loren, *If This Be Sin (The Invisible Glass)*, 55
waitressing/bartending, 163, 179, 186–88
Walker, Jimmy, 67n13
Wall, James M., 122
Warren, Earl, 109
Warren, MI, 174
Warren, Rusty, 104
Warwick, Jarvis, *Waste No Tears*, 56
Washington: anti-porn civil rights law in, 260; censorship in, 64
WAVPM (Women Against Violence in Pornography and Media), 258
Wayne County Prosecutor's Office, 29, 40, 43–44, 96, 117–18, 213, 219–20
Weisberg, Arthur, 230–31
Well-Digger's Daughter, The (film), 81
Wells, Win, "A Gypsy in Asphalt," 102
Wenzel, Mrs. Jacob, 216
Wertham, Fredric, 33, 144
Weston, John H., 252
white flight, 138, 148, 152, 236–37

white supremacy, 79
Wichman, Theodore, 97
Wierzbicki, Anthony, 181–82, 208, 209, 211, 228
Wilcox, Mrs. F. H., 147
Wilder, Thornton, 30
Williams, Ralph, 150
Wittern-Keller, Laura, 83, 98
Wolf, Laurence, 195
Wolfgang, Myra, 186–89
Wolfson, P. J., *The Flesh Baron*, 56
women: canvassing work, 1, 41, 42, 44–45; in Censor Bureau, lack of, 21–22, 121; as customers at topless bars, 171–72; feminist anti-porn movement, 143, 257–60; in Redford's protest campaign, 142–43; regulating bodies of, 158–59, 160–61, *161*, 162–64, 169–70, 178–83, *180*, 185, 189–90, 238
Women Against Violence in Pornography and Media (WAVPM), 258
Wood-Six Theater, 222
working class poor: and elitism of censorship policy, 114–15; and paperback book popularity, 36, 58; and police targeting, 21
WXYZ Radio, 271

X-rated movies, 117, 230, 245. *See also* adult films; adult movie theaters

Young, Bob, 164
Young, Coleman, 272, 274–75, 276, 276–77, 280–81
Youngstown, OH, 46
Young v. American Mini Theatres, 252–54, 256, 277
youth. *See* children and teenagers

Zoline, Larry, 179–80
zoning law: class D cabaret licensing, 178, 190–91; constitutionality of, 215, 247–54; Detroit Model *vs.* Boston Combat Zone Model, 255–57; impact on adult businesses, 254, 256–57; influence outside of Detroit, 254–55, 258, 269n122; and racial segregation, 140; "regulated uses" provision, 210–11, 212, 227, 228, 238, 247–48, 249–50. *See also* licensing law

BEN STRASSFELD is Adjunct Assistant Professor in the Department of Media Studies at Queens College, City University of New York.

For Indiana University Press

Lesley Bolton, Project Manager/Editor
Brian Carroll, Rights Manager
Allison Chaplin, Acquisitions Editor
Sophia Hebert, Assistant Acquisitions Editor
Brenna Hosman, Production Coordinator
Katie Huggins, Production Manager
Dan Pyle, Online Publishing Manager
Rachel Rosolina, Marketing and Publicity Manager
Jennifer Witzke, Senior Artist and Book Designer

www.ingramcontent.com/pod-product-compliance
Lightning Source LLC
Chambersburg PA
CBHW030749250426
43673CB00058B/553